O F 8

STATE AND SOCIETY IN ROMAN GALILEE,
A.D. 132–212

Parkes–Wiener Series on Jewish Studies
Series Editors: David Cesarani and Tony Kushner
ISSN 1368-5449

The field of Jewish Studies is one of the youngest, but fastest-growing and most exciting areas of scholarship in the academic world today. Named after James Parkes and Alfred Wiener and recognising the co-operative relationship between the Parkes Centre at the University of Southampton and the Wiener Library in London, this series aims to publish new research in the field and student materials for use in the seminar room, to disseminate the latest work of established scholars and to re-issue classic studies which are currently out of print.

The selection of publications reflects the international character and diversity of Jewish Studies; it ranges over Jewish history from Abraham to modern Zionism, and Jewish culture from Moses to post-modernism. The series also reflects the inter-disciplinary approach inherent in Jewish Studies and at the cutting edge of contemporary scholarship, and provides an outlet for innovative work on the interface between Judaism and ethnicity, popular culture, gender, class, space and memory.

Other Books in the Series

STATE AND SOCIETY IN ROMAN GALILEE,
A.D. 132–212
Second Edition

Martin Goodman

VALLENTINE MITCHELL
LONDON • PORTLAND, OR

First published in 1983
by Rowman & Allanheld, New Jersey
Second Edition published in 2000 in Great Britain by
VALLENTINE MITCHELL
Newbury House, 900 Eastern Avenue
London IG2 7HH

and in the United States of America by
VALLENTINE MITCHELL
c/o ISBS, 5804 N.E. Hassalo Street
Portland, Oregon 97213-3644

Website: www.vmbooks.com

Copyright © 1983, 2000 Martin Goodman

British Library Cataloguing in Publication Data
Goodman, Martin, 1953–
State and society in Roman Galilee, A.D. 132–212. – 2nd ed.
– (Parkes–Wiener series on Jewish studies)
1. Jews – History – 70–638 2. Galilee (Israel) – History
3. Galilee (Israel) – Civilization
I. Title
956.9'45'02

ISBN 0-85303-380-3 (cloth)
ISBN 0-85303-382-X (paper)
ISSN 1363-3759

Library of Congress Cataloging-in-Publication Data
Goodman, Martin, 1953–
State and society in Roman Galilee, A.D. 132–212/Martin
Goodman. – 2nd ed.
p. cm. – (Parkes–Wiener series on Jewish studies)
Includes bibliographical references (p.) and index.
ISBN 0-85303-380-3 (cloth) – ISBN 0-85303-382-X (pbk.)
1. Galilee (Israel)–History. 2. Jews–History–70–638. 3. Rome–
History–Empire, 30 B.C.–284 A.D. I. Title. II. Series.

DS110.G2 G66 2000
956.94'5–dc21
00-062514

Typeset by Vitaset, Paddock Wood, Kent
Printed in Great Britain by
MPG Books Ltd, Bodmin, Cornwall

Contents

Preface to the Second Edition

State and Society in Roman Galilee was written in the late 1970s as a revised doctoral thesis and only few copies were printed. For years it has been hard for many would-be readers to obtain a copy, and I have therefore thought it right to accept the invitation to reissue it some twenty years after its composition.

I have accepted the invitation, however, with some trepidation. The book is not without faults, as some of its reviewers pointed out, more or less kindly, at the time.[1] It was brash in its dismissal of much earlier scholarship and both rash and dogmatic in some of its own sweeping assertions. Some of its deductions from a small number of rabbinic texts were unwarranted or careless, and in some cases these texts were simply misunderstood. I hope that if I was writing the book now it would be very different.

The justification for this reissue thus lies not in the details but in the overall thrust of the argument. My central claim that the assumptions underlying tannaitic texts are likely to reveal much about the everyday world of the Galilee in which they were redacted still seems to me valid, as does my attempt to locate the rabbis both within the wider Jewish world and in relation to the Roman state. If republication can encourage others to pursue further work along the same lines, this would seem a worthwhile enterprise.

This is not a completely revised new edition, which would have required a wholesale rewriting of large sections of the text. I have left the book as it was, but to avoid misleading new readers I have added in this preface an indication of the advances made by scholars in the main areas on which the book touches, and a note on those topics about which there is continuing debate.

Galilee in the Mishnaic period has been the direct focus of only a small number of large-scale studies since 1983. Most directly comparable to *State and Society* is the Hebrew monograph published in 1991 by Aharon Oppenheimer, which brings together a clear analysis of all the major topics addressed by earlier scholarship on the region in this period, with an emphasis on rabbinic concerns and the rabbinic perspective on Jewish society.[2] Also in Hebrew are the varied studies compiled by Zeev Safrai in 1985.[3] Both books bear testimony to a growing scholarly sensitivity to the wider significance for later Jewish history of the developments in Galilean culture in the second century. It is no accident that in 1989 the First (and, so far, only) International Conference on the History of Galilee in Late Antiquity was convened (in Galilee) by Lee Levine; the papers, published in 1992, touch on many of the issues discussed in *State and Society*.[4]

These new discussions have derived their insights more from novel interpretations of evidence long known than from new sources, but archaeology has also had some impact. The most important finds for Galilean history in this period have been the excavations on the summit of Sepphoris, where a fine Dionysiac mosaic from approximately the late second century has been uncovered close to the early Roman theater.[5] Since Sepphoris was the final residence of R. Judah ha Nasi, the compiler of the Mishnah, this evidence of the sophisticated culture of at least part of the city during his lifetime is highly significant; it is unfortunate that reports of the finds—in which a "Jewish quarter", distinguished by alleged ritual baths, is identified as separate from the area in which the mosaic was found—have discouraged scholars from asking how likely it is that rabbis of this period might have been comfortable to dine in a room decorated with such pagan elegance.[6] Other archaeological finds in Galilee with potential historical significance include underground hiding complexes similar to those found in Judaea[7] and a small number of inscriptions, which have helped in the plotting of the Roman road system in the region.[8] From outside Galilee but from the period of the Bar Kokhba war and just before, the Judaean Desert documentary papyri and leather texts were already known in the 1970s, but their full publication in the last decade has confirmed to a far greater degree their importance in discussions of rabbinic authority and conflicts of jurisdiction, as well as in many other areas of social history.[9]

Despite the impact of such finds, study of Galilee in this period must still start with analysis of the rabbinic and other texts preserved through the medieval manuscript traditions. There is still, of course, much disagreement about how best to do this, but the task itself has now been made much simpler through the publication of a series of invaluable research tools. Greek and Latin pagan texts referring to Jews and Judaism are now easily consulted in the magisterial compendium by Menahem Stern[10] and the Roman legal texts in the collection by Amnon Linder (although little of the material in either compilation is directly relevant for Galileé in this period, a fact which is itself probably significant).[11] There is an excellent guide to the latest scholarship dealing with the date and provenance of rabbinic texts in the updated edition by Günther Stemberger of Strack's *Introduction to the Talmud and Midrash*.[12] Much of the corpus of rabbinic writings from late antiquity is now easily available on CD-ROM,[13] and English-speaking readers can benefit from careful use of the translations of many of these texts by Jacob Neusner and others (with the proviso that no translation can substitute for the original texts, especially when the texts are as difficult to fathom as these; many reviewers have pointed to serious deficiencies, particularly in the translation of the Palestinian Talmud).[14] A focus of continuing debate remains the vexed question of the best way for historians to make use of these rabbinic writings once they have been understood in their original literary context.

The most sceptical approach to the use of rabbinic evidence has been advocated by those who point, correctly, to the date of the medieval manuscripts as the earliest period when the ideas contained within the texts can be firmly stated to have achieved their final form and to have had sufficient significance to attract the attention of the copyist.[15] This observation is significant particularly for those rabbinic works, such as the Palestinian Talmud, for which the manuscript traditions vary alarmingly.[16] It has now become much more common among historians to take into account all manuscript variants, although this new tendency may owe as much to the easy accessibility of variant readings through the publication of many manuscript readings on CD-ROM as to the theoretical possibility that any one manuscript tradition is as good as any other.[17] The hypothesis that all these texts were invented in the Middle Ages is too bizarre to be adopted seriously since it raises the question of why and how medieval rabbis should have concocted texts in which, for instance, even the more obscure tannaim and amoraim are almost always situated in stories and halakhic discussions in the company of their coevals—if the Mishnah, talmuds and midrashim were medieval fictions, they were an astonishing literary achievement.

A modified version of this sceptical approach is more plausible and has potentially serious consequences for the argument in this book. The varied state of the medieval manuscripts may suggest that rabbinic traditions circulated not in the form of whole texts, as in modern editions, but in smaller units which could be (and were) inserted into a number of different, larger compilations.[18] This hypothesis explains well the replication of passages in different works, but it implies that it is wrong to see a hypothetical date of the redaction of the text in antiquity as the fixed point in the third, fourth or fifth century C.E. when everything within the text can be said to have had some significance for the compiler. This is the rationale which led Sacha Stern to use evidence from many different late-antique texts to create a composite picture of Jewish identity in rabbinic society.[19]

There is no doubt that this approach is coherent and may in many cases be correct, but some texts show more signs of careful compilation than others and it is probably best to judge each case separately.[20] Thus Jacob Neusner has insisted, in a series of studies, on the major role of the redactors of many texts in shaping their material to conform to distinctive philosophies[21] and, although it is not always easy to be certain how much the alleged philosophy has been imposed upon the text by its modern interpreter, it is certainly true that most tannaitic texts conform to what appears to be a deliberate shape. It is worth noting that the Mishnaic text at least must have existed in approximately its present form by the mid-third century C.E. because the discussions of the Mishnah found in the Babylonian and Palestinian Talmuds presuppose that a similar text was used by both sets of amoraim. There can be far less certainty about the status of the Tosefta as an independent text, and, although the material it contains must have been extant in some form before the redaction of the Palestinian Talmud, the relationship of the redaction of the Tosefta to that of the Mishnah is still much debated.[22] It is even harder to be certain about the redaction of the tannaitic midrashim, which owe their shape above all to the biblical texts on which they form a commentary.

After all this debate the method outlined in Chapter 1 of *State and Society* still seems to me reasonable, although I would express it now with greater caution. Few historians would attempt any more to compose a biography of any of the rabbis of this period,[23] but it remains clear that the main elements of rabbinic history—who lived when, who was pre-eminent in which academies—are more likely to be true than not,[24] not least because (for reasons still obscure) the attribution of sayings to particular sages remained a matter of great concern throughout the history of late-antique rabbinism.[25] It is still plausible to assume that the tannaitic texts were compiled during the second and third centuries in Galilee and that a refusal to base historical arguments on rabbinic traditions found in later compilations, even when they are attributed in those compilations to tannaitic rabbis, may help to avoid anachronisms. (One of the justified criticisms of State and Society was that, despite my defence of this method, in practice I adopted from secondary scholarship some ideas based on amoraic texts, such as the assertion that rabbis in Judaea before 132 C.E. were generally artisans.[26] On the other hand, it is possible that my exclusion from consideration of all beraitot cited in amoraic texts on the grounds that some of them are fictitious was overly cautious and unnecessarily ignored evidence which might have added details to the overall picture.)

Of recent studies using early rabbinic sources as historical evidence, the most important have concentrated on the way rabbinic society worked and the relationship of the sages to wider Jewish society. Some have studied the careers of individual rabbis[27] and the practical working of their academies.[28] Catherine Hezser has produced a fundamental reinvestigation of the complex networks that linked rabbis, raising the interesting question of the exercise of authority between rabbis themselves.[29] There has been much work in particular on the topic of Chapter 7 of State and Society, which deals with the extent of rabbinic authority over other Jews. The technique of relying on case histories of rabbinic activity to show what rabbis actually did was used independently by Shaye Cohen, with rather similar results to mine,[30] but there has been little agreement with my account of the role of the patriarch. Stuart Cohen[31] and David Goodblatt[32] have both argued forcefully against my view that the patriarchs were not recognized as monarchical leaders by the Roman state until the late fourth century. They contend that the impulse in Jewish society towards recognition of one individual as national leader can be observed throughout antiquity and that, with the cessation of the high priesthood, Jews in Palestine would have quite naturally seen the dynasty of Gamaliel as their natural rulers.[33]

It is probably correct that in State and Society I underestimated the desire of ordinary Jews to find in rabbinic leaders both political and secular guidance. On the other hand, claims that the rabbinic patriarch was treated by the Roman state in the second century as the natural leader of the Jews through whom Rome would govern this unruly nation still seem to me implausible. After the destruction of the Temple in Jerusalem, the Roman state no longer needed to treat the Jews as a single entity at all, any more than any other ethnic or religious group within the empire. Lack of Roman recognition is implied by the lack of consistency in the Greek titles applied to the *nasi* in the third and fourth centuries.[34]

Thus the view argued in Chapter 7 that the state only gave formal recognition to the patriarchs during the fourth century still seems to me plausible. But the significance of this for the spread of rabbinic authority may be more complex than I allowed, for many amoraic stories about the *nesiim* envisage them as distanced from, and sometimes hostile to, the rabbis.[35] The issue is not simple, for stories of friction presuppose some proximity. Since (curiously) no rabbinic evidence about the nature of rabbinic society survives from the late fourth century, it is hard to know how "rabbinic" the *nasi* was by that time, but it is fair to warn readers that my assumption that the descendants of Gamaliel always saw themselves as part of the rabbinic movement, and that this perception was shared by their fellow Jews, is less obvious than I suggested in *State and Society*.[36]

Debate about the significance of what is not in the extant rabbinic evidence has also dominated discussion in the past twenty years of the nature of Judaism in this period. An intense debate between Jacob Neusner and Ed Sanders has centered on the claim by Sanders that it is possible to discern the pattern of religion which underlies the whole rabbinic agenda;[37] in contrast, Neusner has frequently asserted that it is only possible to delineate the Judaism of one particular rabbinic text at a time.[38] On the extent to which non-rabbinic Judaisms continued to flourish after the Bar Kochba war, most of the more recent scholarship has tackled the varied evidence from the diaspora, especially Asia Minor.[39]

In an influential article published in 1984, Shaye Cohen irenically suggested that sectarianism came to an end after 70 C.E. because the rabbis at Yavneh sought not to impose their own brand of Judaism on other Jews but to be all-inclusive—hence the novel phenomenon that the Mishnah records divergent legal views without adjudicating among them.[40] I am happy to be persuaded that the rabbis wished matters to be thus but I am less convinced that they described how things actually were. I have argued that it is a mistake to assume that because rabbinic Jews did not discuss other types of Judaism they therefore did not exist, and that for all we know Sadducees and Essenes might have continued as identifiable groups throughout this period even though there is no clear evidence that they did so.[41] It seems to me just as important now as when I wrote this book to treat the rabbis as a select section of Jewish society with a necessarily partial view and not to expect evidence from other sources (mostly in Greek and Latin) always to link in with rabbinic testimony. With this in mind I am much less certain now than I was then about the relationship of the rabbis after 70 to the Pharisees, a relationship I took for granted (like most scholars) when I wrote the book. There is no unambiguous evidence that the rabbis ever portrayed themselves or their predecessors in earlier generations as Pharisees, and the specific evidence that some individuals did in fact belong to both groups in the first century C.E. is limited to Rabban Gamaliel and his son Simon.[42]

Only loosely connected to the debate about the use of rabbinic texts has been the proliferation of studies of the Galilean economy in this period, although the large books by Gildas Hamel and Zeev Safrai both make programmatic statements about the use to be made of such evidence.[43] Study of the economic history of the Roman empire in general has been intensive over the past two decades, fuelled in part by the application of more sophisticated models, and in part by increased consideration of numismatic and archaeological evidence.[44] Some of this has been incorporated into the general study of the Palestinian economy by Zeev Safrai,[45] but the most important new work specifically on Galilee has been the documentation by David Adan-Bayewitz, through pottery analysis, of the extent of local Galilean trade, although his assertions about the significance of his finds may be exaggerated, since patterns of exchange of common pottery may have only limited value in revealing much about the quantity and quality of trade in general.[46]

On a series of specific smaller issues discussed in passing in *State and Society* scholarship has been exceptionally productive. There have been some good studies of the role of cities.[47] Much has been done on the function and architecture of synagogues,[48] and on the role of women.[49] The debate over the relationship between rabbinic law and other jurisdictions, both Jewish and non-Jewish, continues to focus on the significance of the Judaean Desert documents, with some asserting that these demonstrate the use of non-rabbinic rules and judges by ordinary Jews in the second century C.E., while others dismiss the same texts as the product of marginal Jews in a marginal milieu.[50] In general, all these studies seem to me to have much enriched the picture presented in *State and Society* but do not give any reason to reject what is said there.

In some ways the biggest shift since the book was written has been in historians' appreciation of the nature of Roman rule in the region. Two major studies have revealed the extent to which the Roman state militarized the Near East during the second and third centuries C.E. and Romanized the region through the foundation of colonies.[51] My assertion in Chapter 9 that Rome left Galilee to its own devices may thus seem rather anomalous. The view that Galilee was not involved in the Bar Kokhba war continues to be challenged, in part because of finds in the region of underground hiding complexes similar to those in Judaea,[52] and other scholars have drawn attention to the evidence in rabbinic texts of a Roman military presence in Galilee[53] and of Roman interference in support of Jewish judicial authorities.[54] The material prosperity of Sepphoris, now apparent from recent excavations, must modify my picture of Galilean society as in essence isolated and rural. Nonetheless, the ability of the rabbis portrayed in the rabbinic texts to act and talk as if unaffected by the wider culture of the Roman empire and to treat the Roman state as alien remains remarkable, even if it was as much the product of rabbinic self-absorption (to the point of solipsism)[55] as of genuine political, cultural or social separation.

With these warnings I commend this reissue to the reader, with thanks to Vallentine Mitchell and to the editors of the Parkes–Wiener series for their initiative in bringing it about.

Martin Goodman
Oxford
December 1999

Notes

1. See among the more illuminating reviews those by L. J. Archer, in *JRS* 75 (1985) 303–5; S. J. D. Cohen, in *American Historical Review* (1984): 1315–16; H. G. Kippenberg, in *JSJ* 16.2 (1985): 266–7; S. S. Miller, in *AJS Review* 11 (1986): 249–54; J. Neusner, in *JQR* 81 (1984): 427ff.; P. Schäfer, in *JJS* 36 (1985) 120–21; A. Wasserstein, in *Classical Review* 36 (1986): 108–11; D. Weinberger, in *Classical World* 79 (1986): 202–3. I am very grateful to Helenann Francis, Aharon and Nili Oppenheimer and Seth Schwartz for their helpful comments on this Preface; they are not, of course, responsible for the remaining imperfections.
2. A. Oppenheimer, *Galilee in the Mishnaic Period* (Jerusalem, 1991) (Heb.).
3. Z. Safrai, *Studies on the Galilee in the Time of the Mishnah and Talmud* (Ma'alot, 1985) (Heb.).
4. L. I. Levine, ed., *The Galilee in Late Antiquity* (New York and Jerusalem, 1992).
5. Z. Weiss, "Sepphoris," in E. Stern, ed., *New Encyclopaedia of Archaeological Excavations in the Holy Land* (Jerusalem, 1994) 4: 1324–8; Z. Weiss and E. Netzer, *Promise and*

Redemption: A Synagogue Mosaic from Sepphoris (Raleigh, N.C., 1996).

6. But see S. Schwartz, "Gamaliel in Aphrodite's Bath," in P. Schäfer, ed., *The Talmud Yerushalmi and Graeco-Roman Culture*, Vol. I (Tübingen, 1998), pp. 203–17.

7. Y. Tepper and Y. Shahar, "Hiding Complexes in the Galilee," in A. Kloner and Y. Tepper, eds., *The Hiding Complexes in the Judaean Shephelah* (Tel Aviv, 1987), pp. 279–326 (Heb.).

8. I. Roll, "Survey of Roman roads in Lower Galilee," in I. Pomerantz et al., eds., *Excavations and Surveys in Israel*, 14: 38–40.

9. See especially N. Lewis, *The Documents from the Bar Kochba Period in the Cave of Letters* (Jerusalem, 1989); H. M. Cotton and A. Yardeni, *Aramaic, Hebrew and Greek Texts from Nahal Hever and Other Sites* (DJD xxvii) (Oxford, 1997).

10. M. Stern, ed., *Greek and Latin Authors on Jews and Judaism*, 3 vols. (Jerusalem, 1974–84).

11. A. Linder, *The Jews in Roman Imperial Legislation* (Detroit, Mich. and Jerusalem, 1987).

12. G. Stemberger, *Introduction to the Talmud and Midrash*, 2nd ed. (Edinburgh, 1996).

13. *Bar-Ilan's Judaic Library: Bar Ilan University Responsa Project CD-ROM* (Spring Valley, N.Y., c. 1994).

14. J. Neusner, *The Tosefta Translated from the Hebrew* (New York, 1977–82); J. Neusner and R. Brooks, *Sifra: The Rabbinic Commentary on Leviticus* (Atlanta, Ga., 1985); J. Neusner, *Sifre to Deuteronomy: An Analytical Translation*, 2 vols. (Atlanta, Ga., 1987); J. Neusner, *The Talmud of the Land of Israel* (Chicago and London, 1982).

15. P. Schäfer, "Research into Rabbinic Literature: An Attempt to Define the Status Quaestionis," *JJS* 37 (1986): 139–52; idem, "Once Again the Status Quaestionis of Research in Rabbinic Literature: An Answer to Chaim Milikowsky," *JJS* 40 (1989): 89–94.

16. See P. Schäfer, *Synopse zur Talmud Yerushalmi* (Tübingen, 1991–).

17. E.g., *The Sol and Evelyn Henkind Talmud Text Databank*, published by the Saul Lieberman Institute of Talmudic Research [LIEBINST@JTSA.EDU] contains numerous manuscripts of the Babylonian Talmud.

18. See the series of studies published by Arnold Goldberg from 1977 to the mid-1980s in *Frankfurter Judaistische Beiträge*, listed in P. Schäfer, "Research in Rabbinic Literature," pp. 144–6.

19. S. Stern, *Jewish Identity in Early Rabbinic Writings* (Leiden, 1994).

20. See C. Milikowsky, "The Status Quaestionis of Research in Rabbinic Literature," *JJS* 39 (1988): 201–11.

21. J. Neusner, *Judaism: The Evidence of the Mishnah*, 2nd ed. (Atlanta, Ga., 1988); idem, *The Philosophical Mishnah* (Atlanta, Ga., 1989).

22. A. Houtman, *Mishnah and Tosefta: A Synoptic Comparison of the Tractates Berakhot and Shebiit* (Tübingen, 1996), and "The Job, the Craft and the Tools: Using a Synopsis for Research on the Relationship(s) between the Mishnah and the Tosefta," *JJS* 48 (1997). 91–104.

23. See J. Neusner, *In Search of Talmudic Biography* (Chico, Cal, 1984).

24. M. S. Jaffee, "The Taqqanah in Tannaitic Literature: Jurisprudence and the Construction of Rabbinic Memory," *JJS* 41 (1990): 204–25.

25. On this issue see S. Stern, "The Concept of Authorship in the Babylonian Talmud," *JJS* 46 (1995): 183–95.

26. See S. J. D. Cohen, in *American Historical Review* (1984): 1315–16.

27. See, for example, E. Habas, "Rabban Gamaliel of Yavneh and his Sons: The Patriarchate before and after the Bar Kokhba Revolt," *JJS* 50 (1999): 21–37.

28. Z. Safrai, "Rabbinic Recruitment Policy in the Mishnaic and Talmudic Period: A Sociological Inquiry into Rabbinic Society," *Proceedings of the Eleventh World Congress of Jewish Studies* (Jerusalem, 1994), Div. B, Vol. 1: 25–32.

29. C. Hezser, *The Social Structure of the Rabbinic Movement in Roman Palestine* (Tübingen, 1997).

30. S. J. D. Cohen, "The Place of the Rabbi in Jewish Society of the Second Century," in Levine, ed., *Galilee in Late Antiquity*, pp. 157–73; idem, "The Rabbi in Second-Century Jewish Society," in *The Cambridge History of Judaism*, Vol. 3 (Cambridge, 1999), pp. 922–90.

31. S. A. Cohen, *The Three Crowns: Structures of Communal Politics in Early Rabbinic Jewry* (Cambridge and Sydney, 1990).

32. D. M. Goodblatt, *The Monarchic Principle: Studies in Jewish Self-Government in Antiquity* (Tübingen, 1994).

33. See also E. Habas, *The Patriarch in the Roman Byzantine Era—the Making of a Dynasty*, Ph.D. diss., Tel Aviv, 1991 (in Heb.).

34. M. Goodman, "The Roman State and the Jewish Patriarch in the Third Century," in Levine, ed., *Galilee in Late Antiquity*, pp. 127–39.

35. See M. Jacobs, *Die Institution des judischen Patriarchen. Eine quellen—und traditionskritische Studie zur Geschichte der Juden in der Spätantike* (Tübingen, 1995); L. I. Levine, "The Status of the Patriarch in the Third and Fourth Centuries: Sources and Methodology," *JJS* 47 (1996): 1–32.

36. See S. Schwartz, "The Patriarchs and the Diaspora," *JJS* 50 (1999): 208–22.

37. See E. P. Sanders, *Jewish Law from Jesus to the Mishnah* (London and Philadelphia, 1990).

38. E.g., J. Neusner, *Judaism: The Evidence of the Mishnah*, 2nd ed. (Atlanta, Ga., 1998).

39. See A. T. Kraabel, "The Roman Diaspora: Six Questionable Assumptions," *JJS* 33 (1982): 445–64; P. R. Trebilco, *Jewish Communities in Asia Minor* (Cambridge, 1991); J. M. G. Barclay, *Jews in the Mediterranean Diaspora: From Alexander to Trajan* (323 BCE–117 CE) (Edinburgh, 1996).

40. S. J. D. Cohen, "The Significance of Yavneh: Pharisees, Rabbis and the End of Jewish Sectarianism," *HUCA* 55 (1984): 27–53.

41. M. Goodman, "The Function of *minim* in early Rabbinic Judaism," in Geschichte—Tradition—Reflexion, Bd. 1: *Judentum*, P. Schäfer, ed. (Tübingen, 1996), pp. 501–10.; see also M. Goodman, "Sadducees and Essenes after 70," in S. E. Porter, P. Joyce and D. E. Orton, eds., *Crossing the Boundaries* (Leiden, 1994), pp. 347–56.

42. M. Goodman, "Josephus and Variety in First-Century Judaism," *Proceedings of the Israel Academy* (forthcoming).

43. G. Hamel, *Poverty and Charity in Roman Palestine: First Three Centuries CE* (Berkeley, Los Angeles and Oxford, 1990); Z. Safrai, *The Economy of Roman Palestine* (London and New York, 1994).

44. On different models of how the Roman economy worked, see K. Hopkins, "Taxes and Trade in the Roman Empire (200BC–AD400)," *JRS* 70 (1980): 101–25; P. Garnsey and R. Saller, *The Roman Empire: Economy, Society and Culture* (London, 1987); P. Garnsey, *Food and Society in Classical Antiquity* (Cambridge, 1999). On the use of coins, see R. P. Duncan-Jones, *Structure and Scale in the Roman Economy* (Cambridge, 1997); C. Howgego, "The Supply and Use of Money in the Roman World 200BC–AD300," *JRS* 82 (1992): 1–31. On the use of archaeological evidence for economic analysis, see K. Greene, *The Archaeology of the Roman Economy* (London, 1986).

45. Safrai, *Economy of Roman Palestine*; see also J. Pastor, *Land and Economy in Ancient Palestine* (London, 1997).

46. D. Adan-Bayewitz, *Common Pottery in Roman Galilee: A Study in Local Trade* (Ramat Gan, 1993).

47. A. Oppenheimer, "Roman Rule and the Cities of the Galilee in Talmudic Literature," in Levine, ed., *Galilee in Late Antiquity* (1992); D. Sperber, *The City in Roman Palestine* (Oxford, 1998). Compare G. Fuks, *Scythopolis—a Greek City in Eretz-Israel* (Jerusalem, 1983) (Heb.); S. S. Miller, *Studies in the History and Traditions of Sepphoris* (Leiden, 1984).

48. The bibliography is now huge. See especially L. I. Levine, ed., *The Synagogue in Late Antiquity* (Philadelphia, 1987); D. Urman and P.V. M. Flesher, eds., *Ancient Synagogues: Historical Analysis and Archaeological Discovery*, 2 vols. (Leiden, 1995); S. Fine, *This Holy Place: On the Sanctity of the Synagogue during the Graeco-Roman Period* (Notre Dame, Ind., 1997); L. I. Levine, *The Ancient Synagogue: The First Thousand Years* (New Haven, Conn., 1999).

49. See L. J. Archer, *Her Price is Beyond Rubies: The Jewish Woman in Graeco-Roman Palestine* (Sheffield, 1990); Tal Ilan, *Jewish Women in Graeco-Roman Palestine* (Tübingen, 1995), includes a huge bibliography.

50. See survey of the issue in H. M. Cotton, "The Rabbis and the Documents," in M. Goodman, ed., *Jews in a Graeco-Roman World* (Oxford, 1998), pp. 167–79.

51. B. Isaac, *The Limits of Empire: The Roman Army in the East*, revised ed. (Oxford, 1992); F. Millar, *The Roman Near East 31BC–AD337* (Cambridge, Mass. and London, 1993).

52. See A. Oppenheimer, *Galilee in the Mishnaic Period*, pp. 37–44; B. Isaac and A. Oppenheimer, "The Revolt of Bar Kochba: Ideology and Modern Scholarship," *JJS* 36 (1985): 33–229. W. Eck, "The Bar Kokhba Revolt: The Roman Point of View," *JRS* 89 (1999): 76–89.

53. Z. Safrai, "The Roman Army in the Galilee," in Levine, ed., *Galilee in Late Antiquity*, pp. 103–14.

54. A. Oppenheimer, "Jewish Penal Authority in Roman Judaea," in Goodman, ed., *Jews in a Graeco-Roman World*, pp. 181–91.

55. The term is used by Stern, *Jewish Identity*, pp. 200–23.

Preface to the First Edition

This book originated in a doctoral thesis for the University of Oxford, which was submitted in May 1980. I have changed the text very little before publication, taking note only of the most important work that has appeared in the last two years.

Final publication owes a great deal to a number of institutions. Funds for research were provided by the Department of Education and Science and the Memorial Foundation for Jewish Culture. The Craven Fund financed travel to Israel in 1977. Birmingham University Library has been very helpful in acquiring books for me. Mr. Harry Buglass of the Department of Ancient History and Archaeology at Birmingham drew the map with painstaking expertise and Mrs. Valerie Howard of the same department organized the typing with great efficiency. Above all, the Oxford Centre for Postgraduate Hebrew Studies not only provided excellent facilities for study in a quiet cottage in Yarnton in 1977, but has sponsored this publication within its monograph series.

I have received much help and advice from my examiners, Dr. P. S. Alexander and Dr. A. K. Bowman, and from Professor P. A. Brunt, Ms. Dina Castel, Dr. Claudine Dauphin, Dr. G. Foerster, Dr. B. S. Jackson, and Dr. C. J. Wickham. I owe most of all to my two supervisors, Professor F. G. B. Millar and Dr. G. Vermes, who have given me constant guidance, encouragement, and inspiration. None of them is responsible for the imperfections that remain.

Finally, I dedicate this book to my wife Sarah, to whom I owe much more than thanks.

Birmingham
March 1982

PART I: INTRODUCTION

In the second century A.D. Galilee fostered the formation of rabbinic Judaism. The society that flourished there has laid its mark on Judaism ever since. It is a society that can be fully described, for the large corpus of rabbinic writings makes possible a better understanding of Roman Galilee than of any other area of the empire apart from Egypt. It will become clear in the course of this study that the development of the independent and unique Jewish culture of Late Roman Palestine was encouraged by Roman methods of administration, and that the rabbis can be best understood with a full appreciation of the world around them.

1 Sources and Method

Numerous books have been published on Roman Galilee, and another study needs some justification. It is not to be sought in fresh discoveries, important though some of those are, but in a new area of interest and new ways of using old evidence.

Historians have been interested in Galilee for a variety of reasons, and those reasons are reflected both in the topics on which they lay emphasis and in the methods they adopt. Though some of their products contain brilliant scholarship, none provides a satisfactory account of Galilean society.[1]

The history of Roman rule over Galilee provides the dates that confine this book, for A.D. 132 marked the outbreak of the last desperate Jewish revolt against Rome under Bar Kokhba, while A.D. 212 saw the granting of Roman citizenship to Galileans along with the rest of the inhabitants of the empire. But this history of resistance and accommodation has not tempted classicists to investigate the area in any depth. Roman historians have only recently begun to study the provinces for their own sake, and in the more general history of the empire Galilee is accorded only the most minor of roles. The Greek and Latin historians most readily available to classicists deal with political and military rather than social or economic history, reflecting the interests of the governing class rather than the governed. Following their lead, modern scholars find little to say about Galilee in the peaceful period between the second great Jewish revolt of A.D. 132–135 and the emergence of Christianity in the fourth century as a political force affecting Palestine, and what they do have to say concerns the Roman officials rather than the local inhabitants.[2] Galilee in this period was only a small part of the province of Syria Palaestina and was of singular unimportance in the eyes of the Roman world. Not only did no events take place there of any political impact wider than the boundaries of the area itself, but the lack of more than a few cities on the Greek model caused it to be largely ignored, even in matters of general administration. Roman historians tend to concentrate, like the ancient writers and most extant archaeological evidence, on the lives of the inhabitants of the cities that formed the administrative framework for Roman rule. It is rare for sufficient evidence to survive to write the history of a village society in the Roman world, and only special conditions make it possible for Galilee. That possibility has been generally overlooked by Roman historians up to now. There are, then, some studies of Roman administration in Galilee in this period, but the best are very brief[3] and the others tend to retroject to the second century legislation on early Byzantine Jewry as recorded in the Roman law codes.[4] It is a skimpy picture. The cause is simple: the Hebrew and Aramaic of the rabbinic texts have made them virtually unusable by classicists, many of whom are unfamiliar with those languages.[5]

Students of the development of Christianity can more often overcome the linguistic problems, but their interests lie less in the Galilee of the second century than in the background to Jesus' ministry in the first.[6] An excellent recent study by Freyne, based mostly on Josephus and concentrating on the late Hellenistic and Gospel periods confirms much of the account of Galilean society given here. Our two works can be seen as complementary and mutually confirmatory. But Freyne's observations, like those of most scholars similarly attracted to the subject for Christian theological motives, are less applicable for the period after A.D. 70. By this later period Christianity had shifted its center to the wider Mediterranean and in patristic eyes Jewish history had ended with the emergence of the Church as "verus Israel." Such scholars, therefore, concentrate reasonably enough on the evidence of the Gospels and Josephus, with rabbinic sources used, if at all, only to help fill out the accounts.[7]

For writers on Jewish history it is the emergence of rabbinic leadership after the military defeat and destruction of the Jerusalem Temple in A.D. 70 that is of most importance, and it is the rabbis' own evidence that carries most weight. Most such writers come from the very tradition of learning that those rabbis originated.[8] The result is work of great scholarship but inherent bias and blindnesses, broken only with difficulty by historical insight;[9] it is all too easy to reproduce the pietistic emphasis on the lives of early sages that is found in the sources and in the medieval Jewish historians, above all R. Sherira ha Gaon. What emerges is a history of the rabbinic movement rather than the society in which it was situated. Instead of checking this tendency by using other evidence, most such historians have resorted to ingenious sophistry when rabbinic texts disagree and to implausible interpretation of metaphors when those texts leave lacunae in the account.[10]

Finally, there are the archaeologists. They alone produce new material, and much has been excavated in recent years. Little use is made of the data produced, however, for the science has in many cases become an end in itself. Although discoveries are often correlated with the standard histories of the period, usually no attempt is made to use the archaeological information to reshape the historians' picture.[11]

In the last few years some of these gaps have begun to be bridged. Alon has applied the conclusions of Roman historians about the empire as a whole to the rabbinic evidence and thereby clarified previous conceptions about the Roman administration of Palestine.[12] Lieberman has brought great learning to a study of the evidence found in the Jewish sources for cultural contact with the non-Jewish world.[13] Sperber has recently begun a search in the rabbinic texts for quotations and laws to illustrate generalizations about Roman history in the hope that those generalizations may thereby seem confirmed.[14] A few excavators have begun to insist that their discoveries should suggest an account of late Roman Galilee radically different from the conventional rabbinic version.[15]

What new methods can be used? I shall try here to combine all the evidence—rabbinic, epigraphic, classical, patristic, and archaeological —without affording primacy to any and bearing in mind the inherent bias of each. Though Galilee must be treated as a part of the Roman Empire and similarities to other areas of Roman Syria considered with special attention,[16] I shall insist that Galilee may, in some features, be unique. To aid the elucidation of such unique features, I shall usually ignore parallel evidence from the papyri of Roman Egypt. The structure and problems of Egyptian villages were, in many respects, remarkably similar to those in Galilee, but I believe that such similarities will be all the more striking and confirmatory of the Galilean account if the Egyptian material is not used in the first place to build up that account. From the strictly relevant evidence alone, a full picture of the society of second century Galilee should emerge.

All evidence must be given weight, but it is the rabbinic sources that will prove most important simply because they are so extensive. Any study of this sort will be shaped by its use of those sources.

The rabbinic texts are heterogeneous. The work of religious enthusiasts who believed themselves to have the right to legislate for all aspects of the lives of Jews by virtue of their interpretation of the Mosaic Law, they deal with almost every area of contemporary life. Their aim is to lay down guidelines for correct behavior in all social and economic contexts as well as clarifying the relationship of men to the Divine, but it is this latter religious element of their world view that predominates and engenders an attempt to express not just social regulations but eternal truths. The texts are, then, excellent material for social history, but only with these limitations borne in mind.[17]

The Mishnah is a law code, ostensibly setting out the oral law that was said to have been received by Moses on Mt. Sinai at the same time as the written Pentateuchal law and to have been passed down from him through a long chain of teachers, finally being reduced to order by R. Judah ha Nasi, the rabbinical patriarch of the late second and early third centuries.[18] The law expounded, therefore, purports to be no more than an elaborate expansion of the biblical regulations, though, in fact, quite considerable discrepancies sometimes occur and have to be explained away with complex sophistry. However far back the traditions may go, most of the rulings (*halakha*) recorded in the Mishnah are actually described in the form of debates between rabbis of the mid first to late second century A.D. (the *tannaim*), and there is good reason to suppose a second century origin for many specific interpretations.[19] Like the author of the Pentateuch, the tannaim deal with a wide variety of everyday problems in the relation of man to man and man to God, but the emphasis is different from that of the biblical prototypes: a sizeable proportion deals with Temple ritual and even more deals with the laws of purity in a huge expansion of Leviticus 11–15.

The whole work is in colloquial Hebrew, but in a very stylized formal mode of discourse appropriate to an intention to create in words an eternal metaphysical structure to be imposed on the physical world.[20] It does not prescribe correct behavior, but rather describes that behavior as if it was normal, a not uncommon technique for importing solemnity to legal regulations.[21]

No law code can be complete, and the Mishnah, like all ancient compilations, did not even set out to be. Some of the tannaitic rulings were gathered together slightly later into a separate collection called the Tosefta ("Supplement"), in which much the same topics are covered. It is at times, in effect, simply a commentary on the Mishnah. Very much later, in late fourth century Palestine and fifth century Babylonia, the much more extensive commentaries of later rabbis (*amoraim*) were compiled into the two Talmuds with a different language, Aramaic, and a different, specialized vocabulary using new rules and methods of argument. Since the Talmuds are set out as discussions of the tannaitic Mishnah, they frequently describe and discuss those events of the first and second centuries A.D. to which the Mishnah itself refers.

Apart from the Mishnah and the Tosefta, the tannaim also compiled commentaries (*midrashim*) on the Bible. Of these, four survive: Mekhilta on Exodus (in two versions), Sifra on Leviticus, Sifre Bamidbar on Numbers, and Sifre Devarim on Deuteronomy. These works attempt to expound the biblical text in accordance with rabbinical views of what contemporary Judaism should be like, relating, so far as they can, the law found in the Mishnah to the original biblical statements on which they purport to be founded and trying to extract moral lessons from scriptural stories. At times they slip into pure sermonizing with the narration of parables, tales of worthy sages, and numerous moral maxims.

How can these texts be safely used by historians? The legal regulations found cover most areas of civil, criminal, and liturgical law. The rabbis legislate for the smooth operation of farming, commerce, and industry; for peace within the family and community; and for the purity of the individual and his physical effects before the Divine. It is not the legislation itself that can provide social historians with evidence so much as the assumptions that lie behind that legislation. When a law is issued it can be inferred that the society to which it is addressed could, even if it did not, respond to that law. If certain terms and concepts are used by the jurists it can be assumed that those would have some meaning in contemporary society. There was no point in inventing homilies and laws about everyday life unless that life was recognizably that of the audience. It is in the elucidation of this background that the rabbinic texts are so valuable.

This is a far more limited use to that proposed by previous students of Jewish history. For most scholars cited above, the existence of a rabbinic injunction is taken to indicate that the injunction was obeyed.[22] Though it is recognized by some that there were indeed nonrabbinic Jews in Galilee, it is assumed, from the wishful thinking

of the rabbis themselves, that such Jews were only minority rene-
gades.[23] For me, on the other hand, rabbinic legislation reveals nothing
of society except in the general assumptions it makes—apart from
those occasions when a specific injunction is reiterated by later rabbis,
a sign that the rule has been flouted in the interim. The value of specific legislation lies more obviously in the history of rabbinic thought
and values, itself still far too little studied.[24] It is an undue credulity
about rabbinic effectiveness in social matters that has led to most of
the faults in earlier studies and, in particular, to frequent reliance on
selected single quotations and laws taken out of context to support
theories of social, economic, and religious history.[25]

Finally, it cannot be assumed that the rabbinic tradition was mono-
lithic, that rabbis could not change their social position, political aims,
and even religious preoccupations over the centuries, particularly in
the early years when the traditions of the rabbinical schools were still
in the making.[26] It is by ignoring this that all scholars until very
recent years have treated evidence from the fourth, fifth, or even
tenth centuries A.D. as if it had equal standing with more contemporary evidence of the second century. Because a "rabbinic" society
had long been dominant in Mesopotamia by the tenth century when
R. Sherira wrote, he assumed that the same was true of tannaitic Galilee, but he is likely to have been wrong.[27]

In trying to combat this danger, I shall follow the lead of Neusner
in confining my use of the rabbinic texts to those that are contemporary. The Jerusalem Talmud of late fourth century Palestine and
the Babylonian Talmud of fifth century Mesopotamia may well contain trustworthy traditions about the tannaitic period, but it has been
shown that even those stories and laws that appear most reliable—
because they are ascribed in the texts to tannaim and are couched in
tannaitic Hebrew and Mishnaic formulas (i.e., *baraitot*)—are likely
to be either misremembered in the light of subsequent changes in
rabbinic thought or even deliberately falsified to aid such changes.[28]
Once a reliable picture of Galilee has been evolved from contemporary
evidence it might well be fruitful to comb later sources for traditions
that fit in, but this would take too long to attempt here. Meanwhile,
many familiar episodes and stock passages about second century
Galilee will be omitted here because they come from one of the later
Talmuds.[29] When they disagree with the tannaitic sources they
should, I submit, be regarded as better evidence for talmudic society

than for second century Galilee; when they conform, they may be reinserted by the reader.

Such an emphasis on the use of only select rabbinic texts makes it all the more important to establish precise dating of the compilation of the tannaitic works discussed above and of individual utterances enshrined in them. The presence of a given text in a compilation is itself significant, since one can assume that anything that the compiler included was considered by him *in some way* relevant in his own time.

The Mishnah was compiled, according to all the later tradition, by R. Judah I ha Nasi.[30] There is no reason to doubt the tradition; apart from the rather peculiar tractate *Abot*, none of the rabbis quoted taught at a later date.[31] The date suggested most recently for R. Judah I's death is the early 220s,[32] so the Mishnah would belong near to that date. The text can be considered little changed, despite the possibility that the first compilation was oral and despite some differences between the Palestinian and the Babylonian texts, for a natural conservatism in the treatment of sacred texts, as the Mishnah fast became, is evident in the failure to edit out disagreements, and variant texts occur far more in baraitot that were not considered binding from the beginning.[33]

The corresponding tradition about the Tosefta claims that it was compiled by R. Hiya in the mid third century.[34] This has been widely challenged by scholars, with dates up to the fifth century being proposed.[35] More recently, Neusner has claimed the reliability of the halakhic evidence in the Tosefta on the grounds of its coherence with that given in the Mishnah[36] and this would seem reason enough to date the compilation of the work to the Mishnaic period or soon after in the third century (as the Talmudic tradition claims). An excess of caution in this regard can lead to the perverse assumption that the work is not the tannaitic compilation that it purports to be until its credentials are proved (an impossible condition), so that in Neusner's translation of the Tosefta, he rather surprisingly adopts M. D. Herr's view of a late, c. A.D. 400 date for compilation of the Tosefta, though still treating Mishnah-Tosefta as a "complete and whole system." Herr's dating depends entirely on the existence in the Palestinian Talmud of corrupt versions of baraitot that occur in clearer form in the Tosefta. He explains this as the editing of corrupt versions by the Tosefta compiler after the compilation of the Palestinian Talmud, which would therefore date Tosefta to *after* A.D. 400. But the phenomenon he notes could equally well arise from ignorance among particular rabbis of the text of an already compiled Tosefta—as he himself says, amoraim on occasion also dispute the exact text of Mishnah, whose c. A.D. 200 redaction no one doubts. It is reasonable therefore to argue for an early to mid third century date for the Tosefta compilation: rabbis quoted are tannaitic; halakhic preoccupations are precisely those of the Mishnah (e.g., re *am haarez*, purity, and tithing); the Tosefta's comments on the Mishnah form the *beginning* of some Talmudic commentaries and do not presuppose the *end* (i.e., later amoraic halakha); there is no evident motive for the compilation of the Tosefta after the completion of the Palestinian Talmud, whereas its utility as the first commentary on the Mishnah soon after the latter's publication is obvious; and there are no indications whatsoever of awareness of the new Christian Byzantine Empire as found in later midrash and the Palestinian Talmud itself (e.g., heretics as emperors). Though precise dating of the compilation is therefore impossible, it is perverse to argue for anything later than c. A.D. 250, and it is very likely to be a good deal earlier in the third century.[37]

The tannaitic midrashim appear also to have been compiled in the same period since the last teachers named are tannaitic (pre-R. Judah ha Nasi). It is no argument to put them all in the fifth century just because the compilations are not mentioned as such in either Talmud —why should they be?[38] But more serious is the case against the Mekhiltas. The demonstration by Wacholder that the Mekhilta of R. Ishmael could be a pseudoepigraphic work of the eighth century is an argument that only fails to convince because it would be difficult to infiltrate a semisacred text into an established canon at such a date,[39] and the argument by Shraga Abramson that Md Rashbi differs radically from the other tannaitic texts renders it very suspect.[40] For the other midrashim the main problem has been sorting out the earlier, pre-A.D. 70 midrashim that some passages of the New Testament seem to imitate,[41] but what seems decisive here is the dependence of the *legal* ideas in Sifre on the Mishnah and Tosefta as much as (or, in the case of Sifra, more than) on Scripture.[42] If Neusner is right that the legal traditions begin only *after* A.D. 70, then the *terminus post quem* of the compilation of these midrashim is at least firm.[43] In sum, it would seem wisest to rely on the midrashim less than on the Mishnah and Tosefta, and to use the Mekhiltas as little as possible.[44]

Particular passages in these texts can usually be dated by the rabbis said to participate in them. The rabbis themselves can be put in chronological sequence by what is known of their teachers, pupils, and interlocutors from the texts themselves,[45] though even this is not secure since the habit of attributing a ruling to an earlier or more influential teacher to aid its acceptance is attested,[46] and misattribution might disguise changes in the halakha.[47] One can overcome this by various methods. It is reasonable to assume that if point A is deduced from point B, then point B must be an earlier ruling. If rabbis disagree on the minutiae of a problem, then the general principle must have been conceded earlier. Rules that continue despite their inappropriateness must be relatively early and well-established to be tolerated. Teachings attributed to an early rabbi and then commented on by a later rabbi are thereby partially confirmed for the earlier teacher—and so on. Add to this that the new synagogue inscription from near Beth Shean teaches above all the need to put law into its geographical context,[48] and it can be seen that a history of early rabbinic law will be slow to emerge.

This system will work for rabbinic *law*, but rabbinical *stories*, the *aggadah*, cannot be individually dated even by such means. The rabbi who made the comment is not always quoted, and pseudonymity is likely here too. The same applies to stories *about* rabbis, especially since there seems to grow up something of a pattern in the description of rabbinical behavior, suggesting that all their activities were reported within certain narrative structures, regardless of historicity.[49]

These difficulties in dating particular passages should not cause us too much concern. If the date and place of compilation is accepted, it is probable that all the stories and laws were taken as relevant to second and early third century Galilee and that the details of those stories were comprehensible to members of that society. It is true that when the rabbis cited are from the schools of early second century Yabneh in Judaea and when the discussion recorded seems to belong to a stratum of the argument earlier than that which the editors of the texts themselves considered important, it may well be that the assumptions lying behind the rulings are those of pre-Bar Kokhba Judaea rather than those of Galilee in the later years of the century, though some later influence by Galilean conditions is likely even here. But references to such earlier conditions are rare since most law was refined by the Galilean rabbis.[50] The background to the rest of the rabbinic texts will be the society of R. Judah ha Nasi, the compiler of the Mishnah.

Even after dating several problems remain. It is hard to disentangle secular information from religious texts without a clear idea of the religious intentions of the authors. The history of second century rabbinic Judaism is only now beginning to achieve clarification through the efforts of Neusner and his pupils.[51] Until the source criticism essential for such an analysis has been done and the task completed, there will be a danger that a social historian will mistake for a change in the power relations within a society what is in fact a change in the religious ideology of a small and perhaps unrepresentative group. There is not space to attempt such source criticism here.

It would be useful to know the precise function of the texts at the time of composition, but here, too, there is still controversy with little indication from the texts. The Mishnah may have been an aid to learning for rabbinical students or a law code intended for mass application.[52] If I tend toward the former view it is because of the formalism of the language (which would seem to need an insider's knowledge for comprehension) and because of the considerable nonlegal element included. The Mishnah will not then itself have enjoyed wide circulation, being confined, especially if preserved orally, to rabbinical students alone, but the ideas expressed within the work may both reflect a wider society and have influenced that society through the prestige of the rabbis. The midrashic commentaries to the Pentateuch, on the other hand, are much more likely to have reached a wide audience since they fit well into the first century nonrabbinic accounts of the teaching and exposition of the Mosaic Law in the synagogue.[53] It is eminently likely that the background portrayed in a midrash intended for a wider audience will differ from that in the halakhic works, especially since these latter texts will be prone to reflect the interests as well as the situation of the group for which they were composed. If, then, a class bias emerges, evident in a consistent interest in the problems and status of the *baal habayit*, the male householder, it will be hard to judge whether this reflects an inbalance in society or an inbalance in the group around the rabbinical leaders.

Furthermore, if the Mishnah and Tosefta are reckoned to be the products of an intense religious group for the consumption of fellow believers, is there any reason to expect any of the laws to be even in theory applicable to contemporary social reality? It has been suggested that some of the speculation on purity was only theoretical, a meta-physical construct not intended to affect actual behavior;[54] it is obvious that debates in the second century on the management of the Temple cult could not have had practical significance. Why, then, believe that the civil and criminal law or the regulations over tithing and marriage customs were ever intended for imposition on real people? Only recently has an answer been readily to hand: papyri from the early second century found in the Judaean desert contain marriage and other laws very similar to that laid down in the tannaitic texts and confirm that the rabbis were describing something close to contemporary legal reality, however idiosyncratic a slant they may have put on it.[55] The belief that the rabbinic texts are *completely* divorced from social practicalities is not tenable: the very success of rabbis in spreading the appeal of their artificial world to nonrabbinic Galilean Jews during the third and fourth centuries indicates that their map was seen to correspond in some way to Galilean society itself. The rabbinic law codes are no more and no less divorced from reality than the theoretical formulations of Roman lawyers in the Justinianic *Digest*, and their pronouncements are just as validly used for social history.[56]

Nonetheless it is clearly possible that particular stories might have been invented to demonstrate a legal theory and that particular rulings might owe more to the imagination of jurists than to contemporary conditions. The danger of being misled can be circumvented in various ways. Stories that begin with "it happened that . . ."(ב. . .מעשה) or that contain circumstantial details are probably true since theoretical rulings by a sage would be just as binding as real ones and there was thus no motive for invention. Novelties in the law are likely to indicate social or religious change when it cannot be shown that they spring from the internal logic of the system. Above all, anything in the rabbinic sources will be more credible if it can be corroborated from outside evidence.

The tannaitic texts are so full in their coverage of some aspects of contemporary life that it has seemed to me reasonable to propose solid conclusions on the basis of their silence about particular inci-dents or institutions. No argument *ex silentio* is ever very safe, and those proffered here are suggested with due caution. However, it would seem to me to be a justifiable procedure on topics in which there is considerable rabbinic interest, such as court administration or the relations of Jews to gentiles. I shall therefore conclude that when rabbinic silence on a *prima facie* important matter cannot be shown to be due to lack of concern, it is likely that the matter was not, in fact, important in Galilean society. If there is nonrabbinic contemporary evidence to support this, so much the better. What cannot be justified is the insertion into gaps in the tannaitic evidence of material from the later rabbinic sources; if the talmudic commentaries on the Mishnah discuss matters ignored by the primary texts, then the silence of those texts is all the more likely to be significant.

Numerous other sources that supplement the primary texts have rather different views. The Hellenized Jewish aristocrat Josephus wrote in Greek to inform gentiles about Jewish history and customs and to glorify his role in the first revolt of A.D. 66–70, first on the Jewish, and then on the Roman side.[57] The evidence is, of course, all from the first century and therefore out of date, and the interpretation reflects the views of the sophisticated wealthy of Jerusalem as opposed to those of the inhabitants of rural Galilee, but the geographical information is detailed and mostly reliable, and Josephus presents in himself an excellent case study of the difficulty of straddling Greek and Semitic cultures that afflicted all Jews in Palestine.[58]

The New Testament suffers the same chronological and geographical limitations, losing interest in Galilee after the Gospel accounts. As Josephus may exaggerate the importance of the area he commanded, so there is a danger that the Gospels may exaggerate the importance of the area where Jesus grew up and taught.[59] The Gospels tend to schematize, and there is little circumstantial evidence like that found in Acts that concerns Galilee.[60] Nevertheless, the Galilean rural background of the Gospels can be recognized as that of the rabbis.[61]

Of later Church writings, few that are contemporary refer to Galilee. The *Didache*, an interesting manual for new converts, is implausibly ascribed by some scholars to Galilee, but seems more likely to come from second century Syria.[62] The dialogue of Justin Martyr with Trypho has a useful view of contemporary Palestine, but from the outside. Closer to home but later in date is Origen, whose work *Contra Celsum* was probably written in the 240s in Caesarea to persuade those "unacquainted with Christianity or weak in the faith"[63] against the attacks by the Alexandrian philosopher Celsus in the mid second century against both Christians and Jews. Origen was living in Caesarea, but it is hard to distinguish the views he held in Alexandria from those held later on in Palestine.[64] Some of his remarks in this work and his biblical commentaries are so inaccurate about the Jews in Palestine that his more sweeping statements must be taken with caution,[65] and the familiarity of Caesareans with conditions inland in Galilee cannot be assumed.[66] Similar caution is needed with the evidence of Eusebius of Caesarea in the early fourth century. The *Onomasticon* gives brief details of places in Palestine to illuminate biblical references to them, and the *Martyrs of Palestine*, surviving in a short Greek and a longer Syriac version, gives a highly-colored account of Christian martyrdoms, mostly in Caesarea under Diocletian.[67] But Eusebius does not seem to have scrutinized Galilee too closely, for he claims that Khorazin lay in ruins, whereas the most recent excavations at the synagogue suggest it was still standing after his death,[68] and this despite the proximity of Khorazin to the road leading to Damascus. Later on in the fourth century, the fanatical bishop of Salamis in Cyprus, Epiphanius, devotes a passage to events in Galilee,[69] but this evidence is all rather late for the present purpose, as is that of Jerome in Bethlehem in the 390s.[70]

Of the secular evidence, no Roman historian was concerned with any events in Palestine in the second century apart from the Bar Kokhba revolt,[71] and only incidental information can be gleaned from the pages of Cassius Dio, Herodian, or others.[72] The rather fuller information from the *Historia Augusta* is likely to belong to the late fourth century and deserves little credence.[73] The Roman legal texts referring to this period however, though mostly compiled in the sixth century, are nevertheless useful—the survival of contradictory laws suggests that Tribonian's revision for Justinian of his *Code* and the *Digest* was not very thorough.[74] When other versions of laws survive separately from the codes, they are nonetheless preferable,[75] particularly when, like the fifth century *Syro-Roman Law Book*, they appear to apply to this area of the empire.[76] Similar official and administrative evidence can be culled from the Latin inscriptions set up by the army or as milestones, or, much more rarely, by governors, procurators, or the *coloniae* of the coast, such as Caesarea and Berytus.[77] The quite numerous Greek and Aramaic inscriptions reveal rather more of the culture of Rome's subjects, for both languages are used not only on official city inscriptions (though these are much rarer in Galilee than elsewhere in Syria), but on tombstones and as graffiti, and they express the beliefs, hopes, and fears of ordinary people.[78]

Finally, there is the rapidly expanding evidence provided by archaeology.[79] There has been no full survey of sites in Galilee since the survey of Western Palestine in the 1880s,[80] but many sites have been dug and identified since then. There have been important digs at Beth Shearim,[81] Capernaum,[82] Khorazin,[83] Kh. Shema',[84] and Meiron,[85] and much useful information from digs and local surveys elsewhere.[86] Little of the evidence from these sites is accurately dated. Only recently is any clear pottery sequence being worked out, and the varied terminology of different excavators is frequently confusing—so a second century site may have "Middle Roman," "Roman II and early Roman III" or "Late Roman" pottery on it,[87] and precisely dating a coherent cultural period or phase of occupation to "180 AD to Diocletian" depends largely on coin finds.[88] Most digging is still in search of public buildings rather than for the settlement patterns or the economy of the ancient society being studied,[89] but there is nonetheless a great deal available to correlate with the literary and epigraphic evidence to give a fairly full picture of the society of Roman Galilee in the second century.

2 Geography: Topography and Resources

Topography[1]

Palestine lies in southern Syria between the desert to the east and the Mediterranean to the west, and between the fertile plains of northern Syria and the Sinai desert leading to the irrigated fields of Egypt to the south. The natural divisions of the country itself reflect this position between desert and sea, for Palestine is split into four parallel bands running from north to south: the coastal plain to the west, down which so many armies passed on the way to Egypt and back; the central ridge formed by the hills of Judaea, Samaria, and Galilee; the river Jordan, which brings water from the Lebanon and Anti-Lebanon in the north and, sinking ever deeper into its rift below sea level, flows through the Lake of Tiberias down to the Dead Sea; the eastern range of hills, somewhat less fertile than those on the west of the Jordan; and finally the desert border stretching away into the east. All the features run from north to south—only the occasional broad valley between the hills, like the Jezreel valley on the southern border of Galilee, breaks the pattern. The different sections of the country would therefore nourish varied inhabitants, secluded in the one part or another without overmuch influence from the neighboring areas. And nowhere more so than in parts of Galilee where the hills cut the country off from the coastal plain and the desert is never visible.[2]

Nevertheless it would be wrong to consider Galilee as isolated from the rest of Syria. The great trade routes brought goods along the Mediterranean coast and from the east across the Arabian desert. It was not a trade from which the Galileans themselves profited since it was firmly controled by the desert peoples whose cities reached their peak of prosperity in this period,[3] but they could catch a glimpse of the outside world from the merchants hurrying through to the great entrepôts of the coast and buy the luxury goods they brought from the

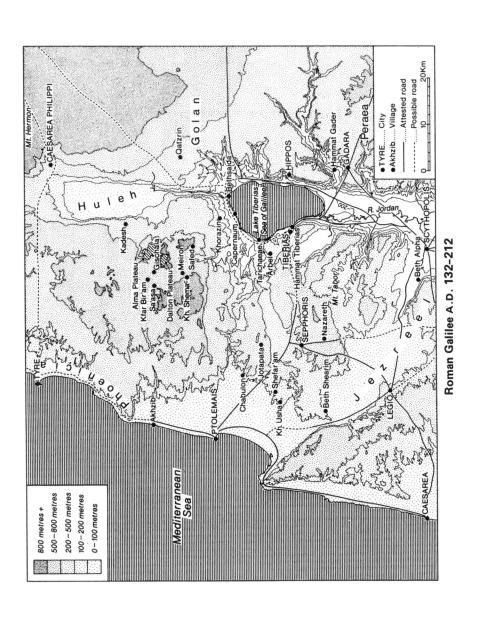

Roman Galilee A.D. 132–212

East through middlemen who bought the caravans' wares.[4] The great road from Damascus to Egypt came down from the Golan plateau just north of the Lake of Tiberias, and passed over the Plain of Arbel on its way southward,[5] and there were quite easy routes going from east to west over the parallel valley of Lower Galilee that connected the area with Akko and the coast.[6] Upper Galilee is rather more secluded —the plateau of Safed and Meiron is difficult of access from the west, south, and east, but the hills to the north leading to Tyre are easy enough to cross, and the main route from Tyre to Damascus via Paneas (Caesarea Philippi) lies only fifteen or so miles away.[7]

Contact with the coastal area was continuous. The borders of Lower Galilee on the west are gentle foothills and in these areas mixing with the coastal population was natural. Nevertheless, the exploitation of the sea, like the desert trade, was hard for Galileans against competition from the inhabitants of the coast, and Galilee, like Palestine in general, was not primarily commercial (as Josephus protested).[8] Only a few Galileans did trade on the sea and were successful,[9] using Ptolemais-Akko, which Josephus describes as the "maritime city of Galilee."[10]

Trade, then, brought the inhabitants of Galilee into contact with both the seacoast and the desert. The Phoenician coast had a well-established gentile population[11] that had long had uneasy but close relations with the interior, both politically (Tyre encroached in c. 43–2 B.C. on Galilee[12]) and culturally (not only did Jesus visit the regions of Tyre and Sidon,[13] but the sick came from there to Galilee to be healed[14]). So, too, for economic relations—Phoenicia used food grown in the inland areas in the first century,[15] though the scarcity of good land in the more mountainous regions may have led to less friendly economic relations at times.[16] Akko, Tyre, and Sidon are the coastal cities most often mentioned in the rabbinic sources of this period. Caesarea appears far less often, despite its size and growing prosperity,[17] both because it is farther away and perhaps for lack either of a large Jewish community or of a rabbinic school.[18]

There were gentile cities bordering on Galilee in the east, too. Much of the range of hills east of the river Jordan had been parceled out between such cities by the mid first century, so that the area gained geographical designation as the Decapolis.[19] These cities had less fertile land than Galilee,[20] but most, like Gerasa,[21] flourished on the proceeds of the caravan trade, and those in the northern part, on the South Golan, even enjoyed an agricultural boom in this period.[22] They presented models of cultured Hellenized living to the Galileans of the neighboring hill range.[23]

To the south, Galilee was separated from Samaria, with whom relations had long been uneasy,[24] by the territories of Caesarea, Sebaste, and Scythopolis (Beth Shean), which took over all the flat fertile land of the plains of Megiddo, Jezreel, and Beth Shean. With Scythopolis in particular relations were close in the second century.[25] Judaea, even if Jews had been allowed to go there,[26] was four days' journey through unfriendly Samaria,[27] and after A.D. 135 contact was rare.

Galilee was therefore susceptible to outside influence from all four directions, but the region was itself large enough to allow for some diversity within it. The area bounded by the Jezreel plain, Litany Gorge, the Jordan valley, and the coastal plain is about fifty miles from north to south and twenty-five to thirty-five from east to west.[28] The area below sealevel around the Lake of Tiberias might seem a quite separate region with its warm, humid atmosphere and fertile plains, but, since Galilean rock is limestone except for the basalt dykes near to and north of the lake, the countryside there seems more similar to the Golan plateau on the east side of the lake than anything else.[29]

But the chief division must be between Upper and Lower Galilee.[30] The plateau beneath Safed is not easy to reach from the valleys of Lower Galilee below, let alone from the Huleh valley to the east. Nor is the land sufficiently fertile for such access to be particularly desirable for its own sake—the small plain between Meiron and Gischala and other plateaus like those of Dalton and Alma are no match for the wide valleys of Lower Galilee such as the Sepphoris plain.

In both Lower and Upper Galilee the hilltops are all accessible, if with difficulty. There are only two exceptionally high mountains: Mt. Hermon to the northeast and Mt. Asamon in western Lower Galilee compared to which nearby Jotapata's formidable hill is easy to climb.[31] Other hills appear bigger than they really are—Mt. Tabor's steep sides obtrude because of its isolation in the Lower Galilee plain.[32] But even the less steep hilltops of Upper Galilee are too infertile for much use to be made of them in antiquity (as now), and it is in the valleys that the country's greatest wealth lies. The main problem in exploiting these valleys is one of drainage. So, the Sepphoris plain, like the Huleh valley, easily reverts to marsh land,[33] but once drainage is achieved (and the Sepphoris plain was certainly cultivated in this period[34]) the land is immensely fertile, as Josephus narrates with pride.[35] The comparatively abundant water supply, from the water seeping through the limestone from the Anti-Lebanon, was, despite the light rainfall, one of the great natural advantages of Galilee;[36] the lack of water the year round from rivers, apart from the Jordan, meant that the trapping and collection of such water seepage was essential to the survival of the inhabitants. Cisterns dug for this purpose are perhaps the most common form of monumental remains left from the Roman period in Galilee.[37] Digging such cisterns was easy in the soft limestone, and many caves are found formed by natural erosion or dug out for burial,[38] so many, indeed, that R. Shimon claimed that if they and the watch towers counted as dwelling places, then the area from Tiberias to Sepphoris must be accounted a continuous suburb.[39] Stories of caves being subsequently used in this way for dwellings are numerous.[40]

The rain, when it came, made the climate temperate and the country green. Extremes were, of course, possible: fires racing at terrible speeds in the evening wind in a hot summer reduced the extent to which an arsonist could be held responsible for his crime,[41] earthquakes were quite common throughout the region,[42] heavy snowfalls were not unknown,[43] and if the rains fell too heavily they could cause widespread damage.[44] However, what the inhabitants feared most was drought. The effect of forty days without rain in the normal rainy season in the autumn could be catastrophic.[45] The whole of the mishnaic tractate Taanit deals with the measures needed to avert such a calamity.

The prayers and fasts required by the tractate were, however, the last resort. In most areas the natural resources could be husbanded by careful planning. A few of the hill settlements had their own spring,[46] but usually wells had to be dug or, more often, cisterns quarried to catch the rain and seepage water.[47] The abundant waters of the river Jordan were of no use outside the river valley, being too far below the level of even Lower Galilee for pumping up for irrigation. So all depended on careful hoarding: cisterns were plastered, cemented, and painted[48] in most settlements[49] for use by individual farmers[50] and could be deep enough to drown a man.[51]

Of other natural resources, Galilee lacked any metals for exploitation,[52] but was well-wooded (which provided cheap fuel) and had in the limestone an easy material for building.[53] Various wild animals are recorded: wolves,[54] deer,[55] moles, mice, and snakes.[56]

Resources

The natural geography of Galilee thus renders it capable of supporting a large population on its fertile soil. The evidence of Josephus and archaeology is that it did so.[57] On what was their economy based?

According to Josephus in the first century, Galilee was very fruitful with large numbers of trees and "no part lying idle."[58] Around Lake Tiberias, walnuts, palms, figs, and olives grew in a perfect climate,[59] and the area north of the lake Capernaum produced grapes as well for ten months of the year.[60] Galilee with Peraea produced tribute of two hundred talents a year.[61]

Josephus doubtless exaggerates,[62] but the picture is essentially correct. The Galilean valleys produced sufficient grain to avoid a need to import, and perhaps more than sufficient on the basalt of East Galilee and the Golan,[63] though the really fertile lands of Phoenicia and the Jezreel valley were not in the control of people who thought of themselves as Galileans,[64] unless Beth Shearim managed to encroach a little into the flat land to the south and east.[65] Galilean grain production was on a smaller scale and intended for the local communities[66] with little fields in the valleys devoted to wheat or barley[67] and sometimes using terraces as in Samaria.[68]

However, Galilee, like other tax-paying areas of the Roman Empire, must have produced exports to exceed imports in order to earn the coin needed to pay Roman taxes, and where Galilee excelled was in the cultivation of olives, which thrived on the soil and were unworried by gentle slopes. Galilean olive oil was famous.[69] Josephus says that it was exported to the north in the first century.[70] Sifre to Deuteronomy records a visit by an *epimeletes* from Laodicea to Gischala via Tyre in the search for oil when supplies ran out in northern Syria and the astonishing ease with which his request was granted.[71] It is significant that the place recorded is in both cases in Upper Galilee, for there, as much as to the south, olive production flourished.[72] As in parts of northern Syria,[73] the prosperity of Galilee in the second century depended on the export of these olives, a market being easy to find since oil in the ancient world was an important fuel and soap substitute as well as food. Numerous oil presses have come to light,[74] and care for the trees could come dangerously close to witchcraft.[75] The temptation for owners was to place them as close as possible to the settlements to help them keep watch over them.[76] Although Josephus records the importance of the industry in the first century, it became increasingly important in the second after the Bar Kokhba war because of the large influx of immigrants, for, with the valleys already intensively farmed, more land could be found only on the more marginal hill slopes where grain would be difficult to grow but olive trees might flourish.[77]

Other crops were purely for a local market: vines, though ubiquitous, were less exceptionally productive. Neatly shaped vineyards[78] are often described—the rabbinic sources are interested in avoiding forbidden juxtapositions of crops on the ground.[79] Wine vats crop up rather less in the sources than the oil presses,[80] perhaps because they are less permanent and less solid structures. Equally local is the market for vegetables.[81]

All this agriculture left its mark on the countryside: watchtowers, oil presses, cisterns,[82] terracing (though this is very difficult to date),[83] field clearances,[84] fences and walls (though perhaps not usually in the valleys),[85] well-trod paths,[86] and numerous enclosures for security.[87]

The country was less well suited to intensive pastoral farming, and it would seem that in most areas cattle were kept only on a small scale. Only the basalt ridges of the north Golan were better used for grazing than agriculture,[88] though one text suggests exceptional meat production in the hillier areas of Upper Galilee.[89] Even small-scale cattle breeding was useful for manure, though there is no evidence for transhumance and perhaps carting from the cattle enclosure was normal,[90] and on the lush grass of Lower Galilee cattle could grow to impressive sizes.[91] But in so heavily cultivated an area there were many difficulties in preventing cattle causing damage to crops—there is mention of cowbells,[92] and in Samaria, which was similarly intensively cultivated, signs of walled roads for livestock traffic have been found.[93] Unlike the desert cattle that wandered loose,[94] most of the halakha about cattle assumes that they are kept in or near to the settlement rather than in distant pasturages.[95]

Though cattle were useful, the most profitable animals to keep were sheep and goats; the problem was that their tendency to erode the countryside was well known.[96] Despite considerable pressures not to raise such "small cattle" for this reason, the continuation of complaints from one generation to the next suggests that herds continued to be common.[97] Kept on the hilltops in summer and in the sheep folds in winter,[98] the sheep and goats destroyed crops and trees and caused havoc when they broke into insecurely fenced fields.[99] But for the landless the relatively easy living provided by sheep and goats was always a greater lure than the eventual well-being of the community on uneroded soil.[100]

Finally, one form of food production of considerable local importance was fishing. The Mediterranean, the Jordan river, and Lake of Tiberias were all intensively fished,[101] the fishermen of the lake probably exporting some of their catch in salted form.[102]

The economy was thus based on agriculture and on olive oil production in particular. Most industry in the area was connected with the processing of that crop.[103] Galilee had no natural resources to encourage other products. Palestinian flax made distinctive textiles whose fame spread abroad to Pausanias[104] and perhaps encouraged the weaving both of silk bought from the caravans bearing it from the East and of wool from the local sheep.[105] But these, like leather tanning and pottery production, were minor industries serving the home market primarily.[106] Glass would seem to have been made in Tiberias in the fourth century,[107] but since the raw materials had to be imported from the Mediterranean coast,[108] it is likely that in the second century most glass production was still centered on Akko,[109] there being no evidence that the Tiberian glass industry had yet begun operations in this period.[110]

PART II: SOCIETY

3 Settlement and Population

Galilee boasted a large population[1] but only two˙cities, Tiberias and Sepphoris.[2] Neither city seems to have been very large,[3] so the majority of the population was scattered over the countryside in villages, described variously in the rabbinic sources as עיר, עירה, or כפר.[4]

Settlement

It would be misleading to see the villages as just offshoots or dependencies of the cities. Tiberias was very much an artificial creation by the tetrarch Herod and enjoyed a less than comfortable relation with the already existing Galilean villages after its foundation.[5] Josephus and the Gospels give the impression that in the first century there was no great difference in the importance of the cities and the larger villages.[6] Admittedly, Sepphoris is called "the strongest *polis* in Galilee"[7] and is sometimes contrasted to "the Galileans" who try to force her into revolt against Rome,[8] but Josephus is prepared to use the term "polis" of many other settlements in Galilee that had no constitutional right to the name: Tarichaeae, Chabulon, Gabara, Gischala, and Jotapata.[9] This is not through ignorance—Josephus can be careful when he chooses and calls Kaphethra in Idumaea a ψευδοπολίχνιον.[10] It may be partly due to the self-important exaggeration of the *Bellum*,[11] and it is true that Iapha, a polis in the *Bellum*, is termed "the greatest κώμη of Galilee" in the parallel *Vita*.[12] But Tarichaeae is still called a polis in the *Vita*,[13] and this emphasis on the size and power of the larger Galilean villages is confirmed by the Gospels—Capernaum and Nazareth are both termed "polis,"[14] and the villages are often called collectively the πόλεις καὶ κῶμαι,[15] or even once, most accurately, the κωμοπόλεις.[16] In this Galilee shows strong similarities to north Syrian and Hauran villages, for inscriptions show that they, too, behaved much like the *poleis*.[17]

It is, then, on these large and, as will be shown, prosperous villages that most attention will be focussed. To the economic, cultural, and political relations between them and the two cities I shall return in the relevant chapters.[18]

Classifying the Galilean settlements by positing rigid distinctions to correspond to the different terms used in the rabbinic sources has led to confusion rather than clarity, particularly when evidence from widely disparate periods is used.[19] If the term עיר at times referred to a large "rural" settlement,[20] and at other times to an "urban" settlement,[21] this neither proves nor disproves the possibility that at other dates it was used to denote an isolated farm.[22] The Latin term "villa" undergoes precisely this change of meaning.[23] Nor is there any sign that the administrative role of a settlement was the primary designation of its name.[24] Three general distinctions of size do however emerge: the כרך (*Kerakh*) or large city, the עיר ('ir, by far the most common), and the כפר (*Kefar*) or small village.[25] These distinctions were doubtless not rigid, but there were differences in living conditions: in the large city young girls spent more time in the baths, whereas in the small villages they were more likely to have to work at the millstone and carry heavy weights.[26] Animal fat was rarely eaten in the small villages, birds and the more exotic sorts of fish and locusts were also rare,[27] and building styles were less lavish.[28] But since it is the 'ir that gets mentioned by far the most often,[29] it would seem reasonable to assume that the data given in rabbinic texts about life in the 'ir applies to the large villages already described by Josephus in Galilee.

Fifty-two such villages have been identified,[30] a great increase in both Galilee and the Golan since the Hellenistic period.[31] The size of the villages is difficult to gauge. Yeivin made guesses of between 100 dunams (c. 10 hectares) and 10 dunams (c. 1 hectare) on 10 sites,[32] but his estimates, based on aerial photography,[33] are considered too small by far by the excavators of Kh. Shema' and Meiron, basing their estimates on limited excavation.[34] The difference is considerable: c. 10 hectares compared to c. 30.[35] Mazar suggested c. 25 acres (10 hectares) for Beth Shearim;[36] Yeivin suggested 6 hectares only at Khorazin where he did excavate.[37]

The siting of settlements in the first century had shown a strong interest in defense. So Gamala, Jotapata, and Gischala are all perched on top of steep, rather uncomfortable hills, as is Nazareth.[38] However, from the second century on, the favored sites for new settlements were further down the hills, on the lower slopes or on small elevations next to level ground.[39] This move toward more comfortable but less easily defended sites also affected some long-established settlements —at both Jotapata and Sepphoris there seems to be second century settlement below the old citadels.[40] Pottery and comments in tannaitic texts would date this change to the early third century at the latest; it is most likely related to the change in political atmosphere after Bar Kokhba and the expansion of population and settlement after A.D. 135.[41]

Josephus had mentioned how closely packed the villages were,[42] and identified sites confirm this. Separate settlements are often found remarkably close together. Hammat Tiberias is less than a kilometer from Roman Tiberias, but clearly a separate village.[43] Khorazin is only two kilometers from Capernaum. Kh. Shema' is so close to Meiron that the Tosefta conflated the two, yet each had a fine synagogue on top of its hill and their distinctness is certain.[44] Villages are particularly close together in Upper Galilee.[45] Some cooperation between them must be conjectured, for even with the fertility of the soil there was a limit to the available good land, and yet disputes between village communities *within* Galilee over land distribution are nowhere recorded. Whether that cooperation was supervised in any institutional fashion is less clear.[46] Such cooperation is the best evidence for a basic similarity of outlook in the inhabitants of these villages, in contrast to often mutually hostile villages elsewhere in Palestine and Syria in the early Byzantine period when divergences in religious preference, including attachment to particular Christian heresies, militated against combined action. This is particularly remarkable since some of the inhabitants of late second century settlements would have been indigenous, and hostility to immigrants who had arrived after A.D. 135 might have been expected.

The shape of the villages is known only from aerial photographs.[47] The danger in using such methods lies obviously enough in the confusion of later settlements with earlier ones. Nevertheless, Yeivin did find that the ten settlements he examined fitted into patterns mentioned in the Tosefta: round, bow-shaped, square, rectangular, or gamma-shaped.[48] Though the particular shape adhered to does take some notice of the topography, so that Khorazin is rectangular with a long main street running along a slight ridge,[49] Kfar Einan, like Meiron, is split into terraces running down the slope of the hill,[50] and only Kh. Usha is found with a network grid in a square shape on its plateau,[51] it seems that at the time of the third to fourth century settlements on the Golan these ·shapes were sufficiently fixed to ignore the topography.[52] What is universally lacking is any careful town planning such as one would expect in a city,[53] and such as is found in neighboring Hippos-Susita;[54] the grids of Meiron and Usha are not rigidly adhered to like that of Dura-Europus.[55]

For the earlier settlements, topography gave the best form of defense,[56] but the new second century villages, like Arbel and Kfar Einan,[57] were not so easily defendable. Surrounding walls might have been expected, but are not found. Sepphoris and Tiberias had built walls in the first century,[58] and some of the villages were similarly fortified during the first revolt.[59] The excavations at Gamala on the Golan have shown the sturdiness of these defenses.[60] In the second century, however, R. Shimon b. Gamaliel remarked that "not every village needs a wall"[61] and it is striking that none has been found from new settlements of this period. It seems to be assumed in the rabbinic texts that the boundaries of a settlement will be clearly defined and that there will be only a limited number of entrances,[62] but rather than a large wall the villages' outside houses might in themselves form a continuous barrier sufficient to exclude small bands of intruders, if not a concentrated attack.[63] Archaeology has revealed only a few exceptions to this evidence of lack of care over defense: the completion of the wall around Beth Shearim in the second–third century[64] and the large rectangular tower in the middle terrace at Meiron that remains firmly dated by Middle Roman pottery (i.e., second century material), but may well be intended for buttressing the side of the hill rather than for any defensive purpose.[65] None of the sites can have been picked to withstand long sieges, even in the first century, since few had a lasting water supply within the inhabited area, as besieged Jotapata found to its cost.[66]

Inside the villages the variety of planning revealed by archaeology and the texts exhibits some general patterns. Each village had a central area with public buildings rather better planned and built than the private dwellings and based, in the third and fourth century sites, on the synagogue.[67] The houses were clustered around courtyards and down alleyways leading off the main streets;[68] at Arbel and Capernaum can be seen traces of larger single complexes rather inaccurately described by the excavators as "insulae,"[69] but the rabbinic texts concentrate on the problems of shared courtyards[70] and the need to cooperate with people living in the same alleyway.[71] The houses themselves varied enormously in size and style, but one can assume that building in the easily available limestone or basalt was always normal; a Mishnah text records in the name of R. Ishmael (so, since he taught in southern Palestine before A.D. 135, presumably not in Galilee) that a small house was 6 × 8 cubits (c. 3 × 4 meters) and a large one 10 × 10 cubits (c. 5 × 5 meters), but this is theory,[72] and Josephus compared the fine houses of the village of Chabulon to those of the cities on the coast.[73] In the archaeology, big, multiroomed houses like MI at Meiron are very much the exception in the sites excavated so far[74] and smaller, even one-roomed houses are common,[75] though it is by no means always easy to distinguish exterior walls from interior dividers. An upper storey seems to be common[76] and so is use of the house roof—olives could be spread out there to dry,[77] and the roof of one house often joined onto that of its neighbor, creating, as still seen in Mediterranean cities, a separate domain above the street,[78] despite the frequent lack of solidity underfoot.[79] Much attention seems to have been paid to the style of the windows—they, says the Tosefta, make a residence desirable[80]—and a number of other texts testify to the diversity available.[81]

Not all the settlement was filled with residential buildings. Texts speak of gardens within the villages, or even vineyards[82] or fields.[83] None of the surveyed sites has revealed such gaps between building complexes, but gardens could well be walled in as at Palmyra,[84] which would make them hard to distinguish from the outlines of houses or courtyards without excavation. Easier to identify have been "industrial quarters"—oil presses at Khorazin and Beth Shearim, workshops at Meiron, and so on.[85] They lie within the village next to the main residential areas, but in Khorazin and Meiron they lie some way further down the hill and at Beth Shearim somewhat toward the west.

Population

Who lived in these villages and what was the structure of their society? Most of the inhabitants were Jews. The designation of Galilee as "of the gentiles" ceased to be appropriate after 103 B.C. when the population was forcibly converted by Aristobulus.[86] In Josephus' time Galilee was almost entirely Jewish,[87] as opposed to the Golan where Jews and

Syrians were mixed[88] with some areas predominantly Jewish and others gentile.[89] The next period when evidence is good is the third century, when the proliferation of synagogues in Galilee, Upper and Lower, can be contrasted to the scarcity of recognizable artifacts of any pagan religion[90] and when Julius Africanus refers to Nazareth as a Jewish city.[91] The impression is confirmed in the early fourth century, for all the Galilean villages mentioned in Eusebius' *Onomasticon* are designated there as Jewish[92] and Epiphanius has a lengthy story about the ineffective attempts of the *comes* Joseph to get churches built in Galilee against the wishes of the local Jews under Constantine.[93] It must be assumed that the Jewish majority remained constant in the second century also.

Estimates of the size of the Galilean population are necessarily speculative, being based on the number of settlements known from extant literary or archaeological evidence multiplied by a figure for each settlement that is derived usually (e.g., by Avi Yonah) from the population density of Galilee in the late nineteenth and early twentieth centuries, for which figures are available. A number around three hundred thousand is a reasonable guess from the fifty-six names recorded after A.D. 135, especially given the maximum of 5,000 for most villages found in the Turkish tax registers of the late sixteenth century.[94] But there is also evidence of a great influx of new people in the early and mid second centuries, and indeed that is what might well be expected given the economic and political pressures on Jews in war-devastated Judaea to move north. The archaeological evidence for this settlement expansion comes primarily from Upper Galilee where the settlement of Meiron began to grow in an organized way during the second century and a separate village was actually built in the third century on the neighboring hill of Kh. Shema'. An expansion is also recorded in Lower Galilee at Beth Shearim and at Khorazin. The literary evidence relates primarily to the settlement of rabbinic schools in Lower Galilee, though again there are some references to rabbis teaching as far north as Meiron in Upper Galilee. But specific attestation is hardly needed: the continued occupation of second century sites into the third century when recognizably Jewish buildings such as synagogues are built makes it clear that the immigrants are not gentile but Jewish, and if some refugees from Judaea were certainly accepted as settlers by the Galileans it would be strange if large numbers did not take advantage of the good land available. The archaeology and, in particular, the shift of the rabbinic schools to Galilee suggests that they did, and I shall proceed on that assumption.[95]

The wealth distinctions in Galilee between classes seem to be much narrower than in other parts of the empire.[96] There are no villas from this period in Galilee,[97] and the bigger town houses that have been excavated are only of moderate size and luxury,[98] but there *are* signs of lavish expenditure in some of the fine mausolea dating to this period in Gischala, Kfar Giladi, and Beth Shearim,[99] though the rabbis hint that most expenditure by the wealthy was on more ephemeral benefits, such as good food and wine and a litter to take the wife to the baths.[100]

How was such wealth gained? Not, it seems, from great *latifundia* like those in first century Golan and Judaea,[101] though the use of bailiffs to manage estates is attested,[102] and there were some wealthier landowners who owned and farmed land in various different areas.[103] Leasing out agricultural land and houses would seem, if the emphasis of rabbinic texts is a reliable guide, to have been the main source of the wealth of the rich,[104] and since most land in Galilee itself was independently owned (see below) some of the land rented out may have been on the Golan, where dense village settlement does not really begin until the fourth century.[105] The extent to which such renting was carried on, and hence the size of the wealthy aristocracy of Galilee, is impossible to determine, for ownership by one man had no effect on the continuation of village life even if the whole of the place was owned by him,[106] and this form of land exploitation leaves no trace on the archaeological record. Much of the limited rabbinic discussion of field rentals admittedly concerns the legal problems created when one of the contractors was gentile, whether it was a Jew renting from a gentile in Syria and wondering about his tithing dues,[107] or a Jew letting fields or vineyards to gentiles in Palestine and wondering about the propriety of so doing—there may be a case of the latter kind in Piga when R. Shimon b. Gamaliel helped decide whether tithes paid by the gentile on the Jew's behalf were valid.[108] Rent was normally a share of the crop[109]—the often harsher form of fixed rent payments whatever the size of the crop was not unknown, but more normal when one of the parties was not Jewish.[110]

To some extent this upper class was doubtless hereditary. Some may have been priests, though it would be rash to follow Büchler in positing a large priestly caste grown rich on unearned tithes.[111] An aristocracy was clearly differentiated in the first century by Josephus, who speaks of the leading men and governors of the Galilean villages[112] as does St. Mark.[113] Their family pride is suggested by the attempt of Justus of Tiberias to damage Josephus by his attack on his family background.[114] The passage in Sifre that asserts that "for all *parnasim* of Israel, their sons stand in their stead"[115] may refer to a continuity of influence in local politics by such families since it can hardly refer to rabbis. Nevertheless, it was notorious that families in Galilee had in general a much less intense interest in maintaining family purity than those in Judaea and Jerusalem since they were comparatively lax in checking on a bride's virginity,[116] and it would be wrong to consider the aristocracy as a closed caste. The leaders of Galilee are the owners of comparative wealth[117] who win political influence through that wealth as owners of some of the land, as prospective lenders of loans,[118] as capitalists able to set up clients in shops for a share in the profits,[119] or as speculators buying up goods to make a profit from a change in the market price.[120]

The upper class was not big. The great mass of the people were *baale batim*, "owners of houses." Such men are envisaged in the texts as small farmers and craftsmen who, whether or not they in fact share or rent their dwellings, are in practice independent controllers of their own livelihoods and nuclear families. That they represent the majority of adult males is an inference from the fact that most of the tannaitic texts deal with laws related to such owner-occupiers.[121] It is with their problems, over responsibility for the upkeep of farms, houses, boundary stones, and so on, that the civil law regulations deal.[122] It is true that the original Pentateuchal laws that are being expounded were intended for farmers of this sort, but it would be perverse to assume that only the comparatively small number of laws regulating landlord-tenant relations had any contact with reality and that the rest was purely theoretical. No attempt has yet been made to discern field patterns in Galilee, but, in the case of houses, it would certainly be strange if most housing was rented given the rarity of homogeneous housing styles in any of the settlements surveyed.[123]

The size of the average farmer's holding is hard to establish. Holdings will have been subject to a continual process of contraction and expansion, with the splitting up of plots through partible inheritance requiring exchange or purchase of other plots to bring the area cultivated to an economical size. There is plenty of evidence from rabbinic texts and Judaean desert documents that such land purchase was common, as was the renting of extra plots by small farmers to bring in an extra income. Estimates of the minimum size that was economical and the maximum size that could be normal can, however, be made, if only with caution. A survey in western Samaria suggested quite small farms of about 2.5 hectares,[124] and farms in Galilee are likely to be similar. A text quoted by Eusebius asserts that two kinsmen of Jesus possessed 4.78 hectares for two families.[125] The 0.1 hectare plots being leased out, probably in the Judaean area, by Bar Kokhba according to calculations based on contracts recovered in the desert, were not necessarily intended to do more than supplement existing farms.[126] The close proximity of one village to another and their high populations suggested by the density of housing would leave little room for large farms if, as seems likely, most of the inhabitants were engaged in agriculture and none traveled long distances to their fields, though this latter assumption is rendered less likely by the references in sixteenth century Turkish tax registers to small unguarded arable areas up in the hills being farmed by the villagers in that period. It is likely also that peasants could survive on farms too small to be viable alone by supplementing their income as hired labor for other farmers or in the nearby cities or by grazing animals up in the hills. It might have been hoped that the Turkish registers, which give both population figures and percentage tax yields for each village and therefore the worth of its produce in each year, might indicate the normal size of farms required to grow such an amount. But the variants in land productivity for each area and each crop would render such estimates too inaccurate to be useful. The more precise figures available from the present day are, of course, useless due to the introduction of modern farming techniques.[127]

There is no reason to suppose that plots in Galilee were uniform in size at any time since the γῆς ἀναδασμός of Nehemiah did not affect Galilee, which was only fully converted in 103 B.C.[128] The size and viability of independent farms was affected by the operation of partible inheritance law, if tannaitic law reflects the law in practice.[129] Sometimes property was too small to split between brothers, though the evidence refers mostly to conjoint ownership of slaves and houses rather than fields.[130] Cooperation between members of an extended family in joint field exploitation does not seem to have been considered a solution to the problem of splitting up farms, for the texts assume that each farmer works with only his nuclear family to help him,[131] apart from occasional hired or bought help.[132] There is little evidence of any kind of the extended family sticking together in this period.[133] One text alone suggests that a young couple might dwell in the same courtyard or house as the husband's parents,[134] whereas there is a striking absence of halakha dealing with relations between a woman and her mother-in-law[135] or with property relations between a man and his father.[136] On the other hand, the texts closely regulate cooperation in bulk buying between a man and his neighbors in the same alleyway or courtyard,[137] and it is to the neighbors, not the extended family, that a man will turn for help[138] or when he needs to borrow farm equipment.[139]

The primacy of the nuclear family as the basic unit of production greatly enhanced the status of women in society. In biblical law, women acted as pawns in the transmission of property from one extended family to another, with strict rules preventing the loss of such property from their original families except through their children.[140] The rabbis, true to their brief, expound this law faithfully.[141] But their own words betray that current practice was often quite different.[142] Testation is common and accepted by the rabbis,[143] and a text from the Judaean desert shows that a man could bypass all the ordinary rules by it and leave his property to his wife.[144] Even verbal orders to witnesses (*fideicommissa*) and the informal wishes of a dying man are considered valid in the bestowing of property.[145] That this could result in powerful women taking control of family property, particularly when there were practical problems in enforcing the rights of the extended family once it was scattered, is clear from the independence in disposing of land and children that, according to their legal correspondence preserved in one of the Judaean caves, a certain Babata and her mother were able to display.[146] The position was considerably complicated by bigamous marriages, which undoubtedly persisted but were apparently rare.[147]

The result was considerable financial and social independence for women even in ordinary poorer circles. When the rabbis insist that a wife be allowed certain minimum comforts by her husband it must be remembered they are only a minimum: food, bedding, new clothes once a year, one *maah* pocket money,[148] freedom to visit her father and go to funerals and feasts and wear a bit of jewelry,[149] and permission to drink wine unless she is very poor indeed.[150] On the other hand, it is clear that women could own a great deal of their own apart from their husband's property. A wife had property inherited from or held for her father and kept separate by her[151] so that the husband would not even always know of the existence of such property.[152] If the wife was considerably richer than the husband he might even be found working for her.[153] Where the wife was at a disadvantage, however, was in her inability to increase her wealth by her own labors. Whatever she earned belonged to her husband,[154] so the evidence of women doing jobs indicates their contribution to the family budget, not independence. Jobs recorded include bread production for sale in the market,[155] and selling bread from a stall in the market; shop-keeping; helping with the harvest; selling from home the poorer quality olives to passers-by (the best quality being taken to the shops); and acting as wet nurses.[156]

Nonetheless, husbands preferred their women to stay at home as much as possible. The Mishnah's list of the standard duties required of a wife are fairly demanding but entirely domestic: grinding, baking, washing, cooking, raising children, and so on.[157] Above all, women were expected to work at the loom, even, according to R. Eliezer and R. Shimon b. Gamaliel, if they had plenty of slave girls to do it for them.[158] All women were allowed out of the house occasionally, to go to the baths (a useful opportunity to examine young girls for suitability as brides),[159] visit friends,[160] do the shopping,[161] and celebrate feasts,[162] but indecorous behavior merited divorce. Alimony was not required to be paid to a wife who shamed her husband by her loose hair, torn dress, or washing in the bath house in public or in the presence of men.[163] As a result of these restrictions women inhabited something of a separate society of their own, excluded from any share in the public life of the community, either secular[164] or religious,[165] and reduced instead to concentration on beauty.[166]

The nuclear family, then, was the primary unit of production and of society. It was aided in production by two other groups: the slaves and the mass of landless poor.

Large-scale use of slaves in agriculture was never common in the ancient Near East,[167] but exploitation of slave labor on a smaller domestic scale was widespread at all periods.[168] A household might have one to four slaves[169] to help in the fields[170] and serve in the house.[171] There are only faint echoes of the chain gangs of imperial Rome—accounts of slaves rowing on board ship or dying because of being attached by a chain to a burning wheat stack.[172] Domestic service brought the slave into very close contact with his master, and the hostile relations recorded of some Italian slaves with their owners would appear to have been rare.[173] In the Tosefta, the new slave marked his slavery by tying the master's sandal and carrying his bathing equipment to the baths.[174] It is typical of his duties as they are recorded: washing the master's feet, carrying him in a litter, supporting him while walking if he is frail, kohling his eyes for him or pulling out his teeth (presumably to stop toothache).[175] A woman slave was in a similar position—working wool for her mistress[176] and becoming at times more friendly with her master than morality would permit.[177]

The trust put in slaves of course varied according to the individual. Slave stewards of wealthier men doubtless existed, as in Greece and Rome,[178] and slave prices and therefore their quality varied considerably,[179] the really cheap slaves being the thieves and those "written down to the *malchūt*" (taken for *angareia*).[180] The origin of the slaves themselves is rarely discussed. Some were the offspring of slave marriages, which are recorded as commercial ventures by their masters.[181] But it is too often asserted that by this date *no* slaves kept by Jews were themselves Jews.[182] Elsewhere in Syria debt slavery is still known,[183] and in the mid first century Josephus records that Simon b. Giora could expect freed slaves in Galilee to fight on the side of Jewish nationalists.[184] Kidnapped Jews were apparently sold openly in the market place as if they were gentile.[185] Nevertheless, this last passage does support the general assumption that at least most slaves could be presumed gentile until proved otherwise.[186] Of these gentile slaves, later sources mention captives imported from Germany,[187] but most of the supply must surely have been from kidnapping and breeding for sale. The mechanisms of the slave market where "men are disgraced and despised because they go naked in the market place" to be sold[188] agree with contemporary Greek descriptions.[189] As for their treatment once bought, the leniency brought about by domestic contact with their masters was by no means absolutely effective and it was not unknown for slaves to run away.[190]

Slaves were useful, but, despite the lack of legal compulsion to feed them properly, it was a waste of the purchase money not to do so, and that could prove expensive.[191] For labor-intensive tasks it was far easier to rely on the landless poor, on the laborer who hired himself out for what work he could get, by period of time worked or by work done, and who had no claims on his employer in the slack times between jobs.[192]

The existence of a class of extreme poor even in the relatively prosperous villages of Galilee is not really surprising.[193] Jewish society never attempted—any more than any other ancient society—to get rid of poverty.[194] What distinguished the Jews was the establishment of charitable institutions for the relief of the poor.[195] The rabbinic regulations for those institutions reveal the numbers and potential violence of these people. Every village had local poor to whom it first owed help,[196] and begging continued even on the Sabbath.[197] Free distribution of food at the harvest time had to be carefully managed to avoid a riot—the poor hang around the field all day shouting to each other "Here's gleanings,"[198] and even if they are technically not eligible to glean, they should have grain distributed to them "for the ways of peace."[199] In the distribution of poor tithe once every seven years, the provision of small quantities at a time is recommended to avoid a rush.[200] On such occasions the poor became an undifferentiated mass and it mattered little whether the beneficiary was a Jew or a gentile.[201]

Many of these poor had no home and traveled from place to place.[202] Such traveling bands of landless men were endemic in Syria.[203] Doubtless they found shelter in the caves and rock tombs that abounded in the area.[204] Many of them were searching for jobs.[205]

There is a great deal of halakha on the use of hired labor and some, at least, is likely to refer to such men.[206] One passage is particularly telling—the evening time is the hiring time,[207] so this passage regulates overeager farmers who go to the village limits toward the close of the Sabbath in order to ensure a supply of workers the following day.[208] The workers had clearly spent the Sabbath outside the boundary— they have, temporarily or permanently, no home. Much halakha deals with the hiring of gentiles and of Jews by gentiles,[209] and some concerns possible impurity imparted to produce by workers not overscrupulous in the observance of purity laws.[210] But there is also evidence of the kind of jobs required—all sorts of agricultural tasks, but particularly the guarding and harvesting of crops[211]—and of the conditions of hire: pay was given by the day and was not large (one or two *selas*);[212] the farmer sometimes fed the workers during the day,[213] even if not the best of food,[214] and gave them drink money,[215] and it was normal, if not universal, to let harvesters eat from the produce on which they were set to work.[216] Pay was given at the end of the day[217]—the workers engaged could not always be relied on to turn up, so prepayment would be rash.[218] The moneychanger might provide the small change needed,[219] and the workers, paid off, would be discharged and left to look after themselves.[220]

Not all the poor were prepared to rely for a living on so casual an income. Some resorted to casual stealing, of grapes from the vineyard or grain from the sheaves.[221] Others took to a more lucrative profession in banditry. Josephus has much to say about λῃσταί in Galilee under Herod and in the first century. They worked in gangs, living in caves in the mountains and escaping to the marshes of the Huleh valley when pursued, meanwhile terrorizing the countryside and supporting entire families in their hideouts.[222] They were well-organized and very hard to suppress.[223] The bandits are usually identified with extremist Jewish nationalists[224] and may well have sympathized with the anti-Roman and anti-rich aspects of the rebellion of 66–70.[225] It is also likely that Josephus is capable of being misleading, at times, in his application of the word λῃστής, as, for instance, in his description of the leading men of Gischala, whom he opposed.[226] Nonetheless, the λῃσταί of Arbel behaved just like other bandits in most parts of the ancient world at most times,[227] and straightforward robbery was surely one of their purposes.[228]

The rabbinic texts suggest the continuation of such gangs into the second century. R. Shimon remarked on gang loyalty,[229] and there are stories of cattle and sheep rustling[230] and even of crop stealing.[231] Some of the bandits were apparently gentile,[232] but most were not, for there is one text that contrasts a field reaped illegally by gentiles to one reaped by robbers.[233] Galilee did not quickly lose its reputation as a haven for banditry.[234] The caves and the marshes provided hiding places too attractive (and the prevalence of homeless poor an incentive too pressing) for all the Galileans to take willingly to peaceful ways. On the hilltops and in more deserted areas Galilee is likely to have nourished a little-known second society alongside the prosperous villages that left their greater mark upon the landscape and literature.

4 Jews and Gentiles in Galilee

Most of the inhabitants of Galilee in the second century were Jews.[1] That there was a gentile minority is likely *prima facie* since there was no mechanism for their exclusion, but how many gentiles there were and how comfortably they lived with their Jewish neighbors is not easy to discover. In the first century, Antipas had deliberately transplanted some of the urban mob of the coastal cities to his new *polis* of Tiberias,[2] but if these people were gentile they do not appear in the narrative of the first revolt. For the other communities within Galilee proper, all the evidence deals with Jews alone. Only the appearance of pagan symbols on the coins of second century Tiberias and Sepphoris gives a dubious hint to the contrary, and this can easily be explained without the need to posit a gentile presence.[3]

With such a dearth of other evidence, the rabbinic sources take on a new importance. They contain a mass of regulations dealing with relations between Jews and gentiles.[4] Can this solve the problem?

The first difficulty to be resolved is whether the rabbis refer in this matter to Galilee at all. They purport to legislate for all Jews in the land of Israel. Other areas are well known to contain a mixture of Jews and gentiles, and it could be to them that the texts refer.

Yabneh, the first home of the rabbis after 70 according to the tradition, lies on the coastal plain close to pagan Ashdod and Lod-Diospolis, a pagan polis.[5] The story about R. Gamaliel using a gentile laundry will refer to Lod.[6] In the cities of the coast, Jews came into close contact with gentiles, whether on visits or as inhabitants.[7] The areas closest to Galilee are known to have had such mixed populations—the Decapolis cities perhaps, though many Jews were massacred in 66,[8] the Golan plateau,[9] and further north into Syria.[10] There is also some slight evidence of a few Jews being in Jerusalem in this period,[11] where they would have been surrounded by gentiles, and from the Dead Sea area come papyri indicating not just coexistence but close cooperation.[12]

With so many alternative settings for general rabbinic statements about gentiles it would be best, were it possible, to rely on reports of actual cases that are specifically attested in Galilee. Unfortunately, and perhaps significantly, there is almost none. A story in Sifre to Numbers records a certain Sabbatios of Ulam, apparently in Galilee, hiring out an ass to a gentile woman with his own services as ass-driver.[13] There was a case in Piga decided by R. Shimon b. Gamaliel that involved the liability to tithes of a crop where the tithing had been done on a Jew's behalf by a gentile (his tenant?), but whether Piga lies in Judaea or western Galilee is not, it seems, certain.[14] There is no other circumstantial story in tannaitic texts that could show absolutely the presence of gentiles in Galilee.[15]

Nonetheless, it might seem premature to dismiss gentile presence in Galilee as negligible, for the sources do attest significant changes, in rabbinic eyes, in the halakha governing relations with gentiles in this period. A new ruling pardons the sinner when wine touched by a gentile is mixed with Jewish wine by mistake and is therefore liable to suspicion as "libation wine"; the leniency is decreed for "the good order of the world," indicating that such an occurrence was considered likely.[16] Another ruling relaxes the degree of supervision a gentile requires when working for a Jew on wine production.[17] An old prohibition on the import of vegetables from abroad in the Sabbatical year is declared null.[18]

Later evidence records the tacit lifting of a ban on the sale of animals to gentiles within the land of Israel at sometime after A.D. 275.[19] Ideas of gentiles as unclean are forgotten in the third century.[20] Some gentile territory is pronounced by the rabbis pure for priests to visit.[21] R. Judah ha Nasi or his grandson decreed with his court that gentile oil is kosher.[22]

What do these changes show? The amount of halakha on relations with gentiles could be produced just by the intellectual curiosity of rabbis about the effect that gentile participation has on a legal system intended for Jews. Leniency toward gentiles might be due to their rarity in Galilee, which made them unthreatening,[23] but in that case why *change* the halakha at all? Alternatively, both phenomena could be due to a need to regulate relations with gentile *slaves*, since circumcision of slaves and their resultant partial Judaisation was considered mandatory by rabbis only after the tannaitic period,[24] and was therefore presumably little carried out before since such an operation on an adult male carries the risk of death.

It can only be said that other explanations are equally possible: that the law reflects a new *rapprochement* with local gentiles, though since they are otherwise unattested this seems to me unlikely; that it reflects recognition of and adaption to the relationships with such gentiles already normal in nonrabbinic circles in Galilee, though the same objection applies. It may be best to describe the kind of evidence that the rabbis provide in the sorts of intercourse they imagine between Jews and gentiles and hope that a clearer picture emerges at the end. If one explanation of the total evidence of rabbinic and patristic texts seems to be preferable, then it will be only tentatively espoused: it seems to me especially likely that there was close contact with gentiles not within Galilee itself (which the Christian writers deny), but on the borders of Galilee where no clear geographical frontier can be postulated, such as in the southwest where the foothills merge into the plain of Megiddo around Beth Shearim and a complete racial division would be hard to maintain, or in the Golan community "swallowed up" in gentile country.[25] The changes in the law may reflect the increased importance of gentile markets in those areas or, more likely, rabbinic recognition of the importance of those markets.[26]

Many of the problems concerning gentiles that the rabbis discuss arise only when Jews and gentiles do live in close proximity. A mixed village ('*ir*) is sometimes envisaged: in such a village guardians of the community's fields might be either Jewish or gentile and there is some likelihood of Jewish produce being mixed with gentile (though the rabbis suggest that the land might be divided between the two groups on an east-west axis).[27] A wife can insist that her husband, on penalty of divorce, move to a place where the majority are Jews,[28] though a place with a gentile majority inside the land of Israel is considered preferable to an entirely Jewish town abroad.[29] Within such villages, Jews could be living in the next house to gentiles and sharing a courtyard (difficulties arise over its use on the Sabbath);[30] dividing a single house between them (problems over purity);[31] sharing an oven for bread baking;[32] and leaving their animals in the same place.[33]

In such cases the Jew would see much of the everyday life of the gentile. He could observe his religious activities[34] or his aberrations,[35] or enter into commercial dealings with a gentile who is both neighbor and friend.[36] The rabbis encourage a limited amount of friendliness. In the Sabbatical year, they say, when Jews should not farm the land, it is permitted to encourage gentiles, who are not so prohibited, to farm.[37] Various rabbinic laws presuppose Jews eating together with gentiles, though not necessarily their food.[38] Politeness to gentiles is considered desirable to promote peaceful relations.[39] A gentile might help in equally friendly fashion—watering his neighbor's animal on the Sabbath[40] or putting out a dangerous fire for him.[41] Common courtesy was to be maintained, according to the rabbis, and Jews should travel with gentiles rather than risk the roads alone,[42] and should demonstrate sympathy in times when gentiles mourned, comforting them and burying their dead.[43] Again, the reason given, "for the ways of peace,"[44] suggests that such relationships actually existed and compelled the rabbis to be lenient against their will.

Friendly contact would ripen into closer relationships. A Jewish woman might lend her blouse to a gentile friend,[45] a man might lend his ass,[46] and there are plenty of comments about financial loans in both directions.[47] Cooperation could extend to joint ownership of vineyards or farms,[48] mutual aid at work,[49] and use of the same storehouse to deposit goods.[50] From such activities might grow a considerable trust, so that a Jew might entrust his goods or family to a gentile guardian to look after after his death (considered acceptable in the Tosefta and Jerusalem Talmud[51] and actually the case in the family of Babata down by the Dead Sea[52]). A Jew might also be appointed guardian by a gentile, a situation similarly envisaged by the Tosefta[53] and perfectly normal according to a third century jurist recorded in the *Digest*.[54]

In general, then, it appears that, despite a fair amount of racial prejudice,[55] the rabbinic texts assume the possibility of close, if wary, relations between Jews and gentiles among at least some of those to whom they wished to appeal. That the increased leniency that the rabbis show reflected actual practice is rendered more likely by evidence of the chief evil that rabbis feared from such contact, that is, intermarriage.[56] Such marriages were doubtless more frequent in the diaspora[57] and the coastal cities than in Galilee, but the concern of the rabbis is most likely to indicate their prevalence also in Galilee or its environs. One passage considers the liturgical position of a proselyte child of a mixed marriage (but this raises interesting problems for the rabbis and so may be theoretical),[58] other passages deal with the religious status of mixed marriages when conversion of the gentile party has been preceded by cohabitation,[59] yet others decry marriage to proselyte girls, whether on religious grounds[60] or (and the practical nature of this observation gives it particular force) because a proselyte girl, unlike a freed slave girl, has relatives who may well be hostile.[61]

Social contact with gentiles is therefore probable, at least in some parts of Galilee; commercial contacts are certain. Commerce in no way relied on social relations, though doubtless facilitated by them, for, even if there were few gentiles within Galilee itself, trade across the borders with the coastal and Decapolis cities is well attested,[62] and much of the evidence that follows will refer to that external trade.

The tannaitic texts discuss in passing a great variety of goods imported from abroad[63] or manufactured on the coast, sold to Jews either in the market places of the coastal cities[64] or by traveling salesmen (תגרים), who could be Jewish, gentile, or Samaritan.[65] Some of the goods found in inland sites may have been specially manufactured on the coast for a Jewish market.[66] On a smaller scale, the texts discuss in detail the problems in ensuring the purity of foods bought from gentiles. Apple wine bought in the market is permitted,[67] but any foods connected with suspect gentile grape wine (suspect through risk of use for libations) are forbidden by the rabbis except in special circumstances.[68] Problems arise in tithing grain bought from a gentile[69] or using vegetables gathered for sale by a gentile on the Sabbath,[70] but all the discussions of special cases seem to assume a general custom of indulging in such trade. Once again, though, no specific cases are given in Galilee or even on its border.

Of trade in the opposite direction the evidence is rather more specific. The large hoards of non-Galilean coins found in various places in Galilee must have been exchanged for Galilean goods,[71] and prohibitions by rabbis on selling certain products to gentiles are provoked only by a desire either to prevent idolatry by the gentiles[72] or to discourage non-Jews from settling in the land of Israel.[73] This leaves a great deal of commercial contact taken for granted,[74] to the extent that, in one Tosefta passage that cites an actual case, gentile market officials are seen as ideal customers for suspect barrels of wine that a conscientious Jew might be too scrupulous to drink but happy to sell.[75]

Some halakha assumed that Jews and gentiles sold not only goods but also labor services to one another. Jewish use of gentile laundries (probably not in Galilee),[76] dyers and millers for flour production,[77] and gentile use of artifacts made by Jewish craftsmen[78] concerned the services of free men contracted for particular tasks. But more humble occupations also crossed the religious and ethnic lines, and Jews and gentiles were found as tenants of each other's farms[79] and as hired workers in the fields and in the workshops.[80] Doubtless a good deal of this involved casual labor only—acting as porter for wine casks,[81] or hiring out an ass for the transport of produce.[82]

At least on the borders of Galilee, then, Jews came into close commercial and probably social contact with gentiles. It is likely, if not inevitable, that this was accompanied by mutual influences in cultural and religious matters; the interests of the sources make religious contact the easiest to investigate.[83]

Within Galilee, there is little evidence of the public practice of pagan cults, which does not automatically preclude pagan beliefs or private rituals. Tiberias apparently boasted a Hadrianeum, but it was probably in ruins in the 230s and its building is most likely to have been a political act only and not grafted onto or having any function as part of a system of existing pagan cults.[84] Coins provide a rather shaky indication of respect for, but not necessarily worship of, Zeus and Hygeia—also in Tiberias—though there is no reason to assume the existence of temples from coin types.[85] But for a good idea of the kind of public cults to which local pagans adhered it is necessary to turn to the surrounding areas.[86]

North and slightly east of Galilee lay the important cult center of Paneas at Caesarea Philippi by the source of the river Jordan. Worship there was of the imperial cult,[87] but the area had long held religious significance in pagan eyes—there was a temple to the golden calf in Daphne,[88] and the local male god in Dan near Paneas drew Greek as well as Aramaic-speaking worshippers in the second century B.C.[89] Farther north lay the flourishing cult centers at Baalbek, where the local Baal-Hadad was identified with Zeus as Jupiter Heliopolitanus and favored with a Roman-style temple of monstrous size,[90] and at Gohariene, 40 kilometers east of Damascus, where a famous temple of Zeus was the center for religious processions under the control of a priesthood.[91] All these were at some distance from Galilee, though their fame traveled far, but to this day the Hellenistic temple of Helios at Tel Kadesh stands prominently on a hilltop on the very border of Upper Galilee.[92]

West of Galilee the coastal cities all achieved a similar amalgam of local semitic cults with those of Rome.[93] Gaza boasted the largest statue of Zeus in the world,[94] and the plentiful evidence of public cults in Caesarea shows great eclecticism in this period.[95] On Mt.

Carmel the local Baal, against whom Elijah fought, was identified with the Baal-Zeus of Baalbek,[96] and such identifications shaped the pantheon of Akko.[97]

To the south, Sebaste-Samaria was a center of the imperial cult from the early third century,[98] but the religious center closest to Galilee and, by chance, best studied, was Beth Shean.[99] Figurines and statuettes found in tombs indicate private allegiances,[100] the excavated temples reveal magnificent public cults.[111] What emerges is similar to the other Syrian cities—an amalgam of Greek-Egyptian, Roman, and semitic cults.[102]

Finally, the cities east of Galilee housed their own cults. Hippos-Susita had a nymphaeum,[103] the festivals at Hammat Gader near Gadara were famous,[104] and excavations at Gerasa have revealed Hellenized local cults alongside Sarapis and Isis and emperor worship as elsewhere.[105]

Evidence for the mode of worship in the public temples is quite plentiful, especially with use of comparative materials from elsewhere in Syria. The Syrian gods, however Greek or Roman the architecture of their temples,[106] retained perfectly "native" forms of worship.[107] Cultic rituals were broadly similar to those of the Jewish God in Jerusalem,[108] with the god kept hidden away except for the rare solemn procession in which he was viewed by the populace.[109] The rabbinic texts add a little to this picture:[110] the possibility of private prayer to the idol in his temple is suggested by a story of prayer to Peor (here a generic name for a pagan god) by a gentile woman before setting off on a journey,[111] and the importance of sacrifices to the gods is indicated by the definition of idolatrous worship, given as taking an object and either washing it, sacrificing to it, putting incense before it, pouring libations to it, or bowing down before it.[112] The rabbinic texts also contain a casual remark that taking a light from an idolatrous altar for use on a festival is permitted.[113] Evidence from nonrabbinic sources is confirmed in the assumption that the places most commonly devoted to worship are either buildings where the god is housed[114] or sacred groves,[115] and that nudity or pollution prevented entry into sacred areas.[116] On the administration of the pagan temples the rabbis are unsurprisingly vague—the generic term כמר to mean "pagan priest"[117] could refer either to a professional or to the aristocratic amateur holding a priesthood as an honor, as was done at Rome,[118] but rabbis were rather more aware of the methods of financing the temples since it was not always possible for Jews in some of these places to avoid contributing. The *fiscus Judaicus* is one obvious example,[119] but t A. Zar. 6(7):1 discusses the problem on a more local level, where flute players collected fees for the upkeep of the temples, shops sold produce and contributed their profits, and treasurers did the rounds raising money. Such ventures might be administered by the government like the fiscus Judaicus itself (in which case the rabbis permitted Jewish contributions with a clear conscience), but it is assumed that other temple administrations might act on their own behalf alone.[120] This passage also gives one of the rare rabbinic scraps of information on the precise ceremonial in pagan temples (namely, the use of flute players). From other sources comes further evidence: public reclining at feasts in times of rejoicing;[121] the spring festival connected with the hot baths at Gadara;[122] and the *maioumas* festival popular all over Syria.[123] Again, what interested rabbis was perhaps only a by-product of the big festivals: the markets that sprung up in cult centers on feast days. On these, the rabbis have a good deal to say, and they seem to have served an important economic function.[124]

The monuments and buildings left by the public cults of the ancient world tempt historians to concentrate on them as if they—rather than the private ideas and behavior of individuals—were the essence of pagan belief. But it was private pagan worship that was more likely to impinge on the life of Jews in Galilee, and the rabbis were well aware of it. Any house might have been used for idolatrous worship, whether custom-built and specially decorated or not, and any stone might have an idol set upon it, whether specially cut and shaped or just plastered and painted for the purpose.[125] In Beth Shean the inhabitants signified their participation in religious festivals by decking out their shops, but some must have refused to take part, for the rabbis recommend that scrupulous Jews patronize undecorated shops to avoid the appearance of connivance in idolatry.[126] In the fourth century Christians had the same problem farther north in Antioch, when the city was lit up with special lamps and doors garlanded for the Kalends;[127] a Tosefta passage notes that worship is by no means universal on the Kalends,[128] and this may possibly be the festival causing the garlanded shops in Beth Shean.

A number of passages assume the use of small figurines of gods kept for private worship, like those found in tombs in Beth Shean;[129]

m A. Zar. 1:4 refers to a continued tendency to worship the dolmens, which still stand in many places in Galilee and the Golan.[130] The objects most likely to be sacrificed to such divinities were cheap, homely things—the white cock for a poor man,[131] food and wine left in front of the idol and sometimes stolen by the hungry.[132]

This sort of religion was on the popular level of the Jewish-influenced magical papyri of Egypt, where pine cones and white cocks took on a special significance.[133] It was a democratic form of paganism, open to all, and the kind of beliefs and practices entailed is evident from a lengthy rabbinic discussion of which common superstitions among Jews are forbidden because they "approach the ways of the Emorites," i.e., are idolatrous:[134] trimming the hair; cutting long hair at puberty; shaving one's head for נודגדון (Gad?); shaving a child at the graveyard; tying a pad to one's hip or a red thread to the finger; throwing pebbles into seas or streams; cavorting by a flame; calling to a piece of bread that one has dropped to return to him; extinguishing a candle flame on the earth to trouble the dead; expecting to have a guest when one sees snuff fall off a candle; and so on. Such beliefs fall into predictable categories: protection against dead spirits and the demons familiar from Christian saints' lives;[135] prognostication from natural events[136] and by deliberate divination;[137] cultivation of certain practices to ensure health and luck;[138] a general animistic belief that all objects have independent wills;[139] and the use of appeals to the spirits in meaningless formulas in times of stress.[140] It is not surprising to find that women, especially, were prone to such practices, particularly in hope of fertility,[141] for public pagan cults as much as those of Judaism excluded women and it was natural for them to turn to such things in compensation.[142]

The rabbis knew that not all paganism was centered on the temples and that pagan festivals could be purely local or even confined to one family.[143] Private celebrations occurred on the day a child came of age, when his hair was ceremonially cut[144] (a ceremony well-attested in Greece, but otherwise unknown in Syria[145]), and on occasions such as recovering from sickness or the attainment of office as a public magistrate.[146] It was much more difficult for Jews on the borders of Galilee, brought into constant contact with their gentile neighbors, to avoid involvement in the happiness of such days than to make a point of not going to Beth Shean, Akko, or Gadara on the fixed days of the year when the great festivals were held.

As a result it is generally true that the rabbis showed much more ignorance and vagueness about public cults than they did about the practices of individuals. They were bewildered by the complexities of polytheism[147] and end up using the term "Merkolis" as a generic name for any idol.[148] One text claims that it is quite permissible for the conscientious Jew to learn to understand foreign religions even if not to follow them,[149] but the rabbis did not use the opportunity sufficiently to enable modern scholars to identify which particular cults they came to know.[150] Instead, they accepted and tried to ignore the proximity of the pagan temples, permitting the reaping of benefits from the big festivals within certain limits designed to avoid the appearance of idolatry,[151] and allowing the sale of one's house for the building of a pagan shrine[152] (though it is only in the Jerusalem Talmud that a text from the late third century states that even helping to build an idolatrous temple may be permitted to Jews).[153] This mildness towards idolatry is reflected by R. Gamaliel in his remark that it was hostility to pagan shrines that brought about the destruction of the Temple in revenge;[154] harshness towards paganism in the Mishnah appears somewhat softened in the later Tosefta[155] and the portrayal of pagan gods as demons, found both in the Talmuds and in the Christian fathers,[156] is not espoused in the tannaitic texts. The *appearance* of idolatry was to be avoided by *Jews*—a Jew should not pay for entrance to temple facilities[157] or go to (or even near) a big city holding a festival,[158] nor should he bend down before an idolatrous temple even to pick up a coin in case he appears to a casual observer to be bowing in worship.[159] But avoidance was the limit of Jewish opposition to idolatry, though the substitution of rude nicknames to describe the centers of pagan worship in place of their real names was also recommended.[160]

Avoidance of the private pagan practices of gentile neighbors could be quite complicated. What happened if the neighbor issued an invitation to a feast in honor of his son? A scrupulous Jew might accept but insist on bringing his own food and servants to wait upon him, though R. Shimon disapproves of going even this far.[161] Gentiles decorated all articles in use with images as a matter of course; if a Jew buys such an object, the rabbis recommended that he should have the seller "cancel" the efficacy of the images by abusing them in some way.[162] A casual joke to a gentile on the day of a pagan festival might be taken to indicate a readiness to participate and should be avoided.[163] The

Tosefta passage already quoted at length[164] indicates the spread of common practices in the regulation of daily life.

If further evidence is needed of contact with gentiles in religious matters, at least, it lies in the numerous indications of gentile sympathy with, and conversion to, Judaism. Many such sympathizers are attested from the period just before the Temple was destroyed,[165] but veneration of an antique and impressive cult involved rather less commitment than that required of sympathizers in the second century. Worship by sacrifice was no longer possible, and veneration by donations to God strictly limited in scope.[166] Instead, what was required was the adoption of specific practices—purity perhaps, observing the Sabbath and so on certainly, and, in the end, self-identification with the local Jewish community. At one point in the second century, in the Bar Kokhba war, such identification was politically dangerous,[167] and at no time was it easy. It is all the more striking that it should have been common.[168]

For the gentile neighbors Judaism was only one of a number of competing attractions in this period in Syria, for the Didache was probably composed for converts from a similar pagan background.[169] The sympathy for Judaism and Christianity was, in some cases, arrived at through theological speculation: some philosophers in the second century were willing to try any new idea,[170] and the conclusion of Maximus of nearby Tyre that the gods have many names but only one nature could lead to sympathy with Judaic monotheism.[171] For such men, Judaism, both scripture and practice, provided another rich quarry for esoteric wisdom and hints for a new morality, and even if they picked out only what was congenial, like Porphyry who approved only of the Essenes,[172] this did not always preclude a real veneration for the religion as a whole. A passage in Sifre records the martyrdom of a "philosopher" who was killed for protesting against the burning of a Torah scroll, probably in the Bar Kokhba war.[173] But for most gentiles the attraction of Judaism, like the attraction of pagan practices to Jews, was on a far lower intellectual plane: the power of Jewish holy men, alive or dead;[174] the magical efficacy of phylacteries[175] and holy books;[176] the repetition of blessings;[177] the donation of money to synagogues to build a visible sign of respect for the Jewish God and win favor.[178] For many pagans this last act could be performed with no feeling of commitment to the exclusive nature of Judaism, and dedications to εἰς θεός could combine Jewish, Christian, and pagan intentions in happy ambiguity. It appears in a Jewish context in Beth Shearim[179] and Damascus,[180] but, according to Epiphanius, it was adapted to Christianity by the Jews of Tiberias in reaction to a miracle wrought through the *comes* Joseph,[181] and it appears frequently on inscriptions from the Antioch area put up, on their house lintels, by Christians in the fourth and fifth centuries, perhaps in imitation of the Jewish *mezuzah*.[182]

Such "Judaizers" were far more common than adherents to the stricter regulations considered mandatory by the rabbis.[183] Though the rabbinic attitude was not consistent, enthusiasm for encouraging conversion was common[184] and occasionally reaches an all-embracing missionary view that eventually at least all the land of Israel would become Jewish.[185] Nevertheless, the traditions that make great rabbis like Meir and Akiba proselytes came very late,[186] and reliable stories about rabbinical students who have converted are very scarce—R. Judah tells of a certain Benjamin from Egypt who studied alongside him under R. Akiba,[187] and there are many stories about R. Gamaliel's pupil Onkelos who is sometimes credited with the literal translation of the Torah.[188] For most gentiles, the less extreme forms of Judaism, which gave comfort while permitting their old secular lives to continue fairly unchanged, were more congenial than the demands of the rabbis.

In any case, even the less extreme forms of conversion could create sufficient problems. The marks of conversion were circumcision and baptism, particularly the former.[189] Circumcision was popularly considered sufficient, at least in the first century, for Josephus was embarrassed by the forcible circumcision of two officials of Agrippa by Josephus' nominal followers as a condition of residence in Trachonitis,[190] and it is presupposed in the second century by Jewish and Roman sources alike.[191] It could be dangerous both in its immediate effect on a man's health and because it was illegal after Hadrian.[192] The conversion of women, which in the first century was more common,[193] avoided the dangers of circumcision but created tension in the convert's family. In either case such tension was perhaps bound to arise when one member of a family voluntarily adopted a new set of civil laws—rabbinic law claimed to regulate inheritance when a convert shared his father's property with his unconverted brother, to the convert's advantage though not scandalously so,[194] and for the zealous the theory of rebirth as a Jew on conversion meant not only that a father had no hold on his son born before conversion, but that marriage between brother and sister would become permissible under Jewish law.[195] To family problems were added extra burdens of taxation—one source suggests that it was proselytes who suffered most from the imposition of the fiscus Judaicus, at any rate in the first century.[196]

Finally, the convert ran the risk of rejection by the very community he wished to join. Admittedly, Galilean Jews lacked the fears for their blood purity that marked the Judaeans[197] since they owed their own Jewishness to the forcible conversions of 103 B.C.,[198] but this did not necessarily overcome the constant prejudice against outsiders. In particular, there was the problem of deciding the authenticity of a conversion. Circumcision did not in itself convert according to some Jews; it needed to be done by the right person with the right intentions, else all the circumcised of Syria could be reckoned Jews.[199] There is no reason to assume that, at any time in the second century, all or even most such conversions were carried out by rabbis. On the contrary, given the far more severe requirements laid on the rabbinical convert,[200] most of the circumcisions that distressed the Roman legislators must have been done by nonrabbinic Jews. The rabbis did not recognize such conversions. As a result, the daughters of such marriages were considered by the rabbis to be gentile, and their children would be reckoned gentile in turn.[201] Perhaps the argument has come full circle: part of the reason for the prevalence of halakha about gentiles, when according to the Christian sources there were no gentiles in Galilee, might be that some of the inhabitants of Galilee who considered themselves Jewish (and were reckoned by outsiders to be Jews) were judged by the rabbis to be gentile.

5 Galilean Village Trade

What has been said in Chapter 2 about large-scale trade patterns between Galilee and surrounding areas should not obscure the evidence
that the Galilean economy thrived to a large extent on internal markets
alone. Oil and a few other commodities were exported; metal, salt,
and luxury goods were imported.[1] But food, as always in the ancient
world, was produced for local consumption, local potteries produced
wares for Galilee and Golan alone,[2] and the hills themselves provided
the raw material for building. It is this internal economy, whose
operation was the subject of a great deal of rabbinic comment and
theoretical regulation, that I intend to examine in this chapter.

The village markets were the main centers for exchange. Most
עיירות[3] could boast a שוק where farmers brought their produce once
or twice a week.[4] The Gospels refer to such markets as ἀγοραί,[5] but
no archaeology has yet revealed in Galilee an open central place on
the model of those in the contemporary πόλις, though presumably
they await discovery in Tiberias and Sepphoris at the very least. Nevertheless, the paved courts in the industrial complex at Meiron[6] and the
open space next to the synagogue at Khorazin[7] both give suitable contexts to what is known about activities in the markets.

Foodstuffs were the commodity sold most often in the market.
Animals, alive[8] or dead,[9] vegetables,[10] herbs,[11] fruit,[12] fish,[13] casks
of wine and oil,[14] eggs,[15] and ready-baked bread[16] were all sold—the
produce of the surrounding countryside. At the same time, craftsmen
within the villages took the opportunity to sell their goods,[17] and the
villages themselves became centers of production.[18]

Bringing in the produce for sale could be a complex and expensive
business.[19] Ass-drivers needed to be hired and paid off on arrival[20] or
before they begin their work (rashly, since they might default and fail
to provide substitutes as rabbinical law insisted they should).[21] Wagons
were perhaps used less often since tracks were unpaved.[22] The impecu-
nious carried their fruit and vegetables on baskets on their shoulders.[23]

Sensible people took food to eat on the way,[24] and though most of the texts warning of the dangers of travel by road come from the Mekhiltas,[25] the Tosefta, too, suggests a need to be wary of robbers.[26] Selling was normally a man's job,[27] but wives also might come to market to sell their bread[28] or olives,[29] and children or slaves could always be used.[30]

Villages as local trading centers encouraged the establishment of permanent shops and facilities for the inhabitants apart from the periodic markets. Purpose-built shops (חנויות) are assumed by all the tannaitic texts.[31] There are references to shops that cluster together (סמוכות)[32] like those on the lowest quarter of Meiron.[33] Such shops served to retail both food (on nonmarket days?) and products manufactured inside the settlement.

Food sold in the shops was much the same as in the market. In some places, only one shopkeeper might have fruit for sale, according to R. Yosi.[34] The best olives were kept for sale in shops,[35] some vegetables were kept there ready for eating,[36] wine and oil was sold over the counter,[37] eggs were available for purchase,[38] fresh bread was sold,[39] and locusts could be bought.[40] Such shops were considered essential to the community, for the rabbis insisted that they should keep working in the intermediate days of a festival.[41]

Shops lay open to the street or to courtyards[42] so that animals wandered near the entrance,[43] sometimes dangerously.[44] Goods such as honey, oil, and wine were packed into standard-sized amphorae[45] and vegetables hung from racks inside the shop.[46] Ready-cooked vegetables were sold to the public from stalls outside,[47] but most business was carried on from behind a counter (תיבה)[48] with customers allowed to wander freely and sit in the shop proper,[49] only the inner recesses being normally forbidden.[50] Credit was frequently given— men would patronize one shop only, so that the shopkeeper would let them buy goods on festivals without the need to hand over money,[51] and the shopkeeper might offer credit to let a man get around a vow not to help an erstwhile friend in any way,[52] the debt being marked up on tablets[53] and money, once received, being stored in a money-box with a slit in the top.[54]

Similar shops sold the produce of craftsmen working to sell to the local community. Some of the craftsmen were probably directly employed by the village authorities, for instance on the erection of public buildings such as synagogues.[55] Most, however, were independent specialists[56] working usually in their own homes; hence the rulings about the craftsman's responsibility for furnaces used in the upper story of his house[57] and the customer's responsibility if he gets hurt by flying chips of wood when he enters a carpenter's workshop without permission.[58] Only certain jobs needed to be carried out on the client's own premises;[59] the craftsman's tools were kept where most often used, in the courtyard at home.[60] If, then, archaeologists have claimed to find "industrial quarters" in excavated sites in Galilee,[61] these indicate the desire of craftsmen to live close to one another to their mutual benefit rather than the design of a capitalist employer. Guilds of wool-weavers, bakers, ass-drivers, boatmen, and flax traders are all attested in Roman Palestine,[62] practicing a sort of communal insurance to set a member of the group back in business if he suffered financial disaster through no fault of his own,[63] and it is anyway not surprising that in the ancient world members of a craft should wish to live and work close to one another. Wool-workers could agree to share in the purchase of any wool that came to the village and bakers might form a combination to settle the weight or price of bread.[64]

Of the crafts practiced, it is possible but tedious to compile a list from the tannaitic sources.[65] Most places had their own pottery— production of fine tableware might be centralized and imported from elsewhere in Galilee and abroad,[66] but coarse pottery for such things as domestic stoves was made locally.[67] Metal workers are attested, though it is hard to know how commonly they were found. There are quite a few references to the tools of their trade in tractates on the susceptibility of utensils to impurity,[68] and the familiarity with blacksmiths' technical terms there assumed would indicate that they were not altogether rare, but, with the need to obtain metal either by import from abroad,[69] or by melting down old utensils, their products will have been expensive and retained as long as possible without replacement, thereby rendering such craftsmen less essential. A sickle was found hoarded, perhaps as a valuable, at Meiron,[70] and no forge has yet been uncovered in any Galilean site.[71] More important were craftsmen for clothes production; most wool weaving was done at home by the women[72] (Josephus reckoned it exceptional that Babylonian Jews did not consider it shameful for men to weave cloth, suggesting that Palestinian Jews did),[73] but dyeing the wool was a specialist activity[74] and tailoring was respectable enough, the craftsman

carrying a needle as a mark of his skill[75] and providing a service sufficiently necessary for the rabbis to demand that he stay at work up to
the last moment before a religious festival to serve the public.[76] Rather
less respectable was the eminently useful craft of the tanners, for
theirs was a smelly job perhaps confined to particular families (two
brothers were tanners in Sidon)[77] and practiced outside and down-
wind of any settlement.[78] One man is said to have tried to offset his
occupational disability by carrying on a spice-dealing business at the
same time as his tanning.[79]

The role of the villages as economic centers attracted to their market places a host of service industries. As places for exchange the
markets needed moneychangers and scribes, and as the places where
the inhabitants regularly met they became centers for cultural and
social life where profit could be gained by selling entertainment, healing, or moral instruction.

Moneychangers were essential to deal with the profusion of different sorts of coin in circulation in Galilee in this period.[80] Old coins
took a long time to drop out of use if they contained pure metal,[81]
and the cities around Galilee churned out bronze coins for use alongside those of Rome.[82] The hoards indicate the availability of city
currencies in Galilee as does the fact that Bar Kokhba chose city issues
to overstrike during the revolt.[83] Good silver coins, such as those
hoarded, had a value above that of their weight and there is second
century evidence that the best of all, from Tyre, became relatively
scarce.[84] It is not such issues but the ordinary bronze city coins and
bronze weights (*perutot*) that are picked up in scattered finds.[85] This
was a monetary economy and there is no trace whatsoever of barter in
the sources. This was an important element in the integration of
Galilee into the wider economy of the empire and was no doubt
partly caused by the need of its inhabitants to earn coin with which to
pay the Roman taxes. But monetarization went very deep: loans, like
payments on divorce, were certainly computed and probably paid in
coin.[85]

In such a monetary economy commerce depended heavily on the
activities of moneychangers.[86] They worked every day in the big
cities (כרך), though only once a week in the smallest villages (כפר),[87]
and were recognized to perform a public service.[88] Slightly discon-
certingly, the specific information about coin changing concerns the
supply of small change to customers with large coin rather than the

exchange of one currency for another—on getting to market with his produce a man would change money to pay off his ass-drivers and workers,[89] and in many, if not all, places a gold dinar would be too valuable a coin to use except for very large purchases and shopkeepers would not accept it.[90] A parable in Sifre concerns a man going to Caesarea who needed 100 or 200 *zuz* for expenses, but took the cash in *selas* for convenience, changing it on arrival.[91] A similar story is told of shopping in Beth Aelias,[92] but such big shopping expeditions were rather different from regular ones in the Galilean villages.

The moneychanger made his profit by varying his buying and selling rates for coin.[93] A parable in Matthew assumes that bankers accept deposits and pay interest on them,[94] but, though this would technically involve the depositor in immoral usury in rabbinic eyes, complaints about such usury are never directed specifically against bankers, which suggests that such behavior was more often found in transactions between private individuals.[95] The moneychanger used a stool as a surface for counting the coins[96] and a pin, presumably to separate the coins without handling them.[97] When exact exchange proved difficult he used minute coins probably specially minted, at least in Caesarea, to make up the differences in currencies[98]—a stock of coin of all kinds was kept in a money box beside him[99] and other coins were displayed in front of him to educate apprentices and as examples of genuine issues.[100] The profession was by no means an easy one. Poorer moneychangers might have to hire genuine coins for making comparisons[101] and would certainly not be able to send issues on request for clients to check for themselves, as the richer ones did.[102] For such men it paid to be very careful. It seems to have been etiquette to receive back coin that had been wrongly exchanged if an expert testified to this,[103] and it was universal for a moneychanger to insist on taking in money brought to him before handing over coin in exchange,[104] but a supply of clients could best be assured by accepting riskier commissions, such as the safekeeping of deposited money (the banker could profit from it if it was given him loose, not tied up in bags)[105] and the responsibility for payment to a client's employees from such a credit account.[106] This latter role of keeping deposits had been one of the chief uses of the Temple while it stood,[107] but there is no evidence of similar hoarding in synagogues,[108] and depositors therefore had to depend on moneychangers such as these, on friends, which could prove costly,[109] or on any man in the village known for his honesty.[110] The lack of complaints against moneychangers suggests that they were remarkably trustworthy because they do not appear in any of the lists given by the rabbis of potentially villainous professions;[111] in the third century, at any rate, they could be men of high moral stature, such as R. Hiya and R. Eleazar b. Pedat.[112]

Hardly less essential services were provided by the scribes. R. Eliezer's assertion that vows not to benefit from a particular man are cancelable if he turns out to be a scribe may refer to teachers of the Law as in the Gospels' "scribes and pharisees,"[113] but in tannaitic texts the term normally designates the public clerks who write out documents for clients in the market places, and Eliezer's assumption that access to such a scribe is essential would not be out of place. As one passed through the market one would hear the voices of scribes reading back to clients the documents they have written for them, thereby letting passers-by know of an impending divorce.[114] Galilean society laid great stress on the use of documents and careful preservation of essential items, like the cache kept by Babata near En Gedi,[115] was normal, especially with papers proving repayment of debt or divorce.[116] It is likely that literacy was not widespread,[117] but anyway the technical terms used in legal documents were safer left to the experts. A Mishnah passage records an old man in a village near Jerusalem before A.D. 70 who used to write out notes in his own hand for his debtors to sign,[118] but all other passages assume the use of scribes for loans[119] and sales,[120] as is confirmed by the documents from the Judaean desert.[121] The scribe kept to conventional formulae to such an extent that he might produce blank forms for divorce, rent, and sale documents,[122] like the blank *actio* found by the Dead Sea,[123] and as a result he could handle a good deal of business, though there was always a danger of his getting documents for different clients muddled up.[124] It was a profitable profession with a fee paid for each document by the buyer or debtor.[125]

Other habitués of the Galilean market places, attracted by the guarantee of a clientele gathered for more strictly economic purposes, provided the social services one might expect of an economic center, contributing to the village economy only in so far as they in their turn brought the inhabitants to the market place to buy goods. So the barbers were recognized to provide a public service,[126] though too frequent use of them was considered morally reprehensible—for R. Yosi b. Halafta it was a sign of the pride of Absalom that he had his hair dressed once a week, even more than the foppish inhabitants of Tiberias and Sepphoris.[127] (The barbershop was openly visible to the public, to the detriment of the client's dignity,[128] but there is no record of barbershops as centers for the exchange of gossip as in classical Greece.) Cruder desires were catered for by prostitutes for a fee,[129] the rabbis reserving moral indignation for the use of gentile prostitutes[130] and homosexual brothels[131]—this last being considered, probably rightly, as a non-Jewish custom only.[132] The girls wore special headdresses and transparent blouses out of doors.[133] Also in the market places practiced the doctors, earning very considerable fees[134] whether professional[135] or freelance (as one might describe those religious healers who concentrated on mental illness).[136] Doctors doubtless lacked the formal training of the Greek medical schools,[137] but some Greek teachings were generally adopted, such as the calculation of the number of limbs in a man,[138] and operations described show a mixture of skilled surgery[139] and physicianship[140] with barbarous healing methods such as eating the lobe of a dog's liver when bitten by it[141] and wearing necklaces and rings to drive off epilepsy.[142] In general the value of going to a skilled doctor was recognized even by rabbis who might expect their religious aid to be called for when physical cures failed, and a distinction was readily made between medicinal cures and those close to superstition.[143]

The prosperous villages of Galilee thus provided their inhabitants with most of the services they required to build up a flourishing society. There was no need to rely on the cities, whether within Galilee or outside, to provide centers for the exchange of goods. If use was nonetheless made of the markets of the surrounding gentile cities, that trade was required only to earn coin to pay Roman taxes and to dispose of surplus goods and produce, particularly oil, and for the purchase of luxuries brought in from outside Palestine.[143a] Transport problems increased over greater distances: safety was never quite guaranteed away from home, so the rabbis prescribed prayers for those walking in dangerous places[144] and for those entering and leaving the bigger cities to ensure safety within.[145] The expense of hiring ass-drivers for up to a week became heavy[146] and only profit was sufficient bait. It was recognized that price fluctuations in different places could profit a man prepared to transport his goods,[147] and professional middlemen, Jewish and gentile,[148] worked in competition but cooperation with the farmers,[149] being prepared to utilize to their advantage the numerous customers promised by fairs held at pagan shrines on feast days.[150]

For such long distance travel, convoys of asses[151] like the camel caravans were used.[152] They kept well clear of all settlements until arrival—there are a number of stories about goods in mid-transport being left outside while the ass-drivers go into a village.[153] Overnight stay was in hostelries similarly placed outside the settled areas;[154] these were essential for the well-being of travelers, for R. Akiba in an uncharacteristicly lenient mood asserts that all innkeepers are to be trusted as witnesses to the death of their customers (and therefore the right of the widow to remarry),[155] which shows considerable confidence in them, and R. Yosi is prepared to let even gentile innkeepers cook food provided for preparation by the traveler.[156] Such inns were rather different from the public hospices erected for travelers by some communities,[157] for these latter seem to have been exclusively Jewish and connected with the synagogues in the centers of the settlements.[158] However, expensive though such large expeditions might be, they were considerably less ambitious than the huge camel caravans that brought goods right across the desert from the East,[159] and this was recognized by the tannaitic texts, which considered the caravans to be a gentile preserve. Traveling with such a caravan, even if only to get shelter for a night, was branded as "going after other gods."[160] Jews might have to join a caravan for journeys to Mesopotamia; hence the rulings on Sabbath regulations for a caravan once encamped[161] and on the keeping of the Feast of Tabernacles by building a booth on top of a camel,[162] but Jews competing with Palmyrenes and Nabateans in importing luxury goods were very rare.[163]

Nevertheless it was the desire to buy those luxury goods that the caravans brought that impelled Galileans to use the bigger city markets on their borders. The Mishnah denotes gold and glass as the most valuable materials for vessels;[164] the gold at least must have been imported into Galilee and would be highly valued not least for this reason.[165] The Gospels attest to the high cost of ointment brought from the East.[166] Pearls were available for purchase only in city markets.[167] Glass came from the coastal workshops[168] and was much prized—broken glass was mended with metal struts[169] and glass objects were carefully preserved.[170] Such shopping expeditions could involve large sums: 100 or 200 zuz in Caesarea,[171] 100 *manehs* in another town according to Sifre.[172]

In return the Galilean farmer could rely on a market for his oil[173] and for selling slaves, though it could be worth traveling from place to place to get the best price—a Jew is supposed to have sold one of his slaves in Lydda, but then traveled to Syria to sell another one.[174] It would not be safe for conscientious Jews to buy wine in city markets since the agoranomos need only have checked a wine barrel to render the contents religiously suspect and therefore in rabbinic eyes forbidden,[175] but conversely, a nearby gentile market was very useful for getting rid of goods whose kashrut was not certain.[176]

The cities were particularly attractive when a fair was held to celebrate a pagan festival, and the number of reported rabbinic restrictions that forbid profit from such occasions indicates the temptation for Galilean Jews to make use of them. Some passages (e.g., by R. Akiba in the early second century) restrict commercial dealings with gentiles on the way to such fairs[177] and forbid the use of meat that may have been sacrificed on a pagan altar,[178] but shopkeepers apparently came from all the surrounding areas to take part (so that a Jew traveling innocently in a caravan might find himself in the midst of a fair by mistake[179]) and all the professional merchants would be aware of which fairs were in operation at what time.[180] Even the villages near the city would become infected with the excitement, so that R. Meir (but not the other sages) reckoned that Jews should not go anywhere even *near* the city for fear of seeming to support paganism.[181] It remained profitable for Jews to use such markets, and all the rabbis could do was to advise that a Jew selling a slave in a fair should be forced to throw the profit away into the Dead Sea,[182] and as with their leniency in permitting the use of pagan flute girls,[183] they circumvent the problem by asserting that a fair is only entirely forbidden if it is clearly idolatrous and not if it is given by the state (i.e., Rome?), the city, or the local aristocrats.[184]

These cities held their markets in Greek-style *agorai*,[185] though it may well be that the bigger cities had more than one market place, perhaps frequented by different parts of the community. This seems to be the case in an odd story about Jews stealing pigs from a gentile market place in Caesarea[186] and a late third century talmudic account of R. Imi in a mixed village going to the "Aramean" market on a Sabbath to get someone to put out a fire, promising payment for the service next day.[187] The texts also suggest the use of large basilicas for holding markets as well as for gentile courts of law.[188] These buildings are a characteristic of cities rather than villages—such are the basilicas used in Ashkelon in the time of R. Judah I ha Nasi for selling wheat.[189] But the term is transferred to large private buildings in Galilee proper, such as the "courtyard of Beth Gaddi."[190] These, too, had public access, which may suggest the use of covered market buildings in some of the larger villages also, though none has yet been excavated.[191] Such buildings could be locked at night[192] and seem always to have doors at either end,[193] but they must have varied considerably in size if the larger ones were too big for a man standing at one entrance to see people entering and leaving from the other.[194]

6 Galilean Village Culture

Galilee could not preserve complete isolation from the culture of surrounding areas. Trade provided bridges for cultural influence to cross and it is evident that the Galileans to some extent succumbed. But to what extent and in what spheres of life, whether willingly or unwillingly, whether uniformly or only in certain regions or classes—such are the questions that this chapter will try to answer.

The Culture of Surrounding Areas

The culture of the cities on Galilee's border in Phoenicia, the Decapolis, the valley to the south and the hills to the north is too easily taken to be pure Hellenism, the fruit of the vision attributed to Alexander the Great and the desire of native city dwellers to conform to the new world order he ushered in.[1] It is not difficult indeed to point to the Greek traits of cities in Syria in this period: Greek language widely used for official purposes in all cities[2] and for private use in some areas,[3] the names of Greek gods worshipped by the locals,[4] some temples and statues in good Greco-Roman style like the temples at Baalbek and Caesarea,[5] the statues imported by the camel load into Palmyra,[6] and a woman being described in the Gospels as γυνὴ Ἑλληνίς, Συροφοινίκασσα τῷ γένει near Tyre.[7]

But the culture of Roman Syrian cities was more complex than a pale reflection of Greece would be. Within the cities, even in the second century, semitic traits remained. Inscriptions show semitic institutions lurking behind Greek terminology in Palmyra and the Nabatean cities: Palmyra kept her tribes[8] and caravan chieftains as leaders,[9] Palmyrenes and Nabateans continued to rely on the "chief of the well,"[10] and disguised continued rule by a long established family with the title "στρατηγός."[11] The Greek name of Beth Shean, "Scythopolis," did not oust the old semitic term.[12] Under Greek terminology there remained the old semitic cults so well-known from

Emesa, Hierapolis, and Baalbek.[13] The gods of Palmyra were numerous and purely semitic;[14] they were worshipped with Syrian feasts led by native priests in the local fashion.[15] The cults of Gerasa were Hellenized but not transformed.[16] And the language: again, Palmyrene inscriptions show the local Aramaic dialect used almost exclusively in private dedications.[17] The use of Greek in official contexts seems to have been largely ceremonial, like that of Latin in Greek-speaking cities dignified with the status of *"colonia,"*[18] for trilingual inscriptions omitted from the Greek and Latin versions information that appears in the Palmyrene, which was thus presumably the version intended to be read.[19] In Beth Shean in the late third century the local church employed a translator to explain Greek sermons in Aramaic—though an inability to understand theological Greek does not necessarily imply a complete ignorance of the language.[20] Language, like religion, reveals a blending of cultures. Three languages were employed in the Judaean desert documents,[21] and Greek and Latin words (especially technical ones) incorporated into Palmyrene[22] suggest familiarity with Greek constitutional terminology, even if not absolute acceptance of the ideas behind them.[23]

Art in Syria follows similar lines as language, with the characteristics of oriental art—linearity, frontality, lack of moulding, and so on[24]—being found untainted in a few places, but more usually curiously mixed with Greek styles,[25] grotesquely at Palmyra,[26] but rather magnificently in the synagogue in Dura Europus.[27]

The precise relation of semitic to Greek culture in Syria as a whole is yet to be clarified. Artistic developments away from Hellenism towards native traditions can be traced in some areas,[28] but by no means in all.[29] A Syriac literary tradition strongly influenced by Greek emerged in Edessa in the second century, recorded largely through the churchmen involved, such as Bardaisan,[30] but any echo farther west in this period is not recorded. The emergence of powerful Palmyrene rulers in the chaos of the third century indicates the continuation of old political structures in the desert city,[31] but it is unwise to assume the same of the cities of the coast, whose identity as distinctively "Phoenician" may not even have been recalled by their second century inhabitants.[32] The relation is one of unequal mixture rather than cultural conflict, and the mixture could constitute something of importance in its own right, as at Palmyra.[33]

Galilee, then, should not be viewed as a semitic enclave surrounded by Hellenism.[34] What needs to be ascertained is simply the particular cultural mixture that evolved and its similarity to or difference from the mixture in nearby areas. One would not expect Hellenism to dominate. In the first century even the aristocratic cosmopolitan Josephus felt himself unfluent in Greek and considered this a national trait.[35] Rabbinic rulings forbidding the teaching of Greek,[36] temporary in intention and ineffective though they may have been,[37] nevertheless reveal that the cultural antagonism of the Maccabean period had not been entirely forgotten in the second century.[38] I shall look for traces of Hellenism in various aspects of Galilean life and try at the chapter's end to evaluate the significance of what emerges.

Language

The question of language presents difficulties. Aramaic was something of a *lingua franca* throughout the fertile crescent[39] and was the medium of communication between Jews in Palestine and those in Mesopotamia.[40] All areas reveal its use to some extent—Jesus on the cross in the first century[41] and, in Lower Galilee, speaking to the daughter of the *archisynagogos* in Capernaum;[42] numerous inscriptions show it in widespread use in Upper Galilee[43] and on the Golan;[44] and rather fewer confirm its use in Lower Galilee.[45] However, inscriptions cannot always make clear whether the language in use is Hebrew or Aramaic,[46] and although there is plenty of evidence that *some* Jews known to the tannaitic rabbis did not know Hebrew,[47] there are sufficient indications that make it likely that Hebrew was spoken in most parts of Galilee in this period. The Judaean texts prove Mishnaic Hebrew to be still a living language in the time of the Bar Kokhba war,[48] and this was unlikely to be just a Judaean phenomenon, for the language was inscribed in Upper Galilee at the Kfar Bir'am synagogue[49] and in numerous places on the Golan.[50] However, Hebrew was always being used here in a religious context, as in the translation of Christian texts into Hebrew reported in Tiberias[51] and not as an everyday language as in the Judaean texts. Exhortatory remarks about the value of speaking Hebrew attributed to various rabbis[52] suggest that this practice was not as firmly fixed as they might wish. It may indeed be precisely in second century Galilee that Hebrew as a living language made the transition from colloquial, secular to literary, religious status.[53] It is noticeable that Lower Galilee lacks such inscriptions altogether apart from the rather

special case of Beth Shearim where the tomb inscriptions are sometimes too short to assign comfortably to either semitic tongue.[54]

To the extent that Hebrew was spoken it cut off Jews from the surrounding peoples, but Aramaic would have been quite sufficient to
make contact, both economic and cultural.[55] There was, therefore, no
need to learn another lingua franca, and it is all the more striking that
Greek is found in use in some parts of Galilee. The rabbinic texts envisaged Jews whose main or only language is Greek and showed singular leniency towards such people, even to the extent of allowing the
vernacular in some of the liturgy.[56] But such comments are more
likely to refer to coastal cities such as Caesarea, where Greek-speaking
Jewish communities were recorded at a later date,[57] than to Galilee,
and precise location of evidence will again be essential.[58]

Most of the inscriptions in Beth Shearim are Greek and not all have
the "public" quality that might render them only dubious evidence
for the language being spoken. Vulgar Greek[59] and even graffiti[60]
attest the presence of Greek speakers, but how many of these were
visitors to the shrine is largely guesswork (though the lack of precise
indications of the deceased's origins in the relevant catacombs may
suggest that most of those buried were local residents[61]) and inscriptions from the Beth Shearim synagogue prove the use of Greek by
locals at least for official purposes.[62] Beth Shearim lies right on the
border between Galilee and the plain leading to the Phoenician coast;
farther east, the evidence for Greek is less decisive. A fourth century
Greek inscription from Sepphoris does not seem to refer to local
men[63] and only a Greek inscription from Tiberias of the same date
assumes use of Greek by locals, assuming in turn that the marble
worker concerned was indeed local.[64] In Upper Galilee there is almost
no evidence of Greek at all, encouraging claims that Greek was never
spoken,[65] though these now need to be modified, even if only very
slightly, in the light of two Greek ostraca recently found in Meiron
and Gischala.[66] But *some* acquaintance with Greek is hardly surprising
given the trading contacts with Tyre that are indicated by coin finds.

The Hebrew rabbinic sources reflect precisely a general knowledge
of a bit of Greek, supplemented in some cases by rather deeper understanding, and of an extensive knowledge of Aramaic, the language
of the Palestinian Talmud. That more than one language might be
in use is assumed more than once: m Sotah 7:1 includes a list of
biblical passages that may be said in any language, t Gitt. 7(9):11

(Lieberman, page 274) discusses not implausibly the validity of a document that five witnesses sign in five different languages.[67] Plenty of Greek words have slipped into the semitic vocabulary used by the rabbis, not always as technical terms,[68] and, though that does not in any way prove that Greek was in use in the same time in the same place,[69] the fact that more Greek-loaned words can be found in the Caesarean portions of the Palestinian Talmud than in the rest,[70] when Greek was known to be commonly spoken in Caesarea,[71] would render it likely that rabbis used Greek words in second century Lower Galilee precisely because they were in common use among at least part of their audience. But in Upper Galilee and probably in the area around Lake Tiberias, Greek was only a thin strand in the linguistic cloth, in marked contrast to neighboring Gadara where the poet Meleager wove his Greek verses; but just as Meleager knew Phoenician to supplement his Greek,[72] it is highly likely that Galilean Aramaic as much as Greek could be adapted for converse with the inhabitants of the coast. In Sifre, a commercial term used in moneychanging is described as "a Canaanite word," that is, Phoenician.[73]

Art and Architecture

Language is a potent carrier of culture, but, given the multilingual society surrounding Galilee, that society could quite well transfer elements of its cultural outlook without needing the adoption of a new tongue.[74] Roman Syria also had its distinctive artifacts and art forms; to what extent did the Galileans adopt them?

All Greco-Syrian art assumed the use of representations of human beings and animals. To that extent a special reluctance to accept artistic influences might be expected among Galilean Jews, as being idolatrous. The biblical prohibition on the making of images had held considerable emotional significance in the first century when Roman legions kept their standards out of Jerusalem in tactful recognition of the law.[75] Herod's subjects disliked the games he held only because of the imagelike trophies awarded to the victors.[76] Such a prohibition could not be easily discarded and there were always zealots who returned to a literal interpretation of its meaning: in Judaea in the early second century one finds lamps with figures deliberately broken,[77] at some date now impossible to know representations of living creatures on the Capernaum synagogue were mutilated,[78] and the Mekhiltas preserved some completely strict teachings.[79] However, the rabbinic texts reveal a growing leniency toward such representations from the tannaitic to the amoraic periods.[80] The Tosefta permits a picture of a possible pagan divine figure to appear on everyday things such as boilers, kettles, pans, basins and so on, but not on precious objects such as jewelry.[81] R. Judah asserted that rings may have any image on them provided it be not in relief or making a relief seal impression, though even this would be too strict for R. Shimon b. Gamaliel, who is said to have used a ring with a face on it as his seal.[82] A Jerusalem Talmud fragment dates new permission to use mosaics to the late third century.[83]

Growing leniency assumes a demand for such forms of art, and this demand is evident in surviving artifacts. In Judaea the reputation of Bar Kokhba as a Jewish nationalist was unaffected by his use of a man fighting a lion as his seal.[84] Seals with a Hercules motif are found from the same area and period.[85] But within Galilee proper the use of representations falls into very limited categories: animal and occasionally human reliefs carved on synagogues dating probably from the late third century in Upper and Lower Galilee[86] and on funerary objects from the early third century and after in Beth Shearim.[87] Of freestanding sculptures or figurines such as those found in neighboring Beth Shean[88] there are no examples, despite rabbinic rulings assuming the possibility of Jews owning such things—a Jew's idol is not forbidden for use unless it has been worshipped by him,[89] a gentile's idol can be used by Jews so long as it will never be worshipped again.[90] No examples survive of painting, despite evidence from Dura-Europos that in some circles synagogue wall paintings had reached a high standard of sophistication.[91] It seems significant that no pottery from Galilee has been found painted with human or animal figures, despite the finding of a bronze ritual bowl decorated with a Greek myth motif in the Judaean desert.[92] The adoption of representative art is less startling when these limitations are borne in mind. The architectural relief in the synagogues was too high up on the buildings and out of the way to embody deep religious significance;[93] many of the motifs are common elsewhere in Syria and it is not really surprising to find religious builders borrowing artistic conventions from sects at variance with them.[94] It is only with the fourth and fifth century mosaics incorporating zodiacs and other pagan motifs that interpretation of the symbolism becomes a pressing need.[95]

Nevertheless, the change in Jewish art in Galilee after Bar Kokhba was dramatic and rapid,[96] and its origins must lie in admiration for contemporary gentile art that came to the artists' attention. Perhaps the habit of collecting pieces of art arose among the more wealthy— there is a Mishnaic discussion about the kind of statues a Jew may own,[97] and a first century red cornelian gem inscribed with a picture of Athena and found in a fourth century context at Khirbet Shema' had presumably been preserved as a valuable, though not necessarily in that place.[98] But most will have come from the artists' impressions from visits to neighboring places where oriental and Greek artistic elements awaited imitation. The choices made in borrowing from those traditions may illuminate the Galileans' attitude to the outside world.

There seems no reason to assert a deliberate preference in Galilee for either the Greek or the oriental elements of contemporary Syrian architecture, for the amalgam of motifs found in Galilean synagogues (from which, of necessity, most arguments must be taken) display just the same mixture of influences that is found in the rest of rural Syria. It is true that no strikingly classical buildings like the public edifices of places like Caesarea survive in Galilee, and this has prompted some historians to posit a prejudice in Galilee toward oriental motifs in preference to Greek.[99] But such prejudice would require knowledge, competence, and a deliberate refusal not to copy Greek architecture, whereas the models actually used by Galilean architects were almost certainly the contemporary *rural* temples in surrounding areas, simply because their styles were easier to copy successfully.[100] Galilean late third century synagogues share with these temples features such as an interest in the facade rather than the interior, and ultimately such architectural elements must have been derived from Rome. But this does not imply direct imitation for any Galilean: the styles were mediated through the buildings in areas such as the Hauran in which the amalgamation of Greek and oriental had already been achieved.[101] Historians search in vain for deliberate acceptance or rejection of Hellenism; for the architects themselves the problem never arose.

Similarly, it would be wrong to exaggerate the Greek influence on Galilean painting and sculpture. What evidence there is suggests that here, too, there was no prejudice in accepting Greek motifs, but such motifs, when found, seem always to have been put to an idiosyncratic local use in imitation of similar acceptance elsewhere in Syria. Beth

Shearim and Khirbet Shema' show that the Syrian use of stone mausolea was taken over by Jews in all parts of Galilee.[102] Up in the hills of
Upper Galilee it is difficult to discern any direct Greek artistic influence at all.[103] Further south, Greek motifs were used but for oriental
purposes;[104] this is particularly true at Beth Shearim where for lack of
an ancient semitic tradition of funerary art, Roman motifs were
adopted and Roman marble coffins imported.[105] The same is true of
contemporary Palmyrene funerary art;[106] and indeed the whole of the
Beth Shearim cemetery must owe a great deal to the taste of the many
Palmyrene Jews buried there in the third century, for they were accus-
tomed to elaborate funerary monuments forming almost a separate
community for the dead and to the use and abuse of Roman artistic
motifs in the process.[107] Greek conventions often provided subject
matter for decoration—the lion's head, wreaths, eagles, and cherubs
of synagogue reliefs,[108] the winged Nikos of a Beth Shearim coffin[109]
and so on; but their use conformed to an oriental tendency to an
impersonal approach and frontality[110] and with adaptations to incor-
porate Jewish elements, the menorah in particular.[111] It has been
tempting to erect a hypothetical separate "Jewish tradition" around
the Jewish elements of Galilean art and to link it to the paintings of
Dura-Europus where the Old Testament scenes prefigure so much
early Christian art,[112] but the subject matter and treatment of Galilean reliefs have so little in common with the Dura-Europus works
that a connection either of imagery or symbolism is impossible. Even
the fourth to sixth century mosaics, apart from the binding of Isaac
portrayed at Beth Alpha, harp on different themes.[113] If a well-
established Jewish art influenced the growth of Christian art, as seems
certain, that art belongs to the diaspora, not to Galilee.[114]

Education

Language, art, and architecture alone are not influential enough to
alter cultural horizons. That can be achieved only by education, one
of the least known and most important aspects of village life in
Syria.[115] What was taught to children in Galilee?

Primary education, according to the Mishnah, began with the
teaching of literacy.[116] Its success was not universal, for the Mishnah
denotes an abbreviated *amidah* for those who cannot read Hebrew
well,[117] and some men could not learn the words required on making

an offering in the Temple.[118] Although the Mishnah considers an inability to read shameful for a man who cannot say the Hallel and has to be prompted by a slave, woman, or child,[119] it is just as common in the Judaean Desert documents for a man to require the scribe to sign for him as for a woman.[120] The general rabbinic tendency to assume literacy must be discounted as a reflection of the highly literate group within which the rabbinic texts were formed, though it may be accepted as normal that all children were taught prayers, learning blessings by rote in the same way as the Hellenized Egyptian children learned their Homer,[121] starting with the Shema and Hallel.[122] At this early stage there would be nothing to stop the girls from joining in, too.[123]

There is scant evidence, but it is likely that teaching was a specialized occupation as in the rest of the Roman Empire by this time.[124] Fathers still had the duty of teaching their sons Hebrew[125] and a trade.[126] This was expanded in the Mekhilta to a wider curriculum of Torah, swimming, and "civics" (a curious mixture),[127] but then it was the professionals who taught these subjects for them.[128] Herod threatened to turn his feeble princes into "country schoolmasters"[129] —evidence that the occupation was both familiar and lowly. Rabbis regulated their employment to exclude bachelors, women, and any man deserted by his wife, for fear of sexual deviancy.[130] The controller of the children, perhaps a *paedagogus* rather than the teacher himself,[131] is termed in one text a *hazan*, standing watch over the children as they read on Friday afternoon.[132] Teaching the Bible to children was sufficiently important to be more than simply the *personal* responsibility of the father. According to the rabbis, a vow not to benefit from another man did not preclude that man teaching the children of the one who had vowed.[133] The teacher sat on a special sort of bench on which things were put, perforated and with the legs not permanently fixed to the flat surface,[134] while the children read their lessons, wrote on boards (presumably covered in wax)[135] and scraps of skin and ostraca. Papyrus was reserved for the more important documents[136] since it would be more expensive once transported to Galilee than its careless use in Egypt suggests it was there. The extant alphabets written out for practicing letter forms are doubtless those of scribes,[137] but those of children would be similar.

Boys in towns in contemporary Egypt, though not necessarily in villages as small as those of Galilee, would, once familiar with Greek letters, become acquainted with a wide range of Greek authors at secondary school and learn to analyze the grammar and meaning of the classic texts.[138] In the first century Jews in Egypt may well have undergone the same curriculum, if Philo is a trustworthy guide.[139] But for boys in Galilee, there is no evidence to suggest that their course was other than entirely Jewish: the learning and critical understanding of the laws of Judaism.[140] The method was the same as in a Greek education, for Josephus' excellence as a student was signaled by his "memory and understanding" in expounding the Law,[141] but there was no room in the syllabus for the Greek classics. The Jew described by Celsus knew the *Bacchae* of Euripides, but Origen denied that any Jew was much acquainted with Greek literature.[142] Josephus tried to learn Greek well, but was admired by the Jews solely for his learning in Torah,[143] and the language used in the literary inscriptions of Justus (a man who, anyway, came from Caesarea) in Beth Shearim is not a schooled Greek despite its reference to Leda and the swan, Homer, and Moira.[144] R. Joshua is said to have prohibited the teaching of Greek at any time,[145] a remark probably rightly taken to refer to the teaching of Greek literature rather than Greek language[146] and confined to the period immediately following the Bar Kokhba war.[147] It is a remark that might have had some practical purpose in a place like Caesarea where Jews learned their prayers in Greek in the late third and fourth centuries,[148] and where Justus picked up a smattering of Greek mythology[149] (though even here Origen in the 240s, himself in Caesarea, can deny that a Jew would know all about Perseus and other Greek heroes[150]), but in Galilee such a prohibition was wasted.

The lack of secondary education put Galilean Jews outside the orbit of the Greek tertiary education in rhetoric, philosophy, or Roman law that could lead to fame or power within the empire, particularly in this period, the peak of the Second Sophistic.[151] Palestine, like the rest of the empire, recognized the utility of rhetoric for ambitious men, for Antipas entrusted his kingdom to the orator Irenaeus[152] and the orator Justus became a powerful secretary to Agrippa.[153] Schools of rhetoric flourished in the immediate vicinity of Galilee, in Gaza,[154] and even closer in Tyre, whence came Aspasius, Paul, Herodian, and the great enemy of Lucian, Hadrian.[155] Jews in Galilee ignored both opportunity and evidence of utility, preferring the ancestral custom of not encouraging eloquence[156] and distrusting it when practiced.[157]

Philosophy was less obviously abhorrent. After all, Philo achieved a comfortable accomodation of Greek philosophy with his religious ideas,[158] and in the third century the affinities of Plato to the Bible were taken for granted by experts in the former field[159] and Christian experts in the latter.[160] Philosophy texts were readily available —Porphyry came from Tyre[161]—and the manner of philosophers, just as important as their subject matter, had long been attractive to Palestinian Jews.[162] But evidence of Cyniclike behavior—long beards, moral maxims, the crying of doom in the marketplace[163]—should not encourage speculation of a close acquaintance by any Galilean Jew with Greek philosophical literature. Attempts to link rabbinic theology to Epictetus are complete failures;[164] the rabbis lacked the basic training in Greek literature required to tackle such texts.

As for the alternative Greek curricula, mathematics and medicine,[165] Gerasa produced one of the greatest of Greek mathematicians, Nichomachus, at the turn of the first century,[166] and Eusebius implies that natural sciences were taught in Beth Shean at the turn of the third,[167] but rabbinic, and probably all Galilean, mathematics were largely unaffected, borrowing only the most simple of methods to aid textual exegesis,[168] while medicine, though a respected profession, never attached itself to academies like those of Cos.[169] As for Roman law, the need to learn Latin meant that no Galilean Jew seems to have been tempted by the highly lucrative legal profession being taught from early in the third century in Beirut.[170]

But if Galilean Jews did not compete as experts in Greek philosophy, they were still quite prepared to act as Greek philosophers did. For them, too, the marketplaces were the normal places for disputation,[171] where Cynics gathered crowds and talked to anyone who would listen.[172] Public displays of philosophical brilliance attracted an audience in Galilee as in Athens.[173] And as Greek philosophers were expected to teach practical ethics as physicians of souls rather than impractical theorisers,[174] so the rabbis meted out moral advice in the midrash they delivered to the wider public on Sabbaths.[175] As a result, there is evidence that rabbis and philosophers had sufficient in common to engage in disputations. R. Reuben, spending a Sabbath in Tiberias in the mid second century, conversed with a philosopher who asked him the definition of a "man who hates" and received the reply: "He that denies his creator."[176] R. Eliezer joined the audience of a heretic (*min*) discoursing in public in Sepphoris.[177] R. Gamaliel entered a theological dispute with a certain philosopher Proclus when accused of inconsistency in using a bath in Akko that housed a statue of Aphrodite.[178] A late compilation of purportedly tannaitic midrash tells of R. Yosi being collared in a marketplace by a gentile couple eager to learn from him about Judaism.[179] It has been noticed that the topics discussed in reports of conversations between R. Judah ha Nasi and an emperor Antoninus are the stock subjects of Stoic philosophers.[180]

In a similar vein were the disputations between Jews and Christians attested in the mid third century by Origen in Caesarea,[181] and clearly by that stage centering on the interpretation of a limited number of troublesome proof texts;[182] the format and the Greek spirit of philosophical enquiry informing such disputations were well illustrated by the dispute of Justin Martyr and Trypho, though that took place on the other side of the Mediterranean.[183] These confrontations seem to have been confined to cities—Gamaliel in Akko, Origen in Caesarea, Reuben in Tiberias, Eliezer in Sepphoris. Perhaps philosophers intent on deflating the pretensions of material culture were less concerned with the comparative lack of extravagance in village life.

Rabbis did not require specifically Greek learning to be equipped to dispute with Greek philosophers. They had their own system of formal tertiary education, the only form of tertiary education attested in Galilee. There is no reason to suppose that any other more Greek form of education was available alongside it unless one insists that the *minim* (heretics) occasionally mentioned in tannaitic texts were local Jews who had such an education[184] or that some of the philosophers just mentioned as operating in or near Galilee were from a similar background. Such possibilities are weakened by the fact that all certainly attested learned Jews of this area and period, including Josephus and the νομοδιδάσκαλοι of Origen, owed their reputations to precisely the kind of expertise in the interpretation of Torah that the rabbis taught.[185] The rabbinic texts were themselves the products of that system, so it is not surprising to find them more illuminating on this than the primary and secondary levels of the education system.

The normal term for the place where advanced students met is the "Beit ha Midrash," in contrast to the "Beit ha Kneset" where the less learned received instruction in formal sermons after the Sabbath reading from the Torah.[186] Doubtless a specific building was usually used, though evidence for this is scant. Nehonia ha Kana said a special prayer on coming in and going out,[187] and the term clearly had a technical meaning by the time it was inscribed on a stone lintel on the Golan.[188] Nevertheless, few details were given about such a building —lighting was by oil lamps,[189] and seating perhaps on straw strewn on the floor for students.[190] No actual buildings have been identified from the second century and the identification of third and fourth century buildings on the Golan as rabbinical schools relies entirely on the assumption that any large formal looking rectangular building that does not have a synagogue's north-south orientation must be such a school.[191] Even the beit midrash of R. Eliezer ha Kappar is suspect, for the stone found on the Golan is not long enough to fit any of the remains of the site[192] and the identifying inscription is poorly incised, more like a graffito than the finely carved reliefs that surround it.[193] One must assume that second century academies did not possess purpose-built buildings, an impression confirmed by stories about the use of a vineyard in Yabneh,[194] teaching in marketplaces and open fields,[195] discussions in private houses,[196] and teaching by rabbis as their disciples followed them on a journey, like the crowd that apparently followed R. Gamaliel from Kezib to Tyre as he walked and taught.[197] No capital expenditure was required for a rabbi to start a school; he could teach in a small village[198] or in a city outside Palestine, as Hanania b. Khinai and Hanina b. Gamaliel taught in Sidon.[199]

Sufficient uniformity is evident to suggest a loose curriculum and rules of conduct for students. Josephus' description of the subjects he was taught as "law and the interpretation of scripture"[200] fits well the content of the Mishnah and midrashim. Both subjects were studied with new intensity in the second century.[201] Law was studied partly as an academic and religious pursuit practiced for its own sake, for details of Temple ritual law being argued in the second century can have had no possible practical value.[202] Wisdom was defined as expertise in legal minutiae, especially, suggests R. Ishmael, in civil law,[203] but the topics most discussed involve purity and tithing, the main preoccupations of the rabbis' Pharisee forebears.[204] The more esoteric and mystical interests of some rabbis figured as important elements in their popular appeal, but never as a major component in their teaching curricula.[205]

Even shorn of mysticism the preoccupations of rabbinical schools were sufficiently esoteric to mark off the student from the rest of the population. The texts assume that the details of law would be known only to a select few—the man who is *ne'eman* (i.e., trustworthy, with regard to purity, tithes, and the avoidance of oaths and jests[206]) would be well known to everyone in the community and could be pointed out to visiting travelers;[207] the wise man's pupil (*talmid ḥakham*) was known as such by his fellow inhabitants,[208] and R. Shimon b. Eleazar suggested that his very status would normally depend upon recognition by them of his expertise in midrash, halakha, and aggadah.[209] Above all, all tannaitic texts assume a division of Jewish society into *haverim*, who keep the purity and tithing laws, and *amme haarez* ("people of the land"), who do not.[210] The degree of separation from the latter group enjoined on rabbinical students varies from text to text, but it is clear that the distinction was reckoned to override class distinctions[211] and depended entirely on education and religious practice. A degree of association was indeed inevitable and was assumed in numerous rulings dealing with purity problems arising from such contact,[212] and a number of texts make it clear that entry into the sect was equally open to an *am haarez* willing to learn,[213] but it was only in the amoraic period that the distinction began to be dropped.[214]

Students could be recognized from their clothing;[215] their cloaks, and the way they walked and spoke in public distinguished them.[216] Origen suggested that they wore *tefillin* (phylacteries) conspicuously,[217] and there is a story about a student who visited a gentile prostitute being rebuked by his own garment's ceremonial fringes and then being asked by the girl to what academy he belonged that assumes that his status as rabbinical student was obvious to her from his appearance (and the miracle).[218] Students were bound to stick together much of the time, not only out of common interests, but also out of a need to eat together in order to ensure purity in food preparation—a great deal of halakha concerns the regulations of groups eating meals in common,[219] to such an extent that table-fellowship can even be seen as the main function of pre-70 Pharisaism.[220] As with all intense religious practices this could involve disruption of family life—a man is permitted by the Mishnah to ignore his wife for thirty days while studying Torah,[221] just as Jesus proclaimed that his service should override family ties.[222]

Rabbinical students, then, formed a separate group within the population, in contact with, and held somewhat in awe by, the ordinary people, and distinguished by way of life, by interests, and by learning. Little has changed since the Pharisees of the first century were described by Josephus as a sect of above 6,000 valued for skill in the Law and believed by the people in matters concerning vows and sacrifice,[223] though it is only an assumption forced by lack of evidence to the contrary that, in so far as rabbis did not simply educate their own sons, their pupils continued to be the sons of the more leisured upper class as in first century Judaea.[224] As early as the first century it seemed to Josephus that Pharisaic education had something in common with that of the Greek philosophical and rhetorical schools: he described Pharisaism in Greek terms[225] and called the Pharisaic teachers "sophists."[226]

Ties between students were close. The caliber of fellow pupils was considered an important element in successful study and old friends from student days were long remembered.[227] Many of the students were members of rabbinical families—Sifre remarks on the good fortune of rabbis' sons who can listen to the rabbi so much more often[228] since even their daughters may imbibe wisdom greater than the average.[229] The Tosefta seems to envisage a privileged position for the "sons of the sages" at court cases and feasts, equal to that of students who may be more learned[230] but come presumably from the local Galilean population instead of the immigrant Judaean families from which the second century rabbis sprung,[231] and in the late third century this discrimination may have become an institution, with the sons of the sages forming a separate semiprofessional class.[232] However, for every student the relationship that really mattered was that between him and his master, his *rab*. "When R. Yosi ha Galili first came to Yabneh to serve the sages," it is suggested that it showed great courage on his part to speak out at all;[233] one should, according to Eleazar b. Shammua, honor one's pupil and fellow student but revere one's master.[234] Respect was called for at all times: protocol in asking after a teacher's health was suggested[235] and elaborate politeness was in order.[236] The title "Rabbi" was much prized,[237] and though it could be accorded to teachers of elementary reading and even instructors in a craft, it is clear that its primary meaning referred to those who taught *hokhma* (wisdom) or *talmud*, i.e., rabbinic learning.[238] The master was *in loco parentis*, permitted to beat pupils[239] and exacting at times both more loyalty than was due a father[240] and services of a servile nature, such as being carried on a litter, having utensils carried to the bath for him, and having his feet washed.[241] The closeness of the tie carried responsibilities. A student should go in general to his own rab rather than any other wise man, according to R. Judah,[242] and the whole dating of rabbinical schools relies on this principle.[243] The teacher assumed responsibility for the beliefs of his pupils and the teaching of wrong opinions was therefore denoted by the Tosefta as equivalent to idolatry.[244]

Lessons were formal, with the teacher orating to the students sitting in front of him. The rabbi laid down the halakha for pupils to learn by repetition.[245] He was expected to put the rulings into a logical order for them.[246] There was a tradition that the less controversial rulings of practical halakha could be entrusted to a deputy, like Zunai the deputy in the academy of R. Gamaliel in Lod,[247] and at some point senior students were expected to start teaching, though not all would want to.[248] However, a good deal of participation by students, asking questions and proffering ideas was also recorded. A Tosefta story gives the flavor of such questioning: when the pupils sat before R. Eleazar, the master's favorite, Issi the Babylonian insisted on a reply on a technical question about sacrifices, and was so excited by Eliezer's reply (because it ensured he was no longer alone in his opinions) that he burst into tears.[249] There is a competitive aura to such stories that emerges even more clearly when students are portrayed putting forward their own ideas: a student explaining a dispute of the Houses before R. Akiba;[250] Judah b. Bathyra giving a tentative ruling on lepers before R. Eliezer;[251] Yosi ha Galili, while still very young, contradicting R. Tarfon before R. Akiba even though they both call him "my son";[252] R. Akiba cursing R. Judah b. Nahman for flushing with triumph at his victory over the old man R. Tarfon (and, according to one account, causing his death by the curse);[253] R. Eleazar changing his mind because of the force of a comparison pointed out to him by his students.[254] Students needed to be kept on their mettle and encouraged to speak out—Yohanan b. Zakkai was said to have given wrong answers occasionally for this purpose.[255] However it seems clear that most of the time the master kept close control over this part of the lessons also, for it was considered a special favor that R. Akiba permitted R. Yosi ha Galili to return later to a subject on which he had already been worsted by other students and Akiba himself.[256]

All this presupposed a fair number of students and well-established methods of teaching. Informal rabbinic teaching in small groups as asserted by Goodblatt for amoraic Babylonia[257] is found in tannaitic texts and was doubtless normal.[258] However, there seems to have been also a fixed hierarchy among the students who sat before the sages and among the sages themselves,[259] and this hierarchy was exhibited at more formal lectures. Such lectures took the form of trials of cases, theoretical or actual, and are described in parts of tractate Sanhedrin in both Mishnah and Tosefta.[260] The passages lay down the order of precedence in a rabbinical court (*beth din*), but, as I shall argue in chapter seven, there was no distinction between the function of rabbinical schools as educational establishments and as courts purveying legal rulings and therefore the picture painted here can be taken to reflect educational as much as legal practice in the academies.[261] Rules of precedence between the rabbis were laid down, the *nasi* (president) receiving most honor and the "father of the court" after him; the students sat with the rabbis' sons and only went out if they really had to. Otherwise they would sit and listen to the proceedings to understand the topic before daring to say anything. Other passages add that rank was marked among the students by the position of their seats, increased expertise being rewarded by permission to move nearer the teacher.[262]

Graduates of the academies came back to hear what was new. So R. Eliezer in Lod asked R. Yosi b. Damaskit what new idea had cropped up in the academy that day,[263] and a similar conversation was recorded of R. Yohanan b. Beroka and R. Eleazar Hisma.[264] It is clear from the latter passage that new teachings were particularly expected on the Sabbath when one rabbi would be given special opportunity to speak,[265] but other passages assume that study was normal every day—a *haver* was likely to be in the beit hamidrash on a weekday if he was not out in the fields.[266] Lessons had fixed times and R. Gamaliel attacked R. Tarphon for arriving late.[267] It was a place in intense use, but a place also of decorum for which respectable dress was required.[268] It was a place of learning, but also a place for brilliant rabbinic displays of erudition and argument.[269]

On the highest level of culture, then, Galilean Jews possessed educational institutions not dissimilar in method to the Greek sophistic ones but quite different in content. Whereas the Greek system concentrated on the perfection of rhetorical style, the Jewish equivalent was the perfection of acute insight into problems in the Law, but just as the Greek academies developed from the private audience of the individual teacher described in Philostratus to the great schools with their enthusiastic student traditions described by Eunapius,[270] so the Jerusalem Talmud reflects the complete institutionalization of the beit hamidrash with the great building at fourth century Tiberias[271] and the excessive zeal of masses of students.[272] The more the Jewish academies flourished, the more Greek culture might be ignored on that plane and the less the temptation for rich young Galileans to become minim.[273]

Entertainment

The same selective adaptation of Greek culture is apparent in less elevated spheres of recreation. Private entertainment provided for family feasts incorporated where it could be afforded the latest fashions popular elsewhere in the Roman world, such as the use of couches for dining and the importation of delicacies to eat (see below, note 395). But more interesting is the extent of Greek influence on public expressions of communal enjoyment.

Theaters in the Greek style were found in many of the cities around Galilee. Sebaste, Gerasa, Hammat-Gader, Gadara, Hippos, and Legio all had theaters by the end of the third century.[274] Theaters have been excavated at Hammat-Gader and Beth Shean.[275] Theaters in predominantly Jewish cities, on the other hand, were rare: they could be found in Herodian Jerusalem[276] and Caesarea,[277] in Sepphoris probably under Herod Antipas,[278] but that was all. This is confirmed by the assumption in rabbinic texts that theaters were hostile, gentile places: R. Meir forbids any Jew to go to gentile theaters because of idolatry, though some rabbis permitted it except when sacrifices were in progress.[279] The reason for such opposition was not a dislike of singing and dancing on the Christian grounds of immorality,[280] though some nearby theaters were doubtless used for the licentious Syrian mime approved by Libanius and Lucian and popular in Caesarea.[281] Bardaisan in second century Edessa seemed to consider singers and dancers essential to civilization,[282] and in fourth century Antioch the local Jews were apparently notorious fans of such spectacles.[283] Nor was the reason for opposition a cultural dislike of Greek or Latin plays, though they, too, were probably performed in some of these theaters—a third century tomb door from Palestine bears an image of a man carrying a tragic mask,[284] and an inscription reveals the World Wide Synod of the Artists of Dionysus performing in Gerasa in the second century.[285] Though a Tosefta text forbids Jews to go to the στρατεῖον and *castra* for the *Atellanae Fabulae*, it was only on the grounds that such pursuits were a waste of time and frivolous.[286] Instead theaters were considered objectionable because of two other uses that were their primary functions in this part of the empire: as places for religious ceremonies and as indications of Roman imperial rule.

Religious use of theaters was indigenous in Syria,[287] in particular for the orgiastic *maiouma*[288] and in the Roman period for the imperial cult,[289] and it was because of the idolatry there practiced that the Tosefta forbade attendance.[290] Political use of theaters was indicated both by the fact that in Syria they were almost always a Roman imposition rather than locally instituted[291] and by the employment of such buildings to house assemblies and *boulai* in the *poleis*.[292] The theater was so essential a part of city administration that the erection of one was one of the few changes made by the emperor Philip in the elevation of his native village to the rank of *colonia* with the name Philippopolis.[293] The theaters came to be identified by the rabbis with everything Roman and bad;[294] the earliest synagogues, used in the same way for political meetings, incorporated some of the features of the Greek theaters, but there is no trace of such an influence in the surviving synagogues of Galilee.[295]

A similar attitude was found among Jews in this period to *stadia* and Greek athletics, according to Bardaisan one of the defining characteristics of specifically Greek culture.[296] Tiberias had a stadium in the first century[297] and Tarichaeae had a hippodrome,[298] and a late talmudic text described Tiberias as joined to Sepphoris by stadia along with castra and a "Syrian monument."[299] There is scattered evidence of an interest in private athletics—going down to the wrestling floor, taking emetics as an athlete,[300] or going running with a scarf over the shoulder.[301] The Jewish aversion to the need for nudity in athletics was not absolute[302] for Philo showed acceptance of such games as absolutely normal in first century Alexandria.[303] However, Galilean Jews completely lacked the interest in *public* displays of athletics and chariot racing that formed an important part of the culture of surrounding cities.[304] Inscriptions reveal that important public games were held at Sidon, Tyre, Caesarea, and Beth Shean,[305] and there were games of particular prestige in Caesarea[306] and Baalbek;[307] in addition, a large stadium has been found outside Gerasa.[308]

The rather less common phenomenon of chariot racing and gladiatorial and wild beast exhibitions indicates their Roman (as opposed to Greek or Syrian) origins. Herod had begun such games near Jerusalem[309] and built a hippodrome in Jericho,[310] while Berytus boasted chariot factions[311] (though the hippodrome in Gerasa was perhaps never used for races[312]). Gladiatorial fights were introduced by and for the imperial cult but never proved very popular with the Syrians[313] and, though Herod built a permanent amphitheater at Caesarea,[314] most such amphitheaters were intended for Roman garrisons.[315] It was only in connection with Caesarea that the local inhabitants were recorded by the rabbis as emptying the markets to watch the spectacle at the circus.[316] Anyway, none of these activities were recorded in second century Galilee and it seems that when they were available (as in Caesarea) the Jews did not go to watch.[317] They were clearly seen to be both gentile[318] and immoral.[319] *Knowledge* of these institutions is nevertheless quite frequently attested, by the gladiator drawn on a Beth Shearim wall (best connected with the Palmyrene owner of the burial hall),[320] by a purity law stating that the covers of a horse can become impure because they are stood on in the *campus*,[321] and by a Mekhilta midrash that seems to reflect a second century Roman innovation in the use of three-horsed chariots in races.[322] Such knowledge may come from the interests of the Romanizing Herodians[323] or from bitter experience as victims of the arena,[324] but not from the entertainment interests of second century Galilee.

Theaters and stadia carried unwelcome political and religious overtones. Baths, almost as characteristic an aspect of Greek culture,[325] did not, as a rule,[326] and every aspect of Greek bathing was adopted with enthusiasm. Most settlements were assumed to contain a bath of some kind,[327] an assumption not yet confirmed by archaeology,[328] though Tchalenko's survey in northern Syria suggests that further digging may reveal more.[329] Some of the evidence doubtless refers to special baths like those at Hammat Gader and near Tiberias, used for health cures,[330] but enough remains to illustrate the wealth of equipment used in Galilean baths as a matter of course—boards, couches, curtains and heating fuel;[331] towels and sponges;[332] strigils with oil;[333] a cold room as well as the main bath;[334] olearium with windows;[335] and a public attendant.[336] There were public baths and private baths,[337] these latter being named after the owner[338] and open to the public for a small fee payable to the attendant with a small token prepurchased in the marketplace.[339] With the lack of Galilean archaeological evidence, it should be recognized that there are a fair number of references to baths in mixed gentile-Jewish cities[340] and that no moral objection was put forward to the use of gentile baths in such places,[341] but it does not seem that gentile baths were the main interest of the considerable volume of halakha since the rabbis proposed rather impractical rules for the use of baths when gentiles were around.[342] Nevertheless, perhaps stories about the gentiles who sell stoned olives at the baths' entrances should be taken to refer only to the poleis outside Galilee.[343] Certainly it seems to be true that the cultural importance of the bathhouse as a meeting place for debate in the noon day heat[344] was singularly absent in the rabbinic corpus where anointing, massaging, rubbing and scraping,[345] and the plentiful use of oil[346] were much heard of, but discussion of anything approaching the intellectual (which in Jewish terms would be bound to be religious) was considered wrong.[347]

Religion

Galileans adopted Greek customs when it suited them and adapted them for local use for education, entertainment, and material comfort. The same is true in the last area to be considered, religious practice.

There is considerable literary evidence for synagogues in Palestine in the first century, in Jerusalem,[348] Caesarea,[349] and Galilee.[350] Archaeological evidence as to the nature of such buildings, however, is inconclusive: apparently public buildings have been identified as synagogues in first century Masada and Herodium,[351] in Migdal located in Galilee,[352] and in Gamala,[353] but they do not, in fact, make their function at all clear.[354] It is only with the so-called "early Galilean" synagogues[355] that buildings are found that clearly held a central religious place in their communities. For our purposes, a date for such synagogues will be of great importance; it is, unfortunately, much disputed.

Numerous synagogues from the Roman-Byzantine period have been identified in Galilee.[356] Few of these are dated epigraphically, and then only to the sixth century.[357] Two distinct styles, incorporating differences in the orientation of the facade towards Jerusalem, were noted by Sukenik in the 1930s and used to posit a method of dating that assumed the variation to reveal a change in building practice brought about by development of the liturgy.[358] This stylistic criterion can be elaborated by noting the difference, apparently resulting from liturgical change, between an early concentration on decoration of the facade of the building and later expenditure in some buildings on magnificent mosaics on the interior floors of comparatively subdued edifices.[359] However, even if the facade type does correspond best to second and third century styles elsewhere in the empire,[360] it is now no longer possible to rely on style alone for dating.[361] Excavation of sealed materials under the floors of stylistically early synagogues has revealed late third century material at Meiron[362] and fifth century material at Capernaum.[363] It must now be admitted that it is all too possible that conservative communities might have continued building religious edifices in an earlier style many centuries after new ideas have appeared elsewhere. It certainly will not do to assume, as has been done, that finds of fragments of "early style" relief in any particular area indicate second or third century synagogues in that area.[364]

Only meager archaeological evidence, then, is left for synagogues of the second and early third centuries. Meiron had as yet nothing.[365] In Beth Shearim a building with large well-cut ashlar lay underneath the mid third century synagogue.[366] The Khorazin synagogue has been dated, unreliably, to the end of the second century.[367] In the Decapolis city of Gerasa, a Jewish public building was destroyed in A.D. 117.[368] These finds are indecisive. It is possible to say only that Galilean society in the second century was at least *moving toward* a system centered around a public synagogue that would dominate the surroundings,[369] even if such a society was not yet fully in being.

Literary texts help reveal the kind of building envisaged, though architectural information is somewhat difficult to reconcile with any of the later or contemporary buildings excavated: the doors of synagogues open only to the east according to the Tosefta, although most of the Galilean synagogues open north or south.[370] Given this discrepancy, it is hardly reasonable to claim rabbinic authority for the prominence of many of the "early" synagogues on the landscape from the Tosefta passage that follows and asserts that synagogues should be built in the highest place in any settlement.[371] What the texts do tell us is the use made of synagogues once they were built and, presumably, the use made of a cleared area of public ground before such building began.

Synagogues in the diaspora served as centers for communal liturgy in partial substitute for Temple ritual from well before A.D. 70.[372] Not so in Palestine, where the Temple cult was paramount.[373] There the synagogues served to house the reading of the Law enjoined by Ezra[374] but for little else of religious importance. The Torah was read[375] with corresponding *haftarah* and explanation,[376] but, so far as the evidence goes, there was no public prayer to go with it, only private prayer that was considered rather ostentatious in a synagogue.[377] Perhaps there was some formality about the reading of the Law, for Pharisees had their πρωτοκαθεδρία (front seats)[378] and there was clearly a ritual involved when Jesus read from the scroll in Nazareth,[379] but there was nothing added to that ritual and no suggestion of any special sanctity attaching to a synagogue. On the contrary, the synagogue seemed to have a secular function—being used for public assemblies[380] and for the hospitable reception of strangers.[381] Above all, the building of a synagogue was presumably not considered essential for a community while the Temple stood since the only pre-70 evidence of a synagogue being built shows it being erected by an individual and paid for out of his own pocket.[382]

It would be surprising if the practice of building new synagogue buildings with a central liturgical function were adopted immediately on the destruction of the Temple. In fact, the tannaitic texts reveal an intermediary stage. The Torah was, of course, still read with haftarah and explanation.[383] The secular use of synagogues continued in the provision of lodgings for strangers[384] and the collection of charity for the poor.[385] The early synagogues appeared to be parts of larger complexes of public buildings in Khorazin,[386] Qatzrin,[387] and Er-Rama.[388] But the main impetus for the development of a full synagogue liturgy was acceptance of the idea that fixed prayers could take the place of the Temple sacrifices. The earliest evidence for this idea comes from the mid second century, though unfortunately from Justin Martyr in Corinth rather than a Palestinian source.[389] Justin also provides evidence of the incorporation of a curse against heretics in Jewish daily prayer, though this may come from the practice of saying private prayers aloud rather than from a formal synagogue service.[390] Only a Tosefta text that seems to describe contemporary liturgy in the synagogue in the singing of the Song of the Sea and the Hallel[391] would suggest a developed form of communal prayer on the model of the Temple services. However, where distinctively synagogal liturgy does emerge very clearly is in the celebration of the annual festivals—the *shofar* sounded at the New Year, the waving of the palm branch at the feast of tabernacles, and, above all, the reading of the scroll of Esther at Purim, for which no Temple celebrations seem to have been instituted in the first place.[392]

If in this period much religious activity still went on outside the synagogue at family feasts[393] and the decoration of the marketplace,[394] and even if the semi-public celebration of marriages, circumcisions, and funerals centered around the homes of the chief participants rather than the synagogue,[395] still it was through their steadily growing liturgical function that Galilean synagogues began to acquire something of the aura of sanctity that had surrounded the Temple. By the late third century, synagogues were found with ritual baths attached, presumably for use before entering the sanctuary,[396] and tannaitic texts already revealed a sense of the holiness of such buildings by restricting the sale of their site.[397] The lower "early" synagogue of Gischala was even found to rest on the site of very early settlement, perhaps an ancient pagan holy place.[398]

The growing importance of the synagogue in Galilee is not a phenomenon for which the internal development of Judaism can by itself provide sufficient explanation. The example of the diaspora communities in surviving without the Temple cult must be part of the answer.[399] The other part lies in the adoption of features of local gentile society. Syro-Greek pagans were used to having temples in prominent positions in their villages and cities for regular religious festivals.[400] The Jews of Galilee slowly took over not only the practice but also, by the third century, the style of building. The "early" style of synagogue architecture was a local variant of religious architecture familiar all over Roman Syria.[401] So similar were these buildings to pagan temples that Jews were warned in a talmudic text not to bow down toward synagogues in case they made a mistake and worshipped before a pagan god.[402] In setting up synagogues as houses for public worship, Galileans used gentile methods for distinctively Jewish worship; as I have demonstrated throughout this chapter, it is clear that outside customs were enthusiastically adopted but always adapted to a fiercely persistent native culture.

Cultural Unity

The same judgment would seem to hold true for all aspects of the infiltration of Greek culture in Galilee, in language, art, education, and religion. The acceptance of things Greek was greatest where it did not affect native traditions at all, as with the use of baths, and least where it affected them the most, as with the Greek insistence on the study of Greek poets as the basis of education rather than the Bible. Artistic and linguistic evidence suggest that Lower Galilee was more Hellenized than Upper Galilee, though whether this also applied to other aspects of life is unproved. Perhaps, however, one more possible cultural distinction should be considered, namely, the gap between town and country. Was the culture of Tiberias and Sepphoris more Greek than that of the surrounding villages?

Such a culture gap has been noted elsewhere in the eastern empire,[403] most relevantly in Palmyra, where far more Palmyrene than Greek was used in the villages, unlike the city,[404] and in Antioch, where John Chrysostom remarked on the different language of the country people who came to his church.[405] A similar gap has been posited for Galilee,[406] but there is not much evidence to support it. In the first century, Tiberias attracted hostility from the surrounding villages because it was founded, at least partly, by wealthy strangers under royal patronage.[407] Sepphoris was hated because its inhabitants stayed aloof from the first revolt.[408] This *political* division was recognized in Josephus' exclusion of citizens of the two cities from those he calls "Galileans,"[409] but it is not necessary to resort to Zeitlin's hypothesis that "Galilean" was not a geographic term but one which denoted a revolutionary group[410] for this usage to be explained satisfactorily in terms of Josephus' need to keep the narrative clear. At any rate, apparent hatred of the cities by the country folk[411] reveals a political dispute, not a cultural split; for that, there is no evidence apart from the curious fact that Jesus never went into either city in his travels around Galilee[412] (though a political reason for this, too, could be posited[413]) and rabbinic remarks on the greater attention paid to bathing in cities in general and to hairstyles in Tiberias and Sepphoris in particular.[414]

On the other hand, once the political divisions had healed,[415] there is evidence for a cultural continuum from city to country as in some other parts of Syria.[416] The cities, like the countryside, used a mixture of Greek and Aramaic—an early inscription from Tiberias is in Aramaic,[417] the Palestinian Talmud was compiled there in Aramaic,[418] and the Mishnah was compiled in Hebrew in Sepphoris.[419] These great rabbinic works reveal the existence of Jewish higher education in the cities and nothing suggests rival Greek schools. Sepphoris had its theater and Tiberias its stadium, both left over from Herodian days, but whether either was used for Greek plays or athletics is extremely doubtful.[420] The only cultural distinction between city and country in Galilee lay in the survival of old Herodian public buildings in the cities, which no village could hope to match in magnificence,[421] not in the size of settlements since some of the villages were quite as large as cities.[422]

Analysis shows a mixture of Greek and semitic cultures in and around Galilee and the need to avoid the assumption that cultural preferences in one sphere of life need be reflected in another. In general, little difference has been detected between parts of Galilee, though Upper Galilee seems less affected by Greek art styles and perhaps by language, and cosmopolitan Beth Shearim on the very edge of the Megiddo plain seems particularly susceptible to such influences from the coastal cities. No distinction has been discerned between classes in Galilee, a fault perhaps of the sources, but quite insuperable; an assumption that nonrabbinic wealthy men were likely to know more Greek and have more cosmopolitan tastes than others would be quite reasonable, but nothing firm is known of such men in this period[423] and the example of Josephus' education in the previous century would suggest that such Hellenization never went very far. There is no reason to suggest that the inhabitants of Galilee felt themselves to be fighting a cultural war. On the contrary, their particular amalgam of the Greek and the semitic produced as coherent and independent a culture as any in Roman Syria.

PART III: GOVERNMENT AND LAW

7   Rabbinic Authority in Galilee

The rabbis came from Judaea in A.D. 132–135 and settled first on the western borders of Galilee before moving to the cities of Lower Galilee later on in the century.[1] They had mostly been artisans, it seems, while in Judaea,[2] and there is no reason to suppose any change in their occupations or social status immediately on arrival in the north[3] —on the contrary, the difficulty in finding vacant land must have pushed the rabbis along with other immigrants even more into service occupations in the Galilean villages. It is remarkable, particularly in the status-conscious society of the second century Roman Empire, that the Jewish intelligentsia of this period were manual laborers, but there is no doubt that this was so.[4] Only toward the end of the second century will some of the immigrant rabbis or their descendants have risen to a higher economic status through patronage by the indigenous richer landowners and through their own secular efforts, and only then will their numbers have been swelled by the adherence to the rabbinical schools of some, if not necessarily many, of the sons of those same landowners in their search for higher education.

In A.D. 135, therefore, most rabbis were immigrants to Galilee and manually employed, owning no land. It is impressive and unusual that within the normal patterns of Roman society such men should have indulged in intellectual and educational activities and that those activities should be recognized as valuable by the rest of society. But what would be even more remarkable would be secular rule by such a manually employed intelligentsia; and yet that is precisely what all scholars accept. The assertion is influenced by the rabbinical claim that Yohanan b. Zakkai inaugurated an era of rabbinic control that lasted in Palestine from just after A.D. 70 until the completion of the Palestinian Talmud and beyond.[5] When rabbis state that their Pharisee forebears administered the Jewish state before 70, Josephus and the Gospels prove them wrong;[6] for the period after 70 there is much less external evidence and the rabbis must be disproved on the basis of what they themselves say.

With the methods outlined in Chapter 1 it is not difficult to find such disproof in the rabbinic evidence. Later stories about rabbinic jurisdiction must be ignored on the grounds that they were inevitably colored by later conditions and legal rulings must only be accepted as reflecting actual conditions when there is some reason to show that they were put into practice—Neusner has, after all, described the way that the purity laws were built up in this period simply by internal logic rather than by case law,[7] and the rulings on Temple ritual clearly had no effect on any behavior after 70.

What is needed is an analysis of case law alone. Since the rabbis were quite prepared to use precedents in the building up of legal ideas, they quoted such precedents whenever they were to hand; but those that did come to hand almost all concerned very limited areas of religious law. Almost no decisions on secular matters were recorded. Since rabbis considered the hearing of court cases to be their prime function,[8] the cases reported should give an accurate picture of their actual influence over Galilean society.

Sphere of Rabbinic jurisdiction

PURITY

> R. Eleazar said: "When I went to Ardaskos I found R. Meir and Judah b. Patyrosh sitting and judging on halakha."[9]

The passage goes on to give the essence of their judgment. It was on the offerings to be brought for impurity caused by taint from blood, a matter of purity only. About a quarter of the tannaitic legal corpus is concerned with details of purity and it is remarkable how disproportionately large is the number of cases cited for this branch of the law.

Utensils made (by mistake) unusable to the scrupulous were often brought to the sages for them to judge whether the owners could justifiably be assured that using them would not be impious. A case came before R. Akiba and his pupils about an olive wood seat.[10] To the pupils' surprise and presumably the owner's delight, Akiba pronounced the seat untainted. According to R. Joshua, a similar case about a loom beam was brought to four rabbis by the beam's owner when they were sitting in the house of Eleazar b. Azariah; the decision was similarly a happy one.[11] On the other hand, the sages successfully prevented the men of Sepphoris using gourds that were not clean,[12] and whether the decision of Gamaliel when a woman came to him after she had put her hands by mistake in the airspace of a pottery vessel was favorable or not is not stated[13] (if not, it would have had to be smashed up). Not all such cases were necessarily brought to the rabbis by the persons concerned—sometimes they intervened unasked. Gamaliel pronounced on the susceptibility to impurity of stoves in Kefar Signah after they had been accidentally baked in a fire[14] and other sages gave a similar judgment about wicker baskets borrowed from their owners.[15]

The most common origin of impurity was a woman in *niddah*, the state of pollution caused by a suspected menstrual flow:

> Again, there was a case of one woman who was weaving a scarf in a state of cleanness. She came before R. Ishmael and he checked her. She said to him: "Rabbi, I know that the scarf is not become unclean, but it was not in my mind to keep an eye on it." While R. Ishmael was checking her, she said: "Rabbi, I know that a thread gave way and I held it together with my mouth."[16]

R. Ishmael proceeded to emphasize the importance of erring on the side of caution in such cases—her spittle had rendered the scarf unclean. Women unsure whether they were in niddah at all came to the rabbis for advice, whether from a rabbi in Sidon,[17] or, in Yabneh, from R. Akiba[18] or a group of rabbis who came to a joint decision.[19] Particularly difficult were cases when women lived in close proximity to one another so that blood spots were difficult to assign. R. Zadok apparently sent a sample of bloody tissue produced by a woman from Galilee to the Yavnean academy for analysis; they had to turn to the doctors for guidance.[20]

Corpses were another source of uncleanness, though rabbis are not portrayed having much to do with cemetery administration (they did not, for example, seem to run the annual check on the graveyards that the Mishnah required of each town):[21]

> There was an occasion when the brothers Judah and Hillel, sons of Rabban Gamaliel, were walking on the border of Oni when they found a certain man in whose field a grave had been opened up. They told him: "Gather the bones up one by one and everything will stay in a state of cleanness."[22]

This is pure advice, and whether the man obeyed is not indicated. In a different case, bones were brought in a box to Yabneh where Teodorus the physician pronounced them not human (he was looking at them in the open air and not in a synagogue, since the impurity could otherwise have prevented Cohanim from coming to hear the Torah).[23] On the whole, however, location and disposal of bodies was a local matter not brought to the academies. In Beth Horin, a local old man discovered a mass grave in a suspected spot by a curious method using a wet sheet.[24] No rabbi was recorded to have indulged in such scientific practices.

In general, practical legislation on purities was an important contribution by the rabbis to Palestinian social life. In the Mekhilta, the verse "There will be for you a law suit" was interpreted as referring to decisions on purity laws.[25] In the same work, the punishment of a judge who received bribes was, if not blindness or destitution, confusion about the laws of cleanness.[26] In Sifre, the "suit concerning blood" in Deuteronomy 17:8 was taken to refer not to murder but to problems about purity.[27]

KASHRUT

There is remarkably little indication of attempts by the rabbis to supervise the production of kosher meat. A long story of R. Tarfon's decision that a cow whose womb had been removed was not kosher, the reversal of that decision by the sages on the advice of Todos the doctor, using evidence from Alexandria, and the assertion by Akiba that Tarfon was not bound to pay damages for the loss of the animal since his decision was given as an expert (*mumheh*),[28] all presupposes regular application to the rabbis for decisions on doubtful cases. Unfortunately the passage is missing in some editions of the Mishnah. Another case when rabbis were asked to judge a particular kashrut problem exhibits them as not only incapable of enforcing a decision, but unwilling even to express an opinion—this was regarding an animal that was slaughtered correctly in Caesarea, but the blood afterwards dedicated to idolatry.[29] It is not recorded whether the rabbis' warning to the men of Mahuz that their way of storing grain rendered their bread unclean had any practical effect.[30]

KILAIM (MIXED KINDS)

In the markets of Sepphoris they used to graft Crustumenian pears onto a native pear tree. A certain disciple found them and said to them: "You are forbidden." They went and cut them off; and they came and asked in Yabneh. They [the rabbis there] said: "Who is this you have come up against? He must be one of the pupils of Beth Shammai."[31]

The unasked-for decision of the rabbinical pupil was followed *before* the Sepphoritans went to check with higher authority and were given a more lenient ruling. Men came also from Arieh near Tiberias to Yabneh to ask about kilaim, and presumably accepted the decision.[32] When R. Joshua visited R. Ishmael in Kefar Aziz, Ishmael sat Joshua down to judge a difficult kilaim case that had come up before him.[33] On the other hand, a case in Zalmon when the rabbis allowed a man to make the best use of the limited land available to him despite the danger of mixed kinds may be purely theoretical.[34] The Mishnaic text stated that: "The case came before them." It was not stated whether the man also came to bring the case.

SHEBIIT (THE SABBATICAL YEAR)

R. Yosi said: "There was an incident when people sowed a field in Sepphoris with onions for the year after the Sabbatical year . . . and the matter came before R. Yohanan b. Nuri and he said: 'If the onions were growing naturally they are allowed. If not, they are forbidden.' "[35]

Yohanan was enforcing the proper observance of the sabbatical year. If the people who brought the matter were the people who sowed the field, the jurisdiction was effective; otherwise it was pure theory. Akiba, according to R. Yosi, took no action when a man planted vines on the sabbatical year. He just declared them ownerless.[36]

TITHES

There are many examples of rabbis expertly checking first-born animals to see whether they are blemished and so need not be handed over to the Cohen.[37] Ila in Yabneh was so expert he was allowed to accept payment for this work.[38] Though he was not himself a member of the rabbinic academy, with whom he sometimes disagreed,[39] he was closely associated with them. R. Shimon b. Gamaliel got help from the sages with one such problem;[40] Akiba and Yohanan b. Nuri

disagreed on a particular case brought to the academy when only the
testicles of the animal were faulty.[41] Akiba decided another such case
that had arisen in the house of a certain Menahem who is otherwise
unknown.[42]

Cohanim were still receiving tithes at the end of the first century at
least, when R. Tarfon came late to the academy because he was eating
tithed produce.[43] The rabbis showed an intense interest in their
proper payment, but had no means to enforce their wishes. R. Yosi
said that he spoke in a case before Akiba when tithed produce had
fallen into a bundle of ordinary food,[44] but the one instance of a man
clearly being made to treat tithes with the proper reverence concerns
Shimon b. Kahana whom the sages in Akko compelled to drink on
board a ship in the harbor the *terumah* wine he had brought from
Cilicia because it was forbidden to bring terumah into the land of
Israel from abroad.[45]

SHABBAT

When Yohanan b. Zakkai was in Arab near Sepphoris he was approached
twice by locals wanting to know whether they had broken the Sabbath by their actions.[46] Yohanan was asked to decide whether they
needed to bring guilt offerings (the Temple was still standing at this
time). These are the only examples of Sabbath problems being brought
to rabbis for adjudication, though Tarfon was asked in general terms
whether an animal that died on a festival could be moved and had to
ask the academy for help in deciding.[47] According to R. Eliezer,
Gamaliel and the elders "came and forbade the use of a door bolt in
the synagogue" of Tiberias on Shabbat, though R. Yosi reckons they
came and permitted it.[48] Whether Gamaliel's instructions were followed is not stated. It seems unlikely since Eliezer and Yosi could
still argue as to what the instructions were. Similarly unrequested and
possibly ignored was the ban declared by the sages on the men of
Tiberias putting a cold water tube through their hot springs on the
Sabbath.[49] On the other hand the decree of R. Judah ha Nasi on the
Sabbath limits of Gader and Hamata seems to have been obeyed—it
was quoted as being of the same validity in practice as ancient local
custom as remembered by an old shepherd.[50] That most rules for
Shabbat were the result of such local custom sanctioned by local
elders seems clear.[51]

IDOLATRY

It once happened that Baytos b. Zunin brought dried figs in a ship and a jar of יין נסך (suspected libation-wine) was broken and fell upon them; and he asked the sages and they declared the figs permitted.[52]

In this case Baytos clearly reckoned the rabbis to be the best arbiters of how close a conscientious man should allow himself to go to the taint of idolatry. All other examples may have had less practical effect —R. Shimon allowed a tree to be used in Sidon despite the idol that had stood underneath it,[53] while other sages tried to prevent the use of wine that had been left in a gentile's possession for too long.[55]

SYNAGOGUE RITUAL

When Hanina b. Gamaliel was in Kebul he told the translator-commentator when to give his version of biblical passages and when to stay silent because the passages contained sensitive material.[55] R. Tarfon stopped a funeral for a man called Aleksa taking place with a full funeral oration on a festival.[56] However most synagogue ritual was not under rabbinic control though the academies' example was doubtless influential. It was the head of the synagogue or the *ḥazan* who apportioned tasks in the synagogue.[57]

THE CALENDAR

R. Akiba said: "When I went down to Nehardea to ordain a leap year I was met by Nehemiah of Beit Deli. . . ."[58]

The academy Beth Din took the place of the Jerusalem Sanhedrin in deciding on the arrival of the New Moon. There are a number of stories about such decisions taken at Lod and Yabneh,[59] and the halakha explains the difference in procedure from before 70.[60]

VOWS

The following is part of the story of Rabban Gamaliel's journey with R. Ilai from Akko to Tyre:

He reached Akhzib, and a man came to him and asked him about changing his vow. Gamaliel said: "Is this a vow not to drink even a quarter log of wine?" He said: "Yes." Gamaliel said: "If so, travel with us until we evaporate our wine." He walked with them until they got to the Ladder of Tyre. He got down from his ass, covered himself, sat down and freed him from his vow.[61]

Rabbis as holy men could release a man from a vow he had taken. They did so in Sidon when a man's vow to abstain from marital relations with his wife threatened domestic concord.[62] When a similar case came before Akiba he ordered the husband to agree to an annulment or else divorce his wife and pay alimony.[63] The husband was displeased but yet consented—he had presumably come to Akiba in the hope of confirming the legality of his vow. A man in Beth Horon in northern Judaea appealed to the rabbis for help when a vow to have nothing to do with his father caused him financial loss, but the rabbis refused to help.[64]

FASTS

Usually called to try to stop a drought, such occasions called forth the best in pious men, who might or might not be rabbis.

> There was an incident when a pious man [*hasid*] was told to pray for rain to fall. He prayed and rain fell. They said to him: "As your prayers have proved successful here, pray again for them [i.e., other places]."[65]

The hasid refused on the reasonable ground that too much irresponsible prayer would bring a danger of flooding. Honi and Hanina b. Dosa were both reckoned by later generations to be rabbis of a sort, and they indulged in such rainmaking.[66] R. Shimon b. Gamaliel thought that a fast was one of the few occasions when a man might *make himself* a talmid hakham in order to help protect the community.[67] The rabbis claimed, perhaps wishfully, some control over the conduct of such fasts. When a man said the whole blessing (as opposed to only a part) in front of the ark in Galilee in the early second century the matter came before the sages, who allowed it.[68] Tarfon allowed a fast in Lod to stop the moment the rains came instead of waiting for the evening.[69] Shimon b. Shetah is recorded as claiming that he would have placed a ban on any unorthodox rainmaker less potent than Honi.[70]

SUBSTITUTES FOR SACRIFICES

Actual cases are lacking, but there is a tradition that Yohanan b. Zakkai and other leading rabbis laid down rules for Jews to follow in those circumstances when a Temple sacrifice had been stipulated but was now impossible, and it is a tradition that must be considered highly plausible since guidance at such times, when guilt feelings would ensue if nothing was done to substitute for the required offering, would be highly useful for all Jews. So Yohanan is reputed to have regulated the consumption of the new harvest since there was no longer an Omer sacrifice and the conversion of proselytes since there was no longer a convert's offering.[71]

Limitations of Rabbinic Jurisdiction

Apart from one exception to be discussed below,[72] such religious questions were the sum total of the tannaitic rabbis' activity outside their educational role in the academies. This judicial activity governed the consciences of individuals, not the good ordering of a community. It could therefore take place in much the same form not only in the semiautonomous villages of Galilee but in Lod or Yabneh in Judaea or even outside Palestine—at least four rabbis studied in Sidon,[73] and cases involving idolatry,[74] purity,[75] and release from vows[76] were all heard and dealt with there.

Neither civil nor criminal cases, then, were decided by rabbis at this time. There *were* Jewish courts in the villages and such cases *did* come before them, but their judges were not rabbis,[77] and in such matters the sages had to be content to discuss problems in the abstract. The relation of the theoretical rabbinic discussions of law to these actual nonrabbinic Jewish courts will be discussed below.[78]

When the rabbis judged, they decided religious matters only. In some cases people with a conscience came to them for decisions[79] and presumably accepted the decisions given, but there is no clear example of anyone accepting an unpleasant decision who had not approached the rabbis in the first place. Nevertheless, as has been said, in religious matters the rabbis tried to impose a strict standard on the nation and were not loath to issue instructions whether requested or not.[80]

Rabbinic religious authority

DISREGARD

It can be seen from the evidence of the rabbis themselves that in practice these instructions were more often ignored than not. The tannaitic texts are largely a record of the struggle to educate the stubborn *amme haarez* and prevent them lowering the standards of the more scrupulous. In almost every area that the rabbis tried to control there were some, and, as far as one knows, a majority, who disobeyed.[81] Noncompliance was far more common and venial in rabbinic eyes than active opposition; it is all the more striking that the failings of such disobedient amme haarez were attacked by the sages much more often than the quite different theological opposition of rival groups such as the *minim*.[82]

Purity laws were those most likely to be ignored because of their complexity, and the Mishnah confirms that they were.[83] If a man failed to observe tithes or the Sabbatical year properly it could be assumed that he would ignore purity laws.[84] It could, in general, be assumed that any worker,[85] olive-treader,[86] or poor man gleaning[87] would be little concerned with the minutiae of purity.[88]

As for kashrut, R. Meir urged that no butcher could be trusted to porge meat properly.[89] His caution was, however, probably excessive and the sages disagreed with him on this point. Another passage gives the procedure to be followed when the whole town sells kosher meat except for one butcher who sells *demai*[90] (meat of dubious kashrut—*not* unkosher meat), and there was a legal ruling that a rebellious (*meshumad*) Jew's meat is kosher.[91] This ruling also said that the meat of a *min* was not kosher, which suggests that apart from the theological views of the butcher there was nothing wrong with it since otherwise the ruling would be otiose. Jewish insistence on kosher food marked them out to gentiles before and after the second century—the Sardians passed a decree to allow the import of suitable food[92] and Origen remarks on Jewish eating habits.[93] Bread was considered by rabbis unkosher when made by bakers in a state of impurity. The *haver* was urged to give such a baker only limited help[94] —it was assumed that he could not be stopped. What is explicitly a later ruling relaxes this rule still further.[95] Presumably unkosher bread was too widespread and the rabbis gave up trying to stop it. As for vegetables, illegal sprinkling with water to make them look fresh made much that was sold impure. All shopkeepers were suspect on this account[96] and no herbs sold in village markets were certain to be kosher.[97] The scrupulous had to buy them straight from the field.

Kilaim, the law of mixed kinds, was generally disregarded.[98] So were the rules for the sabbatical year—these institutions had gone the way of the Jubilee.[99] It was notorious that no one observed them,[100] and the rabbinical rulings had to take into account that "since the transgressors increased" they lived in a society generally lax in such matters. Special venom was reserved for those who actually profited by their sin of breaking Shebiit.[101] The ḥaver was not expected to cut himself off from transgressors in the sabbatical year, so it was presumably not feasible.[102] He was just urged not to help them or profit by their actions.[103] When an entire town failed to keep Shebiit, the rabbis ruled that this should be ignored in distributing charity.[104] This laxness was in marked contrast to the apparent strictness of pre-70 Jerusalem.[105] It was not due to ignorance, for one of the Bar Kokhba contracts from the Judaean desert uses the sabbatical year as a means of dating the period of the lease,[106] and the detailed provisions of the seventh century Rehov mosaic inscription about the sabbatical year in operation near Beth Shean suggests it was taken seriously by the synagogue's users by the middle Byzantine period.[107] Laxness, then, was due simply to the fact that the religious desires of Galilean Jews in the second century did not include any interest in the sabbatical year.

Tithes were similarly ignored.[108] The definition of an am haarez in the Tosefta is one who is not scrupulous about tithes.[109] There were plenty such persons at this time.[110] In the mid second century R. Shimon b. Gamaliel, R. Judah, and R. Yosi were not prepared to eat a meal they were offered in Akhzib until they had checked whether their host was trustworthy regarding tithes.[111] People were suspected of ignoring *terumah*,[112] *bekhorot*[113] (the tithe of the first-born animal), and the tithe of the third and sixth year given to the poor.[114] The days when there was no need to check whether tithes had been given were remembered as a golden age.[115]

Shabbat was less widely ignored. The ruling that a Jew who breaks Shabbat with παρρησία does not count as a Jew for an erub was probably theoretical,[116] and the only real hint that laxness was not uncommon is the comment that bathing was no longer permitted on the Sabbath because transgressors had increased—these transgressions concerned only the wringing out of towels and hardly indicates serious nonobservance of the basic law.[117] For Bardaisan, as for many other gentiles, Shabbat was, along with circumcision, the main mark of Jews.[118] As for idolatry, it was assumed that workers would drink יין נסך (suspect libation wine) and the householder who pays them was told not to interfere.[119] A new ruling that wine made יין נסך by accident could still be drunk suggests that most people were fairly lax in checking on the origin of their wine.[120] Similarly, it may be in response to popular pressure that rabbinic restrictions on the plastic arts were relaxed.[121]

Synagogue ritual was not usually interfered with by rabbis. Dosa b. Harkinas suggests that the amme haareẓ had their own synagogues in which *haverim* should not sit.[122] R. Meir, according to Shimon b. Eleazar, apparently followed an unusual local custom when he sat down to read the scroll on Purim at Tibon.[123] However, this lack of interference was not so much because rabbis *could* not control ritual as because they did not try.[124]

The keeping of "small cattle," on the other hand, meets thorough disapproval. According to R. Ishmael, it was this sin with one other that destroyed the village of Beth Aba in Galilee.[125] However, such sinners were not to be opposed, like heretics, but simply not helped, like gentiles.[126] The laxity was due to the prevalence of the sin. It was so common that some passages simply take for granted that the rule was ignored—in one place a ruling was given on transactions involving small cattle without reproach and on the assumption they were being reared.[127] There is an anonymous comment that the rabbis would have liked to forbid large cattle as well (they were only slightly less damaging to trees), but that this was not done because "one only builds fences that are capable of standing up."[128] That is, any attempt to impose a harsher rule would have been bound to fail.

OPPOSITION

The amme haareẓ were disobedient Jews, but they did not belong to any breakaway religious sect. Such sects, however, doubtless existed as they had in the first century.[129] They were identified by the rabbis as either minim or *meshumadim*.[130]

The minim were Jews[131] whose sin was theological.[132] The precise nature of their theology has been much disputed: Christian contemporaries describing Jewish sects reflected their own Christian concepts of heresy[133] and were sufficiently uninformed to describe the Samaritans simply as sectional Jews,[134] so their evidence must be treated with caution. It will be best to use the rabbinic evidence itself to see what sort of enemies the rabbis conceived the minim to be.

It has been suggested from the rabbinic texts that the minim were those Jews whose theology was overly influenced by Greek philosophy, and certainly some of the ideas attacked by the rabbis do seem to be Greek.[135] It is noticeable that the sort of heretical belief that the rabbis envisaged seems to involve in some cases a system of two or more powers in heaven, in which one power acts as intermediary to the other while both are essentially friendly to the worshipper. Rabbinic concern was directed to prevent open admission of such dualism (hence the restrictions in m Ber. 5:3). It is certain that such views were attractive to some Jews outside Galilee and that they played some role in converting some of the Diaspora to Christianity, and it is likely that their popularity within Galilee was played down by the rabbinic authors with their assumption that their own approach to religion was the *only* one to take. Furthermore, if the rabbinic form of higher education took some time to become standard in Galilee in the second century, there should have been room for the development of such rival philosophies. But it is unwise to try to build up such nonrabbinic theologies into serious competitors for the attention of Galilean Jews for, if they had been so, much more opposition to their ideas rather than merely to the lax practice of amme haarez might have been expected in the rabbinic texts themselves. This is, after all, precisely the period in which Christian self-definition was achieved through the exclusion of theological concepts defined by patristic writers as heretical. The rabbis were not interested in doing the same thing: the dualism that they opposed was too unorganized and vague to evoke concentrated attention. And so it is that no fuller account of such philosophies can be safely ventured. Only in the amoraic texts can the gnostic and Christian ideas of the third and fourth centuries be seen to elicit a response from the rabbis of Galilee. Tannaitic comments on minim were either allusive or abusive or both. It is anyway more than likely that the rabbis conflated different groups in their attack on the theological opposition. But one suggestion can usefully be made: if the picture of Galilee drawn in Chapter 6 is correct, it would be most unlikely that any sophisticated Greek philosophy was dangerously (in rabbinic eyes) current in Galilee itself, and therefore minim would have culled their ideas, not in Galilee, but in the cities of the coast, and Galilean *minut* would be only a pale reflection of the Hellenistic Judaism of the Diaspora.

This is only a hypothesis, but it is certainly preferable to the wilder hypothesis that the minim were Jewish Christians promulgating a special form of Galilean Christianity.[136] Epiphanius states that in the early fourth century there were no Christians at all in the Jewish settlements of Galilee, including Tiberias, Sepphoris, Nazareth, and Capernaum,[137] and that a Jew converted to Christianity had to take refuge outside Galilee in Beth Shean.[138] Upholders of the Christian identification of the minim therefore have to claim that Galilean Christianity was too different from Epiphanius' belief for him to recognize it as Christianity at all. This form of Christianity, according to such scholars, would be more than a simple interest in Jesus like that shown by the non-Christians who pointed out the cave and manger in Bethlehem,[139] or the Gadarene hill off which the swine fell, to pilgrims,[140] or by the copying of St. John's Gospel into Hebrew in fourth century Tiberias,[141] but would be an indigenous product of the disciples of those who went to Galilee after the Crucifixion[142] and followed the leadership of Jesus' family after his death.[143] It is suggested that their theology remained Jewish while the main Church, centered on Jerusalem and soon the Greek Diaspora, was transformed.[144] Of such a Judaizing tendency in Syrian Christianity there is plenty of evidence outside Galilee, particularly from Origen in Caesarea,[145] and Epiphanius knew of such a group and called them "Ebionites";[146] but there is nothing whatsoever to connect them with *Galilee*. Unless Epiphanius is to be convicted either of self-contradiction or of denying the name of Christian to the Ebionites (whom he, in fact, considers specifically as a Christian heresy), then his statement that there were no Christians in Galilee in his time should be considered to include them also.[147] With this background, excavations at Capernaum and Nazareth fail to prove the presence of Jewish Christians in those places: Corbo's dig at Capernaum showed that the eventual fifth century church was built on a first century private house (the "House of St. Peter"),[148] but quite failed to show that the house was used for sacred purposes before the date of the fourth century enlargements[149] since pilgrim graffiti could belong to any time before the fifth century building of the church—as likely one year as three centuries.[150] The same is true of structures under the fourth century church at Nazareth.[151]

At any rate the minim were vehemently opposed[152] and considered by the rabbis at times as if they had sunk to Samaritan status,[153] so that, whatever their precise theology and however many of them there were, it is clear that the rabbis were forced to consider them a real but (compared to the amme haareẓ) minor threat. The meshumadim (rebellious ones), on the other hand, were considered worthy to be classed as Jews, in contrast to the minim[154] (though they, too, were excluded from celebration of the Passover according to the Mekhilta[155]). These were presumably ordinary Jews whose laxness had gone too far, not for theological reasons but for lack of interest—Jews such as Tiberius Julius Alexander.[156] Not surprisingly, the rabbis attacked them much less than they did the minim since there was less point in doing so and they posed only a passive threat. But, as far as the rabbis were concerned, neither group was as worrisome as the amme haareẓ who, far from enthusiastically opposing rabbinic Judaism, apathetically refused to espouse the customs and ideas demanded by that religion.

ACCEPTANCE

Rabbis, then, attempted to control Jews in Galilee only in religious rather than secular matters, and even in this sphere were largely unsuccessful in this period in imposing their decisions. Was there any area at all in which rabbinic ideas were generally accepted?

Some basic laws were fairly universally kept, the meshumadim and perhaps the minim excepted. There is an unascribed Mekhilta statement that Jews were martyred for refusing to forsake Shabbat, circumcision, learning of Torah, and *tebillah* (ritual immersion), and that as a result these practices had been preserved among them;[157] this agrees with Justin's description of Judaism as involving Shabbat, circumcision, the keeping of the set feasts, and washing after suffering sexual uncleanness.[158] Shabbat was universally kept—if a Jewish court denied its importance the denial would be reckoned ridiculous.[159] Apart from those who succumbed to Roman pressure, there is no evidence of failure to circumcise.[160] There were no rabbinic complaints of nonobservance of sexual purity laws and the number of *mikvehs* (ritual baths) identified on first and second century sites suggests that they were scrupulously kept[161]—perhaps because these laws were securely in the control of the women and could be used by them for psychological advantage over their husbands.[162] In the same way there seems to have been widespread use of tefillin[163] and kosher meat.[164] One can assume that in all these matters rabbinic advice or instruction would not be unsympathetically received by all.

Nonetheless, all these religious activities *could* be carried on satisfactorily without rabbinic interference. There were very few aspects of widely accepted religious practice where rabbinic authority was essential; the only clear case was regulation of the calendar. In this matter there is no evidence that rabbinic decisions were ever challenged.

It would be hard to overemphasize the importance of the calendar in the growth of rabbinic authority.[165] It was because of their dispute over the calendar that the Qumran sect considered the Temple authorities to be sinful heretics.[166] Most Jewish ritual must be performed at set times. Without a clear idea of the date all Jews with religious conscience would live in a state of permanent guilt. When the Temple Sanhedrin could no longer give them certainty they accepted the authority of the self-appointed rabbinic Sanhedrin with relief. This was the only religious function performed by the rabbis that was genuinely needed by the rest of the Jewish nation; the later dispute with the Babylonian academies shows its continued importance.[167] The rabbis' right to dissolve vows was apparently also not disputed (surprisingly if it was already exercised before the destruction of the Temple, when release from a vow would lose the Temple the income of a duly performed sacrifice), but this activity would, of course, affect only those rash enough to repent of serious vows.

This strictly limited jurisdiction was wielded by the rabbis on the basis of their prestige within the community. Their predecessors, the Pharisees, had been respected for their morality and learning and had "persuaded the people" as a result;[168] it was a respect shown openly by the title "Rabbi" and seats of honor on public occasions.[169] In the same way, a *talmid ḥakham*, like the wealthy, was recognized as such by the people of his town.[170] Hence the moral force of rabbinic rebukes: a man might ignore the ḥasid who told him to stop fouling the road, but the pious man was vindicated by a miracle.[171] The sages may have had to rely on similar divine intervention when they told Nehoniya to stop digging cisterns on the public highway[172]—the Tosefta does not say whether he obeyed them or not.

Rabbis came to be seen as almost superhuman holy men.[173] Hillel, Yohanan b. Zakkai, and Akiba are all said to have lived for 120 years.[174] The performance of miracles involving transmutations of the contents of stored casks like that of water into wine at Cana are recorded of R. Judah and R. Yosi.[175] Prestige depended above all on skill in expounding the Law. Asceticism, so important a part of the power of John the Baptist, Jesus, and the Essenes[176] and clearly a common feature of much intense first century Judaism,[177] was not practiced by the rabbis, and Origen denies that 'raving prophets' were any more to be seen.[178] On the other hand, all tannaitic rabbis lived in an artificial holy world of purity taboos by which their view of the world was colored,[179] and some rabbis increased their reputation by skill in esoteric mysticism, based loosely on biblical texts and revealed only to a select few.[180] Both *hekhalot* and *merkabah* mysticism were practiced by the end of the third century,[181] and if it is right to suggest that Palestinian apocalyptic texts were connected with later merkabah speculation,[182] then such practices go back at least to the first century, along with speculation on the form of the Deity (*shiur komah*)[183] and the mystical meaning of the Song of Songs.[184]

Such religious reasons for rabbinic prestige must be sought because rabbis' social status was likely to have told against them. Tannaitic rabbis do not seem to have been particularly wealthy themselves[185] and did not usually associate with the wealthy;[186] they were self-employed craftsmen[187] unable to live without such employment since their educational role did not bring any reward in financial terms.[188] They tended to associate with those of their own class rather than the established Galilean aristocracy, except, perhaps, for their immediate students.[189]

The moral superiority of being holy men was reinforced both by the rabbis' claim to absolute authority and the pomp with which they enacted important decisions. The rabbinical court in Yabneh held formal sessions in imitation of the old Sanhedrin.[190] The reverence accorded to the Nasi and the Ab Beth Din—the mass of sages sitting in judgment in the Academy and the crowd of students listening—was calculated to inspire confidence in their decisions.[191] Not many laws were explicitly ascribed to a decision of a rabbinic beth din rather than to that of an individual rabbi, but those that were became important: sikarikon regulations,[192] the decision that Caesarea might be treated as part of Eretz Israel for purity purposes,[193] and, above all, regulations about the calendar.[194] Despite all this, however, there is no evidence that these decisions were any more widely obeyed than the decisions taken more informally. Is it likely, for example, that no Cohen entered Caesarea until R. Judah I's beth din allowed him to do so?

It is worth asking whether rabbinic control grew at all firmer during the second century. The answer will be that it did not, and that at first sight the rabbis seem to have lost even their slight religious control almost entirely after the Bar Kokhba war. Out of over sixty cases of tannaitic rabbis exercising jurisdiction, only six can be shown to have occurred after the rebellion;[195] and of these six, three concern cases in Sidon or Damascus, which leaves only two purity judgments and one decision about a first-born animal ascribed to the tannaim in Galilee after the war.[196]

This evidence would suggest that rabbinic jurisdiction, after a mild flourish in religious matters between revolts, died away after Bar Kokhba, and was only resuscitated at a much later date in the early third century. Many of the sages had been killed in the war in Judaea,[197] and the Roman prohibition on *semikha* (ordination) at that time reflected the break up of the schools and a delay in their reestablishment farther north in Galilee.[198] It is only in the late third century that there is evidence of increased rabbinic authority. The rabbis sent out by R. Judah Nesiah had much greater authority than any of those considered here. They were sent out to teach the Law and reprimand negligent local community leaders,[199] and in one case even to take over "sermonizing, judging, being ḥazan, acting as scribe, teaching Talmud, and doing all the needs" of a village.[200] In this case the villagers treated the rabbi as omnipotent and set him up on a tribunal, and his head was turned by the prospect of power.

If the rabbis had lost even the minimal power portrayed in the tannaitic sources for over a hundred years and only then regained power to such a degree, it is surprising to find no echo of this in later writings, but so far as I can tell there is none (though *explicit* admission of this lack of authority would not be expected because the rabbis' claim to have been the natural leaders of the nation since Yohanan was consistently presented). Furthermore, it must be admitted that tannaitic concentration on the exploits of earlier rabbis might be explained as a desire to lend prestige to a particular legal stance since, although rabbinic decisions could not *always* create precedents since they conflicted too often, the judgments of a previous generation did have a special prestige. An argument based on a Yabnean or Lyddan opinion might be considered more weighty than one based on that of a contemporary, though actual pseudo-epigraphy within the tannaitic texts seems to be rare and easily spotted.[201]

Nonetheless, I would prefer the simpler explanation of the evidence, that rabbinic influence, which was never great in secular matters until the late third century, also suffered a decline in religious matters until the end of the tannaitic period at the beginning of that century, only picking up with a change in the religious ideas that the rabbis tried to encourage.[202] Furthermore, the causes should not be hard to find: dislocation of the Judaean schools by the war, the lack of a base in Galilee (hence the movement of the schools between Usha, Beth Shearim, Shefar'am, Sepphoris, andTiberias[203] penetrating progressively farther into Galilee and away from the Mediterranean coast), the low status of rabbis in Galilean society as immigrants and manual laborers,[204] and, above all, the lack of sympathy among Galilean Jews for rabbinic extremist piety.[205]

The Patriarchate

With so limited a role for the rabbis in secular affairs, it would seem likely that the power of the leading rabbi, the *nasi* or patriarch, has also been exaggerated. The origin of the office of nasi was dated by Büchler, Halevy, and others[206] to the first known of the *zugot*, who are in their turn ascribed to about 150 B.C.[207] Graetz thought the office was begun even earlier,[208] and Mantel has recently expressed a careful preference for this view.[209] The evidence for placing the office in this early period is all found in rabbinic texts and the dispute can be decided only by juggling with a number of statements of equal authority. However, when one comes to consider the *political* power of the nasi at any time up to the destruction of the Temple, it becomes clear that, as with the other rabbis, the evidence of Josephus and the Gospels overrides that of the rabbinic texts and that neither rabbis nor Pharisees nor nasi controlled the Jewish state other than by moral exhortation.[210] At what time after 70, then, did the nasi become the effective ruler of the Jewish nation?

Mantel says that it was soon after 70; the nasi took over as the natural leader of the nation with the destruction of all other Jewish institutions.[211] Juster and Avi-Yonah say the mid second century; Antoninus Pius put the nasi in power because he wanted a puppet government to control the Jews after the Bar Kokhba war.[212] Juster quoted in support of this theory the example of other client kings in the Roman Empire, though this one would have no army, no mint for coinage, and no fixed borders to his territory and would be coming to power in a period when the administrative use of client kings was becoming increasingly rare elsewhere.[213] Safrai asserts that "unrecognized" rule began under Antoninus Pius with R. Shimon b. Gamaliel, but that it was at the end of the century, with R. Judah ha Nasi, that Roman official recognition was given to patriarchal control.[214] It becomes apparent that all these are no more than guesses and that what is called for is a new look at the evidence, much of it lying in patristic sources and the Theodosian Code, but, above all, in rabbinic references to the functions of the nasi.

Examination of the tannaitic evidence reveals a nasi to have been not much different from the other rabbis already described. The word "nasi" is found only rarely in tannaitic texts[215] and the title "ethnarch" or "patriarch" not at all before the third century.[216] Apart from the very schematic and suspect list of the pairs of sages claimed in m Abot to have controlled the Sanhedrin before 70,[217] the term is not used as a title applied to any particular rabbi until the references to R. Judah ha Nasi, the compiler of the Mishnah.[218] Later rabbis were to assign the title to a number of sages of the tannaitic period, and in particular to those of the family of Hillel, in a characteristic attempt to portray conditions of the second century as similar to those of the fourth,[219] but their efforts are misleading. The term was used by the early second century rabbis mainly in a general sense to refer to any man who is "lifted up" above his fellows—when Hillel explained the law of Passover particularly well, he was appointed "nasi" by his pupils (and continued to teach them),[220] and at the funeral of R. Gamaliel the burning of costly garments was permitted because such extravagance was allowed at the funerals of *nesiim* as of kings.[221] At other times the word still seems to carry connotations from its use in Ezekiel to refer to a mythical Prince of Israel associated with the High Priest.[222] According to one Tosefta text it refers simply to the president of the Sanhedrin—be it the powerful body of pre-70 Jerusalem or the pale rabbinic imitation in Yabneh.[223]

At no time before R. Judah is the title unequivocally assigned by the rabbis to a contemporary rabbinic ruler of Israel—in striking contrast to the term when used by the leader of the rebellion of 132–135, Bar Kosiba.[224] There can be no doubt that Bar Kosiba was a genuine secular ruler and his use of the term "nasi" renders it all the less likely that a rabbi claiming the title at the same time also held secular power. It must either be assumed, against the evidence, that Bar Kosiba was in league with rabbis and the rabbinic patriarch stood down temporarily in his favor,[225] or that the rabbinic nasi claimed power but had no following outside his own limited circles,[226] or, as here suggested, that no rabbi was yet making such claims.[227]

The hypothesis, then, is that a nasi in this period was no more than any important rabbi. Confirmation may be sought by examining in some detail the actual activities of the rabbis who were reputed in later talmudic sources to have been nesiim, and, above all, the activities of the second century members of Hillel's family, Rabban Gamaliel (fl. c. 80–c. 117) and his son, R. Shimon b. Gamaliel (fl. c. 140–170).[228]

Rabban Gamaliel is attested to have been in close control of the calendar,[229] an activity in which, according to the Mishnah, the authority of a nasi is vital.[230] He proclaimed national fast days[231]—again it is attested that a nasi is needed to participate in fasts to make them effective.[232] He ruled his beth ha Midrash, controlling the appointment of teachers[233] and presiding even at lessons at which a junior teacher carried out the instruction.[234] He was much honored by his fellow scholars, causing consternation when he insisted on serving them at a meal.[235] He had some contact with foreigners, conversing with the ἡγεμών Agnitos[236] and two soldiers apparently sent to investigate the activities of his academy,[237] and discussing the ethics of his position when in the bath of Aphrodite in Akko with Proclus the philosopher.[238] He traveled both to Syria[239] and to Rome[240] and made many journeys, as far as is known on private business, within Palestine.[241] Otherwise, both he and his son were occupied in dealing with the same sorts of cases as those that involved other tannaitic rabbis—details over the observance of the Sabbath,[242] purity laws,[243] the cancellation of vows,[244] the interpretation of legal documents,[245] tithes,[246] and the Sabbatical year.[247]

Of neither man is any mention made of wider powers. No tannaitic source shows either of them presiding over the Sanhedrin,[248] controlling administration either in Palestine or the Diaspora,[249] sending out apostles to far off communities,[250] collecting funds,[251] appointing judges,[252] ordaining rabbis,[253] or enjoying political recognition from Rome.[254] In so far as they enjoyed prestige it was from their wealth, considerable compared to that of other rabbis,[255] from their learning in rabbinic law, and from their control of the calendar.[256] Their influence over nonrabbinic sections of the populace will have been as negligible as that of other rabbis, except in so far as their comparative wealth enabled them (unlike their poorer fellows[257]) to mingle with the upper class of Galilee[258] and to associate with the aristocrats of nearby gentile cities and the Roman administration,[259] and thereby to pick up something of their leisured Greek ways.[260]

It is only with R. Judah ha Nasi (fl. c. 170–c. 220) that a figure more like a ruler emerges. He is the first to whom the title "nasi" is consistently applied in tannaitic sources.[261] Like his father and grandfather, his primary interest lay in religious matters—his learning in rabbinic law was recognized by the canonic authority accorded to his compilation, the Mishnah, and it is evident from that work that questions of purity and tithing were among his greatest preoccupations.[262] To that religious authority, the later talmudic tradition is unanimous in adding an administrative control much stronger than that ascribed to Judah's predecessors.[263] It is likely that they were, at least partially, right.

In R. Judah's case the silence of the tannaitic sources about his secular power is no longer an argument against his having wielded such power since much of the tannaitic material was compiled either by Judah himself or before his time.[264] On the contrary, it is likely that the few general remarks about the privileges of the nasi in tannaitic texts in fact refer to him. He is portrayed as very much in control of the Sanhedrin,[265] as the Tosefta claims a nasi should be,[266] and is capable of creating important new law by personal decree in conjunction with his court.[267] It is with him that the hereditary principle in the appointment of the nasi seems to become fully established—his sons may be poor scholars, but they lead by virtue of their descent alone.[268]

The same factors aided R. Judah in his rise to prominence as had helped his predecessors in their lesser success. His wealth was proverbial.[269] He controlled the calendar despite attacks from Babylonian rabbis.[270] He aided his prestige by emphasis on the nobility of his birth, claiming to be descended on the maternal side from King David.[271] He behaved like a Roman aristocrat in his insistence on *salutatio* from his *clientes*.[272] He came into close contact with a Roman emperor, Antoninus.[273]

Such a background would still seem by itself unlikely to convert a religious to a secular leader. Despite his aristocratic trappings, R. Judah was a religious intellectual and his followers were primarily religious zealots.[274] Two factors extended his influence. First, the Roman Empire of the early third century was used to the rise to power of intellectuals in the Second Sophistic movement through abstruse expertise.[275] Secondly, R. Judah's prominence coincides with a general increase in acceptance of rabbinic leadership within Galilee encouraged by changes in the demands that rabbinic Judaism made. In the early third century, rabbis put aside their interest in purity as a way of reaching sanctity.[276] Insistence on the payment of tithes lessened[277] and the Sabbatical year ceased to be considered of such importance.[278] These changes were calculated to increase rabbinic popularity, and R. Judah led in their introduction.[279]

How far this new acceptance went can be ascertained from the testimony of Origen in the mid third century.[280] Origen's evidence needs to be considered in its context in the three passages where it is to be found. His statement that the patriarch Iullus gave him advice on the order of the psalms[281] reveals little of the patriarch's secular power since, even if this man is the nasi,[282] the only characteristic indicated would be his knowledge of religious matters. On the other hand, in the two other passages Origen makes striking allusion to a patriarch apparently of considerable secular influence.[283]

In the *De Principiis*, a theological work, Origen writes that "some say that a King from Judah still exists and is the '$\dot{\epsilon}\vartheta\nu\acute{\alpha}\rho\chi\eta\varsigma$.' "[284] This ethnarch is likely to be the nasi since the term is almost certainly the Greek form of the Latin word *patriarcha*,[285] but the passage is not therefore decisive in establishing the nasi's power in the third century. The remark is a commentary on the passage in Genesis that states that "the sceptre shall not cease from Judah"[286] and is part of the midrashic polemic so common in the Jewish and Christian academies of contemporary Caesarea.[287] All that it indicates is that Jewish theologians (i.e., rabbis) *claimed* that the nasi had the right to rule all Israel, which is clear enough anyway from the amoraic texts themselves.

More important is a passage in Origen's letter to Africanus about the historicity of the story of Susanna.[288] Africanus had claimed that the death sentence passed by the Babylonian Jews on Susanna was totally implausible since the Jewish nation was in captivity at the time. Origen sets out to refute this claim.

> But you say, "How could they who were in captivity pass sentence of death?" . . . The answer is, that it is no uncommon thing,

when great nations become subject, that the king should allow the captives to use their own laws and courts of justice. Now, for instance, that the Romans rule and the Jews pay the two drachmas to them, we, who have had experience of it, know how much power the ἐθνάρχης has among them (παρ᾽ αὐτοῖς) and that he differs in little from a king of the nation. Trials (κριτήρια) are held according to the Law (Torah), and some are condemned to death. And though there is not full permission for this, still it is not done without the knowledge of the ruler, and we found out about this to our certainty when we spent much time in the country of that people.

Origen may of course be exaggerating, for it is in the interests of his argument to do so. The need to remind Africanus, a Palestinian Jew by birth and perhaps even now living in Emmaus,[289] about the patriarch would indicate that his influence was certainly geographically limited. The doubt expressed about the legality of patriarchal trials shows that the nasi was no client king under the aegis of Rome. On the other hand, the argument would be ruined if the patriarch was not genuinely a figure who *could* appear as powerful as a king and who held trials in which at least once the death sentence had been passed. It would not seem to follow necessarily from Origen's words that patriarchal power had extended far beyond the rabbinical circles in which even third century patriarchs primarily moved. Presumably those who submitted to a death sentence rather than appealing to Rome were religiously committed to rabbinism. But Origen's remarks do suggest that either patriarchal power had begun to grow or rabbinical circles had themselves begun to widen.

The hypothesis is confirmed by stories recorded in the Talmudic sources about the powers of the nesiim of the late third century.[290] R. Judah Nesiah, for instance, appointed judges for communities in Palestine,[291] sent rabbis out to found new schools,[292] wore royal clothing,[293] and used a police force of armed slaves.[294] With the attention of the Roman administration directed elsewhere in the third century political crisis, the patriarch began to establish political control over many of the Jews in Galilee in much the same way and for the same local cultural reasons as other leaders of eastern states at the same time.[295]

However, only in the late fourth century did Rome take any cognizance of this new local ruler in Galilee. It is then that, for the first time, a patriarch is revealed in the Latin and Greek sources with wide powers over Jews in the Diaspora as well as Palestine[296] and with Roman support for his rule.

Patriarchal control outside Palestine is indicated by the institution of the apostolate, the sending of messengers all over the Mediterranean to collect money for the patriarch's use.[297] The custom is clearly attested for the 390s,[298] but not in the full sense before. Justin in the second century[299] and Eusebius in the early fourth[300] mention messengers being despatched from Palestine, but assume them to bring reports on doctrine rather than demands for money. Such apostles are the figment of Christian polemic.[301] Epiphanius, writing in the 370s,[302] asserts that the convert Joseph went to Cilicia in the time of Constantine not only to announce the death of one nasi, but also to collect the tithes (ἐπιδεκατά), presumably for the dead man's successor.[303] Reliance on so wayward a witness is unwise[304] and he is very liable to be retrojecting present conditions onto a colorful story of past events, but at any rate the passage suggests unofficial collection of dues by the 370s. The more formally instituted apostolate presumed in the letter of the Emperor Julian to the patriarch in the 360s would be closer to the position in the 390s, but the text is widely considered spurious on stylistic grounds.[305] Talmudic texts, significantly, give no overt clue, for they are completely silent about any such institution.[306] The evidence, and lack of it, can be explained. It seems likely that in the fourth century the rabbis under patriarchal leadership felt sufficiently confident of their authority in Palestine to request funds from Diaspora Jews. Those Jews may or may not have paid up,[307] but in the 390s the request for charity received Roman state support and became in effect an official tax.[308]

It is not by chance that the apostolate first appears fully fledged in the 390s. It is precisely then that Roman sources of many different kinds reveal knowledge of a Jewish patriarch of considerable power. Now, if at any time, is found the client ruler recognized by the Roman state.[309] This patriarch was of sufficient prominence for the contemporary author of the *Historia Augusta* to write jokes about him.[310] The Theodosian code speaks of him as a man of high rank[311] with special privileges from Rome[312] and the right both to appoint administrators over Jewish communities[313] and to put into practice Jewish law.[314] Wealthy and rapacious,[315] he can tangle with a Roman governor and still win, with imperial support.[316] He is in correspondence with the great sophist Libanius, exchanging civil, cultured letters of patronage in the manner of Late Roman aristocrats.[317] Eight such letters survive, all written after 388—further evidence of his recent rise to prominence since Libanius was then aged 74 and yet is not recorded as writing to the patriarch in any of his voluminous earlier correspondence.[318]

Reasons for this innovation in the 390s can be found. It might be speculated that Theodosius would show interest in supporting a strong Jewish religious leader given the need for Jews, still officially protected as a *religio licita*, to defend themselves against the Christian attacks that his own antipagan legislation encouraged.[319] At any rate, when the patriarch's presumption in trying to usurp too much power brought his downfall between 415 and 429,[320] there was no reason for Jews in Galilee to suffer.[321] All that it meant was that Rome's brief experiment was over.

8 Local Administration in Galilee

Village Administration

If Jewish villages in Galilee had some sort of hierarchy to provide leadership and administrators in local affairs, from the foregoing chapter it will be clear that such leaders were not rabbis.[1] There is sufficient evidence to suggest both that there were such leaders, and who they were and what their function, though the nature of the sources will impose caution in coming to conclusions.

The rabbinic texts have many references to the men who lead the people. Some such comments, however, will refer not to Galilee but to mixed Jewish-gentile communities where the Jewish leaders could only have limited jurisdiction under gentile authority.[2] Such communities in mixed cities are known both in Palestine before A.D. 70[3] and outside Palestine throughout Roman rule.[4] Roman laws and Josephus combine with inscriptions to give a fairly clear picture of the hierarchy in these minority Jewish communities. Leading men had authority either by virtue of age[5] or wealth[6] and bore titles borrowed from their Greek environment—ἄρχων,[7] βουλευτής,[8] φροντιστής,[9] πρεσβύτηρ,[10] names that survive in synagogue inscriptions and attest the centrality of synagogue buildings as a practical focus for a community without any other physical delineation. The inscriptions proudly proclaim the extent of the leaders' expenditure on behalf of the community in erecting such buildings.[11] Leadership of the synagogue with the title of ἀρχισυνάγωγος seems to be the top post in the Diaspora communities[12] and liturgical functions within the synagogue are highly prized;[13] so much so that Roman legal texts refer to synagogue functionaries as "ἱερεῖς" (priests) in the early fourth century and offer immunity from public service on behalf of the Roman state.[14] The exact details of the administrative structure of Jewish communities in mixed cities would require a separate study. What is important for present purposes is an awareness of the possibility both that rabbinic texts may at times refer to mixed cities (especially since some halakha was formulated before A.D. 132 in the mixed cities of Lod and Yavneh),[15] and that the Jewish leaders in such places probably controlled only liturgical and perhaps charitable matters.[16]

Galilean villages had a great deal more administration to do. If Josephus' description of Galilee is still pertinent, all Upper Galilee lay outside the χώρα of any πόλις,[17] which would encourage, as in Bashan, Hauran, and Trachonitis, the growth of efficient government on the village level,[18] either completely independent or in some sort of coalition under a μητροκωμία.[19] Even if the city χῶραι had expanded,[20] comparison with other villages in the rest of Syria would suggest that the cities interfered very little in village life. The cities usually sent tax men (*mokhsin*) to gather in their revenues,[21] but otherwise Syrian villages ran their own affairs, with village councils and assemblies, public buildings, and local magistrates.[22] A few villages may have been wholly owned by large landowners,[23] but again these men are not recorded as interfering and were presumably content with rent. Even if much of Palestine had been converted into imperial land after 70 (which I believe unlikely),[24] there is evidence from elsewhere in the empire of fully developed village administration under the control of an imperial official.[25] It should not, then, be surprising that the tannaitic sources *assume* a well-regulated administration for the Jewish villages of Galilee.

The Tosefta asserts that the people of an עיר were competent to control their synagogue, their market prices, and the wages of their workers.[26] They could stipulate a fine for anyone seen frequenting a particular person or the Roman authorities. They might also fine anyone who let his cow graze among sown crops.[27] Passages assert their responsibility for checking roads after the rainy season,[28] digging public cisterns,[29] marking the boundaries of cemeteries, and so on.[30] Archaeological evidence helps confirm the importance of at least one of these functions, that of controlling the cemeteries. Though only a few of the less magnificent catacombs at Beth Shearim are second century[31] and the idiosyncracies of the necropolis there are partly due to Palmyrene influence,[32] it is still significant that an authority for supervising the cemetery is assumed by inscriptions[33]—though the ability of that authority to impose its control is not certain, for there are no inscriptions threatening fines for disturbers of the dead, whereas these are found in many other areas of the empire.[34]

Tombs were privately owned[35] and often very rich,[36] but public interest was involved in the need to regulate ceremonies at the cemetery[37]
and in the demarcation of burial areas to prevent accidental pollution
to passers-by.[38] The lavishness of some of the memorials on graves
indicates their importance in the eyes of the inhabitants[39] in Galilee
no less than surrounding gentile areas.[40]

Public decisions on matters of this kind seem to have been taken
by the community as a whole, meeting in assembly. Assemblies were
held on Mondays and Thursdays when the court also sat.[41] There is
no certain indication that these assemblies discussed political matters
rather than filling a purely religious function, but Josephus' story of
the spontaneous meeting in the synagogue of Tiberias on Shabbat suggests that religion and politics were not felt to be mutually exclusive[42]
and that the twice-weekly meetings may well have discussed local
affairs as well as listening to the Law.[43] Village building projects such
as those for a synagogue will have required decisions about sources of
income, especially if this was derived partly from common land, as is
likely by analogy,[44] and there is evidence that financial matters were
not considered inappropriate at such times.[45]

The magistrates of the village were the *parnasim* (from the root
פרנם meaning "assign") and the *gabbaim* (from גבי , meaning "collect")
and they operated either singly or, just possibly, in groups of seven.[46]
The chief function of both officials was to administer public charity,
but this should not distract attention from hints of a wider role for
the parnasim. Close inspection of inscriptions has shown that the chief
role of *all* village officials in Syria was to supervise village finances and
building projects.[47] The Jewish magistrates were no exception.

The parnasim both collected and distributed money[48] given to
them by the villagers for the care of local and vagrant beggars.[49] In a
town with a gentile minority they are urged to include the gentiles
in both the collection and the distribution of charity to preserve the
peace.[50] A ruling is given that a *parnas* distributing in a village not his
own must give to the local poor;[51] this does not imply that parnasim
were professionals (i.e., rabbis), for the definition of citizenship of a
town is residence of one year[52] and this rule would thus apply to any
newcomer appointed as parnas before his year is up. This is not to
deny that rabbis could, as trustworthy men, be asked to act as parnasim of their or another village as they certainly were in the third
century.[53] Apart from charity work the parnasim, according to a late

second century rabbi, had the final word in building projects in the village—a new synagogue or a marketplace.[54] Add to this the tradition that anyone appointed as parnas of the public "weighed like a mighty one among the mighty"[55] and it is clear that fairly powerful local individuals are being discussed. The impression is confirmed by the frequent assumption that it was normal, but not inevitable, for the post to have been kept in particular families, the leading and probably the richest families of the community.[56]

The gabbaim dealt with charity cases only and the normal translation "treasurer" is correct. They too both collected and distributed money,[57] but a good deal more detail is given of the way they operated. They carried a bag of money (כיס) in public places.[58] When distributing to the local (and also presumably the vagrant) poor they would announce this in public.[59] Collecting funds might involve entering citizens' houses in their absence, presumably for nonpayment,[60] and it is interestingly asserted that when a gentile (city official inspecting? Roman soldier?) accompanied them on such forays they would be more embarrassed to tell lies about their activities inside the house.[61] There is clearly a danger of confusing these treasurers with those recorded under quite different names as collectors of funds for the Temple while it still stood[62] and of overemphasizing the institutional character of charity in these villages (voluntary charity, commended as a virtue, continued to exist[63]). But enough remains to confirm the gabbaim as important local officials.

These magistrates did not have absolute powers but were in some way related to the members of the local village court, the beth din. The precise nature of that relationship is nowhere made explicit, although the normal practice elsewhere in the Roman Empire would make it likely that they acted as the leading members and the executive of the beth din. It seems certain that most, if not all, villages had such courts[64] and that, though their primary function was legal,[65] they also had an administrative role. Like the βουλαί [66] in other villages they controlled the daily administration. Care of roads, cisterns, graveyards,[67] even in theory *Kilaim*[68] might be entrusted to them and their (servile?) agents. They ordered legal abortions for raped girls[69] and seem to have given licences to doctors to practice.[70] Their judicial competence in theory covered the whole criminal and civil legislation of Mishnah-Tosefta. In particular they had care of orphans and widows and were responsible for appointing guardians for them when the dead men had failed to plan for such a contingency.[71] According to the Babata documents, this is the same function as the βουλή of Petra fulfilled;[72] the only distinction would have been the greater ability of the Petrean body to enforce its decisions.[73] The beth din similarly oversaw the marriage laws[74] and other contracts, all of which could take place "before the Beth Din" for greater security.[75] The many criminal offenses were punished by whipping.[76] The courts had their officers, some of them almost certainly slaves. There are many references to the "messengers of the beth din" carrying out their instructions.[77] When an עיר (i.e., village) was sold, the *santer* (public guard) was sold with it;[78] the אנקלמוס (οἰκονόμος) was not considered so integral a part of the town.[79] Both officials are frequently assumed in later texts, particularly the Jerusalem Talmud.[80] In some cases the man appointed by the court to carry out executions is called *hazan*,[81] but what connection this man had with the identically named official who apportioned tasks in the synagogues[82] or the ἄζζαν on an Apamean inscription is not clear.[83]

The relation of synagogue administration to assembly, beth din, and the work of the magistrates cannot be traced with certainty.[84] Outside Palestine, synagogue officials appear to have been the leaders of the community.[85] In so far as the synagogue was jointly owned by the inhabitants,[86] one would expect the same to be true in Galilee. The Gospels speak about the ἀρχισυνάγωγος of Galilean villages and Capernaum in particular as important men who control activities in the synagogue,[87] but the Gospels are themselves largely the product of Diaspora Judaism.[88] The rabbinic references to a "head of the synagogue" (ראש בית הכנסת) must surely have a similar reference: two passages reveal him as responsible for controlling precedence in the public readings to be made in the synagogue[89] and one passage concerns a particular head of the synagogue in Akhzib on the Mediterranean coast who unwittingly infringed the rule over the tithes owed on the produce of his vineyard in Syria.[90] Of course, Akhzib lies outside the purely Jewish area of Galilee, but the evident need for some sort of hierarchy in the synagogue makes the applicability of the Tosefta texts to Galilee very plausible. One inscription alone backs it up: from Sepphoris, a stone bearing the title ἀρχισυνάγωγος.[91] Another Galilean inscription, however, has the title of the other synagogue official who appears in the rabbinic texts, that of חזן;[92] though again the only evidence of his precise synagogue function comes from outside

Palestine—he is said to have conducted the public liturgy in the huge synagogue of Alexandria by waving a scarf so the congregation would know when to say "Amen."[93] All in all, it would seem that community control over the synagogue was exercised by officials selected for that purpose, but that there is no reason to assume that they had any considerable secular power.

In the same way, community control over market prices and weights and measures is assumed by a number of texts for essential foodstuffs such as grain,[94] and the officials responsible for such control are named, in imitation of Greek market officials, as ἀγορανόμοι.[95] It is possible that such references, in which Jewish *agoranomoi* are clearly distinguished from gentile,[96] may refer to Jewish market officials in mixed cities,[97] but such officials are almost certainly attested in village markets in third century Baetocaece[98] and there is every reason to expect that markets such as those of the Galilean villages needed such supervision.[99] However, the role of the agoranomos was clearly very limited, and there is again no reason to posit a wider administrative role—that Agrippa in first century Tiberias had the same title and perhaps function is curious, but it was hardly the source of his influence, which was due entirely to his royal birth and transcended local boundaries.[100]

This, then, is the administrative structure assumed in the tannaitic writings. Unfortunately, not a single case is described in which the Jewish magistrates are shown acting in their role or a nonrabbinic beth din shown in session.[101] Why, after the skepticism shown toward the claims examined above, that the rabbis themselves controlled the whole nation, should there be any reason to believe them in this instance? There *are* reasons, not decisive but persuasive.

First, the silence of rabbinic sources about actual cases involving nonrabbinic magistrates and courts is far less damaging than their silence about their own jurisdiction. The decision of a local beth din did not, for the rabbis, have the authority as a precedent that a rabbi's decision had; there was no point in quoting such cases, so they did not.

Second, there is a striking similarity between the village administration unearthed by Harper in the Hauran and that described in the rabbinic texts.[102] Semi-autonomous villages[103] are found preserving native Semitic tribal structures[104] inside a democratic framework,[105] building places for public village worship[106] and sometimes for public entertainment,[107] and appointing magistrates to oversee the spending of the money.[108] The intervening level of administration by a council (beth din) is less often paralleled—the only examples are the γερουσία from Castellus in Lydia, which functioned alongside an ἐκκλησία,[109] and possibly the κοινόν in Agraine.[110] But as for the magistrates, not only the functions, but also the names, crop up in other Syrian villages. Harper records a similar vagueness and overlapping of roles to that evident in Galilee.[111] Similarity of roles, though not etymology, suggests that the parnas may be considered the same *sort* of magistrate as the προνοηταί found in later Syrian village inscriptions;[112] the fourth century synagogue inscription from Tiberias stating that "Iullus προνούμενος carried out everything" may reflect this similarity too.[113] But perhaps the clearest link is provided by a Tosefta passage that introduces the *apamalatos* as an official similar to the gabbai.[114] Transliteration of the term into Greek reveals the ἐπιμελητής of numerous Syrian villages[115] who is found overseeing the building of temples and looking after their accounts.[116] The parallels may prompt further comparisons. Many of the Syrian villages were grouped around a main μητροκωμία,[117] and combined for religious purposes on occasion.[118] In Lower Galilee the two Galilean *poleis* may have taken the place of the *mētrokōmia*, but in Upper Galilee four of the villages seem to have been considered more important than the rest[119] and inscriptions from the fourth to sixth century synagogue in Hammat Gader reveal that, in popular sites such as this, similar cooperation was found between Jewish villages in the erection of a synagogue, perhaps in default of a wealthy local community.[120]

Third, parnasim appear in documents from the Judaean desert. Although they were in friendly contact with the Bar Kokhba military administration, there is no evidence that they were military officials. The two parnasim of the village of Beit Masiko give a certificate to a local man attesting that his cow legally belongs to him to prevent its confiscation by Bar Kokhba's chief of camp.[121] At Ein Gedi, a parnas is found leasing out land.[122] He may have been acting on behalf of Bar Kokhba, like the untitled Hillel b. Garis recorded elsewhere as farming out land to a large number of tenants that had probably previously been under imperial control.[123] On the other hand it is possible that he was arranging for the receipt of revenue for his village from its public land. This required detailed control by the village's magistrates, as a stone from Castellus in Lydia testifies.[124] Harper pointed out that the income from rents was, with private benefactions, probably the main source of village income for the upkeep of buildings and so on.[125] Since some village buildings, like the Galilean synagogues, were extremely impressive, the income must have been considerable, though I know of no evidence from Galilee itself of villages owning land.

Fourth, parnasim were certainly powerful figures in the later third century when the Jerusalem Talmud records an attempt to ensure that only rabbis should be appointed to the post.[126]

What was the relation of the rabbis in their academies to these administrators of the community? Parnasim were not necessarily rabbis since the Jerusalem Talmud recalls a third century struggle for them to become so, and a passage in Sifre says that the place of all parnasim is taken by their sons,[127] which suggests that they were important local men, not imported academics. As for the treasurers, the gabbaim, it is assumed that they were not rabbis. No treasurer was trusted to be pure—they are Jews but not ḥaverim.[128] On the other hand, gabbaim knew enough about purity laws to avoid touching anything when entering the house of an ḥaver.[129] Another passage clarifies the position: in the past any ḥaver accepting a post as treasurer was excluded from his ḥavura (accepting was evidently voluntary), while a new ruling permitted a ḥaver to become a treasurer but temporarily suspended him from his ḥavura.[130] Something about being a treasurer, perhaps consorting with all those impure poor, would have rendered any man unclean.

Nor were the courts under rabbinic control, despite the mass of laws evolved by rabbis for their edification.[131] According to Mekhilta, R. Joshua said that the judges of a town should always be the rich who are free from the need to work;[132] after such a remark, R. Eleazar of Modiim's contention that they must "practice the words of the Torah" sounds hollow.[133] Another Mekhilta passage defines "men of worth" who are suitable to act as judges as עשירים ובעלי ממון, the wealthy.[134] Certain classes were excluded from such duties, such as the despised shepherds,[135] always suspected of immorality. Just as the courts of pre-70 Jerusalem were outside Pharisaic control,[136] so the rabbis could do nothing but curse when Beth Aba in Galilee entrusted civil law cases to single arbitrators instead of to the courts of three that the rabbis stipulated.[137] Such single judges may even have been more common than the rabbinic ideal since they are what many passages in the Gospels assume.[138] It is noteworthy that when R. Ishmael asserted that illegal behavior in Beth Aba was one cause of the village's destruction, he added another more plausible economic cause—that the villagers allowed goats to destroy nearby woodland. It suggests that the issue of the number of judges desirable in the courts was a live one in Ishmael's day, in the 120s.

And yet the legal exhortations of the rabbis were not entirely ignored.[139] Hillel's concept of the prozbul was certainly used—it is incorporated in a mid first century admission of debt found in the Judaean desert.[140] Other such documents embody rabbinic rulings for divorce,[141] marriage,[142] and sale procedures.[143] To a certain extent, what the rabbis claim as new inventions or rulings may simply be an acceptance by those rabbis of laws already in use among the rest of the people. According to a late (talmudic) source, for instance, this is precisely what R. Shimon b. Gamaliel did when allowing the form of a διάθεμα, common in Greek law, to be used by Jews.[144] The new form was allowed alongside the Semitic form of *matana* in gift giving.[145] However, this cannot explain Hillel's evident influence in the case of the prozbul. The relation of the rabbis to the courts is easily explicable in terms of the relation of *iurisprudentes* to a legal system.[146] Not unlike contemporary Roman lawyers such as Ulpian from nearby Tyre, the rabbis spent their time codifying the law as they saw it, inventing problems to solve according to the principles they evolved from these laws, adding a strong element of what they would like the laws to be, and making the results known to the nonacademic public. And like that of the Roman iurisprudentes, their advice was sometimes followed and sometimes, perhaps more often, not.

Occasionally a problem of legal complexity would crop up for which the rabbis' advice, based on their expertise, would be asked. A man worried that his divorce might not be valid came to ask R. Ishmael and R. Leiyi, who were sitting together in a house, whether particular evidence would be sufficient.[147] R. Gamaliel in Legio declared a divorce with two Samaritan witnesses legal.[148] An unfortunate man who betrothed five girls when jokingly giving them some figs (the gifts were construed as valid betrothal gifts) came to the sages for legal advice on how to escape from his mess.[149] A creditor who wanted to recover a debt from its guarantor came to R. Ishmael to check on his legal rights. It was a difficult case—R. Ishmael gave the wrong answer and changed his mind on the advice of R. Shimon b. Nanos.[150] R. Yosi in Sepphoris "pronounced kosher" (*heksher*) by mistake a document that was dated to a Shabbat or Yom Kippur, again presumably on being asked to lend the authority of his legal learning to one party in a dispute.[151]

There is only one reported case that suggests a more positive role in the administration of justice for tannaitic rabbis. It concerns R. Akiba and so is most likely to have occurred in the mixed city of Yabneh.[152] On this occasion a man had unloosed a woman's hair in the street and when she came to Akiba to complain he condemned the man to pay her 400 zuz. This punishment was by no means theoretical, for the man went to great lengths to try to escape it. He asked for time to pay and then tricked the woman into showing her shamelessness by having a jar of perfume broken in the street when she was passing. When she took off her headdress to make use of the perfume he went off to Akiba with his witnesses to insist that if she was prepared to bare her head for her own profit then she was so immodest that she did not deserve damages for what he had done. Akiba replied that her actions did not make his behavior any the less culpable and that the fine still stood. It is interesting that the man did not appeal to the gentile authorities; the story is best explained if the man was one of Akiba's pupils and the woman came to ask him to discipline his student. At any rate, the story is far too isolated to upset the general picture of the secular powerlessness of the rabbis, and it is quite legitimate to explain it in this way.

For the rest of the cases, they all concern legal advice given to clients. The incident with Akiba indicates the way in which the trust placed in rabbis enabled their influence to grow until they occupied a position of great power by the fourth century,[153] but all the other texts reveal that in the second and early third centuries the rabbis were only aspiring,[154] and that the rich men of the Galilean villages still remained as firmly as ever entrenched in control of their communities.[155]

City Administration

The *polis* of Tiberias would seem to have had an administrative system identical to that of other Greek cities, with ἄρχων, βουλή and ἐκκλησία,[156] and once Sepphoris no longer had the special distinction of being the center of Agrippa's dominions[157] one can assume, by analogy with other Syrian *poleis*, that the same was true there.[158]

The inhabitants of both cities were mostly Jews,[159] as were the ruling magistrates. In the second century there was no problem for Jews in becoming members of a city *boulē* or becoming a city *archōn* without giving up Jewish practices[160] and not only was Tiberias ruled entirely by Jews before 70[161] but Eusebius claims that in the early fourth century all of Sepphoris-Diocaesarea was also Jewish.[162] The only reasons for suggesting that Jewish rule had been supplanted by gentile after Hadrian[163] are the early third century rescript of Severus and Caracalla that Jews might at that time serve on municipal councils (wrongly taken to indicate a new policy rather than the reiteration of an old policy after a particular challenge),[164] the possible attempt, on Roman instigation, to build a temple in honor of Hadrian (an attempt never completed),[165] and the types on second century coins issued by both cities. The name "Diocaesarea" is used on Sepphoris coins in the second century only after Hadrian,[166] some Sepphoris coins may show a temple of the Capitoline Triad,[167] and there is a Tiberias coin type with an image of Victory stamped on it.[168] The edict and the temple inspired by Roman propaganda clearly have no force in the argument. The coins are no more convincing on closer examination: there is a contrast between earlier and later city issues,[169] but this indicates no change in status, for the later Capitoline temple and the image of Victory may well have been chosen simply as inoffensive images by a Jewish aristocracy fearful of offending the Roman authorities after the bloody Bar Kokhba war and therefore choosing the safe types favored by neighboring cities.[170] As proof of this, the earlier types such as the Tiberias Hygeia and the city goddess type minted under Trajan are no more Jewish in iconography.[171]

The administrative structure of both poleis assumed the existence of an upper class to staff it. Such an aristocracy is attested before 70 by Josephus[172] as the class that fills the places on the city's βουλή.[173] It includes the "ten most powerful men" (δεκάπρωτοι) who have effective control.[174] A fifth century inscription reveals a man of similar high local standing in Sepphoris.[175] For the period in between one can rely only on probability and rabbinic allusion.[176] A parable in Sifre rings true: if a man defied a βουλευτής in the marketplace, people would reckon him a fool, since the βουλευτής could hit him, tear his clothing, and throw him into prison.[177] The power of the βουλευτής, the passage continues, is exceeded only by that of the קטרון (centurion?) and the הפתם (governor)—the Roman military and civilian government.[178] As to precisely who these aristocrats were, the sources are rather vague. In the first century they were simply wealthy local landowners.[179] In the second century there is no reason to suppose a change—if Justus of Tiberias survived the first revolt unscathed, the same is likely to have been true of his fellow aristocrats with their equally uneasy reluctance to join the rebellion. But other questions, such as the number of families involved in administration, are unanswerable.

What can be ascertained is the relation of the city administrators to the society of Galilee in general; in particular, the extent to which the cities of Galilee, like those elsewhere in the empire, controlled and exploited the villages within their territory.[180]

How much territory ($\chi\omega\rho\alpha$) did Tiberias and Sepphoris control? Learned estimates have been made.[181] The premises are dubious: that milestones, both those found in fact and those apparently used by Eusebius in his *Onomasticon*, give the distance to the polis in whose territory the stone itself lies.[182] It clearly need not be so—the stones were set up to help long-distance travelers (who else would need them?) by giving the distance to the nearest big town, whatever the administrative position of the area in question. Rabbinic texts refer to the $\chi\tilde{\omega}\rho\alpha\iota$ of Hippos-Susita[183] and of Akko[184] but not to those of the Galilean cities. A favorite method of fixing territorial boundaries has been to chart those areas that are exempted by rabbis from the requirement of giving tithes on the grounds that they are no longer inside the borders of the land of Israel.[185] But why the rabbis should alter religious rulings in this way to fit in with administrative changes by the secular power is not clear.

There was, perhaps, no reason why the rabbis should have been particular about the administrative status of any particular village. It has been pointed out that attempts to assert that there were economic barriers between city territories are not obviously borne out by the ceramic evidence.[186] There was no apparent culture gap between the cities and the countryside.[187] Whatever the city, the villages within its territory retained considerable autonomy, as is described above.[188] Josephus in the first century (with the interests of a Romanizing politician close to the city aristocracies) and the lists of bishops in the Byzantine period (with the main interest of their authors being in Church administration) both concentrate on the city administration as if it was the most important level of government in the area, just as the city aristocrat Aelius Aristeides did in Asia Minor.[189] But it is a misleading picture they give, and it would be misleading to conclude from them that Lower Galilee was "urbanized" and Upper Galilee was rural and Semitic simply because the latter probably did not lie inside the χώρα of any polis.[190] The impact of a city on its territory was, according to the rabbis, negligible. Tax collection was the city's only important function. The provision of security, a market for goods, or a coinage to facilitate exchange had comparatively little effect on its villages.[191]

Tax collectors appear in the rabbinic texts as *mokhsin*, from the Semitic word *mekhes*, meaning "tax". They are clearly Jews: texts discuss both the problems for a collector who wishes to repent but cannot repay money illegally exacted[192] and the possibility of accepting charity from such a man when he is at home but not when he is at work (since at work the money offered may not be his to give).[193] It is a continuation of the system recorded in the first century by the Gospels and Josephus,[194] and, as then,[195] collectors were despised[196] but perhaps, according to a story in the Jerusalem Talmud, still rich.[197] Some texts assume that they were corruptible and prone to favoritism.[198] The method of collection emerges from the texts and appears variable: Matthew collected taxes in Capernaum seated ἐπὶ τὸ τελώνιον [199] (the תיבה [bench] of the rabbinic texts?)[200] but other passages seem to envisage the men as mobile, taking forbidden goods from a man transporting them on an ass[201] or requisitioning the ass itself in return for another one.[202] Presumably the first method was used to collect the regular direct tax, since a passage that discusses the binding nature of evidence given to mokhsin that a man is one's son rather than slave seems to refer to a census like the Roman one,[203] while the second method seems to indicate some sort of customs duty that could be avoided by hiding goods—clothes,[204] pearls,[205] and perhaps bigger things[206]—at the time of search. If such concealment was effective at evading tax a sort of checkpoint on a road or a spot-check on travelers seems to be envisaged. In all cases it was considered essential to keep hold of the tax receipt given, this being a piece of paper of standard size[207] that ought in theory to have been useful only until checked by the mokhes but in practice, according to R. Judah, was still needed after that to show to the man who received the tax.[208] In either case, the purpose of the collector's needle referred to in t Kel. B.M. 3:9 is obscure.

Because the mokhsin were Jews it is most likely that they were city officials rather than direct employees of the Roman administration. A passage in Sifra has R. Shimon claim that such jobs tend to continue in the same family,[209] which would agree with other evidence of the use of city aristocracies to collect taxes under the empire.[210] It is more than likely that both city taxes and imperial taxes were being collected by the same men: local city taxes are attested in the Hellenistic period[211] and in the imperial period in other Syrian cities.[212] They are perhaps suggested in Galilee by the expectation that mokhsin will not tax produce that they are told is *terumah* (heave offering)[213] and just possibly by the position of Capernaum, where Matthew sat, which was probably on the edge of the territory of Tiberias;[214] Roman taxes are suggested by references to the Roman census procedure[215] and the general use of city authorities for direct tax collection throughout the empire.[216] Taxes for either local or Roman benefit could justifiably have roused the opposition voiced by the rabbis, though perhaps Roman taxes were more likely to elicit the response that in discussions with mokhsin it was rabbinically permissible to lie on oath as much as one wished.[217]

Elsewhere in the empire cities also played an important role in the preservation of order both within their own boundaries and in the surrounding countryside.[218] Such a role is assumed by Josephus for Palestinian cities in the first century: the city governments controlled riots in the cities of Caesarea and Dora[219] and could use prisons for troublemakers[220] and debtors,[221] and the local authorities were expected to apprehend brigands near Beth Horon.[222] One must assume the continuation of such a role despite the slight evidence, for there is no reason for its discontinuance. The קסדור (*quaestor*) who came to the beth midrash of R. Akiba in time of danger was clearly gentile since he terrified, and since he sported a Latin nonmilitary title was most likely to have been a magistrate from the new *colonia* Caesarea;[223] he would not in that case have been acting within the χώρα of his own city.[224] A passage in Sifre states that anyone who insults a βουλευτής would be a fool since he would get thrown straight into prison;[225] a late text records Eleazar b. Shimon helping the Roman government to arrest robbers.[226] If the city police force was less efficient than it might have been, the explanation may lie in R. Judah's assertion that each village had its own סנטר or watchman, who was presumably a public slave since he could be sold.[227] Harper found no evidence of a local village police in Syrian inscriptions,[228] but the existence of such an institution would help explain the lack of city interference in village affairs.

On the other hand, the issue of coin was one function that no village ever tried in competition with the cities. The cities coined to advertise their prestige and to enjoy a small profit on the sale of minted coin at a higher rate than the raw material, so that the right to coin became a highly valued privilege granted by the Roman government.[229] Thus the rebels in both Jewish revolts indicated their independence from Rome by minting their own coins, only for their coins to be judged of dubious validity when the revolts failed.[230] But during the periods of political stability the Galilean villagers relied on city mints to supply their monetized economy. Roman issues were nothing like sufficient for these demands so that in the western empire where city mints were not found recourse was had to private forges.[231] This circumstance would have given the cities decisive control over the economies of their territories had it not been for the prolific mints of other cities in competition. For, if the contents of the hoards found in Galilee are a good indication, it would seem that even villages in the immediate vicinity of Sepphoris and Tiberias felt no necessity to rely on the coinage of those cities, but preferred the products of the mints of Tyre and elsewhere.[232]

Altogether, the role of the cities in the Galilean economy seems very slight. The villages were largely self-supporting and exports were as much to cities on the fringes of Galilee as to the Galilean cities themselves.[233] There is no evidence of a parasitic city aristocracy of any size reliant on an income from estates to maintain a luxurious lifestyle as there was elsewhere in the empire.[234] It must surely be significant that the numerous references to city markets by the rabbis refer to gentile cities outside Galilee, that there is no evidence at all of any difference in occupation between city and country dwellers,[235] and that, though Tiberias and Sepphoris doubtless shared with some of the other cities the advantage of a greater variety of goods than the villages could offer, it is never actually attested that this was so.[236]

The importance of the Galilean cities lies, then, purely in their administrative role, in particular with regard to relations with the Roman government. In this, the Greek patina of the polis was all-important. Semitic forms of society might well have continued underneath as they did in Bashan, Edessa, Gerasa, and so on,[237] but it was the *form* of an oligarchic βουλή representing a δῆμος that provincial governors liked to deal with, and that is what the cities provided.[238] Both cities had a βουλή,[239] and Tiberias is likely to have continued to appoint an ἄρχων and δεκάπρωτοι[240]—it is permitted to date a divorce document by the magistracy of a particular archon[241] as in the Syriac deed of sale from Edessa.[242] If the Roman authorities, when acting tactfully, wished to institute any policy it would have been through these city authorities; and because the prestige of the cities depended on Roman support they could in general be relied upon. Rome, after all, could rescind the prestigious right to mint coins;[243] alter the boundaries of a city's territory;[244] prefer one city to another in their constant rivalry for greater prestige (Tiberias was traditionally opposed to Sepphoris and Hippos);[245] and finally and most ignominiously, demote even the greatest of cities from city status to that of a village.[246]

9 Roman Administration

Galilee in the second century lay in the province of Judaea to which the new title of Syria Palaestina was given after the Bar Kokhba war.[1] The province lay in the control of a legate of praetorian rank until c. A.D. 120 when the post was upgraded to consular status with the introduction of two permanent legions.[2] The importance of the province in Roman eyes is indicated by the high status of many of the legates appointed[3] and by the large military force stationed in Jerusalem and Legio, as much for possible Parthian campaigns as to prevent internal rebellion.[4] Administration here, as elsewhere in the empire, was based on relations with the local *poleis*,[5] a policy which led to the encouragement of a "spread of urbanization", that is, the granting of city status to a number of villages in Palestine that could as a result be more trusted to enforce the wishes of the Roman governor.[6] The governor himself seems to have spent most of his time in his *praetorium* in Caesarea,[7] not, perhaps, so much because this was formally the capital of his province,[8] as because Caesarea boasted facilities for his comfort and easy communications to all parts of his province as well as to the rest of the Mediterranean; from there he imposed his rule through a small bureaucracy[9] and the network of cities.

The much closer control over their subjects exercised by the Ptolemaic kings was continued by the Romans in Egypt[10] but seems to have collapsed in Palestine, probably under Hasmonean or Herodian rule.[11] Reminiscences survive in the use of the term "toparchy" as a geographical designation in Josephus[12] and the legal texts of the early second century from the Judaean Desert,[13] though it is no longer current in Eusebius' *Onomasticon* of the early fourth century.[14] At times it appears that these toparchies may be part of the *polis* system, equivalent to χῶραι,[15] but this supposition is rendered unlikely by the failure of any source, including the lists of toparchies provided by Pliny and Josephus, to mention Sepphoris as the center of a toparchy,[16] by the disagreements between Josephus and Pliny in their lists for

Palestine as a whole,[17] and by the complete absence in the rabbinic sources of the mention of any official, such as the *nome strategus* found in Egypt, to administer such a region.[18] Instead, Josephus ascribes the control of toparchies to villages not attested otherwise as administrative centers of any kind.[19] Scholars who assume a continued role for toparchies in Palestine administration are forced into wild guesses to explain their eventual disappearance.[20] They should be more surprised than they are by the fact that Upper Galilee, which had no polis, also had no toparchy assigned to it by either Josephus or Pliny;[21] but once it is recognized that the term in Palestine, as largely in Roman Egypt itself, was purely geographical, it is evident that so small an area is perfectly well described as "Upper Galilee" without need of further designation by division into toparchies.[22] The vagueness of Josephus and Pliny is now understandable, as is the very rough Hebrew version of one toparchy name in a Judaean desert document.[23]

Roman administration was, in contrast to the Ptolemaic, loosely applied. It was haphazard in all respects, apart from the collection of tribute, relying on the initiative of the provincial officials rather than on the governor to get anything done.[24] I shall argue that this was also the case in Galilee for most of the period under consideration; but clearly not at the period's beginning when Rome was enmeshed in the suppression of the revolt of Bar Kokhba.

For that part of the period the rabbinic texts reveal a vivid recollection of a "time of danger" (שעה של סכנה).[25] Stories about that time display a rare feel for history in what are mostly ahistorical writings.[26] In this time of danger, it is said, any outward sign of Judaism was dangerous.[27] There was religious persecution aimed particularly at circumcisions (leading to apospasms[28]) but also affecting all other public forms of religious behavior.[29] Those who died are considered martyrs,[30] whether killed by crucifixion[31] or any other unpleasant method,[32] and are glorified to such an extent that some rabbis seem to believe suffering positively desirable.[33] Stories praising the deaths of great men were current even in the tannaitic period[34] though they were more common in the fourth century, when they follow, either in imitation or in competition, patterns similar to that of Christian martyrdoms of the same period.[35] But once the killing was over, it was in the legal sphere that the rabbis attest most disruption to society: documents, even those proving divorce or debt, had been lost,[36] land had been confiscated or seized in the turmoil,[37] there were captives to be ransomed (with agonizing choices between one prisoner and another for the ransomer with limited means).[38] These rabbinic comments are those of close witnesses to the tragedy who also show remarkable acquaintance with the tactics of Roman armies in quelling revolts—from the use of a πολέμαρχος sent especially to quell the revolt after experience elsewhere in the empire[39] to the intricacies of siege methods.[40] Realistically, they also assess the comparative harmlessness of a visiting squadron passing rapidly through a settlement in wartime as compared to a leisurely detachment enjoying the local produce in a time of peace.[41]

The rabbis, then, had a close acquaintance with the revolt. But the rabbis came from Judaea, and the very fact that they migrated to Galilee would in any case indicate their suffering.[42] Was Galilee similarly involved in the revolt? There are strong reasons for believing that it was not.[43] All sources agree that Judaea was at any rate the center of the revolt,[44] and archaeology has shown that the Judaean desert was the site of its end;[45] the onus is on those who believe that it spread more widely than that to prove their case.[46] A hoard of Syrian tetradrachms was hidden in Tiberias at some time after A.D. 120, and may have been hidden because of the war,[47] inscriptions at Gadara and Beth Shean indicate a fear of the Jews among the local pagans in this period[48] and, in so far as one can date the minting precisely and tell from so small a sample, no coins seem to have been issued from Tiberias or Sepphoris during the revolt.[49] But that is all the evidence, and at most it indicates only mild unrest in Galilee in sympathy with the Judaean rebellion.[50] In contrast, as an indication of quiet in Galilee throughout the period, there is the apparent careful selection of troops by Bar Kokhba, suggesting only a small guerilla army rather than a nation on the march,[51] the titles αὐτόνομος, πιστή, and φίλη given to Sepphoris under Antoninus Pius,[52] the lack of Galilean coins found overstruck by the rebels[53] and the lack of coins of the revolt in many Galilean sites.[54] Above all, there is the complete lack of evidence of destruction of any kind from any of the sites that have been dug up in Galilee from this period. Against such testimony the obscure reference in one of the Dead Sea papyri to "the Galileans" (הגלילאים) can hardly be taken as a reference to Galilean refugees who have escaped to Judaea, unless one assumes that in the absence of a general rising in Galilee those Galileans who did sympathize with Bar

Kokhba would have been all the more vulnerable to persecution by the Romans.[55]

But even if Galilee escaped armed conflict the area could hardly avoid the ill will toward Jews that inevitably followed so severe a rebellion.[56] It is by no means easy to distinguish the results of the rebellion from its causes,[57] but some seem clear enough. The ban on going up to Jerusalem was a keenly felt disability and remarked on by Christian authors,[58] even if a few pious Jews evaded it by the end of the century;[59] but it was an ideological rather than a practical loss since few of the functions of the Temple cult had, in any case, been feasible since 70 and by 135 very few Jews would even remember the Temple.[60] The ban on circumcision is widely attested[61] and likely to have been a cause rather than an effect of the revolt,[62] for even though it was almost certainly not originally aimed against Jews in particular[63] and by the time of Antoninus Pius effectively enforced only against smaller minorities like the Samaritans[64] and those gentiles trying to convert to Judaism,[65] nonetheless the relaxation of the ban by Antoninus Pius[66] was certainly needed, for it struck at a part of Judaism universally observed.[67] The special tax on Jews instituted by Vespasian in 70 was almost certainly still being collected at this date.[68] The hazard of violent expropriation of property by Roman officials was a natural concomitant of war conditions farther south and the large military presence that resulted.[69] The report by many later sources that rabbinic ordination (*semikha*) was achieved only with difficulty and in secret is likely to be correct[70]—but the traditional legend that the rabbis escaped the ban by migrating about two miles from Usha to Shefar'am is singularly implausible given the easy nature of the terrain in the Galilean foothills,[71] and a better explanation would be that Roman governors were quite capable of hostility toward any clubs or organizations that, because they lay outside their direct control, might be suspected, however unreasonably, of fomenting dissent.[72]

The temptation to exaggerate the effect of this post-revolt persecution must be resisted since vicious retaliation against rebellious subjects was not a normal aspect of Roman policy, wooing by "Romanization" being considered preferable.[73] Stories of violence in Palestine before the war[74] and of the martyrdom of proselytes in particular[75] have no parallels after the middle of the century. Even at the height of the disturbances the Jews came in theory under the protection of Roman law[76] and the long held privileges granted to religious practices such as the Sabbath and abstaining from pagan worship remained intact, perhaps in consideration of the interests of pacific Diaspora communities.[77] This was in contrast to occasional persecution and martyrdom of Christians in the same period.[78] Jews were still excused military service even in time of conscription.[79] Furthermore, those restrictions that were imposed were quite easily broken: the reiteration of the ban on circumcising proselytes assumes the continuation of the practice,[80] semikha did in fact continue and by the mid century was carried out in the open (because the rabbinic academies were so patently politically harmless?), and the learning of the Torah continued throughout the period.[81] The Galilean economy flourished and the rabbinical schools with them. Contemporary Christian authors are unanimous in their envy of Judaism as a *religio licita*[82] and consider that Jewish martyrs have been unknown since the Maccabees.[83] This last contention is doubtless exaggerated but seems to be basically correct; the similarity between fourth century accounts of Jewish martyrs under Hadrian and Christian martyrs under Diocletian is most simply explained as Jewish competition with the Christian stories in an attempt to appropriate some of the glory that martyrs have always borne since the Maccabees.[84]

In general then, Galilee after 135 can be treated as an example of an ordinary Roman province[85] and evidence from rabbinic sources about the Roman administration of their country will provide valuable insight into the way that Roman officials affected the area they governed.

Few emperors visited Galilee in person. There is a Mekhilta midrash that has Trajan present at the trial of the proselytes Julian and Pappus,[86] but the sources about these two characters are all late apart from this one, and this particular story is hard to fit in with Trajan's Parthian campaign.[87] Hadrian visited Palestine in c. 130[88] and a new road from Legio to Sepphoris was built to aid his journey.[89] The revolt of Avidius Cassius in 175 was centered in Syria and Palestine and Marcus Aurelius is reported to have passed through in its aftermath.[90] In the early third century Severus Alexander visited Caesarea[91] and at the end of the century Diocletian's visit to Galilee caused quite a stir.[92] These visits caused excitement among the locals: one Mekhilta passage compares the progress of the Lord through Egypt to that of a king,[93] another describes the setting up of statues and pictures and striking of medals that went on when a king arrived,[94] and others mention the hypocritical praise that a king received as he entered a province surrounded by his soldiers and great pomp.[95] The Mishnah acidly remarks that the altars for worship of an emperor were set up only when he was in the vicinity.[96]

Not that the emperor could actually get much done in a province on such a visit. The number of cases he could deal with was clearly limited.[97] R. Shimon relates a parable about the rashness of a man who intentionally insulted the emperor in his hearing in order to catch his attention[98]—not altogether implausible if he were in desperation. Only in later legend does the emperor stop to converse with beggar girls near the baths of Hammat Gader.[99] Normal contact was only with the aristocracy of the Greek cities, with the emperor gaining popularity both from the granting of privileges[100] (a procedure accurately recorded in a parable in Sifre in which the people of a city ask a king to make their city a *colonia* when they reckon the time is ripe for requests because two of the king's enemies have just fallen before him),[101] and from the granting of funds for building projects both in cities[102] and even occasionally in villages.[103] For the rest, the emperor might have heard appeals from his subjects[104] or settled complicated legal issues,[105] but only in those exceptional cases that reached him.[106]

In all this, Galilee was similar to other provinces of the empire. But in those other provinces the place of the emperor was usually taken by the provincial governor who would make regular visits to the larger towns in all areas under his control to hear cases brought by his subjects.[107] In Galilee, by contrast, there is no evidence of the governor being regularly seen. The silence of the rabbis may be purely fortuitous, but an explanation is possible. Caesarea, by the coast, was an attractive residence.[108] Treated as a capital,[109] it was seen by the rabbis as the place from which Roman government emanated[110] and exercised a certain fascination as a place of magnificence.[111] Even so, occasional visits elsewhere must surely be presumed as it was normal among governors of Syria: in the first century, Petronius had received Jewish delegations first at Akko and then at Tiberias,[112] while the governor Quadratus heard a case in the Judaean village of Lod,[113] and from the second century comes a story about a man who followed a מלך ("king," here surely meaning "governor") from Akko to Tyre to Sidon to Antioch to persuade him to come to the ruler of Akko, a story which seems to reflect the often exhausting waiting and traveling required of applicants to the courts under the assize system.[114] But this story does not refer to regular assizes being held in the cities of Galilee and it must be assumed that Galileans were expected to travel instead to coastal or Decapolis cities for judgment, if not all the way to Caesarea.[115] Two indecisive statements of *halakha may* indicate more frequent visitations but they are too vague to carry much weight: R. Judah discusses the advisability of using a bath that has been kept hot over the Sabbath for a visiting רשות ("authority") or of buying vegetables that have been gathered by others over the Sabbath for such a man.[116] The man concerned is clearly a gentile and of great power since the Sabbath had been broken for him, and R. Judah's comments suggest that such occurrences might be expected in the mid second century, but no precise inferences can be drawn.

The governor promulgated his orders by means of notices posted up in public places, probably only in the major cities[117] and including the provincial edict that announced the basis of his rule.[118] So a Tosefta passage permits the reading of letters (מכתבים) set up in a big city (כרך) even on a Sabbath when they affect the safety of the State[119] and a passage in Sifre reveals that edicts were left on display for some time, for once a διάταγμα is old no one cares about it, whereas everyone rushes to read a new one.[120]

The governor's areas of interference were normally much like those of the emperor himself[121] and the same was probably true in Galilee. In Syria governors are found interfering in city politics[122] and village building projects,[123] and the Mekhilta[124] states that "people in a city (מדינה) only like a governor (strictly, מלך , i.e., king) when he builds them a well, brings a water supply and makes war for them."[125] In Galilee, as elsewhere, access to the governor could bring rewards— there is mention of a betrothal being made conditional on one party "speaking concerning you (עליך) to the governor (שלטון)."[126] But it is surely significant that the governor emerges as such a distant figure in the rabbinic texts and that not even his control of the census, which of all his jobs could cause most friction,[127] finds mention. Certainly there is no evidence at all for the kind of close government, on Ptolemaic lines, by a representative of the provincial governor that is envisaged by Avi-Yonah for Upper Galilee and the Golan,[128] and in the absence of such evidence what seems to emerge is a very loose form of haphazard Roman administration.

The Roman army, unlike the civilian rulers, made its presence felt.

As yet there have been almost no discoveries of material remains of Roman forts in Galilee and it must be assumed that most troops who entered Galilee were stationed in nearby Legio, which belonged to the VI Ferrata.[129] It would be surprising if Roman forts the size of the Byzantine complex at Beth Yerah remained untraced;[130] permanent second century military camps are not difficult to identify and the failure to do so can be taken as significant.[131] From Legio to Lower Galilee at least was not a difficult journey, particularly given the network of roads built by the military from the first to the third centuries[132] linking Sepphoris to Legio, Ptolemais, and probably Tiberias, hence possibly to Damascus and certainly to Scythopolis and Gadara,[133] and intended not just for particular campaigns or journeys of the emperors but in general for the more efficient policing of the area in time of peace.[134] In partial confirmation of this view of the importance of the road system, Upper Galilee, where no military roads led, can boast only one tile of Legio VI Ferrata to attest the presence of *any* Roman soldier in the second and third centuries,[135] as opposed to the epigraphic evidence of soldiers buried in Lower Galilee, particularly Tiberias.[136] Details of relations between soldiers and local civilians must therefore be taken as most likely to refer to Lower Galilee.

In areas of the empire where large concentrations of soldiers were stationed it was normal for relations with the civilian population to be very close in both the economic and the social sphere, even if from the second century such relationships were not always without friction.[137] Elsewhere in Palestine, which as a province had an abnormally large number of troops,[138] papyri from the Judaean desert reveal that because of the Roman fort in the middle of the Jewish village of Ein Gedi[139] there was a close commercial relationship with the soldiers, loans by soldiers to locals being recorded in A.D. 124 and probably A.D. 171.[140] Soldiers are found elsewhere in Syria even to have interfered in local politics—either as police in the course of their duties,[141] or as patrons to protect villages through their influence,[142] or by providing a workforce to build constructions considered important by the governor and therefore usually for the benefit of the big cities.[143] Most contact with soldiers was less pleasant and concerned the exaction of dues payable to the army, the *annona*, and of forced labor and transport, *angaria*, both in Syria[144] and, as will appear, in Galilee.[145] In Galilee, the rabbis complain that even in time of peace an army visit could be disastrous—to such an extent that the shofar should be sounded as a national emergency,[146] for a visiting squadron could be relied on to sample any wine left lying around[147] and could only be pacified, according to a story about R. Judah b. Baba being compelled to break the laws of a festival to avoid the troops running amok among the townsfolk, by elaborate hospitality in food and drink.[148] It was neither wise nor safe for a Galilean to oppose the wishes of a centurion, for his power to punish those who offended him are said in one parable to have been even greater than that of a *bouleutes*, a city councillor.[149]

Galilee, then, shared with the rest of Syria the less pleasant effects of the military rule of the Roman administration. What Galilee lacked, and Syria had, was the close social contact to make up for it that neighborliness might have brought. Tombstones in Tiberias suggest that some soldiers were possibly stationed there, though rustic lettering makes it unlikely that there was a permanent fort.[150] Sepphoris in the first century had a Roman garrison during the first revolt[151] and, though there is no reason to suppose a continuous army presence since then, two rabbinic stories do suggest Roman soldiers in a camp near Sepphoris at a later period. One, in Tosefta, describes the "men of the *castrum* of Sepphoris" (אנשי קצטרא) putting out a fire for a Jew on the Sabbath[152] and another, much later in the Jerusalem Talmud, has a Roman (רומיי) living next door to the Sepphoritan R. Yonathan in the late third century and remarking on his handling of a court case.[153] The earlier story ties in with the rest of the tannaitic evidence in consistently seeing Roman soldiers as the inhabitants of camps (castra or στρατιαί)—according to R. Nathan in c. 180, a Jew should not go to the camp (אצטרטון) to watch frivolous Roman comedy shows[154] or indeed ever go at all except to save lives or chastity,[155] even though his property may be held there, confiscated and out of his control.[156]

These hostile passages reveal the main reason why fraternization was so rare compared to the rest of Syria where the overclose relation of the Syrian army to its civilian population was notorious,[157] for it is clear that *all* Roman soldiers are assumed to be gentile.[158] Indeed, despite ad hoc levies of Jews by the rebel Avidius Cassius in 175,[159] a Palmyrene Jew portrayed in legionary garb in a graffito in Beth Shearim,[160] an apparently Jewish *primipilarius* or *praepositus* recorded in the third century in Kefar Giladi,[161] and evidence from the Roman law codes that by the late *fourth* century there were Jews in military service,[162] for most Jews there was no possibility of signing on as soldiers because of the need to break the Sabbath. Thus one of the prime means by which provincials might become reconciled to Roman rule, namely by fraternization or intermarriage with Roman soldiers and especially by entry into the army,[163] was closed to the Jews of Galilee. The legions of Palestine concentrated on pacified Judaea and the desert frontier rather than Galilee[164] and veterans settled near their service posts in the colonies established in volatile areas[165] rather than venturing into unmilitary Galilee on retirement.[166]

Given so limited an experience of the Roman army one would expect few insights into its organization from rabbinic texts. Rabbis were fascinated by the discipline of the army—such as the execution of a centurion who deserted despite the huge financial rewards that awaited him if he remained faithful (centurions are seen as very wealthy)[167] and, if a number of Mekhilta passages can be trusted, they had a fair idea of the organization of the army into *numeri, turmae, actores*, and so on.[168] Especially revealing is their knowledge of special duty troops such as *speculatores*[169] whose task as intelligence agents in Galilee must have been crucial in preventing unrest if there were as few garrisons stationed there as I have suggested;[170] it is the *speculatores* who are recorded as having carried out executions[171] and, in the Mekhilta, are referred to as the glass used by kings to help them to see, a sophisticated pun on *speculum*.[172]

The point of all this expensive administrative machinery was, for Rome, the preservation of peace and the making of profit, the first being necessary for the second. With peace imposed in Palestine the Roman government concentrated on extracting goods and services from the land and its inhabitants, or so at least it seemed to the Jews who lived there.

In Palestine as a whole there was a considerable increase after 70 in land owned directly by the Roman state.[173] Some of this land can be located, in Judaea,[174] Jericho, and Peraea[175] and probably Ein Gedi;[176] it was land that had either belonged to the Herodian royal house and passed directly to Rome or been expropriated in retaliation for revolt.[177] How much of this land lay in Galilee? Before 70, the royal Jewish house owned private estates throughout Palestine in areas of great fertility—Hyrcanus had villages in the plain of Judaea,[178] Berenice had grain collected from her villages in the plain of Jezreel stored in Beth Shearim.[179] It is reasonable to assume that such estates became imperial domain—the valley of Jezreel was under the control of the legionary headquarters at Legio in the second century.[180] It is true that Galilee itself and the Golan lay, before 70, under the *rule* of Herodian princes and that those princes treated Upper Galilee and the area east of the lake with great freedom—*as if* it was crown domain,[181] but from there it is a long step to assert that it actually *was* private Herodian property. Why, for instance, if this was the case, was *imperial* grain stored in Upper Galilee villages in 66?[182] If Galilee contained imperial land it must have been confiscated by Rome, presumably after the revolts since the area was not attractive enough to have been annexed otherwise, and this too is unlikely: Josephus does not specifically include Galilee in the area confiscated by Vespasian[183] and if there were no disturbances in Galilee in 132-5 there is no reason to posit confiscation then.[184] So claims that Upper Galilee and the Golan were imperial estates need close scrutiny[185] and are found to rely on the argument that, by the sixth century, the lists of bishops' sees mention Upper Galilee and the Golan ($\tau\epsilon\tau\rho\alpha\kappa\omega\mu\iota\alpha$ and *Clima Gaulanitis*) in addition to the Galilean cities and that, since these areas must therefore lie outside the territory of those cities, it can be assumed that they were imperial property.[186] The argument holds good for the sixth century when all land within the empire lay either on imperial estates or within the territory of one or other of the cities[187] but is decidedly weak for the more fluid conditions of the second and third centuries. There is no reason why in this earlier period land could not be farmed by independent villagers in these comparatively out of the way places without any interference from the State apart from the sending of soldiers to collect taxes;[188] it was a feature of the later, more rigid imperial administration that comparatively marginal land, of little interest to city councils or beyond their control, was put under the rule of imperial officials and annexed as imperial property, but it is not proved for this time also.[189] Certainly there is no word in tannaitic sources of direct imperial rule by a representative of the governor such as Avi Yonah suggested,[190] and Smallwood's view that after 70 all the Jewish peasants were *coloni* but came to think of themselves as owners of their land paying tax rather than rent[191] is, though ingenious, unnecessary. The halakhic problems over tithes on produce technically owned by the emperor but farmed by Jews are considerable, so it is significant that only one text deals with them:

according to R. Yosi, when products were being made for kings, all that
was harvested had the status of *demai* (doubtful tithe) when the majority
of the workers were Jews but needed no tithes at all when a majority of
the workers were gentile.[192] The picture conjured up is of a large workforce on an imperial estate, perhaps on the fringes of Galilee, since
there are gentile workers too; it would have been a relevant problem
for R. Yosi to discuss in Sepphoris for the benefit of Galilean Jews
living on the fringes of the Jezreel valley, but shows by contrast that
the huge bulk of agricultural law in the rest of the tannaitic corpus
assumes that land farmed by Galileans was genuinely their own.[193]

The most direct form of exploitation, expropriation of land, was
thus probably not used by Rome in Galilee.[194] Instead, Rome imposed a variety of taxes, each resented to a degree by the Jews.

The census aroused complaints at its first imposition[195] and resentment continued, directed against the local Jews who helped in its
collection.[196] Josephus records the release from land tax (*tributum
soli*) on the land granted him in Judaea as a great honor.[197] This was
a tax paid in kind—it may have been such imperial grain that was
stored up in large quantities in the villages of Upper Galilee in 66[198]
and a rabbinic text discusses the need to separate tithes from produce
of a field hired from a Samaritan before giving a portion to the centurion.[199] Another text describes men coming from the "house of the
king" (בית המלך) to take a man's harvest as a punishment or tax
(אונס).[200] Caesar had allowed Jews not to pay taxes in the Sabbatical
Year, but it is likely that this privilege had ended by the second century since there is no mention of it in discussions of the nonobservance
of the Sabbatical Year laws.[201] The *tributum capitis* was particularly
heavy, being probably at the special Syrian rate of 1 per cent on capital.[202] Added to this was the special Jews' tax of two drachmas, payable since 70.[203] According to an inscription, it required especially
appointed bureaucrats to supervise its collection.[204] As well as all
these regular taxes there was the burden of customs duties;[205] a possible market tax on each village market (though there is no evidence
for this in rabbinic sources—perhaps the markets were too small?);[206]
the exaction by Roman courts of fines agreed on by the parties in civil
cases[207] as well as the confiscation of goods in criminal cases;[208] and
the probable imposition of a tax on the earnings of the gentile prostitutes, whom the less scrupulous apparently frequented.[209] Given all
this, it is not surprising that Roman taxation was much resented.

Tacitus remarks on Jewish complaints about the burden of Roman taxes in the first century[210] and the rabbis declare that every tax put on Israel by the gentiles was accounted to them as innocent blood[211] and that the only aim of a governor on entering his province was to extract as much money as possible from it.[212]

Resentment was particularly reserved, however, for two other forms of taxation especially disliked because they were irregularly exacted by the military. They were the *annona* and the system of enforced service to the state called *angareia*.[213] The annona was the ad hoc exaction of supplies taken by the army for its own use or that of fellow soldiers elsewhere;[214] such exactions might have included animals (which were then as good as lost)[215] and bread dough delivered by the victim once it had been cooked.[216] Angareia was a temporary levy of services for a particular job, whether in the form of a loan of transport or of physical labor—a passage in Sifre considers that there is little difference for a conquered people between paying taxes and giving forced labor.[217] Angareia was an ancient form of exploitation known to the Gospel writers: compare "if someone *angareuei* you one mile, go with him two,"[218] the story in Mark of Jesus borrowing a foal by having a disciple say that "ὁ κύριος" had need of it and would send it back,[219] and the soldiers who *angareuousin* Simon of Cyrene to carry the cross.[220] The system is assumed normal by the rabbis even as they resent it: if an ass was taken for angareia, the hirer was deemed not responsible.[221] The Jerusalem Talmud has a story about R. Zeira in the late third century being taken to the *palatina* in order to transport a myrtle bough[222] and asserts that a man could positively expect to have his ass or donkey seized for angareia to Lod or Tyre if he stood with it in an overconspicuous place.[223] More passages may attest the danger of being pressed into forced labor: if two brothers in partnership have one of them "fall into service" (נפל לאומנות) then they must both share the cost since this was through no fault of the brother chosen[224] and another asserts that a slave who is marked down for state service will be a bad buy.[225] According to the Jerusalem Talmud, a man might be pressed into service while standing quietly in the marketplace.[226] Apart from transport only a few texts indicate the kind of work expected of the unlucky victim. A Jew might be pressed into service (נדהק) working at a flour mill with a gentile or a woman in a state of impurity,[227] there is a story in Tosefta of a chain gang (קולר, *collare*) of both Jews and gentiles going all the way to Antioch on some business and returning together,[228] and R. Yohanan b. Zakkai asserted, according to the Mekhilta, that, for failing to repair the roads leading to the Temple, the Jews of Palestine were now required to repair the towers and forts that led up to the great cities of Rome (though if this is literally true they are not credited for their efforts on extant milestones).[229]

The nature of Roman administration as described here led to a fairly antagonistic view of Rome in tannaitic texts.[230] The destruction of the Temple and the death of many Jews in the revolts produced not only a sense of national guilt[231] but also speculation by the same rabbis on the possible annihilation of Israel's enemies.[232] Both reactions owe much to the religious and mythical background into which the rabbis tried to fit the Roman Empire,[233] and both were compatible with a practical pacifism like that of the pre-70 Pharisees[234] precisely because Roman government was exercised at a considerable remove from their Jewish subjects and left them largely to their own devices in Galilee. After 135 there does not seem to have been any political disaffection in Palestine until the fourth century,[235] and the remarkable disinclination to take advantage of the third century political anarchy by rebellion indicates a grudging contentment with the economic prosperity under Roman rule.

Passive acceptance of a Roman administration consisting largely of tax collection was a different matter from active participation in the empire. A desire for such participation came slowly, perhaps not until the third century.[236] It was expressed, as elsewhere in the empire, by attempts to influence the ruling power by seeking contact with Roman officials, so that, instead of simply suffering maladministration and complaining, the provincials themselves became enmeshed in the machinery of government.[237]

Josephus provides much evidence of such collaboration with Rome within the Palestinian Jewish aristocracy before the first revolt.[238] The collaborators were wealthy, spoke some Greek, and considered the revolt a tragedy that brought destruction to property and prestige.[239] The same was surely true of the Galilean upper class of the second century,[240] particularly those in Lower Galilee who entered the councils of the cities.[241] Greek cities by definition had close contact with the Roman government through their role in the collection of taxes, and so too did their leading citizens since they could not afford to ignore the kind of protection that such contact offered them against illegal exactions and other losses in time of unrest.[242] However, it was not, in the second and early third centuries, a collaboration that brought Jews into the Roman government itself as it did to many other local aristocracies in the empire.[243] There is no discussion in the Talmud of what posts Jews may and may not hold in the service of Rome as there is in the writings of early church fathers,[244] and there is only one inscription, from a huge mausoleum in Kfar Giladi, to show that in the mid third century the son of a wealthy man whose natural language was Hebrew could be a *primipilarius* or *praepositus* ($\pi.\pi.$) with a tombstone inscribed in Greek.[245] It is from this mid third century period that rabbinic evidence shows the rabbis themselves having closer contact with Roman officials, not only in philosophical discussions[246] but also in political matters, with Roman official posts even being offered them by the fourth century. Thus, while R. Gamaliel is said only to have got permission from the governor to Syria (permission, i.e., רשות, to teach?),[247] R. Eleazar is said by a late source to have been rebuked by a fellow rabbi in c. A.D. 160 for helping to arrest bandits for Rome,[248] and the tradition is related of R. Judah ha Nasi that he remained loyal to Rome throughout his life and even that he helped Caracalla in his Parthian policy through the Babylonian Jews.[249] By the late third century R. Abbahu in Caesarea is found to be on good terms with the Roman governor[250] and in the following century the position of patriarch was officially recognized by the Romans by the bestowal of a high Roman rank.[251] At this late date the holding of such rank was clearly fully acceptable in Galilean society; this is confirmed by the fourth century Sepphoris synagogue that refers to a *scholasticus* of *comes* rank whose father was also a *comes*.[252] The rabbinic evidence of closer contact from only the mid third century, after all Jews were Roman citizens,[253] would not itself be decisive since this also reflects the growing political influence of the rabbis themselves inside Galilee, but negative evidence from the lack of inscriptions by Galilean aristocrats in the second century and the failure of any of the larger villages of Upper Galilee to win the city status they could surely have had on request[254] suggests that this picture of little enthusiasm for embroilment in Roman affairs is essentially correct.

Part of the reason for this would undoubtedly lie in the lack of rhetorical training for the sons of the city aristocracies, if I have given the right account of their education above.[255] Approaches to Roman officials were effectively made only in person and, if possible, eloquently.[256] It was something that the aristocrats of Judaea had attempted before 70[257] though recourse to a hired orator was necessary then, too, on occasions.[258] Stories collected by M. D. Herr of embassies to Roman dignitaries by rabbinic sages[259] do not reveal a similar relationship to that between Greek sophists and the Roman hierarchy elsewhere in the empire, despite Herr's claim to this effect.[260] Even if all the more fantastic details that he accepts from late stories were true[261] they would reveal no more than the prickly relationship between curious and uncomprehending Romans and the exponents of a strange religion—not the stuff of city politics. If the sages or anyone else in Galilee wished to influence Roman policy, they, like the high priest opposed to St. Paul,[262] would have had to hire a rhetor to speak for them. A parable in Sifre describes how a rhetor hired by an individual spends most of his speech in praise of the king and slips in his client's request only in the middle of his oration.[263] Rhetoric was not an academic exercise that appealed to the rabbis or perhaps any Galilean Jew,[264] but in the empire of the second century a failure to speak Greek reasonably well blocked all avenues to influence apart from army service, which was already closed to Jews.[265]

With Roman rule kept at arm's length, how much did Galileans know about Rome or the emperors? The emperors' reigns provided a convenient method for the dating of documents, though this method was only one used among many. According to the Mishnah, documents could be dated by the Persian, Greek (i.e., Seleucid) empires, by the building of the Temple or from its destruction, as well as by the Roman system.[266] The "Roman system" could of course mean the consuls of the year as it does in one of the Aramaic deeds from the Judaean desert,[267] or the date of the founding of the province,[268] as well as the year of the emperor's tribunician power.[269] It is perhaps significant for demonstrating the comparative unimportance of the Greek cities in Galilean administration that dating by the city era, normal in surrounding areas,[270] is not found in Galilee,[271] apart from a Tosefta text that permits dating by the province (הפרכין, i.e., eparchy, or הורבריינות (archon?)).[272] The dating of extant documents seems to vary cheerfully between such eras as that from the destruction of the Temple[273] to the full official Roman formulas, and those cases when Roman dating methods are borrowed would not seem to have had much effect on local knowledge of what went on in Rome

—how much did it matter to a Galilean even if he did know the names of the consuls in Rome to put at the head of his documents? The propaganda effect of coins in use was similar:[274] subtle information in the changes of imperial coin types would not reach Galilee if the coin hoards found reflect normal circulation, for many of those from the second century are local city rather than Roman state issues[275] and the city coins give no more than the name and bust to identify the emperor.[276]

Ignorance, then is to be expected in Galilee in all matters concerning Rome except for those institutions and officials who directly affected the province. Knowledge of such things was equally shaky elsewhere in Syria where other languages besides Greek were widely spoken. So in Palmyra, the Greek οὐηξιλλατία (*vexillatio*) is translated in a bilingual inscription as לגינה (*legio*)[277] and in the *Lex Vectigalis* Corbulo's title of κράτιστος (*clarissimus*) is loosely translated by כשירה (or does this show knowledge of the original Latin?).[278] However, Palmyrene and Nabatean translations and transliterations can be remarkably accurate in official contexts with consistent transliterations for *eques* (הפקא),[279] *consularis* (הפטיקא),[280] ἡγεμών (היגמננא),[281] and so on,[282] and can even be imaginative in some of the versions offered, such as קרח בארגונה for "bestow the purple,"[283] רב משריתא for *praefectus castrorum*,[284] and מעמננא for ἐπανορθωτής.[285] This last use reveals, however, that even in official contexts there was a certain inconsistency in Palmyrene usage, since *corrector* is translated elsewhere not only by מעמננא but also by מתקננא or the transliteration אפנרתטיא.[286] This may suggest that the other terms were sometimes used with no real understanding of their meaning. At any rate it reveals sufficient fallibility for one to expect many more signs of vagueness in less official texts if they survived. This is certainly what is found in Palestine: the legal documents from the Judaean desert are very accurate in all that concerns Roman officialdom[287] whereas when a rabbinic text enumerates the Romans on whom Israel will take revenge when the time comes the list is meaningless (ὑπατικοί, ἡγεμόνες, χιλίαρχοι, centurions, *beneficiarii*, σύγκλητοι, *matronae*, all given in stilted transliteration),[288] and recourse is generally had to the blanket term *reshut*, meaning "the authorities."[289] Given this vagueness it is surprising to find the rabbis making use of Roman definitions of provincial borders, and perhaps even of the limits of city territories in the formulation of their laws of evidence;[290] the fact that this is the case shows that such boundaries were clear enough to provincials, though it is obscure how they were marked and how accurately they were laid down.[291]

This was the boring aspect of Roman administration, and perhaps no one not involved in it could be expected to understand the ramifications of rank. What interested provincials was life at the top, and the tannaitic texts give a unique insight into provincial speculation about the way the emperors lived and worked. The many stories and parables about kings offer, however, numerous pitfalls in trying to extract rabbinic views about the emperors.[292] Some refer to the Herodians,[293] some to a hoped for Jewish king of the Davidic line,[294] and some perhaps to a Hellenistic king whether Ptolemaic or Seleucid.[295] Some doubtless are fairy stories elevated to a more interesting level by the use of royal personages as the main characters.[296] Nonetheless, it seems reasonable to assume that the main pattern for regal behavior in the minds of second century rabbis would have been that of the Roman emperors, and the compatibility of some details they describe with what is known from Greek and Latin sources would confirm this.[297]

Only the broad outlines of the emperors' administrative role were clear to the rabbis. Even official city and village inscriptions are sometimes found to be confused about imperial titles;[298] the rabbinic texts do not even try to understand and are content with the designation "king" (מלך). Rabbis distinguish only a very few individual emperors (Nero, Vespasian, Titus, Hadrian, "Antoninus," and at a later date Diocletian, all remembered for specific reasons)[299] whereas the other emperors are lost in stereotype. The function of kings seems to be the waging of war, dynastic struggle, and the control of family and advisers. For many of the parables the war is staged in a desert where lack of water and provisions leave the king at the mercy of his soldiers[300]—in Palestine, imperial Parthian and later Sassanid campaigns were the main lure that brought emperors into the vicinity, and then almost always to fail. One would not expect the details of the campaigns to emerge but rather their common factors; it is noteworthy that Mekhilta stories are consistent in this respect with those of the more trustworthy tannaitic texts.[301] Similarly, dynastic struggles, the other main cause of imperial visits,[302] feature prominently in the rabbinic picture. R. Judah remarks that any king or ruler (שלטון) without power in Rome reckons that he has nothing[303] (perhaps the ability of emperors to rule without visiting Rome was realized earlier by provincials than emperors, who proved ready to forego Rome only when forced to do so in the third century).[304] In Sifre, Shimon b. Yohai gives a parable that seems to involve an ἀντικαίσαρ (אנטיקוסר) and his troops,[305] and R. Hoshaya in the mid third century describes a king expelling his ἐπίτροπος so that the inhabitants know which of them to call "Domine."[306] The rest of the imperial power structure was only vaguely understood: of the imperial entourage, the importance of the king's advisers in policy making was appreciated[307] but nothing of the importance of relations with the senate apart from one text that stresses correctly the premium placed by emperors on good birth in deciding whom to favor.[308] Frequent references to kings leaving their subjects (and family) in the hands of an *epitropos* while abroad have no real parallel in Roman administration;[309] on the other hand, finance is seen, accurately enough, to be managed through hoards of treasure and leased-out land.[310] It is in the effect of emperors on the provinces that true insight is found: emperors were known to travel from province to province[311] and to cause a stir on arrival, with altars set up especially for the occasion[312] and, according to the Mekhilta, with the inhabitants showering flattery upon them[313] —when Diocletian visited Tyre in c. 295, R. Hiya b. Abba broke the halakha to catch a glimpse of him.[314] Finally, it is recognized by the rabbis that emperor worship, known from other sources to be enthusiastically performed in Palestine and its environs,[315] is both prevalent and sincerely felt,[316] though the astonishing lack of any diatribe against humans who set themselves up as gods may well reflect a rabbinic, rather than common provincial, inability to identify the object of worship with the emperors they otherwise discuss.[317] It is perhaps a similar lack of identification that enabled Jews cheerfully to swear by the emperor in a number of extant documents without sign of a bad conscience at the possibility of idolatry[318]—such swearing was specifically permitted by second century rabbis.[319]

So much for the limits of rabbinic knowledge of the emperors. This by no means exhausts rabbinic statements on the subject; the rest is fantasy and speculation about imperial private life.

The most common motif is that of the bad son and the difficulty the king has in controlling him, the normal setting for the stories being the palace and, in particular, the *triclinium* where they dine,[320] and the general theme being the charmed position of sons in the eyes of their fathers.[321] Sons are portrayed as struggling for parental favor[322] and the succession[323] and as liable to rebel against their fathers.[324] It is a muddled reflection of Julio-Claudian court intrigues and the problems of Marcus Aurelius with Commodus or Severus with Caracalla and Geta,[325] with perhaps a dash of Herodian history and a layer of contemporary social observation of the behavior of Roman aristocrats in Palestine. (As, for instance, in the prominence in the stories of pedagogues as the confidants of the kings in the rearing of their beloved sons.)[326] The emperors were conceived of as living romantic lives. R. Judah remarks that any Roman emperor will feel the need to build palaces and villas (פלטוריות וחווילאות)[327] and that these will be magnificent—with the emperor himself hidden away in an inner sanctum behind curtains covered with precious stones[328]— and sometimes with astonishing architectural quirks, such as the palace built on boats.[329] The midrash is full of illustrations of this sort. They do not fit together into a coherent picture, which should not surprise, nor do they always tally with imperial behavior as known from sources closer to the emperor. Some of the descriptions drift into fantasy, others are purely artificial for the sake of the parable in which they are incorporated. For many it is not possible to find a neat category of any kind. But enough remains, particularly in the prolific examples of Sifre, to show the sort of fascinated speculation about the rulers of the empire that would be indulged in in the villages of Galilee.[330]

Roman rule rested lightly on Galilee from the mid second century. What interference there was was resented but recent history was sufficient justification for that. What strikes the modern observer is rather the lack of Roman interest. There was no attempt to encourage Romanization of the province as there was in some newly conquered areas of the West in the first century.[331] Nor was there any system of intensive garrisoning to hold down a hostile population as in contemporary Wales.[332] Instead, Rome left Galilee to develop her economy and culture in peace. Jews were treated no more harshly than any other subjects of the empire who had tried to revolt and failed. The ruling power had no interest so long as political stability was maintained. It is an attitude that characterized imperial provincial policy at the height of imperial rule, the Antonine era. Self-satisfied Roman aristocrats, city bred no matter their country of origin, saw only the glittering cities of the empire.[333] All over the empire there were rural areas like Galilee that opted out, and, being therefore of no concern to Rome whatsoever, were left to grow in peace.[334]

10   Conflicts of Jurisdiction

Jews living in Roman Galilee were subject to at least three different administrative systems, each of which claimed jurisdiction over their lives and over any civil or criminal case in which they might be involved. Any single dispute or misdemeanour could, in theory, be decided in the Roman, the *polis* or the village court or, if those involved were rabbinical students, by the rabbis. A conflict of jurisdiction would seem inevitable. Even worse, there was the possibility of a conflict of laws.

The possibility of such disputes was even greater after 212, when all inhabitants of the empire became Roman citizens, but they were also likely before that date since it is probable that Roman jurisdiction and law was often applied even to non Romans by the provincial authorities when cases came before them (see below). How serious these conflicts were in practice, and the procedures taken to mitigate their effect will be investigated in this chapter. This is a question of considerable importance for all provinces of the empire and notoriously difficult to answer even for areas of comparative abundant evidence.[1] If, despite the unique nature of the Galilean source material, conclusions are nonetheless tentative, the attempt will still be worthwhile.

The limits of those sources should first be admitted. No actual case is reported in tannaitic texts of the decision of one court being overturned by another or of a verdict reached by one set of legal rules being discarded in accordance with a different set. Nor do the Judaean Desert documents, despite references to more than one jurisdiction, show a conflict between those judicatures. Only at a later period do a very few examples emerge. One is in the Jerusalem Talmud and concerns a woman by the name of Tamar who lost a criminal case in Tiberias in c. A.D. 290 at a tribunal of rabbis. She appealed against the verdict to the governor in Caesarea, only to have the appeal court of three rhetors prevented from hearing the case by the influence of

R. Abbahu with the governor when he intervened on behalf of his col-
leagues.[2] Another story, in the Babylonian Talmud and therefore of
particularly dubious authenticity in discussing Palestine, concerns
R. Banaah in c. A.D. 220 being locked up by the authorities after a
complaint was brought against him by the unlucky sons who lost an
inheritance suit that he decided in accordance with rabbinic but not
Roman law.[3] According to the Roman law codes, a certain Cornelia
Salvia, who had left her property to the Jewish community in Antioch,
was prevented in A.D. 213 from having her wishes carried out because
so vague an entity was not acceptable as the recipient of a legacy in
Roman law,[4] and in A.D. 204 two, apparently Jewish, traders who
had refused to surrender stolen merchandise that they had bought in
good faith (the relevant criterion in Jewish law) were compelled to
give the goods back to the original owner in accordance with Roman
law.[5] That is all the direct evidence, but the preponderant silence is
by no means decisive given the theoretical nature of rabbinic claims
to jurisdiction at this stage, which would prevent any of *their* deci-
sons coming into conflict with Greek or Roman law.[6] The evidence
suggests that there was an increase in conflict after the tannaitic
period (and therefore after the *Constitutio Antoniniana*) and perhaps this was inevitable,[7] but the earliest case cited belongs to A.D.
204, and that should encourage the belief that in certain public areas
of civil law, such as the rules that governed trade, conflict was possible even when most of the empire had not yet received Roman
citizenship.

This belief is strengthened by the assumption among the tannaim
that such a conflict was *possible* even in areas of family law. According to a Mishnah text, the gentiles might force a Jew to divorce his wife
—but illegally, in rabbinic eyes, unless they make clear as they do so
that this is what the Jews want him to do.[8] A Tosefta text asserts
that *halizah* (refusal to marry a dead brother's wife) is illegal in front
of a gentile court unless the authority of a rabbi is given as a warrant.[9]
A *baraita* in the Babylonian Talmud has a warning by R. Tarfon against
the use of gentile courts for anything at all.[10] Two Mekhilta texts contain the same sort of idea: the punishment for perversion of Jewish
law is that Jewish women and the next generation of men will go to
other, non-Jewish courts[11] and R. Eleazar b. Azariah is said to have
denied the validity of gentile court decisions even when they were in
accordance with Jewish law.[12] The rabbis were aware that the law

of these courts as well as their personnel differed considerably from that of the rabbis. They appear to have known that Roman law did not recognize the Jewish distinction in liability between an ox that has gored and one that has not,[13] and, in the Jerusalem Talmud and therefore post A.D. 212, that Romans reckoned a son and daughter equal as a man's heirs.[14] R. Shimon, again according to the late Jerusalem Talmud, considered that a gentile divorce was valid, presumably showing an awareness and approval of the relevant gentile legal forms.[15] But, in general, conflicts of this kind have to be ascertained not so much by explicit statements of the conflict of legal concepts as by the areas of "illegal" behavior that the law codes are most intent on opposing: the hidden assumptions that the emperors declared invalid in Roman law in rescripts quoted by lawyers and preserved in the codes and the Digest can be pieced together into a coherent *Volksrecht*, a body of traditional local law,[16] and the hidden assumptions against which the rabbis struggled can sometimes be found to have made good sense in Roman or Greek law.[17]

That separate jurisdictions did indeed exist is fairly clear. Many, if not all, of the Galilean villages boasted a local court.[18] The evidence comes, obliquely, from the rabbinic texts. R. Ishmael attributed the destruction of Beth Aba in Galilee to their judging civil cases with only one judge rather than three.[19] Another passage compares the past, when a Jewish court could put Jews to death for sexual offences and admonish gentiles, to the present, when both are only admonished.[20] Numerous texts *assume* the beth din as the central authority in each עיר.[21] Furthermore, if R. Judah was correct in assuming the participation of a court in the signing of a *prozbul* (to enable the Sabbatical Year to be ignored for a loan with a clear conscience),[22] then papyrological evidence of the existence of the prozbul institution lends weight to the argument that there were such courts.[23] If gentiles were permitted by the rabbis to force a Jew to do "what the Jews tell him to do" then there must have been such Jewish institutions to tell the Jew in the first place.[24] The entire rabbinic corpus assumes the existence of Jewish judges and their fallibility.[25] But the clearest proof of all comes from the Judaean Desert documents, not just because they include civil law otherwise known only in the tannaitic texts and distinctively Jewish,[26] but also because the use of Hebrew in contracts would have made them unnecessarily hard to enforce in a non-Jewish court.[27] Small communities like these did have their own law courts in Syria three centuries later, for the Syro-Roman law book assumes that village magistrates or local priests are the first authority in civil and criminal cases—note that this code saw no conflict between a concurrent ecclesiastical and lay court system.[28]

Who were these judges? They were not rabbis, for many texts complain of their corruptness and lack of knowledge of Torah.[29] Wealthy members of the aristocracy are assumed as judges by some texts[30] and the complaints of some rabbis that judges *ought* to be pious and learned as well as rich only point up these failings and the conservatism of those rabbis who are prepared to accept the status quo.[31] Fallible local judges are not unexpected. The Gospels assume that each polis had a fallible κριτής,[32] and Josephus in his schematizing account of his rule of Galilee in the first revolt claims to have put seven men in each "city" to try lesser cases.[33] A village system such as the tannaim describe could hardly have survived without a means of resolving disputes. But Josephus' claim does raise the more difficult issue of the method of appointment of such judges. Josephus' own action was of course exceptional and in time of war (if it happened at all), but is one to assume that in normal times a judge's office was held by virtue of ancestry or wealth alone?[34] Alon asserted that the municipal administration was responsible for judicial appointments,[35] meaning, presumably, the magistrates of Sepphoris and Tiberias in Galilee, but there is no evidence to support this. Rabbinic appointment can be ruled out by the complaints of the rabbis themselves. However, a number of passages do discuss the need for care in the selection of judges: Deuteronomy I: 17 "Do not be partial in judgment" is interpreted to mean that the appointer (ממונה [mamoneh or memuneh —literally "appointed"?]) of judges should not appoint rich or powerful characters if they do not know the Law[36] and other passages assert that "they" should appoint a beth din in every settlement.[37] No single Jewish individual seems likely;[38] but whether the appointment would have been the duty of village magistrates, village assembly, or some other such body (even co-option by the court?) is quite unclear, though the generally democratic nature of other village institutions would suggest that ultimate authority might have lain with the assembly, hence the general warnings to *all* Jews about care in judicial appointment.[39]

The kind of case dealt with by the courts would normally, and perhaps only, have concerned private civil law.[40] This seems to have been the case elsewhere in the empire, so far as the evidence goes;[41] in particular, the papyri show that Greek and Egyptian local law continued to be used extensively in marriage, contract, and inheritance matters under Roman rule.[42] These are the concerns of those Judaean Desert documents that use the Hebrew language or Jewish law: contracts,[43] marriage law,[44] and inheritance.[45] Tannaitic texts suggest that the courts also dealt with slave manumissions[46] and, of course, divorce.[47] There is no negative proof that criminal cases were not also dealt with, only the restrictions on valid judgments introduced by the tannaim that would *in practice* make such jurisdiction impossible: no enslavement or imprisonment of debtors permitted,[48] no condemnation for assault or murder without prior warning and two witnesses,[49] and so on. No judicature could ever apply such rules and still keep control effectively, and they seem to have served instead as a screen to protect the rabbis from the embarrassment of admitting that Jewish courts could not enforce decisions in criminal cases when the city or Roman courts could intervene[50] and when Jews were almost certainly deprived of the death penalty.[51] Decisions in civil disputes were doubtless hard enough to enforce—Sifre describes how the messenger of the court had to observe the same etiquette as the individual creditor and stand outside the debtor's house when coming to extract a pledge for an unpaid loan.[52]

Procedure in the courts seems to have been fairly simple. It is hard to decide how much of the Mishnah and Tosefta on Sanhedrin applies to village courts rather than the great tribunals of pre-70 Jerusalem, but at any rate the detailed accounts of courts of 23 or 71 clearly cannot apply to a village beth din of three, one, or seven.[53] Judges apparently sat while the parties stood before them, nothing being said until both sides were present and prepared.[54] It may well be that the kind of law used was similarly simple—customary law, precedent, and common sense.[55] There is remarkably little evidence of Jewish judges imposing any specifically non-rabbinic civil law, and what there is comes from late sources,[56] but this does not mean that rabbinic lawmaking was accepted, but rather that the rabbis codified the law *as it was actually practiced*. The rabbinic codification of civil law was not published in the Mishnah until the end of our period,[57] so there was not at this time any standard rabbinic code for non-rabbinic judges either to accept or to reject. Even once codified, the compilations did not purport to be comprehensive any more than any other ancient law code; the Mishnah rather discusses in detail specific legal cruces.[58] The basis of village law was set out in the Bible, and Josephus records the widespread horror among Jews when Herod tried to end the biblical procedure for punishing housebreakers.[59] Additional legal rulings, in so far as they appear in the Judaean Desert documents, were introduced to deal with more complex economic, and different social, relations: new rules recorded in the papyri are almost all attested by the rabbis at the same date as actual practice in marriage,[60] divorce,[61] gift,[62] loan,[63] sale,[64] and rent,[65] and are either logical extensions of old Semitic law for new conditions[66] or introductions from Greek legal practice.[67] What all the papyri show is that rabbinic law reflected actual law, and that, even if a later rabbinic idea may well have reflected much earlier actual practice (as in an Amoraic mention of the law that lies behind the admission of debt in DJD II no. 18[68]) or an early rabbinic idea still have been found in actual use long after the rabbis themselves have given it up,[69] nevertheless rabbinic discussions were in general intended to clarify existing practice rather than to create an entirely new civil code. For the same reason, rabbinic assumptions that Jewish courts might have some influence over local gentiles should not be too quickly dismissed as purely theoretical since much Jewish law in practice was simply Semitic common law that could be recognized all over the Syrian region.[70]

In relation to these courts the rabbis acted as *iurisprudentes* rather than as an alternative legal system.[71] Nevertheless, they could and did act as *juges isolés*[72] at least in religious matters, for those who came to them for arbitration, a form of dispute settlement widespread in the empire but emerging in the sources usually only on recognition of its validity by the Roman State, which might come late or not at all —in A.D. 317 Constantine recognized the slave manumissions that had gone on without interference *iam dudum* in churches.[73] Like that of the rabbis, the arbitration of Christian holy men in fifth century Syria was held to be binding by local society whatever its status in Roman law.[74] Rabbinic power lay in the rabbis' personal status as holy men who should not be affronted since contravention of their decisions could bring disfavor or even a curse.[75] Such a power could attract gentiles as well as Jews to bring cases to rabbis: according to Sifre, R. Ishmael would hear cases involving both Jew and gentile and be prepared to use Jewish or gentile law (but would always favor the Jew!),[76] while R. Shimon b. Gamaliel said that the choice of the legal system should be that of the gentile who comes for judgment.[77] Again, no case is given of such arbitration, but the possibility is not unlikely in the context of rabbinic aspirations to spread their influence in the second and third centuries.[78] The rabbis wanted to take over local administration, including the village courts. By adhering in civil law to local custom and by showing a remarkable lack of formalism in their demands for legal behavior,[79] they eventually succeeded in doing so.

The flourishing independent Galilean villages thus had independent courts working in a basically Semitic legal system into which some Greek ideas had crept.[80] Was there another tier of legal administration between these courts and the Roman assizes? There is scattered evidence that elsewhere in the empire in this period the *poleis* that formed the background to the provincial system also had their own courts.[81] Was this also the case in Galilee? Did Tiberias and Sepphoris have their own courts and, if so, what was their relation to the village courts and what kind of law did they enforce, Semitic, biblical, or Greek?

Most cases heard by city courts elsewhere in the empire involved commercial, family, and inheritance law.[82] Severus refers to the practice of city courts giving the burden of *tutela* of orphans to unwilling citizens,[83] and through their archives for contracts the city courts kept jurisdiction over sales of slaves and perhaps some other commodities.[84] Some cities may have reserved the right to hear criminal trials also, as at Ephesus, where St. Paul could be tried by either the ἀγοραῖοι or the governor,[85] but no such cities are well attested after the early second century.[86] It is precisely family and property law that seems to fall within the spheres of competence of the *boule* of Petra in the court cases carried on by Babata: the Nabatean and Jewish guardians of a Jewish orphan were appointed by the boule according to an extract from the *acta* still preserved, and Babata's actions over her husband's estates are likely to have come before the same court;[87] it is action for debt that the Gospels assume as the most likely reason for a man to come before an *archon*.[88]

Given their importance elsewhere it is disappointing to find the rabbinic texts almost entirely silent about distinctively city courts in Galilee. Any of the general comments showing awareness of gentile jurisdictions could of course refer to the gentile cities in the region of Galilee—the Mishnah asserts that a woman imprisoned by gentiles for debt (על ידי ממון) was not likely to be raped (i.e., her captors are not Roman soldiers),[89] a Tosefta text considers ḥaliẓah before a gentile court not valid unless at the behest of a Jewish court,[90] R. Eleazar b. Azariah referred to the courts of gentiles giving legal decisions.[91] But these texts cannot refer to the courts of Jewish Tiberias or Sepphoris.[92] Other evidence is ambiguous. A passage appears in some editions of the Tosefta discussing the purity of נמסיאות (νομοσία?), envisaged as buildings as large as basilicas and presumably connected with law;[93] a rather muddled text in the Tosefta and the Jerusalem Talmud describes how a criminal[94] is sent from one official to another in order to ensure proper punishment, until he arrives at the provincial governor who puts him to death, but it is just as likely that the obscure terms used for the officials (בעל רצועה, בעל זמרה) refer to Roman military personnel as to city magistrates.[95] It only slightly off-sets this general silence that the rabbis show some small knowledge of court procedure in Greek law—the κατήγωρ and παράκλητος in a legal image,[96] the term "sycophant" to describe an informer,[97] the use of an ἀντίδικος to stand up for the defendant in court,[98] though all such usages may have become simply part of colloquial *koine* by then. At the most such knowledge might show imperfect acquaintance with Greek-style city courts outside Galilee. It gives no reason to suppose the existence of such courts in Tiberias and Sepphoris themselves.

The best explanation for this reticence would be that, since comparative evidence makes it overwhelmingly likely that these cities did have courts of some kind, rabbinic lack of interest in them must indicate either that these courts did not deal with matters which interested the rabbis (and, given the wide scope of the Mishnah, it is hard to see what such matters could be) or that the rabbis viewed the polis courts as of equal standing only with those of the villages. Tiberias and Sepphoris would have courts like other communities in Galilee. Their jurisdiction, like that of the village courts, would cover the local population and anyone else who applied. There was no reason for them to have any higher status in rabbinic eyes. Above all, the cities must have administered a legal system reasonably similar to that of the villages to have elicited no rabbinic opposition. They too must have had a Semitic system rather than a Greek one, and if they were used more often by those with difficult cases to settle it would have been purely because of the city courts' greater ability to impose their decisions through their influence with the Roman authorities.

It should not surprise if the Galilean poleis administered Semitic rather than Greek law. The degree of Hellenization of private law will have varied considerably between different cities in Syria in the same way as their general culture. Some Greek elements are easy to find: the main element in the Volksrecht of the Syro-Roman law book is Greek,[99] the second century parchment contract from Dura under Parthian rule contains good Greek law,[100] and the Syriac slave sale from third century Edessa is basically Hellenistic apart from the language.[101] On the other hand, Dura and Edessa were both *originally* Greek foundations, unlike those in Galilee, and many of the legal notions disapproved of by the Roman authorities after 212 were clearly not Greek but Semitic.[102] ·The law of the Syro-Roman law book is largely Semitic in such matters as intestacy,[103] while the requirement by the Petran boule that an orphan should still have a guardian when aged 22 does not accord exactly with either Greek or Roman law but seems to have been local law analogous to that in contemporary Egypt.[104] The Edessan slave sale had both a Semitic ruling with regard to the probationary period required for the sale to be complete[105] and a Semitic form of signing the document and a Semitic κυρεία clause.[106] Finally, a slave sale from Ashkelon was full of semitisms in formulation.[107] It emerges from the Judaean Desert documents too that law in local use was a mixture of Greek and Semitic elements, with both Greek form and Greek content used in conjunction with Semitic legal concepts and language.[108] The cases cited above from elsewhere in Syria should show that this was not just a peculiarity of village law but also the law enforced by the city courts. Probably those poleis that retained a greater proportion of descendants of Greek colonists still aware of their origin would have preferred a more Hellenized law—as was the case in Roman Egypt[109] and doubtless the reason for the Greek kind of law in Dura-Europus.[110] It is also possible that in some cities a *choice* of law was permitted if the phrase "κατὰ δίπλωμα Ἑλληνικόν" in a third century slave sale from Bostra indicates the existence of alternative Semitic or Greek (or Roman?) sale formulas all recognized by the city.[111]

Perhaps the best solution to the confusion is that suggested by H. J. Wolff on examination of the Judaean Desert papyrus hoard: that the Roman administration required Greek cities to use Greek forms and language in their legal proceedings[112] just as they required the cities to have Greek constitutions on the surface,[113] but that the legal concepts applied remained entirely local in all matters concerning marriage, property, contract, and wills.[114] How Greek or Semitic the content of the law was will have depended on the customs of the local population. Outside Galilee some of the cities were perhaps sufficiently Semitic to recognize marriage customs similar to those of the village courts;[115] within Galilee, city law was precisely the same as village law, the mixture of Jewish and Greek elements that is preserved in the civil law of the Mishnah.[116]

If it is correct that the law in use was identical, was there any reason for Jews from the Galilean villages to use the city courts at all? To some extent, the answer is that there was no reason, whence the rabbinic reticence. But the cities did have greater Roman backing, as elsewhere in the empire, and they had an efficient and trustworthy court administration, in particular in the secure preservation of documents in archives for presentation to the court when disputes arose. The archives were repositories for public documents (particularly regarding taxation) and for private contracts, and were found in Greek cities in all the eastern empire including Syria.[117] They were also found in Jerusalem before 70.[118] In Sepphoris the royal archives attested before 70 are likely to have become the city archives after, as at Edessa.[119] The rabbis have much to say about the use of such archives. They tend to talk about gentile archives (i.e., those in the surrounding non-Jewish cities) but this is only because the rabbis wish to show the extent of their leniency in permitting their use to almost anyone at almost any time, precisely because they are so essential: according to the Mishnah, all documents that were deposited (עולים) in the archives of the gentiles were valid except for divorce and emancipation documents,[120] and R. Shimon is reported to have permitted even those so long as they have been drawn up by experts, gentile or not.[121] The Tosefta allows a Cohen to render himself impure in order to give evidence and be judged in the archives of the gentiles,[122] from which it is clear that the function of the archives in deciding law suits was central. It seems that sales involving gentiles were especially reckoned to require witnessing in the archives, perhaps because of mutual suspicion. One passage mentions sales of land, houses, vineyards, animals, and slaves all being registered;[123] to make a gift of land safe from challenge it must be recorded and sealed in the archives—the duty of the donator according to Tosefta and a parable in Sifre;[124] a Jew forced to sell his house to gentiles for idolatrous purposes will nonetheless accept the money and write out a document for the archives to record the sale;[125] documents showing loans on interest between Jews are openly deposited in the archives to the rabbis' disgust;[126] marriage documents were recorded in the archives[127] as were manumissions[128] and, probably, wills.[129] These were city institutions under the control of paid officials who were clearly considered trustworthy. They are not named in the rabbinic texts[130] but can be presumed nonetheless, as they are attested by Josephus and the Edessan documents and, above all, by the Syro-Roman law book of later date.[131] It is evident, from the number of documents hoarded by Babata and from the reiterated insistence in rabbinic texts on the need to hold on to the evidence of divorces, contracts, and so on, that absolute reliance on the archive copy was not wise, but the utility of such depositories was not denied.[132]

Alongside both these local jurisdictions the Romans claimed authority to hear any case they chose. What cases did they hear in practice, and why? Which officials acted as judge and what laws did they implement?

Governors in most provinces tried only those cases in civil law that applicants succeeded in bringing to their notice while they were on their regular but infrequent visits to the assize towns in their area.[133] Such visits were particularly rare in Galilee, if they occurred at all,[134] so that, although it was inherent in a governor's position that he should hear such cases of civil law[135] and the one talmudic passage that seems to deal precisely with such visits refers to cases involving widows and orphans,[136] it usually needed the influence of someone like Julia Crispina, the opponent of Babata, to get a civil case heard before the governor.[137] Rabbinic passages recount instead criminal cases, involving sacrilege, brigands, kidnappers, and thieves, as the business of the governor, as Ulpian did in neighboring Tyre:[138] the governor's concern was the maintenance of public order by law as well as by brute force.[139] Sacrilege included tomb violation as indicated by the first century inscription, possibly from Nazareth, in which the καῖσαρ threatens *capitis damnatio* for interference with the dead.[140] As for brigands, a rabbinic story tells of the execution in Cappadocia of a robber who had operated in Judaea.[141] The Mekhilta describes how a king punishes λῃσταί by prison, execution, or crucifixion.[142]

Rabbis, then, saw governors, when acting as judges, mainly as judges in criminal cases and therefore as essentially hostile. The *commentarii* of the governor, efficient records of trials,[143] were seen as traps from which escape was impossible.[144] The king sitting up on his tribunal (βῆμα) dispensing punishment was a favorite character in parables,[145] the tribunal seen as a reinforcement of his insolent and worldly pride.[146] The evidence for torture and beatings is only found in later rabbinic texts.[147] Instead the rabbis dwell on the unpleasant punishments, with no mention of any of the more lenient legal penalties, such as deportation, that crop up in the Roman legal texts,[148] perhaps because they are reserved by the second century for *honestiores*.[149] Instead there is plenty about the death penalty,[150] and, especially, execution by the sword.[151]

With such a view of Roman administration, Galileans would rarely voluntarily have entrusted their civil law suits to the governor's decision. A parable in Sifre describes how the Romans were to be approached when necessary: a rhetor (לוטייר) hired by the individual concerned would stand by the tribunal and begin to praise the governor (מלך) and his good judgment. After a while he would mention the request of his client, only to revert as rapidly as possible to praise and flattery.[152] It was the method used by the sophist Apuleius in his contemporary speech against a criminal charge for using magic[153] and, as for him, it doubtless often worked well.

The governor was the only Roman administrator entrusted with general jurisdiction over both civil and criminal law, and in Galilee he was a far-off figure little frequented. More junior Roman officials might come into closer contact with the Galileans and, as elsewhere in the empire, usurp jurisdiction—the practical weakness of governors, with their power limited because of lack of time to apply it, led some of them to delegate to procurators in their provinces[154] and led some procurators to usurp a governor's role for the same reason,[155] a process that received steadily increasing imperial recognition during the second and third centuries.[156] Procurators in Palestine in this period were of high rank[157] and could without a doubt have heard cases involving their business (namely, the all-important collection of taxation),[158] but there are only a very few muddled rabbinic passages referring to their jurisdiction being invoked in any specific matter. A Sifre parable concerns an ἐπίτροπος (procurator) against whom the local people (בני מדינה) spoke, only to be told that the king would take complaints against his procurator as directed against him personally.[159] A Mekhilta passage states that the decree of an *epitropos* can be revoked by a χιλίαρχος, δεκουρίων, ἡγεμών, ἔπαρχος, ὑπατικός, or emperor[160]—putting a procurator on a lower level of authority than a number of military officers as well as the governor. Only in the fourth century is there a talmudic description of appeal from a *centenarius* (i.e., junior procurator) to the governor (*eparchos*).[161] This sparse crop of evidence suggests that Roman officials may have steered clear of hearing cases involving Galilean Jews unless they really needed to, though soldiers may be found setting up informal courts as elsewhere in the empire at this time if the *chiliarchos, dekouriōn,* and *hēgemōn* in the passage cited above were indeed Roman military officers.[162] In this case too, however, it was unlikely that Jews would willingly call in military arbitration and it would be unnecessary for soldiers not actually stationed in the area to try criminal cases rather than to take the accused to Caesarea, which was not so far away.[163] This passage must be viewed as exceptional.

As for the kind of law enforced, it seems almost certain that in criminal cases no Roman official would ever enforce any law other than that of Rome, whether judging Jews as Roman citizens or *peregrini* (or indeed *dediticii* if they ever were such),[164] however modified that law might have become, particularly after 212, through the pressures of local custom.[165] So, for example, it was Roman law that was applied to non-Roman Jews in first century Alexandria for cases of murder and adultery.[166]

On the other hand, there is evidence from Egypt that in *civil* cases involving marriage and succession some cognizance might, on rare occasions, have been taken of local customs. If any one Roman citizen was involved, Roman law always applied,[167] but in suits between Egyptian Greeks it seems that recourse might have been had to Egyptian practices, the ignorant Roman judge using the good offices of a local lawyer to explain the rules.[168] In this way the harshness involved in the application of Roman law when many provincials were ignorant of the terms of that law[169] could be offset. In general, too, there are indications from outside Egypt that the institution of a less formal *ius gentium* for foreign private suits in a Roman forum[170] enabled judges to take account of local custom when they so wished[171] and especially when it was politically advantageous to Rome.[172] Even at those periods after A.D. 212 of greatest insistence on the formalities (as under Diocletian),[173] modification of the Roman law was still permitted for the sake of the provincials.[174] Similar leniency during the period when many of Rome's subjects were still not Roman citizens is suggested in the sources—use of languages other than Latin and Greek in contracts was permitted[175] and the validity of contracts was upheld even when they were not drawn up correctly.[176]

The same pattern of occasional partial recognition of local law is likely in civil cases in Roman Palestine. The problem will be to evaluate the extent of the practice. The evidence, unfortunately, is inconclusive.

Those surviving contracts from the Judaean Desert that involve Roman soldiers or veterans as well as locals all, as might be expected from the Egyptian parallels, use Roman law, presumably at the instance of the Roman party and presumably for enforcement by the Roman courts. So, a loan by a soldier to a Jew, probably in A.D. 171, had interest on repayment stipulated as "ἐκ διατάγματος"[177] and the loan of sixty denarii borrowed by Judas of Ein Gedi from a centurion against a mortgage on his father's house had Roman terms.[178] So far as can be deduced from the fragmentary papyrus copy of a report of the verbal process before a Roman court, Roman law was invoked in a dispute between the Jewish women Salome and Miriam and a veteran over property boundaries.[179]

But this does not surprise. It is in Roman arbitration between locals that, as in Egypt, use of local law might be looked for.

There are hints in the Judaean Desert documents that such recognition of local law might be found in Palestine—but the hints are not decisive because there are also strong suggestions of Roman insistence on adherence to Roman legal forms. A phrase in a sale of wine stipulates that the fine for breaking the contract should be paid to "our lord Caesar" (למרנא קיסרא),[180] but, annoyingly, the present inadequate report of the papyrus gives no indication of the other terms of this wine sale. If the terms were those normal in local law, then that was presumably the law invoked by the governor or whomever to extract the fine; if Roman law, it is remarkable that Aramaic speakers are found using it. On the other hand, another document from the same hoard would indicate that Roman courts in fact applied only Roman law: the blank forms for an *actio* against an orphan's guardian preserve in good Greek almost the exact text of Gaius 4.42–52[181] and were intended for use in Babata's lawsuit before the governor.[182] Roman law for trustees and guardians was radically different from Jewish or Greek law, and Jews might justifiably have hesitated to take on such burdens voluntarily if it involved entanglement in a Roman legal morass. It is therefore all the more striking here that Babata's insistence on Roman forms was even more severe than that found elsewhere in the empire. Why should Babata want such a document unless the Roman authorities demanded it? It is possible to find other answers, but none is really satisfactory. Perhaps she nourished a hope that the adjudicator chosen by the governor after formal application would be given a sufficiently loosely-worded formula to enable him to take account of local legal custom,[183] but this cannot be proved. Attempts have been made to confirm this hypothesis by pointing to the insertion of the term "ξενοκριταί" in the Greek translation of Gaius in place of *iudex* in the original but, despite its possible literal meaning of "alien judges," this word is still too little understood to justify conclusion from its appearance alone that such assessors were expected to use local law.[184] All in all, the Judaean Desert evidence still leaves the question open.

Rabbinic evidence is of only little help in clarifying the position. Some texts suggest that, in at least some cases, strict Roman law was applied in contravention of local custom since Roman legal actions may appear occasionally in rabbinic sources as ground for complaint. One explanation given for attacks on the *mazikin* (oppressors) so hated by the rabbis is that they had confiscated property from others for non-repayment of loans on interest, a process of *cessio* quite natural in Roman law but an anathema to Jews of this period.[185] Other texts, however, support the contrary thesis of Roman enforcement of local law. These passages envisage the possibility of a gentile court compelling a man to carry out the decision of a Jewish village or rabbinical court with regard to divorce and halizah,[186] and have been explained as examples of the Roman administration following local law with, presumably, the advice of rabbis as *iurisprudentes* for the interpretation of Jewish custom.[187] But this is not the only possible explanation. I have suggested above that the gentiles concerned here were not Roman but from nearby cities, like the Petran βουλή which dealt with Babata.[188] Alternatively, if Roman courts were indeed involved, the texts may show only the occasional congruence of Roman verdicts based on Roman law with Jewish verdicts based on Jewish law[189] or, more positively, that in cases where Roman law had no view (such as halizah) the Roman administration was occasionally indeed prepared to follow local desires in the interests of the good order of the province.[190]

But it needs to be stressed that all the evidence—Egyptian, Judaean, and rabbinic—of Roman cognizance of local law in civil cases can show this adherence to have been the case only on exceptional occasions. Roman governors had no training in comparative law. There was no requirement in Roman constitutional theory for such cognizance to be taken. There is no trace in any Palestinian evidence of the *systematic* use of local lawyers, rabbis or otherwise, in provincial administration. It must be assumed that, whatever the exceptions, Roman courts usually used Roman law.

The prevalence of Greek and Semitic law in Roman Galilee would have been due, if this account is correct, to the success of the population in keeping their affairs, particularly those concerning the family and inheritance, out of the governor's court and thereby avoiding conflict. It was not always possible: the law used in appointing the guardians of Babata's son was local but a Roman tribunal would presumably have used Roman law to judge the case,[191] and a passage in the Tosefta already cited may envisage a criminal being passed for punishment from a city court to the governor.[192] The result was bound to be a growing awareness by each judicature of the legal concepts of the other systems, so that, even though none of the judicatures had any *formal* procedure for taking cognizance of foreign law, nonetheless the practice of ordinary people in trying to comply with those other laws filtered back to the judges who tried the cases in which they were involved and led one system to influence the other.

Much work has been done by legal historians to trace such influence between Roman and Jewish or Jewish and Greek law.[193] Many similarities have emerged: *lex talionis*, *usucapio*, funeral restrictions, *traditio clavum*, and other Roman concepts are apparent in Jewish law[194] as are Greek usages such as the διαθήκη for gifts in anticipation of death.[195] It is plausible that the separate tiers of jurisdiction in contemporary Palestine caused some of these similarities through their influence on one another, but clearly it is not necessarily the right explanation since others might be equally valid: parallel growth of Roman and Jewish law from the second century B.C. under Greek scholarly influence on the categorizing of material[196] and in response to similar problems in society; unacknowledged borrowing of Jewish ideas by scholars of Roman law in the new university at Beirut[197] or of Roman ideas by rabbinic iurisprudentes in the creation of an artificial system; Roman use of legal concepts borrowed from oriental sources, including Carthage, at the very beginning of the development of Roman law;[198] the borrowing of specific Greek ideas by both Roman and Jewish lawyers at roughly the same time because those ideas were proving useful when put into actual practice.[199] It is more likely in all this that complete legal institutions from one society, such as inheritance or the *peculium* of a slave, would be imitated by another society, than that specific rules would be transfered, unless those rules, like the valid ways of making a sale,[200] affected everyday life.

There seems no certain way to pick among these options but good grounds for asserting that conflict of jurisdiction *could* be one of the more important methods of influence. Evidence from Egypt shows precisely this sort of influence by Roman and Greek law on native Egyptian customs in the second century.[201] The Jewish evidence shows plenty of Greek influence in the tannaitic texts and Judaean Desert documents[202] but similarities to Roman law only in texts after the third century.[203] If similarity is partly accounted for by influence and influence by conflicts of jurisdiction, then this change in Jewish law would support, however tentatively, the hypothesis that Roman jurisdiction was invoked only rarely in the period here discussed, only to be drastically increased after 212.

PART IV: CONCLUSION

11   The Second Century and After

In Roman Galilee of the second century A.D. Greek and Semitic elements were combined within a Jewish framework to produce a coherent culture. Galilee differed little from surrounding areas in this since throughout Syria such Greek and Semitic traits were to be found mixed in a similar fashion. If there was nonetheless variety in Syria, it lay solely in the different emphasis given to one ingredient or the other in the cultural fusion: in Phoenician cities and Antioch, and particularly in places like Dura-Europus where a Greek colony was the foundation of the community, Greek characteristics predominated, whereas in the desert communities of the Nabateans and Palmyrenes the native tradition remained strongest. Second century Galilee, despite geographical proximity to some of the former group, was culturally more akin to the latter.

That this was so was due in no small measure to the nature of Rome's rule. The Romans left Galilee alone. Indifference was not caused by the unruliness of the Jews,[1] for there is no sign of intensive garrisoning of Galilee itself.[2] Nor was it the result of pressure on the administration to divert attention elsewhere. Though the third century preoccupation of the Roman state with frontier wars and its consequent ignoring of interior provinces helped to *confirm* Galileans in their idiosyncratic culture (especially since the concomitant comparative impoverishment of cities through taxation levied by means of, and therefore largely from, the city aristocracies rendered less attractive the benefits of urban life, which depended to a great extent on the voluntary contributions to city finances made by such aristocracies),[3] it is nonetheless significant that Galilean culture was formed in the stable conditions of the *second* century. The causes of Roman indifference were more basic than these and concerned Rome's ideology for ruling her empire: governors still operated on the amateurish principles left over from the Republic,[4] intervened only when essential for the preservation of order or income from taxation, and otherwise stayed content to enjoy the leisured life of Roman aristocrats and leave the natives in peace.

The looseness of Roman rule in Galilee was created by the desire of the inhabitants. It was the provincials who had to call in Rome to sort out their disputes or answer their requests, and elsewhere in the empire this is common. But from bitterness caused by two revolts the Jews of Galilee did not wish to do so. In striking contrast to the continued intensification of voluntarily increased Hellenization by villagers elsewhere in the eastern empire in their search for πόλις status,[5] the Galileans opted out. Such refusals to participate in the life of the empire are less well documented outside Galilee—it is precisely the participants who get into the Greek and Latin sources.[6] But the Jewish sources suggest that others also may have opted out and left no trace. By the second century Roman interest in cultural imperialism, the evidence for which is anyway very weak and confined to the west, seems to have waned completely. Cities that were founded then received the status not from Roman policy but of their own will, through Hellenization or as a particular favor from a specific emperor. For the others, nonparticipation was demonstrated not by the deliberate snubbing of Roman art, architecture, or language (since in Galilee all these show signs of Roman, or at least Greek, influence),[7] but by the deliberate adoption of a native system of education in which no attention was paid to the teaching of the Greek classics and in which no pupil was ever taught an interest in Greek rhetoric.[8] It was this last lack that disqualified Jews in Galilee from the Roman administrative service that would otherwise have welcomed them, and it rendered even their aristocrats strange and unfamiliar to Roman officials. Education was the decisive element in alienation from Rome; a similar rejection of Greek education led to the emergence of a distinctive provincial culture elsewhere in Syria in the fourth to fifth centuries.[9]

Roman Galilee, then, is a useful paradigm for Roman provincial history. The detailed inspection of one village society will not necessarily indicate the features to be found in other villages elsewhere in the empire, but from such a study it should become clearer what questions can be validly asked about life in such communities, about the interaction of geographical, economic, and cultural factors in the shaping of the world view of their inhabitants, and about the relation of the rural communities of the Roman world to the Roman state. It remains to be seen whether separate studies of the rural settlements of

Asia Minor or north Syria would come to similar conclusions from their far more meager evidence.

For scholars of Jewish history, the place and period give this study a particular importance. The methods here adopted offer peripheral insights—like a new way of checking on the reliability of those *baraitot* in the Talmuds that purport to refer to the second century and whose sociological assumptions can be examined for accuracy in the light of the more reliable information collected here; a check of this sort on the king parables found in the Mekhiltas suggests that they are more reliable than Wacholder's study intimated.[10] But second century Galilee is worth studying also for its own sake, because it witnessed the society that shaped traditional rabbinic Judaism.

Galilee before Bar Kokhba had been something of a backwater in religious terms. The area had had only limited contact with the Temple cult,[11] following a lackadaisical religious practice of synagogue readings and Sabbath observance[12] with only the occasional excitement of mildly heretical holy men to whip up religious fervor.[13] It was a country of Semitic village culture apart from implanted cities such as Tiberias with their greater knowledge of the Hellenistic world outside[14] and their greater freedom from the traditional Galilean paranoia about gentile enemies on the borders of their territory.[15] Most Galileans, as Freyne has recently shown from the evidence before A.D. 70, regarded the production of fertile crops as of primary interest and saw religion, from Temple pilgrimages to fasts during drought, as means towards that end. Galileans kept the ancestral Law and worshipped the Jewish God, but they had no interest in the eschatological fervor stirred up around the Temple cult in Jerusalem, and they were not involved in the speculative framework built around the Law by the Pharisaic forebears of the rabbis.

The two Jewish revolts brought Galilee firmly into the center of the political, social, and religious life of the remnants of the Palestinian Jewish population. The immigration of huge numbers of Jews after the two revolts brought shock, and rapidly a boost, to the economy.[16] It brought, too, the wider cultural horizons of Judaea and the rabbis as a ginger group to Galilean Judaism. From 132 to 212 the economy developed to the flourishing state enjoyed in the third century. Galileans achieved an independent confidence and relaxed their hostility to external trends in art and architecture. The more worldly-wise Judaean immigrants settled not only in the already superficially

Hellenized cities but also in the villages of Upper and Lower Galilee, bringing with them new ideas and expertise as artisans that in turn helped to fuel the Galilean economy.

Among these immigrant Judaeans were members of the rabbinical schools. Over this period they grew steadily in influence among the inhabitants of Galilee, an influence that consolidated into secular power only in the mid third century and that was recognized by Rome only in the fourth.[17] This process of acquiring power changed the nature of the religion that the rabbis purveyed and effectively created the present form of rabbinic Judaism.

Immigrant rabbis preaching a religion based on purity and tithes were greeted with no enthusiasm by Galilean farmers.[18] The wealthy might be prepared to use rabbis as educators for their sons but did not want them as arbiters of their religious consciences.[19] The economic demands made by rabbis on farmers were heavy. Purity laws required the destruction of impure earthenware and some other utensils[20] and much time and care in checking foodstuffs in storage and cooking, and tithing took a sizeable portion of agricultural produce. The Sabbatical year cut a farmer's income by a seventh more or less; the laws of *kilaim* prevented the most efficient use of precious land.[21] Rabbinical decrees forbade the export of grain, wine, and oil surpluses from Palestine.[22] Galileans, it seems, were not prepared to accede to the rabbis' demands, especially since the rabbis of the second century were on the whole artisans unaffected themselves by many of the agricultural laws that they tried to impose on the farmers.[23]

Toward the end of our period a few of the richer rabbis seem to have understood the obstacles in the way of their authority being accepted when they too, like most who wished to invest in ancient times, put their money into land and became farmers. So R. Judah ha Nasi is said to have owned huge estates[24] as did the wealthy R. Yannai from Sepphoris in the mid third century.[25] Furthermore, the descendants of the artisans who had come from Judaea in the aftermath of war were joined as rabbis by students from among the local population. Many of them will have been the sons of the Galilean landed aristocracy since they are the most likely sector of the community to have been able to afford the leisure for study in the rabbinic academies of Sepphoris and Tiberias. This change in the economic status of rabbis brought a change in their attitude towards priorities in the Law. It is no accident that R. Yannai and the family of the Nasi are precisely the rabbis whom the later tradition records opposing the rabbinic laws that fell hardest on the farmers: R. Judah ha Nasi excluded areas from the theoretical boundary of Eretz Israel in order to exempt them from the Sabbatical year laws[26] and is reported to have wanted to abolish *Shebiit* altogether;[27] this being prevented, his son R. Gamaliel and R. Yannai between them nevertheless lifted the restrictions on the Sabbatical year so far that in the end ploughing and sowing ceased to be forbidden and only reaping continued to be banned.[28] Furthermore, from the mid third century it seems that scrupulous attention to the purity laws and to the payment of tithes ceased to be viewed by rabbis as *the* crucial characteristic of an acceptable religious Jew.[29] Study and discussion of purity laws and the laws of tithing continue in the Yerushalmi, but since it is clear that the division of Jews into the scrupulous and the less scrupulous was no longer considered the most important factor it must be assumed that, although careful observance was considered by the later Talmudic rabbis to be good and praiseworthy behavior, it was viewed as supererogatory piety rather than as the duty of *every* Jew.[30] That is, the dropping of the clear distinction between *am haarez* and *haver* was a step toward the ignorance of purity laws found among many religious Jews in the Middle Ages. It is of a piece with the relaxation of rabbinic strictness in other cases: usury was permitted in cases of need or for the purposes of charity[31] and there was an end to the theoretical rabbinic ban on the export of wine and fruit outside Palestine[32] as well as a relaxation of the ban on gentile oil.[33]

An explanation is needed of such changes in rabbinic law, for they amount in effect to a complete change in its direction. Instead of the tannaitic insistence that observance of tithing and purity laws marked out the truly religious Jew and was therefore incumbent on all Jews, the third and fourth century rabbis seemed to relax vigilance and, while still elaborating the fence around the Law, seem to view with equanimity breaches of correct purity and tithing behavior by other Jews with whom they came increasingly into contact. If keeping the tithing and purity laws was considered mandatory by the rabbis for every Jew in the second century, it needs to be explained why they ceased to stress this in the third and fourth.[34] This is a problem that has been noted before and there is a conventional answer that the economy required "normalizing" to offset the strain of an economic crisis in the third century,[35] while it has even been asserted that gentile oil was permitted because Galilean Jews were suffering without such essential commodities.[36] The whole of this study goes to show the conventional answers wrong, because there was no such economic crisis in Galilee. On the contrary, the economic gains of the second century were consolidated in the third into a confident and wealthy village culture.

The demands of the rabbis changed because the prosperous farmers of these Galilean villages were prepared to accept rabbinic religious and secular leadership only when such change had come about. Even in the second century the rabbinic world view ought to have had certain attractions for Jews in Galilee, for it made a virtue of, and gave sense to, the need for protection of national identity and group solidarity against external hostility that Palestinian Jews were bound to feel after the bloody failure of two revolts and the accompanying surge of anti-Jewish feeling among the gentiles of nearby cities. Galileans might be expected to have been prepared, and indeed glad, to accept the essence of the view of self and society that the rabbis offered, to be happy to see the inclination they instinctively felt for living among Jews and away from gentiles elevated by the rabbinic system to the status of a search for holiness, and to be reassured that correct behavior at the table and in bed could bring the expiation and blessing on them and their farms that the destroyed Temple had once ensured. But the synagogues were beginning to offer an easier way of reaching the same end, as the gradual attribution of sanctity to synagogue buildings shows, and in the second century the attraction of rabbinic teachings was hampered by the heavy economic burdens that the rabbis demanded in observance of tithes and the Sabbatical year, to the benefit only of priests who no longer served a useful liturgical function. The rabbis, not least those who had attained a natural secular influence through acquired or, in the case of indigenous Galileans, inherited wealth, wanted to be recognized throughout Galilee as the political and religious leaders of society. When that society rejected their religious demands they modified those demands until they became what society wanted.

The result was a more relaxed religious view of the world. The rabbis of the fourth century cheerfully permitted the portrayal of the sun god on the floor of the Hammath Tiberias synagogue and their chief representatives, the patriarchs, conversed on easy social terms with Greek pagan orators and Roman governors. The modification of the ideals of the tannaim reflected the influence of a prosperous Galilean population on the intense scholars who had come up from Judaea, and it was a modification that therefore succeeded in winning the support of that population. Rabbis of the fourth century stressed precisely those areas of the Law—the Sabbath, circumcision, *kashrut*, and *niddah*—that Galilean Jews had kept *before* the rabbis had become their spiritual leaders. The rabbis explained and sanctified, using the careful structure built up by the tannaim, the ordinary and long-established behavior of the Galilean peasant communities, and those peasants were therefore prepared to accept that pious behavior was within their own grasp and that the insights of the rabbis applied not just to special holy men but to every Jew. It was then that rabbinic Judaism won their support and that of the Jewish nation.

Notes

Chapter 1

1. For general accounts of the Jews in this period, see E. M. Smallwood, *The Jews under Roman Rule from Pompey to Diocletian* (Leiden, 1976); M. Grant, *The Jews in the Roman World* (London, 1973); J. Juster, *Les Juifs dans l'Empire Romain: Leur Condition Juridique, Économique et Sociale*, 2 vols. (Paris, 1914); G. Alon, *Toledot haYehudim be Eretz Yisrael be Tekufat haMishnah vehaTalmud*, 2 vols., Vol. 1 (2nd ed., Tel Aviv, 1967), Vol. 2 (Tel Aviv, 1961) (Heb.); M. Avi-Yonah, *The Jews of Palestine: A Political History from the Bar Kokhba War to the Arab Conquest* (Oxford, 1976). Specifically on Galilee is S. Klein, *Eretz haGalil miyeme haaliyah miBavel ad hatimat haTalmud*, edited by Y. Eltizur, (Jerusalem, 1967).
2. E.g., Smallwood, *Jews*. Only 39 of the 545 pages of this book discuss Antonine and Severan Palestine, and they concentrate mainly on relations between Rome and the Jews (p. 467, n. 1).
3. A. H. M. Jones, *The Cities of the Eastern Roman Provinces*, 2nd ed., revised by M. Avi-Yonah et al. (Oxford, 1971), pp. 274-81 [hereafter *CERP*].
4. Cf. abuse of fourth-century material by J. Juster, *Les Juifs* 1: 391, despite his awareness of the problems (ibid., 1: 393).
5. Rabbinic texts are ignored by M. Rostovtzeff, *The Social and Economic History of the Roman World*, 2nd ed., 2 vols. (Oxford, 1957), especially pp. 664-65. M. Heichelheim tried to use them in T. Frank, ed., *An Economic Survey of Ancient Rome*, 5 vols., 1933-40, Vol. 4 (Baltimore, 1938), pp. 121-258, but not systematically. Cf. A. N. Sherwin-White, *Roman Society and Roman Law in the New Testament* (Oxford, 1963), p. v: "Scholars attempting to deal with two worlds of this magnitude need two lives."
6. E. Schürer, *History of the Jewish People in the Age of Jesus Christ*, 2 vols. so far, English ed. based on 4th German ed., 1909, revised by G. Vermes, F. G. B. Millar, and M. Black (Edinburgh, 1973-79), ends his account in A.D. 135.
7. So, for example, J. Jeremias, *Jerusalem in the time of Jesus*, trans. by F. H. Cave and C. H. Cave (London, 1969), and S. Freyne, *Galilee from Alexander the Great to Hadrian 323 B.C.E. to 135 C.E.* (Notre Dame, 1980). Freyne's study of the period from A.D. 70 to 135 rests on unreliable and secondhand use of the rabbinic evidence (see my review in *JJS* 32 (1981): 205-6).
8. E.g., see I. H. Weiss, *Zur Geschichte der jüdischen Tradition (Dor Dor veDoreshav)*, 5 vols. (Vienna and Vilna, 1883-93), or, more recently, A. Oppenheimer, *The 'Am Ha-aretz: A Study in the Social History of the*

Jewish People in the Hellenistic-Roman Period, translated by I. H. Levine (Leiden, 1977); H. Mantel, *Studies in the History of the Sanhedrin* (Cambridge, Mass., 1961).

9. Most brilliantly by A. Büchler in, e.g., *The Political and the Social Leaders of the Jewish Community of Sepphoris in the Second and Third Centuries* (Oxford, 1909). Many of his conclusions are confirmed below by different methods.

10. For a more detailed attack on the historiography of the slightly earlier period, see the tough but not undeserved strictures of J. Neusner in *Rabbinic Traditions about the Pharisees before 70,* 3 parts (Leiden, 1971), 3: 320–66. For ingenious implausibility, A. Büchler, *Studies in Jewish History* (London, 1956), p. 160, is a fine example.

11. E.g., there are attempts to identify from literary texts fourth-century disasters to explain the destruction at Khorazin or Meiron (Z. Yeivin, "Excavations at Khorazin," *EI* 11 (1973): 157 (Heb.); E. M. Meyers, C. L. Meyers, and J. F. Strange, "Excavations at Meiron in Upper Galilee —1974, 1975: Second Preliminary Report," *AASOR* 43 (1976): 97–98), but the apparent evidence for the fifth century dating of the Capernaum synagogue (V. C. Corbo, S. Loffreda, A. Spijkerman, and E. Testa, *Cafarnao,* 4 vols. (Jerusalem, 1972–75), 1: 163) is believed by, e.g., G. Foerster, "Recent Excavations at Capernaum," *IEJ* 21 (1971): 209, not to be likely to alter the contradictory gloomy picture in literary sources but to be *necessarily incorrect* because of conflict with that picture.

12. E.g., see G. Alon, *Jews, Judaism and the Classical World* (Jerusalem, 1977), pp. 458 ff.

13. S. Lieberman, *Hellenism in Jewish Palestine,* 2nd ed. (New York, 1962) and idem, *Greek in Jewish Palestine* (New York, 1942).

14. D. Sperber, *Roman Palestine 200–400: Money and Prices* (Ramat Gan, 1974); and idem, *Roman Palestine 200–400: the Land: Crisis and Change in Agrarian Society as reflected in Rabbinic Sources* (Ramat Gan, 1978). This is a hazardous and not always successful undertaking. The rabbinic sources are so radically different from the classical evidence that only wishful thinking can correlate the two, and Sperber's method seems designed to obscure the perception of unique factors in Palestine that do not apply to the rest of the empire (but see *Roman Palestine: Money and Prices,* pp. 101–11, where he achieves this for prices in Palestine compared to those elsewhere).

15. In particular the excavators of Khirbet Shema' and Meiron; cf. the whole issue of the journal *Explor: A Journal of Theology* 3, no. 1 (Winter 1977), and E. M. Meyers, A. T. Kraabel, and J. F. Strange, eds., "Ancient Synagogue Excavations at Khirbet Shema', Israel, 1970–72," *AASOR* 42 (1976): 258.

16. Much information on Roman Syria can be deduced from inscriptions (see G. M. Harper, "Village Administration in the Roman Province of Syria," *YCS* 1 (1928): 105–68) and the lives of the saints (see P. Brown, "The Rise and Function of the Holy Man in Late Antiquity," *JRS* 61 (1971): 80–101).

17. Useful introductions to these texts can be found in H. L. Strack, *Introduction to the Talmud and Midrash,* translation of 5th German edition (Philadelphia, 1931): Schürer, *History* 1: 68–118.

18. m Ab. 1: 1–18; Schürer, *History* 1: 76; On dating in general, cf. E. P. Sanders, *Paul and Palestinian Judaism: a Comparison of Patterns of Religion* (London, 1977), pp. 63 ff.

19. So J. Neusner, in an extensive study of the laws of purity, *A History of the Mishnaic Laws of Purity*, 22 parts (Leiden, 1974-77) 21: xiii, arguing from indications of deliberate organization in the final form of the tractates.
20. Ibid. 21: 12, 302-88.
21. Ibid. 21: 307-8.
22. E.g., Alon, *Toledot* 2: 56, and passim. For theories on the *ammei haarez*, see below, pp. 102-4.
23. A. Oppenheimer, *'Am Ha-aretz*, pp. 18-22.
24. Such a study has only just begun. J. Neusner has begun, in *Purities* and his even more recent studies concerning women and Temple worship (J. Neusner, *A History of the Mishnaic Law of Women*, 5 parts (Leiden, 1980), and *A History of the Mishnaic Law of Holy Things*, 6 parts (Leiden, 1980)), the careful tracing of the development of ideas. Sanders, *Paul and Palestinian Judaism*, gives a good account of the assumptions of the tannaim in their work. For older methods, cf. the scholarly but historically almost useless compilation of rabbinic beliefs in E. E. Urbach, *The Sages: Their Concepts and Beliefs*, translated by I. Abrahams (Jerusalem, 1975).
25. Examples are numerous. Avi-Yonah, *Jews*, p. 105, n. 97, is a particularly blatant case.
26. See above, n. 21.
27. So J. Neusner, *The Rabbinic Traditions about the Pharisees before 70*, 3 parts (Leiden, 1971) 1: 1; idem, *Purities* 21: 3: "apologetic."
28. L. Jacobs, "How much of the Babylonian Talmud is Pseudepigraphic," *JJS* 28 (1977): 46-59; see B. M. Bokser, *Samuel's Commentary on the Mishnah: its Nature, Forms and Content* (Leiden, 1975), for early adaptions of Mishnah in Amoraic Babylonia.
29. In many cases this will cause my account to differ considerably from that given in, e.g., S. Safrai and M. Stern, eds., *The Jewish People in the First Century: Historical Geography* . . ., Compendia Rerum Judaicarum ad Novum Testamentum: Section One, 2 vols. (Assen, 1974-76) [hereafter *Compendia*]. When the reason is solely my refusal to use late texts, I have avoided purely destructive argument *ad hominem*—the principle, once established, does not need reiteration.
30. Strack, *Introduction to Talmud*, p. 3.
31. Schürer, *History* 1: 76. Pirkei Abot, according to B. Z. Dinur, "The Tractate Aboth (Sayings of the Fathers) as an Historical Source," *Zion* 35 (1970): 2-3 (Heb.), is late third century, with the last two chapters added even later.
32. S. Safrai, "The Nesiut in the Second and Third Centuries and its Chronological Problems," in M. Jagendorf and A. Shinan, eds., *Proceedings of the Sixth World Congress of Jewish Studies*, vols. 1-3 (to be completed in 5 vols.) (Jerusalem, 1975-   ) 2: 51-57 (Heb.), suggests that R. Judah was still alive in A.D. 222.
33. Oral transmission: Lieberman, *Hellenism in Palestine*, pp. 83-99; for differences between Palestinian and Babylonian texts, see W. H. Lowe, *The Mishnah of the Palestinian Talmud* (Cambridge, 1883); for variants in baraitot, see above, n. 25.
34. Strack, *Introduction to Talmud*, p. 75.
35. M. D. Herr, in *Encyclopedia Judaica* 15: 1284.
36. Neusner, *Purities*, builds up a coherent picture of tannaitic ideas of purity from Mishnah and Tosefta alone; see 21: 15-16.
37. J. Neusner, *The Tosefta translated from the Hebrew*, 6 divisions, *Sixth Division: Tohorot* (Leiden, 1977), p. 10.

38. M. D. Herr, in *Encyclopedia Judaica* 11: 1269.
39. B. Z. Wacholder, "The Date of the Mekhilta de-Rabbi Ishmael," *HUCA* 39 (1968): 117–44. But cf. the acceptance of the "rediscovered" Zohar in thirteenth-century Spain: G. Scholem, *Major Trends in Jewish Mysticism* (New York, 1941), pp. 156 ff.
40. S. Abramson, "A new fragment of the Mekhilta de-Rabbi Shim'on bar Yohai," *Tarbiz* 41 (1971–72): 361–72 (Heb.).
41. Schürer, *History*, 1: 90; G. Vermes, *Scripture and Tradition in Judaism: Haggadic Studies* (Leiden, 1961), pp. 3–4.
42. Sanders, *Paul and Palestinian Judaism*, pp. 68–69.
43. A. J. Saldarini, " 'Form Criticism' of Rabbinic Literature," *JBL* 96 (1977): 264.
44. Cf. conclusions below, Chapter 11, n. 10.
45. Weiss, *Geschichte*, is the classic compilation.
46. Cf. Jacobs, "Babylonian Talmud as Pseudepigraphic," pp. 57–58.
47. Neusner, *Purities* 21: 5–6, and all Neusner's recent work.
48. Y. Sussman, "A Halakhic Inscription from the Beth-Shean valley," *Tarbiz* 43 (1973–74): 88–158 (Heb.). The inscription, from the seventh century, lays down the laws about the Sabbatical Year for the Beth-Shean area, with significant additions to the corresponding text in the Jerusalem Talmud.
49. D. Ben Amos, "Narrative Forms in the Aggada: Structural Analysis," (Ph.D. diss., Univ. of Indiana, 1967). Cf. parallel problems in the study of Byzantine saints' lives: E. Patlagean, "À Byzance: Ancienne Hagiographie et Histoire Sociale," *Annales* 23 (1968): 106–23.
50. Neusner, *Purities* 21: 13, and passim; idem, *Pharisees before 70*, 3: 3, on the general reliability of attributions after 70 and especially after 140.
51. See above, n. 24.
52. Strack, *Introduction to Talmud*, p. 24.
53. E.g., Matt. 9: 35; Mark 1: 21.
54. Neusner, *Purities* 21: 309 ff., 322 ff.
55. P. Benoit, J. T. Milik, and R. de Vaux, *Les Grottes de Murabba'at*, Discoveries in the Judaean Desert, Vol. 2 (Oxford, 1960), pp. 67–280 [hereafter DJD 2]; Y. Yadin in N. Avigad et al., "The Expedition to the Judaean Desert, 1961," *IEJ* 12 (1962): 235–57; and H. J. Polotsky, ibid.: 258–62.
56. Compare the unreality of some Qumran texts, e.g., *The War Rule* (G. Vermes, *The Dead Sea Scrolls in English* (Harmondsworth, 1962), pp. 124–48, and his comments on pp. 123–4); for the possible relations of "artificial" views of society to that society, see J. Z. Smith, *Map is not Territory* (Leiden, 1978), especially p. 309. For the use of the *Digest* for social history, see J. A. Crook, *Law and Life of Rome* (London, 1967).
57. The best introduction may be found in T. Rajak, "Josephus: Jewish History and the Greek World," (D.Phil. thesis, Oxford University, 1974), forthcoming as idem, *Josephus: The Historian and his Society* (London, 1983).
58. Ibid., passim, especially pp. 40, 45–46.
59. So in particular the Greek Luke with his talk of *poleis*; see below, pp. 128–34.
60. A. N. Sherwin-White, *Roman Society and Roman Law in the New Testament* (Oxford, 1963), p. 122.
61. G. Vermes, *Jesus the Jew: A Historian's Reading of the Gospels* (London, 1973), p. 48.
62. Text in K. Lake, ed., *The Apostolic Fathers*, 2 vols. (Cambridge, Mass., 1912), Vol. 1; discussion of origins in *Oxford Dictionary of the Christian Church*, s.v. "Didache."

63. Origen, *c. Celsum* praef. 6; for the date, cf. H. Chadwick, *Origen: Contra Celsum* (Cambridge, 1953), pp. xiv–xv.

64. N. R. M. de Lange, *Origen and the Jews: Studies in Jewish-Christian Relations in Third Century Palestine* (Cambridge, 1976), pp. 8–9.

65. E.g., Origen, *c. Celsum* 8. 69: "Jews have not a plot of ground nor a habitation left . . . for their sins."

66. De Lange, *Origen and the Jews*, p. 28, is not justified in claiming that: "There is no doubt that Origen visited all the important centres of Jewish scholarship." Cf. the problems faced by Joseph of Tiberias in the fourth century (Epiphanius, *Panarion* 30. 4).

67. Eusebius, *History of the Martyrs in Palestine*, edited by W. Cureton (London, 1861).

68. Eusebius, *Onomasticon* 303; Yeivin, "Excavations at Khorazin," pp. 144–57.

69. Epiphanius, *Panarion* 30. 4–12.

70. Much of Jerome is heavily influenced by Origen and it might be possible to extract third-century evidence from his works, but it would be difficult.

71. Sources for this are gathered in S. Applebaum, *Prolegomena to the Study of the Second Jewish Revolt (A.D. 132–135)*, British Archaeological Reports Supplementary Series, Vol. 7 (Oxford, 1976).

72. Cf. Avi-Yonah, *Jews of Palestine*, pp. 35–53; Smallwood, *Jews*, pp. 467–506.

73. Avi-Yonah, *Jews of Palestine*, p. 52, n. 22; cf. R. Syme, *Emperors and Biography: Studies in the Historia Augusta* (Oxford, 1971), pp. 263 ff.

74. H. F. Jolowicz and B. Nicholas, *Historical Introduction to the Study of Roman Law*, 3rd ed. (London, 1972); cf. A. M. Honoré, "Imperial Rescripts A.D. 193–305: Authorship and Authenticity," *JRS* 69 (1979): 51–64.

75. In S. Riccobono et al., eds., *Fontes Iuris Romani Anteiustiniani*, 3 vols. (Florence, 1968), Vol. 2 [hereafter *FIRA*].

76. Ibid., pp. 751–98; K. G. Bruns and E. Sachau, eds., *Syrisch-Römisches Rechtsbuch aus dem fünften Jahrhundert* (Leipzig, 1880).

77. Smallwood, *Jews*, pp. 546–57, for a list of governors in this period, mostly from inscriptions.

78. See below, Chap. 6.

79. Including the new papyri from the Dead Sea region: Y. Yadin in N. Avigad et al., "The Expedition to the Judaean Desert, 1960," *IEJ* 11 (1961): 40–52; B. Lifshitz, ibid.: 53–62; Y. Yadin in N. Avigad et al., "Expedition, 1961,": 235–57; H. J. Polotsky, ibid.: 258–62; DJD 2: 67–280.

80. C. R. Conder and H. H. Kitchener, *The Survey of Western Palestine: Memoirs of the Topography . . .*, 7 vols. (London, 1881–88), Vol. 1, *Galilee*; for the Golan, cf. M. Kochavi, ed., *Judaea, Samaria and the Golan: Archaeological Survey 1967–1968* (Jerusalem, 1972) (Heb.).

81. B. Mazar (Maisler), M. Schwabe, and B. Lifshitz, *Beth She'arim: Report on the Excavations during 1930–40*, 2 vols. (Jerusalem, 1973–74), Vol. 1, *Catacombs 1–4* [hereafter, *Beth Shearim*].

82. Corbo, Loffreda, Spijkerman, and Testa, *Cafarnao*, vols. 1–4.

83. Yeivin, "Excavations at Khorazin," pp. 144–57.

84. E. M. Meyers, A. T. Kraabel, and J. F. Strange, "Synagogue at Khirbet Shema." The whole of *AASOR* 42 is devoted to the report of the excavation.

85. C. L. Meyers, E. M. Meyers, and J. F. Strange, "Excavations at Meiron in Upper Galilee—1971, 1972: A Preliminary Report," *BASOR* 214 (1974):

2-25; E. M. Meyers, C. L. Meyers, and J. F. Strange, "Meiron Second Preliminary Report," pp. 73-108. The final Meiron report appears in E. M. Meyers, J. F. Strange, and C. L. Meyers, *Excavations at Ancient Meiron, Upper Galilee* (Cambridge, Mass., 1981).

86. E.g., the survey of twelve sites in E. M. Meyers, J. F. Strange, and D. E. Groh, "The Meiron Excavation Project: Archaeological Survey in Galilee and Golan, 1976," *BASOR* 230 (1978): 1-24; excavations at Horvat ha-'Amudim are reported in L. I. Levine, ed., *Ancient Synagogues Revealed* (Jerusalem, 1981), pp. 78-80; and excavations at Nabratein by E. M. Meyers, J. F. Strange, and C. L. Meyers are reported in *IEJ* 31 (1981): 108-10.

87. J. F. Strange, "The Capernaum and Herodium Publications," *BASOR* 226 (1977): 66-67.

88. E. M. Meyers, A. T. Kraabel, and J. F. Strange, "Synagogue at Khirbet Shema'," p. 6, in discussion of Khirbet Shema' stratum II.

89. Exceptions are Z. Yeivin, "Survey of Settlements in Galilee and the Golan from the Period of the Mishnah in the Light of the Sources," (Ph.D. diss., Hebrew Univ. of Jerusalem, 1971), based on aerial photography; the excavations at Meiron and Khirbet Shema'; the work noted in n. 86; the surveys of late Roman and early Byzantine settlement on the Golan by C. Dauphin, which are not yet published. G. Tchalenko, *Villages Antiques de la Syrie du Nord: le Massif du Bélus a l'Époque Romaine*, 3 vols. (Paris, 1953-58), shows what could be achieved in this direction.

Chapter 2

1. G. A. Smith, *The Historical Geography of the Holy Land* (London, 1894), pp. 413-63, is still the clearest introduction, but there is also a good description in S. Freyne, *Galilee from Alexander the Great to Hadrian 323 B.C.E. to 135 C.E.* (Notre Dame, 1980), pp. 3-21. See also E. M. Meyers, "Galilean Regionalism as a Factor in Historical Reconstruction," *BASOR* 221 (1976): 93-101. See my map on p. 18.

2. Smith, *Historical Geography*, p. 431; D. H. Amiran, "The Population of Galilee," *Yediot* 12 (1954): 233 (Heb.) notes the tendency of modern Galilee to contain minorities unaffected by trends elsewhere in Israel.

3. M. Rostovtsev, *Caravan Cities*, translated by D. Talbot Rice and T. Talbot Rice (Oxford, 1932), but cf. occasional Jews in caravans, and M. Avi-Yonah and E. Stern, eds., *Encyclopedia of Archaeological Excavations in the Holy Land*, 4 vols. (London and Oxford, 1975-78) 2: 421 [hereafter *EAEHL*]: a Phoeniciarch is found in Gerasa, showing trade links with Phoenicia.

4. Sifre Deut. 354, p. 415, re middlemen in Lower Galilee, i.e., Zebulon.

5. Smith, *Historical Geography*, p. 427.

6. Ibid., p. 426.

7. Ibid.

8. Josephus, *contra Apionem* 1. 12, 60-68; see L. Jacobs, "The Economic Condition of the Jews in Babylon in Talmudic Times compared with Palestine," *JSS* 2 (1957): 349, on the decline in trade in Judaea after 70.

9. The Tiberian commercial depots at Rome: *IGR* I 132, 1384. Rabbinic awareness of long-distance sea trade carried out, presumably, by Jews: m B.B. 3: 2: R. Judah, re a Jew in (probably) Spain for over a year; m Hall. 2: 2: a ship carrying a cargo of food from abroad; m Ket. 5: 6: sailors

only need to make love to their wives every six months, cf. m Ned. 3: 6; Sifre Deut. 203, p. 239.

10. *BJ* 2. 188–89; cf. m Gitt. 7: 7: the natural port for going abroad is Akko.
11. Smith, *Historical Geography*, p. 415.
12. *AJ* 14. 314; hence M. Antonius tells the Phoenicians to support his candidate for ruling Palestine: *AJ* 14. 323.
13. Matt. 15: 21.
14. Matt. 4: 24: "all over Syria."
15. N. Jidejian, *Sidon through the Ages* (Beirut, 1971), p. 84, re Acts 12: 20–21.
16. S. Applebaum, "The Struggle for the Soil and the Revolt of 66–73 C.E.," *EI* 12 (1975): 125–8 (Heb.): re struggle between Upper Galilee villages and Tyre for land.
17. Apollonius of Tyana *Ep.* 11: Caesarea is μεγίστη τῆς Παλαιστίνης ; cf. L. I. Levine, *Caesarea under Roman Rule* (Leiden, 1975) p. 42.
18. Levine, *Caesarea*, p. 45.
19. S. T. Parker, "The Decapolis Reviewed," *JBL* 94 (1975): 437: *not* a political league.
20. *BJ* 3. 44 ff., re the Peraea; Sifre Deut. 301, p. 319: R. Yosi haGalili states that *Ever haYarden* does not flow with milk and honey.
21. C. H. Kraeling, ed., *Gerasa: City of the Decapolis* (New Haven, 1938), p. 40.
22. Cf. the sudden increase in small settlements revealed in M. Kochavi, ed., *Judaea, Samaria and the Golan: Archaeological Survey 1967-1968* (Jerusalem, 1972), pp. 245–46 (Heb.).
23. See below, p. 64.
24. *BJ* 3. 307 ff., on the lack of cooperation in the first revolt; there are few Jewish synagogues, if any, in Samaria before the fifth century: G. Foerster, "Ancient Synagogues in Eretz-Israel," *Qadmoniot* 5 (1972): 39 (Heb.). Cf. F. F. Hüttenmeister and G. Reeg, *Die antiken Synagogen in Israel*, 2 vols. (Wiesbaden, 1977) 2: 552: late fourth century.
25. M. Avi-Yonah, "Scythopolis," *IEJ* 12 (1962): 123–34; B. Lifshitz, "Scythopolis: L'histoire, . . . ," *ANRW* II (Principate) 8 (1977): 262–94.
26. Avi-Yonah, *Jews of Palestine*, pp. 50–51, for the decree forbidding it; but cf. ibid., pp. 79–81, for the breaking of the rule by a few.
27. *Compendia* 2: 686; cf. Luke 9:52 for Jesus going up to Jerusalem via Samaria.
28. Smith, *Historical Geography*, p. 416.
29. Ibid., p. 440.
30. Cf. Josephus in *BJ* 3. 35.
31. *BJ* 3. 158, on Jotapata's position.
32. *BJ* 4. 54 ff.: easily defended.
33. Smith, *Historical Geography*, p. 418, n. 2.
34. *Vita* 397: a battle takes place on it.
35. *BJ* 3. 42–43: a fine description.
36. Smith, *Historical Geography*, p. 417.
37. Cf. C. R. Conder and H. H. Kitchener, *The Survey of Western Palestine*, 7 vols. (London, 1881–88), Vol. 1, passim.
38. Ibid.
39. t Erub. 4(6): 11 (Lieberman edition [hereafter, "L."], p. 108).
40. Sheltering in caves: t Nidd. 8: 6 (Zuckermandel edition [hereafter "Z."], p. 650); hiding in them: *BJ* 1. 304, re the caves of Arbel; 3. 336. Some

caveṣ are reported to be vast: see t Erub. 3(4): 13 (L., p. 101), and G. Duncan, "The Sea of Tiberias and its Environs," *PEQ* (1926): 69, re a tunnel reputed to be 14 miles long under the Tiberias palace; "Excavations in Palestine, 1932-3," *QDAP* 3 (1934): 175: a large cave 2½ kilometres south of Nazareth.

41. t B.K. 6: 22 (Z., p. 356).
42. *AJ* 15.121: in Judaea in 32 B.C.; E. M. Meyers, A. T. Kraabel, and J. F. Strange, eds., "Ancient Synagogue Excavations at Khirbet Shemaʿ, Israel, 1970-1972," *AASOR* 42 (1976): 6, re A.D. 306 earthquake possibly destroying Khirbet Shemaʿ; t B.M. 11: 7 (Z., p. 395) on liability for earthquake damage.
43. *BJ* 1. 304: Herod takes Sepphoris in deep snow; m Mikw. 7: 1: the men of Medeba in the Peraea used snow instead of water for their mikveh.
44. t B.B. 6: 11 (Z., p. 406): torrential rain is a disaster to the state; t B.M. 11: 7 (Z., p. 395): destruction of houses by heavy rainfall envisaged.
45. m Taan. 3:1, on the forty days; Sifre Deut. 306, p. 336: "Water is life"; *AJ* 15. 304: unrest against Herod after famine caused by the drought.
46. Conder and Kitchener, *Survey*, pp. 209-17, 265-69; cf. Jotapata's lack of water. Most springs lie outside the settlements—see M. Har-El, "The Zealots' Fortresses in Galilee," *IEJ* 22 (1972): 125: the spring inside Gamala itself is exceptional; C. L. Meyers, E. M. Meyers, and J. F. Strange, "Excavations at Meiron in Upper Galilee—1971, 1972: A Preliminary Report," *BASOR* 214 (1974): 3: Meiron shares a spring with Khirbet Shemaʿ; *EAEHL* 1: 299: Khorazin spring is c. 300 meters east of city; *Beth Shearim* 1: 20: the nearest spring to Beth Shearim is 1.5 km. away; cf., in general, m M. Kat. 1: 1.
47. See above, n. 37. Mt. Tabor had insufficient devices for trapping water and was thus indefensible: *BJ* 4. 61. Reaching the water level with a well was clearly easier in some areas than others: in Samaria (John 4: 7); the discovery of water by digging transforming a property: MdRi Beshallah 2: 143-46 (R. Yosi haGalili).
48. MdRi Nezikin 11: 53.
49. m B.B. 4: 7: it is assumed that each עִיר contains many such.
50. m Toh. 6: 6: the path leading to them is רשות היחיד .
51. m Yeb. 16: 4.
52. Nearest mines: copper mines near the Dead Sea ("Notes and Queries," *PEQ* (1926): 56-57).
53. Well-wooded: Smith, *Historical Geography*, p. 419: oaks; *BJ* 3. 162: Vespasian using wood for attack on Jotapata; used for fuel: MdRi Vayassaʿ 1: 60: a man going up a mountain to gather wood. Some trees were large enough to provide overnight shelter: m Erub. 4: 7, of a man caught out over Shabbat. Some were doubtless planted by the locals: m B.B. 2: 7, re their distance from settlements.
54. m Taan. 3: 6 (eating children in Peraea).
55. m M.Sh. 3: 11: if eaten, were they trapped first to be killed in kosher fashion? Cf. m M. Kat. 2: 5 on use of hunting.
56. m M. Kat. 1: 4 (moles and mice causing damage); m Yeb. 16: 6: snake killing a man.
57. *BJ* 3. 43 and below, Chap. 3.
58. *BJ* 3. 43.
59. *BJ* 3. 516 ff.
60. *BJ* 3. 519.

61. *AJ* 17. 318.
62. See Chapter 1, n. 57.
63. *Compendia* 2: 639; though, according to the Mishnah, the finest flour came from Haphora in Lower Galilee.
64. Cf. Eunapius, *Vit. Phil. et Soph.* 462, re corn exported to Byzantium from Phoenicia.
65. S. Applebaum and M. Gihon, eds., *Israel and her vicinity in the Roman and Byzantine periods* (Tel Aviv, 1967), p. 17: if grain was Beth Shearim's main product it must have been grown down in the plain.
66. m B.B. 2: 8: regulations for the threshing floor and its proximity to the settlement.
67. MdRi Amalek 2: 119-20.
68. *Compendia* 2: 645; cf. 2: 639.
69. *BJ* 2. 592. S. Applebaum, *Prolegomena to the Study of the Second Jewish Revolt (A.D. 132-135)*, British Archaeological Reports Supplementary Series, Vol. 7 (Oxford, 1976), p. 23, with quote of R. Yosi on oil scarcity in Galilee is extraordinary; the point of the comment may be precisely the awfulness of war conditions that could make even Galilee short of oil. On the effect of Roman taxation demands on the production of a surplus, see K. Hopkins, "Taxes and Trade in the Roman Empire," *JRS* 70 (1980): 101-25.
70. *BJ* 2. 592, re the profit made thereby by John of Gischala.
71. Sifre Deut. 355, p. 421.
72. E. M. Meyers, C. L. Meyers, and J. F. Strange, "Excavations at Meiron in Upper Galilee—1974, 1975: Second Preliminary Report," *AASOR* 43 (1976): 80: workshop for olive oil in Meiron in the second century.
73. G. Tchalenko, *Villages Antiques de la Syrie du Nord: le Massif du Bélus à L'Époque Romaine*, 3 vols. (Paris, 1953-58) 1: 25-46, presents many archaeological parallels. The economies of both areas were remarkably similar, both being limestone regions next to basalt, close enough to city markets to flourish but otherwise out of the way.
74. Z. Yeivin, "Two Ancient Oil Presses," *Atiqot* 3 (1966), pp. 52-63 (Heb.).
75. t Shebi. 1: 10 (L., p. 168) insists that painting trees red to help ensure their fertility is not "the ways of the Amorites."
76. m B.B. 2: 7: Abba Shaul legislated against this presumably to stop over-crowding.
77. *Compendia* 2: 645, 674.
78. E.g., m Kil. 4: 6; Matt. 21:33 on planting a vineyard.
79. Cf. Leviticus 19:19.
80. E.g., m Toh. 6: 6.
81. Sifre Deut. 317, p. 360: a monster turnip and cabbage produced in Sepphoris.
82. Conder and Kitchener, *Survey*, passim; cf. Tchalenko, *Villages Antiques*, passim.
83. *Compendia* 2: 645.
84. m. Shebi. 3: 7: moving stones from the fields to work there.
85. m B.B. 1: 2: "not usually in valleys."
86. E.g., m Toh. 6: 6: to wine presses.
87. t Arak. 4: 13 (Z., p. 547); t Erub. 2 (3): 9 (L., p. 94), re בורגנין guarding fields; t Erub. 2 (3): 15 (L., p. 97), re the מגדל for the same purpose; t Ohol. 18: 12 (Z., p. 617) suggests a בורגן might have considerable space inside.

88. *EAEHL* 2: 453.
89. Sifre Deut. 116, p. 175: "it happened in Upper Galilee that they used to buy up for a guest (Tosefta: "old man") a pound of meat a day," clearly considered a huge amount.
90. *Compendia* 2: 653.
91. Sifre Deut. 317, p. 360: an ox weighing 40 *litrae* in Sepphoris.
92. t Kel. B.M. 1: 14 (Z., p. 579).
93. *Compendia* 2: 656, n. 1; cf. Sifre Deut. 93, p. 88: R. Judah b. Baba interprets "Corn in your fields for your cattle" as "between the boundaries," i.e., of agricultural land?
94. t B.K. 8: 10 (Z., p. 362).
95. Cf. MdRi Kaspa 2: 97: an ox has gone astray if it is found outside the settlement boundary. But halakhic problems were more likely to crop up when cattle were near settlements, so this is not conclusive.
96. See Chap. 7 below.
97. Ibid.
98. m B.K. 6: 1: sheepfolds.
99. m B.K. 6: 2.
100. Particularly common with the influx of immigrants after 135? Cf. p. 32, below.
101. Sifre Deut. 39, p. 79: the products of each area had a distinctive taste.
102. The name of Tarichaeae ("salt fish") suggests preservation for export. Josephus mentions 330 small boats on the lake (*BJ* 2. 635).
103. E.g., E. Meyers, Kraabel, and Strange, "Synagogue at Khirbet Shema'," p. 16: at Khirbet Shema'; Applebaum and Gihon, *Israel and her vicinity*, p. 16: at Khorazin.
104. Pausanias 5. 5.2; cf. *Compendia* 2: 654.
105. *Compendia* 2: 682: Applebaum suggests local silk worms.
106. Some Galilean pottery is in a distinctive style found only in Galilee and the Golan: E. Meyers, Kraabel, and Strange, "Synagogue at Khirbet Shema'," p. 170 ff. The proliferation of laws about tanneries (*Compendia* 2: 682) is due to their unpleasant smell and the need for close regulation by the community.
107. Applebaum and Gihon, *Israel and her vicinity*, p. 17.
108. Sometimes in semi-processed form, cf. the great glass slab in the museum at Beth Shearim.
109. Akko: *BJ* 2. 189–91; *EAEHL* 1: 18: a glass furnace found there.
110. *Compendia* 2: 681; cf. the lack of glass making in Khirbet Shema': E. Meyers, Kraabel, and Strange, "Synagogue at Khirbet Shema'," p. 118.

Chapter 3

1. *BJ* 3. 43: "well populated."
2. Excavations at Sepphoris: L. Waterman, *Preliminary Report of the University of Michigan Excavation at Sepphoris, Palestine* (Michigan, 1937); at Tiberias: G. Foerster, *EAEHL* 4: 1171–77. E. Schürer, *History of the Jewish People in the Age of Jesus Christ*, 2 vols. so far, English ed. based on 4th German edition of 1909, revised by G. Vermes, F. Millar, and M. Black (Edinburgh, 1973–79) 2: 172–76, 178–82.
3. Waterman, *Excavations at Sepphoris*, p. v.; *EAEHL* 4: 1171.
4. Cf. *Compendia* 2: 641; see below, p. 28. More inhabited sites in Galilee in Roman times than any other period: S. Applebaum and M. Gihon,

eds., *Israel and her vicinity in the Roman and Byzantine Periods* (Tel Aviv, 1967), p. 17; possible overpopulation: S. Applebaum, "The Struggle for the Soil and the Revolt of 66-73 C.E.," *EI* 12 (1977): 125-26 (Heb.).
5. *AJ* 18. 36-37; little is known about the founding of Sepphoris.
6. On the size of villages, cf. the exaggeration of *BJ* 3. 43: "never less than 15,000 inhabitants."
7. *BJ* 2. 511; cf. *AJ* 18. 27: " πρόσχημα of all Galilee," though cf. Jotapata as "the strongest polis" (*BJ* 3. 111).
8. E.g., *Vita* 30-1, 39.
9. Tarichaeae: *BJ* 2. 252; Chabulon: *BJ* 2. 503; in general, αἱ πόλεις : *BJ* 2. 570: 3. 32; Gabara and Gischala: *BJ* 2. 629; Jotapata: *BJ* 3. 111.
10. *BJ* 4. 552.
11. The account of Josephus's activities in Galilee given in *BJ* consistently portrays him as more important than he is in the corresponding passages of the *Vita*.
12. *BJ* 3. 289 and *Vita* 230.
13. *Vita* 97.
14. Matt. 9:1: Capernaum; Luke 2:4: Nazareth (but Luke is prone to this, cf. Luke 9:10 and Mark 8:23 in contrast on Bethsaida).
15. E.g., Matt. 9: 35.
16. Mark 1: 38.
17. Libanius *Oratio* 11. 230; G. Harper, "Village Administration in the Roman Province of Syria," *YCS* 1 (1928): 105-68.
18. Economic: Chap. 5; cultural: Chap. 6; political: Chap. 8.
19. E.g., *Compendia* 2: 641-44.
20. Ibid., p. 641.
21. A. Alt, "Die Stätten des Wirkens Jesu in Galiläa territorialgeschichtlich betrachtet," *ZDPV* 68 (1949): 52-3.
22. *Compendia* 2: 641; Applebaum suggests (ibid., 2: 643) that the term was transferred from the Hellenistic farmsteads to Roman villages, but, if there was such a shift, it is surely more likely in the opposite direction, from the villages to Byzantine farms.
23. J. Percival, *The Roman Villa: An Historical Introduction* (London, 1976), p. 31.
24. *Contra Compendia* 2: 644. See the sensible, if uninformative, reserve of Z. Safrai, "Marginal Notes on the Rehob Inscription," *Zion* 42 (1977): 19-23 (Heb.), in interpreting עיר in the Rehob inscription as a "villa, village or large townlet, either dependent on an urban centre or itself a centre of population and administration."
25. The distinction is made, e.g., in Sifre Deut. 180, p. 223.
26. t Nidd. 4: 9 (Z., p. 648): hence the lower pudenda develop first in the city whereas the upper develop first in the small village.
27. m Uktz. 3: 2, 3, 9.
28. t Ohol. 14: 3 (Z., p. 611): windows are only used for ventilation in the כפר .
29. Well over one hundred passages in Mishnah; כרך is found in only eleven passages; כפר in only twelve passages.
30. M. Avi-Yonah, *The Jews of Palestine: a Political History from the Bar Kokhba War to the Arab Conquest* (Oxford, 1976), p. 19.
31. E. M. Meyers, J. F. Strange, and D. E. Groh, "The Meiron Excavation Project: Archaeological Survey in Galilee and the Golan, 1976," *BASOR* 230 (1978): 18.

32. Z. Yeivin, "Survey of Settlements in Galilee and the Golan from the Period of the Mishnah in the Light of the Sources," (Ph.D. diss., Hebrew Univ. of Jerusalem, 1971), p. v.

33. Ibid., p. v.

34. E. Meyers, Strange, and Groh, "Meiron Archaeological Survey," p. 22, n. 3.

35. Ibid. Also Khirbet Shema': c. 1 hectare compared to c. 4.

36. *Beth Shearim* 1: 14.

37. Applebaum and M. Gihon, Eds., *Israel and her vicinity*, p. 16.

38. B. Bagatti, *Excavations in Nazareth: From the Beginnings till the XII Century*, translated by E. Hoade (Jerusalem, 1969), p. 9.

39. E.g., Meiron, Khirbet Shema', Beth Shearim, and Usha.

40. E. Meyers, Strange, and Groh, "Meiron Archaeological Survey," pp. 5–6.

41. As in the end of hilltop towns in northern Roman provinces; though not, it seems, as there, as a result of deliberate government action. For expansion of population and settlement in the second century, see below, p. 32.

42. *BJ* 3.43.

43. G. Foerster, in *EAEHL* 4: 1173; despite rabbinic rulings to enable the Sabbath limits to extend that far, cf. t Erub. 5(7): 2 (L., p. 111).

44. E. M. Meyers, A. T. Kraabel, and J. F. Strange, eds., "Ancient Synagogue Excavations at Khirbet Shema', Israel, 1970–1972," *AASOR* 42 (1976): 15.

45. Ibid., p. 17.

46. Y. Soreq, "A Rabbinic Evidence of the *Tricomia* in Palestine," *JQR* 66 (1976): 236, suggests that many villages formed economic, cultural, and political units in groups of three, hence the name "tricomia." The hypothesis is attractive but the evidence is weak.

47. Yeivin, "Survey of Settlements," p. xi.

48. Ibid., p. vii; cf. t Erub. 4 (6): 4–6 (L., p. 105).

49. Yeivin, "Survey of Settlements," p. iv.

50. Ibid., p. x; C. L. Meyers, E. M. Meyers, and J. F. Strange, "Excavations at Meiron in Upper Galilee—1971, 1972: a Preliminary Report," *BASOR* 214 (1974): 12.

51. Yeivin, "Survey of the Settlements," p. x.

52. C. Dauphin, "The Golan in the Mishnaic and Talmudic Period," typescript recording briefly the survey of 1978, p. 3: Khushniyye in a square, Deir Kaffukh and Naffakh in a rectangle, Qasrin, Farj, and Ed-Danqalle in a curve.

53. Yeivin, "Survey of the Settlements," p. xx.

54. *EAEHL*, s.v. "Hippos."

55. C. L. Meyers, E. Meyers, and Strange, "Meiron Preliminary Report," p. 5, and E. M. Meyers, J. F. Strange, and C. L. Meyers, *Excavations at Ancient Meiron, Upper Galilee* (Cambridge, Mass., 1981), pp. 76–77.

56. See p. 28.

57. Yeivin, "Survey of the Settlements," p. 77, for plans.

58. *BJ* 2. 574; *Vita* 156; although the Tiberias wall was *probably* rebuilt in the second and the third centuries; cf. G. Foerster, "Tibériade: Communication," *RB* 82 (1975): 106.

59. *BJ* 2. 573; Josephus takes the credit, but most of these fortifications cannot be identified archaeologically.

60. Personal inspection of excavations in progress by S. Gutman, September 1977.

61. m B.B. 1: 5.
62. t Erub. 5 (7): 4 (L., p. 122).
63. m Arak. 9: 6: it is common for an עיר חומה in Galilee to have its roofs form its external wall—(but the Cambridge ms. reads גנות (gardens), not גגות (roofs)); cf. Yeivin, "Survey of Settlements," p. xix, for examples in Khorazin, Khirbet Shema', Arbel, and the Medaba map.
64. *Beth Shearim* 1: 16.
65. *EAEHL* 3: 860, and C. L. Meyers, E. Meyers, and Strange, "Meiron Preliminary Report," pp. 20, 80.
66. *BJ* 3. 186; and p. 21 on water supply.
67. Yeivin, "Survey of Settlements," pp. vii–viii.
68. Ibid., p. xi; *Beth Shearim* 1: 16, for Beth Shearim.
69. A. Segal, ed., *Ancient Sites of the Holy Land in the Classical Period: Selected Plans* (Beer Sheva, 1978) (Heb.), plan 20, but based only on aerial photographs; V. C. Corbo, S. Loffreda, A. Spijkerman, and E. Testa, *Cafarnao*, 4 vols. (Jerusalem, 1972–75) 1: 171 ff.
70. E.g., m B.B. 1: 5: responsibility for the courtyard door and gate house; m Maas. 3: 5: difficulty of guarding property against thieves and embarrassment of eating while being watched in an over-public courtyard.
71. E.g., m Erub. 7: 7: cooperating over the 'erub to let everyone carry objects in the alley on a Sabbath; but *Compendia* 2: 729 claims that the counrtyard is the basic unit of cooperation.
72. m B.B. 4: 4.
73. *BJ* 2. 504: Phoenician architecture?
74. Meiron MI in E. M. Meyers, C. L. Meyers, and J. F. Strange, "Excavations at Meiron in Upper Galilee—1974, 1975: Second Preliminary Report," *AASOR* 43 (1976): 76–83; but cf. D. Saltz, "Surveys, Salvage and Small Digs in Israel," *ASOR Newsletter*, no. 10 (May 1977): 3: fine house in Migdal.
75. Z. Yeivin, "Excavations at Khorazin," *EI* 11 (1973): 145: plan of settlement and houses.
76. E.g., m Erub. 9: 4; cf. *Compendia* 2: 730; m Ohol. 11: 4: looking out of an upstairs window at a burial party.
77. m Toh. 9: 6.
78. m Erub. 9: 1: "all the roofs of a town are one domain" for Shabbat.
79. MdRi Shirata 8: 72: "wood, stone or mud"; m Betz. 5: 1: hatchway in roof; Mark 2:4: making a hole in the roof to let down a paralytic in Capernaum.
80. t B.M. 8: 33 (Z., p. 391).
81. With glass? Cf. *Compendia* 2: 734; m B.B. 3: 6: Tyrian and Egyptian styles; t Ohol. 14: 4 (Z., p. 611) on varied sizes, etc.
82. m Ter. 8: 3: adjoining the courtyard; t Arak. 5: 14 (Z., p. 550).
83. m Arak. 9: 5: but suggested, in context, as an extreme.
84. H. Seyrig, *Antiquités Syriennes*, Extracts from Syria, 6 vols. (Paris, 1934–66), no. 1, "Les Jardins de Kasr el-Heir," 1: 1–3.
85. *EAEHL* 1: 299; E. Meyers, C. Meyers, and Strange, "Meiron Second Preliminary Report," p. 80.
86. Schürer, *History* 1: 217–18; G. A. Smith, *The Historical Geography of the Holy Land* (London, 1894), p. 415. I do not find convincing the detailed arguments of S. Freyne, *Galilee from Alexander the Great to Hadrian 323 B.C.E. to 135 C.E.* (Notre Dame, 1980), pp. 37–38.
87. *BJ* 3. 41: "encircled by foreign neighbours."

88. Cf. *BJ* 4. 2, re Gamala.
89. M. Har-El, "The Zealots' Fortresses in Galilee," *IEJ* 22 (1972): 123-24: the Jewish Golan, e.g., Gamala, as opposed to, e.g., Hippos-Susita.
90. On synagogues, see E. L. Sukenik, *Ancient Synagogues in Palestine and Greece* (London, 1934); on paganism, see below, pp. 46-51; cf. G. Foerster, "Ancient Synagogues in Eretz-Israel," *Qadmoniot* 5 (1972): 39 (Heb.).
91. Bagatti, *Excavations in Nazareth*, p. 18.
92. Such designation is specifically stated only occasionally, but cf. Eusebius, *Onomasticon* 250, re Dabeira.
93. Epiphanius, *Panarion* 30, 4 ff.
94. Avi-Yonah, *Jews of Palestine*, p. 19; W. D. Hütteroth and K. Abdulfattah, *Historical Geography of Palestine, Transjordan and Southern Syria in the Late Sixteenth Century* (Erlangen, 1977), p. 47. Cf. ibid., pp. 56-61 for changes in settlement between the sixteenth century and the survey of western Palestine carried out in the 1880s.
95. Early second century: Meiron (E. Meyers, C. Meyers, and Strange, "Meiron Second Preliminary Report," p. 74: "before the middle of the second century C.E."), and Beth Shearim (*Beth Shearim* 1: 20); mid second century: some parts of Upper Galilee later in the century (E. Meyers, Kraabel, and Strange, "Synagogue at Khirbet Shema'," p. 258), and Khorazin (*EAEHL* 1: 299). Cf. S. Klein, *Neue Beiträge zur Geschichte und Geographie Galiläas*, Palästina-Studien, Vol. 1 (Vienna, 1923), p. 40: rabbis in Meiron, Upper Galilee. Hütteroth and Abdulfattah, *Historical Geography*, p. 45, note a similar massive increase in population from 1525 to 1553. Their whole picture of Galilean society is remarkably similar to that given in this study: closepacked villages with stable settlement, especially in the hilly areas, and an economy based on local grain production with olive oil exports (ibid., pp. 47 and 84).
96. Cf., for example, the wealth of Pliny the Younger (R. P. Duncan-Jones, *The Economy of the Roman Empire: Quantitative Studies* (London, 1974), pp. 17-32); note, in contrast, the fantasising about the גדולי הדור in A. Büchler, *The Political and the Social Leaders of the Jewish Community of Sepphoris in the Second and Third Centuries* (Oxford, 1909), pp. 7-12. Stories about wealthy people in tannaitic works look back to the first century and Judaea (e.g., Sifre Deut. 305, p. 325), whereas the Jerusalem Talmud has many stories about the contemporary vast wealth of, e.g., R. Yannai. Sherwin-White comes to similar conclusions to mine from the Gospel evidence in A. N. Sherwin-White, *Roman Society and Roman Law in the New Testament* (Oxford, 1963), p. 141.
97. *Compendia* 2: 643, n. 3: Hellenistic "large fortified farms" are reported from western Galilee but have not yet been published; contrast the finds in Beth Shean: *EAEHL* 1: 225.
98. See p. 31, re the two Meiron houses.
99. F. Vitto and G. Edelstein, "The Mausoleum at Gush-Halav," *Qadmoniot* 7 (1974): 50; Israel museum gold from Kefar Giladi; cf. Applebaum and Gihon, eds., *Israel and her vicinity*, p. 17, and N. Avigad, "The Tomb of Jacob's Daughters near Sepphoris," *EI* 11 (1973): 41-44 (Heb.): "comparatively rare"; in Samaria also (S. Applebaum, "Judaea as a Roman Province: The Countryside as a Political and Economic Factor," *ANRW* II (Principate) 8 (1977): 366).
100. Sifre Deut. 307, p. 17.
101. Golan: *Vita* 33, 47, 58; Judaea: before 70, according to H. Kreissig, "Die

landwirtschaftliche Situation in Palästina vor dem Judäischen Krieg," *Acta Antiqua Acad. Scient. Hungaricae* 17 (1969): 223-54; after 70, Josephus' own land in the Judaean plain (*Vita* 422).

102. t Yom Tob 4: 9 (L., p. 303): an ἐπίτροπος ; similar figures are frequent in parables, e.g., MdRashbi Shemot p. 2, 1. 14 ff.

103. m Dem. 5: 7: a householder with gardens in different עיירות ; cf. t Yom Tob 4: 9 (L., p. 303): man with his produce in another עיר has an agent to look after it.

104. Cf. the parable in Matt. 21: 33, re the vineyard owner; for rented houses: m B.M. 2: 3; t B.M. 8: 32 (Z., pp. 390-91); for rented courtyards: m B.M. 5: 2.

105. *EAEHL*, s.v. "Golan."

106. E.g., Zamarid village near Gamala (*AJ* 13. 23 ff.); it is assumed by t Peah 1: 13 (L., p. 45) that a man can bequeath his עיר ; y Yeb. 8: 1, 34a: a man buys an עיר of slaves from a gentile; cf. A. H. M. Jones, *The Greek City from Alexander to Justinian* (Oxford, 1940), p. 272, for the continuation of village organizations under great landlords, including the emperor.

107. m Hall. 4: 7.

108. t Ter. 1: 15 (L., p. 111): c. A.D. 150, but Pagi is apparently near Petah Tikva, not in Galilee, according to S. Lieberman, *Tosefta Ki-fshutah: A Comprehensive Commentary on the Tosefta* (New York, 1955-   ), in the commentary on t Ter. 1: 15.

109. The renter is termed '*aris*: t Dem. 4: 30 (L., pp. 83-84); m Hall. 4: 7.

110. t Dem. 6: 2 (L., p. 94): gentile lets to Jew; m B.M. 5: 6: "Iron flock" terms that should only be imposed on a gentile, which suggests that such terms were considered more onerous.

111. Cf. Büchler, *Political and Social Leaders*, pp. 27, 69; tithes and offerings still brought: *Compendia* 1: 406; A. Oppenheimer, *The 'Am Ha-aretz: a Study in the Social History of the Jewish People in the Hellenistic-Roman Period*, translated by I. H. Levine (Leiden, 1977), p. 43.

112. *Vita* 79: οἱ ἐν τέλει .

113. Mark 6: 21: Herod makes a feast for his own officials and οἱ πρῶτοι τῆς Γαλιλαίας .

114. *Vita* 1-6: Josephus protests that his family tree is well attested and high class.

115. Sifre Deut. 162, pp. 212-13.

116. *Compendia* 2: 760.

117. Büchler, *Political and Social Leaders*, pp. 7, 34.

118. Lending to tenants for seed corn: m B.M. 5: 8 (profiting by this would be usury for the creditor); t B.M. 5: 13 (Z., p. 382): credit for shop or sea trading ventures forbidden, but to cover against crop failure is allowed.

119. t B.M. 4: 11 (Z., p. 380): one opinion approves of the renter getting half the profits and a wage, another insists on two-thirds profits and a wage to avoid usury; cf. m B.M. 5: 4.

120. m B.M. 5: 7 considers this usury; t A. Zar. 4: 1 (Z., p. 465) forbids hoarding in a famine; cf. Dio Chrysostom, *Oratio* 46, with the same problem.

121. For the dangers of this assumption, see above, p. 12.

122. The division *Nezikin* in both Mishnah and Tosefta. Possibly tenants, if free enough, could also have had such responsibilities.

123. Yeivin, "Survey of Settlements," pp. xi-xii. Again, in theory, tenants might be ordered to build houses in different styles, but there is no evidence for this.

124. *Compendia* 2: 657.
125. Ibid.
126. Ibid. Cf. DJD 2: 122-34, no. 24, which gives the amount of rent payable. But perhaps the land rented was bigger but infertile (hence the low rents), or the Jewish administration generous.
127. Compare *Compendia* 2: 646, which suggests that a Judaean settlement has fields 1½ kilometres away. For small, distant plots being farmed, see Hütteroth and Abdulfattah, *Historical Geography*, p. 29; for impossibility of estimating, even with use of the Turkish evidence, the average or minimum farm sizes needed for each family unit, ibid., p. 76. The survey of western Palestine carried out in the 1880s does not include figures for the amount of land farmed.
128. Nehemiah 5: 11-12; for conversion, cf. p. 31.
129. On this problem in general see below, Chap. 7. On partible inheritance, see Deut. 21: 16; Num. 27: 1 ff.
130. Perhaps because of legal problems arising when property of this sort is shared: m B.B. 10: 7, re bath-house or olive press left to brothers; m B.B. 9: 4: brothers as joint holders; *Compendia* 2: 730.
131. Wife and children: see below, n. 156 (going to market, etc.); Mark 1: 20 (unmarried sons of Zebedee in boat with father).
132. See pp. 39-40.
133. *Contra* Safrai, in *Compendia* 2: 732, re living arrangements, and M. Gil, "Land Ownership in Palestine under Roman Rule," *RIDA* 17 (1970): 27, re land ownership, both being highly speculative with little evidence.
134. t Erub. 5 (7): 10 (L., p. 113), on the need for an erub for it to be permissible to use the courtyard on Shabbat; m Erub. 6: 7 concerns sons sleeping in separate houses around the same courtyard, but they were, perhaps, married.
135. E.g., re ritual obligation in separating Hallah offering or lighting Sabbath lamps for the household.
136. Unlike Roman *patria potestas*, Jewish law permitted an adult son to enjoy absolute ownership; cf. *Compendia* 1: 514.
137. E.g., m Erub. 6: 5.
138. m B.M. 5: 10: mutual aid in weeding and hoeing.
139. MdRashbi Mishpatim p. 206, 1.15; for a price, cf. m Ter. 11: 9.
140. L. Epstein, *Marriage Laws in the Bible and the Talmud* (Cambridge, Mass., 1942); in general, cf. J. B. Segal, "The Jewish Attitude towards Women," *JJS* 30 (1979): 121-37.
141. The ethos of patriarchal succession still pervades the parables.
142. m B.B. 8: 5: the position of sons in inheriting can be changed, but only so long as the words "by inheritance" are omitted at the ceremony; ibid.: if someone leaves all to an outsider and ignores his sons, "the sages take no pleasure in him," but it is legal.
143. R. Yaron, *Gifts in Contemplation of Death in Jewish and Roman Law* (Oxford, 1960).
144. Babata's father to her mother: N. Avigad et al., "The Expedition to the Judaean Desert, 1961," *IEJ* 12 (1962): 247.
145. Yaron, *Gifts in Contemplation of Death*, pp. 46 ff.
146. Babata's mother was given property by her husband, but Babata simply usurped the property of Judah (Avigad et al., "Expedition, 1961," p. 247).
147. Justin Martyr, *Dial. c. Trypho.* 141; Babata may share a second husband with Miriam (Avigad et al., "Expedition, 1961," p. 248); but cf. *Compendia* 2: 748-50.

148. m Ket. 5: 8.
149. m Ket. 7: 3-5.
150. t Gitt. 5: 11 (L., pp. 267–68); t Ket. 5: 8 (L., p. 74): a "nice" girl does not drink wine.
151. Gil, "Land Ownership," p. 21; cf. DJD 2: 114 ff., no. 21: the contract that "the daughters will be fed from *my* properties" (my italics) suggests that the wife's property might usually be used. Sifre Deut. 301, p. 320: a man bringing first fruits from the property of his wife.
152. m Ket. 8: 2: inherited secretly.
153. m Kidd. 3: 6.
154. *Compendia* 2: 761.
155. t Hall. 1: 8 (L., p. 276): at home, since the baker will also sell the produce of other women.
156. m Ket. 9: 4; m Yeb. 15: 2; t B.K. 11: 7 (Z., p. 370); t Nidd. 2: 5 (Z., p. 642); m Hall. 2: 7.
157. m Ket. 5: 5.
158. Ibid.; cf. m Sot. 6: 1: women chatting as they spin yarn by moonlight.
159. m Ket. 7: 8.
160. m Toh. 7: 9: Eliezer b. Pabi teaches re women being suspected of lifting the lids of their friends' pots to examine the contents; t Ket. 7: 4 (L., p. 79): borrowing kitchen equipment.
161. Particularly craftsmen, according to t Kidd. 5: 14 (L., p. 297), such as net makers, wool dealers, weavers, perfumers, millstone grinders, tailors, hair-dressers, and clothes washers, who all come into frequent contact with women.
162. m Ket. 7: 5.
163. t Ket. 7: 6 (L., p. 80); whether she is actually bathing at the same time as the men or committing some lesser sin of indecency is not clear; cf. S. Lieberman, *Tosefta Ki-fshutah*, ad loc., with parallel passages in later texts.
164. Sifre Deut. 13, p. 21 gives this a pseudoreligious backing in a midrash. Only exception: a woman could be an orphan's guardian if specifically appointed by the husband (m Ket. 9: 4).
165. Cf. J. B. Segal, "Popular Religion in Ancient Israel," *JJS* 27 (1976): 22, on the resulting "unofficial" religious ideas rampant among women. In this context, Sifre Deut. 29, p. 45, in which R. Joshua likens God to a pregnant woman, is extraordinary for rabbinic literature. *Contra* Safrai, in *Compendia* 2: 920, re women in synagogues.
166. m Ned. 9: 10: marrying for beauty; m Ned. 11: 1: necessity of cleanliness; t Ket. 7: 9 (L., p. 81): bad breath and body odor preclude marriage; m Pes. 2: 1: cosmetics; m Shab. 6: 1: ornaments (cf. the finds at Meiron); m Shab. 6: 3: scent; m Shab. 6: 6: pierced ears; m Shab. 8: 4: depilation with quick lime.
167. I. Mendelsohn, *Slavery in the Ancient Near East . . . from the Middle of the Third Millennium to the End of the First Millennium* (New York, 1949), p. 109; E. E. Urbach, "The Laws regarding Slavery as a Source for Social History of the Period of the Second Temple, the Mishnah and Talmud," *Papers of the Institute of Jewish Studies, London* 1 (1964): 1–94.
168. Didache 4: 10 assumes it; m B.M. 7: 6: even a hired worker might have his own slave.
169. Mendelsohn, *Slavery*, p. 119; m Ket. 5: 5: four is considered a great deal.
170. Sifre Deut. 308, p. 74: "men buy slaves to bring them food."

171. Luke 17: 7: same slave combines both roles; MdRashbi Bo, p. 38, 11. 12-13: according to R. Nehemiah, Jews in Egypt did both as slaves.
172. m B.B. 5: 1; m B.K. 6: 5.
173. Mendelsohn, *Slavery*, p. 121, notes that there are no records of Eastern slave revolts.
174. t Kidd. 1: 5 (L., p. 277); cf. John the Baptist with Jesus (Mark 1: 7, etc.).
175. MdRi Nezikin 1: 57-62; MdRashbi Mishpatim, p. 177, 11. 35-36, though this latter passage may be referring to what the *master* should do *for* the slave if he has injured him.
176. m Ket. 5: 5.
177. *Compendia* 2: 749.
178. Cf. Matt. 25: 14 ff.
179. MdRi Nezikin 11: 12-14.
180. t B.B. 4: 7 (Z., p. 403).
181. MdRashbi Mishpatim, p. 162, 1. 6: breeding by master; MdRi Nezikin 2: 4: *one* wife for slave, not indiscriminate mating; m Tem. 6: 2: R. Judah approves of taking a fee for lending one's slave as a stud for another man's slave girl.
182. E.g., J. H. Heinemann, "The Status of the Labourer in Jewish Law and Society in the Tannaitic Period," *HUCA* 25 (1954): 269.
183. M. I. Rostovtzeff and C. B. Welles, "A Parchment Contract of Loan from Dura Europus on the Euphrates," *YCS* 2 (1931): 67: Dura in c. A.D. 122 still has debt slavery, as does Egypt. Cf. Sifre Deut. 320, p. 367: gentiles enslaving Jewish debtors.
184. *Compendia* 2: 627.
185. t B.K. 8: 1 (Z., p. 360).
186. Cf. t A. Zar. 3 (4): 11 (Z., p. 464).
187. y Shab. 2: 9, 39a.
188. Sifre Deut. 320, p. 367.
189. E.g., the parody in Lucian *Vitarum Auctio*, passim.
190. MdRi Pisha 1: 82-84: running into a cemetery to stop the master following if he is a Cohen.
191. MdRashbi Mishpatim, p. 161, 1. 8.
192. m B.M. 9: 11: by time spent; t Peah 2: 17 (L., p. 48): by job.
193. Extreme poverty: Vita 66 " ἄποροι"; *Beth Shearim* 2: 78-80, no. 99: "son of Isaac" "πενηχρός"; m Ber. 6: 8: boiled greens as the whole meal (theory only?); m Kel. 28: 8: clothes made out of scraps; t B.K. 7: 13 (Z., p. 359): stealing from hunger.
194. Matt. 26: 11: "the poor are always with us."
195. For the rather different aims of the *alimenta* in Italy, see Duncan-Jones, *Economy of the Roman Empire*, pp. 294-300.
196. MdRi Kaspa 1: 17-18.
197. m Shab. 1: 1; m Toh. 7: 9 (begging in general).
198. t Peah 1: 6 (L., p. 43), giving details of problems arising from inefficient distribution.
199. t Peah 3: 1 (L., p. 50).
200. t Peah 4: 2 (L., p. 56).
201. m Gitt. 5: 8: "let the gentile poor take gleanings, for the ways of peace"; t Peah 3: 1 (L., p. 50): gentile poor receiving gleaning.
202. m Peah 5: 4: the sages assert that when a householder travels he becomes a poor man, i.e., this is part of one definition of poverty; m Peah 8: 7:

giving journey money to travelling poor; cf. t Erub. 3 (4): 17 (L., p. 103), re poor man marking his Sabbath limit with his feet.

203. P. Brown, "The Rise and Function of the Holy Man in Late Antiquity," *JRS* 61 (1971): 84.

204. See Chap. 2 above; cf. Epiphanius, *Panarion* 30.8.2, re tombs in rock caves with many (live?) inhabitants.

205. It is possible that the evidence for landless unemployed being hired on an occasional basis applies to urban dwellers from the cities surrounding Galilee seeking seasonal employment as at Rome, rather than to permanent poor in Galilee. But Galilee was overpopulated (see above, p. 27), there is evidence of cave dwelling, and unemployment had been a problem before 70 in similar circumstances in Jerusalem (*AJ* 20. 219–22).

206. Some of the laborers being hired may have owned small farms but needed extra work to add to their income. If farms were mostly small (above, pp. 34–35) and grew smaller with subdivision between heirs (above, p. 35), many families may have needed such a supplement. But would they need to travel so far that they became temporarily homeless in looking for work? Given the small size of Galilee, this seems unlikely, and the home-less hired worker would therefore belong to a class of permanently home-less poor.

207. t A. Zar. 7 (8): 10 (Z., p. 472); though cf. Matt. 20: 1 for early morning hiring for a vineyard.

208. m Shab. 23: 3.

209. Cf. p. 45, below.

210. m Toh. 10: 3.

211. MdRi Shirata 8: 61–63: ploughing, weeding, sowing, hoeing; m B.K. 10: 9: guarding crops; m Maas. 2: 7: processing figs; m M. Kat. 2: 1: pressing olives; t Erub. 3 (4): 9 (L., p. 100): shepherds; t A. Zar. 7 (8): 1 (Z., p. 471): grape harvest; and many other passages.

212. MdRashbi Mishpatim, p. 175, 1.26.

213. m Ned. 4: 4: from a communal bowl; t Ber. 5: 24 (L., p. 29) for workers in the home; t Dem. 5: 14 (L., p. 89): money in lieu (a dinar).

214. m B.M. 7: 1: "bread and beans"; cf. m Hall. 1: 8: dog's dough of shepherds.

215. t A. Zar. 7 (8): 10 (Z., p. 472).

216. m B.M. 7: 6: special terms for higher pay for not eating.

217. Matt. 20: 8.

218. m B.M. 6: 1; m M. Kat. 2: 1.

219. m Shebi. 5: 8.

220. MdRi Shirata 8: 61–63: a nice summary of the system.

221. t Peah 3: 11 (L., p. 54) (grapes); t Peah 2: 5 (L., p. 46) (grain); cf., in general, B. S. Jackson, *Theft in Early Jewish Law* (Oxford, 1972).

222. *AJ* 14. 159–61, 415, 417, 421–30, 432. On brigands, cf. R. Macmullen, *Enemies of the Roman Order* (New Haven, 1967), Appendix A.

223. *Vita* 105; *Vita* 246: the brigands' stronghold.

224. E.g., M. Stern, "Zealots," in *Encyclopedia Judaica Yearbook* (Jerusalem, 1973), pp. 132–52.

225. Cf. P. A. Brunt, "Josephus on Social Conflicts in Roman Judaea," *Klio* 59 (1977): 149–53.

226. *BJ* 4. 84.

227. Dio mentions the brigand Claudius overrunning Palestine and Syria around 195 (E. M. Smallwood, *The Jews under Roman Rule from Pompey to*

Diocletian (Leiden, 1976), p. 489). See also Macmullen, *Enemies*, Appendix B, pp. 255–68.

228. Confirmation of this can now be found in an excellent article by R. A. Horsley, "Josephus and the Bandits," *JSJ* 10 (1979): 37–63.

229. MdRashbi Mishpatim p. 212: the term is *"gazlanim"* as opposed to *"ganavim"* (robbers).

230. MdRi Nezikin 16: 14; m B.K. 6: 1; t B.M. 8: 18 (Z., p. 389).

231. m Peah 2: 7–8 and Sifre Deut. 43, p. 101.

232. m Erub. 4: 1: kidnapping; m Ter. 8: 11: stealing a loaf; m Ter. 8: 12: rape.

233. m Peah 2: 7.

234. Cf. *BJ* 2. 581.

Chapter 4

1. See p. 31.

2. *AJ* 18. 36–38; cf. M. Avi-Yonah, "The Foundation of Tiberias," *IEJ* 1 (1950–51): 161.

3. Cf. M. Avi-Yonah, *The Jews of Palestine: A Political History from the Bar Kokhba War to the Arab Conquest* (Oxford, 1976), pp. 46–47. M. Simon's statement in *Verus Israel: Étude sur les Relations entre Chrétiens et Juifs dans l'Empire Romain (135–425)* (Paris, 1948), p. 49, that Tiberias was full of pagans in the time of Judah II, i.e., late third century, is pure speculation. For a different explanation of the coins, see below, p. 129.

4. See below, pp. 43–44.

5. M. Avi-Yonah, *The Holy Land from the Persian to the Arab Conquests (536 B.C. to A.D. 640): A Historical Geography* (Grand Rapids, 1966), p. 147.

6. m Shab. 1: 8, 9.

7. Caesarea: H. Bietenhard, *Caesarea, Origenes und die Juden* (Stuttgart, 1974), p. 8, suggests that only a few Jews were there in the second century, but the halakha may look back to the close contact of the first century (*AJ* 20. 173, etc.); Akko: t Pes. 2: 15 (L., pp. 146–47), re R. Gamaliel walking from Akko to Kezib and meeting a gentile; m A. Zar. 3: 4, re R. Gamaliel meeting a (pagan?) philosopher in the baths of Aphrodite; Sidon: t Yeb. 14: 7 (L., p. 53), re Abba Yudan of Sidon telling a story about Jews and gentiles deep in conversation while travelling.

8. *BJ* 2. 477 ff.

9. *BJ* 3. 57; continued mixed population in the second century is suggested by the later synagogues built close to the flourishing gentile city of Hippos-Susita.

10. *BJ* 7. 43; m Hall. 4: 7: Jew renting land from a gentile in Syria; Libanius *Oratio* 47. 13, re area round Antioch.

11. S. Safrai, "The Holy Congregation in Jerusalem," *Scripta Hierosolymitana* 23 (1972): 62–78.

12. N. Avigad et al., "The Expedition to the Judaean Desert, 1961," *IEJ* 12 (1962): 261: the orphan's guardian and Julia Crispina.

13. Sifre Num., p. 171, 1.15, Balak 131: 11. K. Kuhn, *Der tannaitische Midrasch: Sifre zu Numeri* (Stuttgart, 1959), p. 516, n. 87, asserts that Ulam is twelve miles east of Sepphoris.

14. t Ter. 1: 15 (L., p. 111); S. Lieberman, *Tosefta Ki-fshutah: A Comprehensive Commentary on the Tosefta* (New York, 1955–   ), ad loc.

15. I assume, *pace* A. Büchler, *Studies in Jewish History* (London, 1956),

p. 247, that contemporary *minim* are all Jews; cf. G. Vermes, *Post-Biblical Jewish Studies* (Leiden, 1975), p. 175 ff.; see below, pp. 104-7.

16. t Gitt. 3: 7 (L., p. 257).
17. t A. Zar. 7 (8): 1 (Z., p. 471): permission to harvest grapes with gentiles.
18. t Shebi. 4: 16 (L., p. 183): dried, pressed, or fresh. For general relaxation of Sabbatical Year rules, see below, p. 179.
19. G. J. Blidstein, "The Sale of Animals to Gentiles in Talmudic Law," *JQR* 61 (1970-71): 197.
20. G. Alon, *Jews, Judaism and the Classical World* (Jerusalem, 1977), p. 188.
21. E.g., t Ohol. 18: 2 (Z., p. 616): effort at leniency by R. Shimon; t Ohol. 18: 15 (Z., p. 617).
22. m A. Zar. 2: 6; though whether W. A. L. Elmslie, *The Mishnah on Idolatry: 'Abodah Zara* (Cambridge, 1911), p. 38, is right to attribute this to "the paramount importance of the trade in oil" is another matter; see below, Chap. 11, n. 33. A. Oppenheimer, *The 'Am Ha-aretz: a Study in the Social History of the Jewish People in the Hellenistic-Roman Period* (Leiden, 1977), p. 65, attributes it to a need to "facilitate co-existence with the gentiles."
23. The rabbis were not worried that Jewish settlement in Galilee might be threatened, for, whereas the *sikarikon* laws were lifted in late second-century Judaea to encourage Jews to live there, they remain in force in Galilee (t Gitt. 3: 10 (L., pp. 257-58)); cf. Lieberman, *Tosefta Ki-fshutah*, ad loc.; y Gitt. 5: 6, 31a; *contra* S. Applebaum, "Judaea as a Roman Province; the Countryside as a Political and Economic Factor," *ANRW* II (Principate) 8 (1977): 388-89, and S. Klein, *Eretz haGalil miyeme haaliyah miBavel ad hatimat haTalmud*, ed. by Y. Eltizur (Jerusalem, 1967), p. 58 (Heb.), re *mazikim*.
24. S. Zeitlin, "Slavery during the Second Commonwealth and the Tannaitic Period," *JQR* 53 (1962-63): 210.
25. t Kil. 2: 16 (L., p. 212): Lieberman, *Tosefta Ki-fshutah*, ad loc.
26. Cf., also, the close contact with gentiles of the Tyre region portrayed in the Gospels (Mark 3: 8); m A. Zar. 4: 12 mentions commercial relations in Scythopolis (see B. Lifschitz, "Scythopolis—l'histoire . . .," *ANRW* II (Principate) 8 (1977): 285-86). For a different general hypothesis, see p. 53 at the end of this chapter.
27. t Dem. 6: 14 (L., p. 97).
28. t Ket. 12: 5 (L., p. 98).
29. t A. Zar. 4 (5): 3 (Z., p. 466).
30. m Erub. 6: 1; t Erub. 5: 19 (L., p. 115): all gentiles in the courtyard except one or two Jews; MdRashbi Bo, p. 23, 1. 5: a Jew rents a house in his courtyard to a gentile.
31. t Neg. 6: 4 (Z., p. 625) and t Dem. 6: 13 (L., p. 96): inheriting a gentile's house together (Onkelos).
32. t Hall. 2: 3 (L., p. 279): the doughs get mixed; see also, m Hall. 3: 5.
33. t Dem. 1: 20 (L., p. 66): a Jew should not bind his animal where a gentile's is kept. Cf. J. Neusner, *Eliezer b. Hyrcanus: the Traditions and the Man*, 2 parts (Leiden, 1973) 2: 297: Eliezer may have introduced new leniency. (John 4: 9 reflects harsher relations; see also Origen, *c. Celsum* 2. 1: Peter was frightened to be *seen* eating with gentiles by Jews.)
34. MdRi Kaspa 4: 18: prohibition on referring to a Jew's house by its geographical location by a pagan temple.
35. Sifre Deut. 81., p. 147: R. Akiba claims to have seen a gentile feed his own father to a dog.

36. t A. Zar. 3 (4): 14 (Z., p. 464). The Tosefta wants to distinguish dealings with such gentiles from those with gentiles who travel from place to place.
37. m Gitt. 5: 9.
38. m A. Zar. 5: 5: Jew eating with gentile is invited to "come and drink" and may be embarrassed into sinning by drinking unkosher wine; m Ber. 7: 1; 8: 8: regulating responses to Grace after Meals when said by a Samaritan. Passages concerned with buying a gentile's house, e.g., t Ohol. 18: 7 (Z., p. 616) re check for abortions in the walls to ensure purity, suggest close proximity.
39. m Gitt. 5: 9: one should greet a gentile in friendly fashion for "the ways of peace."
40. m Shab. 16: 8.
41. m Shab. 16: 6; y Shab. 14: 7, 47a records three actual cases of this in Galilee, but in the fourth century.
42. E.g., m Shab. 24: 1: gentile can be given stuff on the road if the Sabbath draws on.
43. t Gitt. 3: 14 (L., p. 259).
44. Ibid.
45. m Nidd. 9: 3: problems of purity.
46. t Pes. 2: 14 (L., p. 146).
47. m B.M. 5: 6. Jews lend to gentiles: t A. Zar. 7 (8): 5 (Z., p. 471) (grapes as security); t A. Zar. 1: 1 (Z., p. 460) (R. Joshua b. Karha, teaching in post-Hadrianic Galilee on problems encountered if proper documentation is not ensured); Sifre Deut. 113., p. 173 (it is a positive duty to extract debts from gentiles). Gentiles lend to Jews: Sifre Deut. 320, p. 367 (gentiles who lend are said to enslave their debtors); DJD 2: 240-43, no. 114, records a debt of a Jew to a Roman soldier in Ein Gedi by the Dead Sea.
48. t Peah 3: 12 (L., p. 54); t Shebi. 3: 12 (L., p. 177): helping to avoid the restrictions of the Sabbatical Year.
49. t A. Zar. 7 (8): 1 (Z., p. 471): harvesting grapes with gentiles is permitted, though it was forbidden "in former times" (בראשונה); m Dem. 3: 4: leaving fruit in the care of gentiles; m Shab. 1: 7: helping gentile to load an ass; t B.M. 2: 27 (Z., p. 375): looking after a gentile's ass; MdRi Kaspa 2: 121: using one another's ass for transport.
50. m Maksh. 2: 10.
51. t B.M. 5: 20 (Z., p. 382); cf. H-P. Chajes, "Les Juges juifs en Palestine, de l'an 70 à l'an 500," *REJ* 39 (1899): 44, and y B.M. 5: 5, 23a.
52. Avigad et al., "Expedition, 1961," p. 260. The guardian was appointed by the Petran *boule*.
53. t B.M. 5: 20 (Z., pp. 382-83).
54. *Digest* 27. 1. 15. 6.: Modestinus, saying that the imperial constitutions only forbid such guardianship if the ward may come to some harm through Jewish indoctrination.
55. t Ber. 4: 18 (L., pp. 22-23), about the nasty smell of Arabs (i.e. Nabataeans and desert caravaneers?), but the vehemence of the Mekhiltas against Ishmaelites was one of the arguments for a post-Islam date (cf. MdRi Bahodesh 11: 26-27); note also the assumption in some texts that all gentiles are on the verge of committing rape (Sifre Deut. 363, p. 396, of Ammon and Moab east of the Jordan).
56. Intermarriage is the chief fear: L. M. Epstein, *Marriage Laws in the Bible and the Talmud* (Cambridge, Mass., 1942), pp. 145-219.

57. E.g., Acts 16: 1: Timothy is son of a pagan father and a Jewish mother. She may be a proselyte.
58. m Bikk. 1: 4.
59. m Yeb. 2: 8 (gentile girl); t B.B. 7: 1 (Z., p. 407): gentile man in such a position cannot claim as legitimate his children born before conversion, according to rabbis.
60. t Hor. 2: 12 (Z., p. 477) (R. Eleazar b. Zadok).
61. t Hor. 2: 11 (Z., p. 477).
62. See below, p. 19.
63. E.g., Bithynian cheese (m A. Zar. 2: 4: R. Meir and sages agree one should not eat it).
64. See below, p. 61.
65. t Dem. 4: 20 (L., p. 81): merchant coming from any religious group but never being trustworthy for tithes; t A. Zar. 3: 14 (Z., p. 464): buying goods of a travelling gentile.
66. So J. Brand, "Indications of Jewish Vessels in the Mishnaic Period," *EI* 9 (1969): 41: Sidonian cups and lamps deliberately left unfinished to avoid susceptibility, in rabbinic eyes, to impurity.
67. y A. Zar. 4: 12.
68. E.g., m A. Zar. 2: 4: gentile's bottles and grape seeds; m A. Zar. 2: 7: locusts sprinkled with wine in the market to keep them fresh.
69. m Dem. 5: 9.
70. m Maksh. 2: 6.
71. Kh. Shema': E. M. Meyers, A. T. Kraabel, and J. F. Strange, eds., "Ancient Synagogue Excavations at Khirbet Shema', Israel, 1970–1972," *AASOR* 42 (1976): 168 (Tyre); Khorazin: Y. Meshorer, "Coins from the Excavations at Khorazin," *EI* 11 (1973): 158–62 (Heb.) (Hippos, Caesarea, and Tyre).
72. m A. Zar. 1: 5: no selling white cocks, etc.
73. m A. Zar. 1: 8: no selling plants while still attached to the land (R. Judah); t A. Zar. 2: 8 (Z., pp. 462–63): R. Meir and R. Yosi agree that selling land to gentiles in Israel is wrong but debate the permissibility of letting fields.
74. R. Eliezer even allows the making of ornaments for idolatry for reward (m A. Zar. 1: 8), but others disallow.
75. t A. Zar. 7 (8): 6 (Z., p. 471). The sages were asked to rule.
76. m Shab. 1: 8: by R. Gamaliel.
77. t A. Zar. 7 (8): 11 (Z., p. 472); m Dem. 3: 4.
78. t A. Zar. 1: 3 (Z., p. 460).
79. m Hall. 4: 7 (in Syria); t Dem. 6: 2 (L., p. 94) are both of Jews renting from gentiles, but the reverse is also considered (t A. Zar. 2: 8 (Z., pp. 462–63).
80. Agricultural work by Jew for gentile: t A. Zar. 1: 3 (Z., p. 460) (prohibition on working for a gentile on his festival unless he is too far away to be pleased); t Kil. 2: 16 (L., p. 212), re Beth Ana. Agricultural work by gentile for Jew: t Peah 3: 1 (L., p. 50) prohibits the use of gentiles for reaping if the reason is that the Jewish farmer is mean on gleanings; but J. H. Heinemann, "The Status of the Labourer in Jewish Law and Society," *HUCA* 25 (1954): 263, suggests this is rare; industrial work by Jew for gentile: m A. Zar. 5: 1 (in general, but wine production is the main topic because of the ethical problem in helping to manufacture unkosher wine); t Hall. 1: 3 (L., p. 274); t Pes. 2:5 (L., p. 145), industrial work by gentile for Jew: m A. Zar. 4: 10 (wine production again); t A. Zar. 4 (5): 11 (Z., p. 467) (gentile may work in a Jewish cheesery or bakery).

81. m A. Zar. 5: 3.
82. t Dem. 4: 26 (L., p. 83) (gentile ass driver taking grain from threshing floor to village); Sifre Num. p. 171, 1.15, Balak 131 (Galilean Jew hiring both ass and his own services as driver to gentile woman—an actual case).
83. See now the survey in M. Hadas-Lebel, "Le paganisme à travers les sources rabbiniques des IIe et IIIe siècles: Contribution à l'étude du syncrétisme dans l'empire romain," *ANRW* II (Principate) 19. 2 (1979): 397–485.
84. Epiphanius, *Panarion* 30. 12: Hadrianeum site still identified in the fourth century; y A. Zar. 4: 4, 27a, according to S. Applebaum, *Prolegomena to the Study of the Second Jewish Revolt (A.D. 132–135)* (Oxford, 1976), p. 6: pulled down in the 230s.
85. S. Applebaum and M. Gihon, eds., *Israel and her vicinity in the Roman and Byzantine Periods* (Tel Aviv, 1967), p. 15. Hygeia is an obvious type, connected with the hot baths nearby.
86. J. Teixidor, *The Pagan God: Popular Religion in the Graeco-Roman Near East* (Princeton, 1977).
87. Since Herod: *AJ* 15. 363.
88. *BJ* 4. 3.
89. Communication by A. Biran in "Notes and News," *IEJ* 26 (1976): 205.
90. N. Jidejian, *Baalbek: Heliopolis, "City of the Sun"* (Beirut, 1975), pp. 6, 23, 26.
91. F. Millar, *The Emperor in the Roman World (31 B.C.–A.D. 337)* (London, 1977), p. 455.
92. From personal observation under the guidance of Dr. Gideon Foerster.
93. In general, Eusebius, *Praep. Evang.* 1. 10. 55, on continued Phoenician city and village cults; H. Seyrig, *Antiquités Syriennes*, Extracts from Syria, 6 vols. (Paris, 1934–66), no. 10, "Note sur le culte de Deméter en Pales-tine," 1: 56–61: Demeter, associated with Isis and Serapis, being found in Lod, Akko, Caesarea, etc.
94. *EAEHL* 2: 417.
95. L. I. Levine, *Caesarea under Roman Rule* (Leiden, 1975), p. 42: Serapis, particularly after Hadrian; less public Mithraeum (*Compendia* 2: 1099).
96. M. Avi-Yonah, "Mount Carmel and the God of Baalbek," *IEJ* 2 (1952): 118–24.
97. *Compendia* 2: 1073.
98. E. M. Smallwood, *The Jews under Roman Rule from Pompey to Diocletian* (Leiden, 1976), p. 490: Severus and Caracalla establish it.
99. The main component of the *Compendia* article on paganism is the Beth Shean material; cf. A. Ovadiah, "Greek Cults in Beth-Shean/Scythopolis in the Hellenistic and Roman Periods," *EI* 12 (1975): 116–24 (Heb.).
100. *EAEHL* 1: 221.
101. *EAEHL* 1: 219: first century A.D.
102. A. Ovadiah, "Greek Cults in Beth-Shean," p. 116.
103. *EAEHL* 2: 522.
104. *EAEHL* 2: 469, from Epiphanius, *Panarion* 30.5.7.
105. Hellenised local cults: M. I. Rostovtzeff, "La Syrie Romaine," *Revue Historique* 65 (1935): 26; others: C. H. Kraeling, ed., *Gerasa: City of the Decapolis* (New Haven, 1938), p. 56.
106. See above, n. 90, on Baalbek.
107. F. Millar, "The Background to the Maccabean Revolution," *JJS* 29 (1978): 4, re Hierapolis and Baalbek; see also Lucian, *De Syria Dea* 12 ff.
108. E.g., Herodian 5. 3. 3–6, on Emesa.

109. Seyrig, *Antiquités Syriennes*, no. 23, "Deux Inscriptions grecques de Palmyre," 2: 111.
110. General introduction to the rabbinic evidence on this can be found in S. Lieberman, *Hellenism in Jewish Palestine*, 2nd ed. (New York, 1962), pp. 128–38.
111. Sifre Num. p. 171, 1.16, Balak 131; cf. Matt. 6: 7 on the habit of the pagans (ἐϑνικοί , i.e. *goyim*) who βατταλογοῦσιν in their prayers.
112. t Sanh. 10: 2 (Z., p. 430).
113. t Yom Tob 4: 7 (L., p. 302): cf. Sifre Deut. 70, p. 134: R. Shimon says that the pagans have burnt offerings; BJ 2. 289: Greek provocation in Caesarea by sacrificing birds at synagogue door.
114. E.g., t A. Zar. 6 (7): 2 (Z., p. 469), on the problems of a Jew who gives his house over to be used for idolatry, whether voluntary or forced; t Erub. 4 (6): 7 (L., p. 106) adds the possibility that an idolatrous temple *may* (but need not) have a place in it for the priests to live in. (Lieberman, *Tosefta Ki-fshutah*, ad loc., suggests that this is the ἄδυτον, but it surely refers to living-in quarters.) Cf. my comments above, on temples for the gods.
115. m A. Zar. 4: 3: ruling that Jews should not pay fees to use the garden or baths attached to an idolatrous temple unless they also have other secular owners (to show that worship is not intended)—it is clear that fees are not always requested; Elmslie, *Mishna on Idolatry*, pp. 54, 60–61: the term "asherah" means a living tree in Mishnaic Hebrew, a post in Biblical Hebrew; for comparison: M. Gawlikowski, *Palmyre, 6: Le Temple Palmy-rénien* (Warsaw, 1973), p. 30 (ἱερὸν ἄλσος of Aglibol and Malakbal in Palmyra); Daphne near Antioch; Justin Martyr, *Discourse to the Greeks* 4: gardens in temples in Samaria.
116. m A. Zar. 3: 4: R. Gamaliel knows this.
117. Like the כמר of Bel in Palmyra (J. Cantineau, J. Starcky, and J. Teixidor, *Inventaire des Inscriptions de Palmyre*, 11 fascs. (Beirut and Damascus, 1930–65) 9: 29, no. 19).
118. E.g., in first-century B.C. Chalcis, where the kings call themselves ἀρχιερεύς (Jidejian, *Baalbek*, p. 21).
119. See below, Chap. 9, n. 203.
120. One can only deal with those bodies so long as they מעלין שכר למדינה .
121. *AJ* 19. 356 ff.: to celebrate Agrippa's death in Caesarea and Sebaste; Justin Martyr, *Discourse to the Greeks* 4, re Greek religion in Samaria with public banquets, flutes, anointing, and gardens.
122. *EAEHL* 2: 469, from Epiphanius, *Panarion*.
123. *EAEHL* 2: 427, re Gerasa. Is this what was going on in Hammat Gader? (See above, n. 104.) Cf. M. I. Rostovtsev, *Caravan Cities*, trans. D. Talbot Rice and T. Talbot Rice (Oxford, 1932), p. 76, on religious use of theatres.
124. See below, Chap. 5, nn. 177 ff.
125. m A. Zar. 3: 7.
126. m A. Zar. 1: 4.
127. Elmslie, *Mishna on Idolatry*, p. 108: John Chrysostom complains.
128. t A. Zar. 1: 4 (Z., p. 460).
129. *EAEHL* 1: 221; cf. Apuleius, *Apologia sive Pro se de Magia* 63 with his little god figure, and V. Sussman, "An oil lamp from the Beit-Nattif work-shop," *Atiqot* 6 (1970): 82–83 (Heb.): lamp from Eleutheropolis (third to fourth century) with similar decoration to figurines of the Syrian Goddess in Beit Nattif cistern.

130. E.g., Khorazin (*EAEHL* 1: 299).
131. m A. Zar. 1: 5: cf. Elmslie, *Mishna on Idolatry*, p. 9.
132. t A. Zar. 6 (7): 12 (Z., p. 470).
133. S. Lieberman, "Palestine in the Third and Fourth Centuries," *JQR* 37 (1946-47): 50, on m A. Zar. 1: 5.
134. t Shab. 6 (7)–7(8) (L., pp. 22-29).
135. t Shab. 6 (7): 1 (L., p. 22): shaving child at graveyard; ibid. 6 (7): 2 (L., p. 22): dousing candle on earth; ibid. 6 (7): 4 (L., p. 23): blocking up window with them; ibid. 6 (7): 7: touching the coffin of a dead man to see in the dark; cf. P. Brown, "The Rise and Function of the Holy Man in Late Antiquity," *JRS* 61 (1971): 89 and passim.
136. t Shab. 6 (7): 2 (L., p. 22): snuff falling off a candle; ibid. 6 (7): 6 (L., p. 23): call of a crow as a bad omen; ibid. 6 (7): 16 (L., p. 25): snake by bedside will predict future children.
137. t Shab. 6 (7): 7 (L., p. 23): turning clothes inside out or sitting on a broom in order to dream.
138. E.g., t Shab. 6 (7): 7 (L., p. 23); eating dates to avoid cataracts in the eye.
139. E.g., t Shab. 6 (7): 8 (L., p. 24): sitting on a plough to persuade it to work easily and not break; cf. Sifre Deut. 60, p. 126 (R. Akiba): any high mountain, hill or good tree is bound to house idolatry.
140. Appeals to spirits: t Shab. 6 (7): 3 (L., p. 23): "He whose hands and feet are light," called on to help with new work or newly made dough; t Shab. 7 (8): 2 (L., p. 25): דגון וקודן (Philistine god Dagon according to R. Judah); ibid. 7 (8): 3: דני, דנן (Dan, according to R. Judah). Meaningless formulas: t Shab. 6 (7): 10-12 (L., pp. 26-27): חדא , uttered when shielding light by a wall, pouring water into public areas, or throwing iron into cemeteries; t Shab. 7 (8): 1 (L., p. 25): ימיא וביציא (R. Judah permits), but some formulas have familiar meanings, e.g., מרפיא ("Health") (t Shab. 7 (8): 5 (L., p. 26) and שתו והותירו ("Drink up") (ibid. 7 (8): 7).
141. t Shab. 6 (7): 17, 19 (L., p. 25): using baby birds as a sort of sympathetic magic; ibid. 6 (7): 18: using eggs squeezed against a wall.
142. J. B. Segal, "Popular Religion in Ancient Israel," *JJS* 27 (1976): 1-22, on the religious beliefs of Jewish women in the biblical period.
143. t A. Zar. 1: 4 (Z., p. 460).
144. m A. Zar. 1:3.
145. Elmslie, *Mishna on Idolatry*, p. 24; cf. Lucian, *De Syria Dea* 60.
146. t A. Zar. 1: 4 (Z., p. 460). But interpretation of שלטון as "public office" is uncertain.
147. Sifre Deut. 43, p. 97: R. Isaac claims that "if the names of idolatry were examined singly, there would not be room in all the world for them."
148. S. Lieberman, "Palestine in the Third and Fourth Centuries," *JQR* 37 (1946-47): 46, 53-54, suggests that Mercury is picked out because he is identified with Hermes Trismegistus of the magical papyri. Lieberman points out that all the rabbis interested in Merkolis had reputations for mystical speculation. But identification of Hermes-Thoth with the stone heaps at street corners was hard enough for pagans and surely impossible for rabbis—such idols seem very out of place in the rarified world of Greco-Egyptian magic.
149. Sifre Deut. 170, p. 217.
150. Though a late text suggests that R. Akiba may know about the practice of incubation in temples (A. Büchler, *The Economic Conditions of Judaea after the Destruction of the Second Temple* [London, 1912], p. 6).

151. See below, Chap. 5, on markets; m A. Zar. 2: 3 (one can use meat being taken to the fair but not being brought back), etc.
152. t A. Zar. 6 (7): 2 (Z., p. 469).
153. y Shab. 9, 57a: R. Zeira and R. Abbahu; m A. Zar. 1: 7, forbidding aid in building various pagan edifices is rather stricter, particularly about the place in bath-houses used to house the idolatrous statue.
154. Sifre Deut. 61, p. 126.
155. Elmslie, *Mishna on Idolatry*, p. 20.
156. Ibid., p. 42; Brown, "Holy Man," p. 89.
157. m A. Zar. 4: 3.
158. t A. Zar. 1: 5 (Z., p. 460): opinions differ on how scrupulous Jews should be about this.
159. t A. Zar. 6 (7): 4 (Z., p. 469).
160. Ibid.
161. t A. Zar. 4 (5): 6 (Z., p. 466).
162. t A. Zar. 5 (6): 3 (Z., p. 468).
163. t A. Zar. 1: 2 (Z., p. 460).
164. See above, notes 134–41.
165. *BJ* 5. 562–63 (votive offerings by Augustus); *BJ* 2. 412–13 (general); John 12:20 (Passover); Acts 21:28 (charge of bringing Greeks into the Temple); all reflected in Sifre Deut. 254, p. 416: "lots of people came to Palestine for trade in Jerusalem but converted and brought sacrifices."
166. See n. 178 below, on donations to synagogue buildings.
167. Dio 69. 13.2 and N. Avigad et al., "The Expedition to the Judaean Desert, 1960," *IEJ* 11 (1961): 46, no. 11, on תירסים בר תינינום, for evidence that some gentiles took the risk.
168. See Simon, *Verus Israel*, p. 323 ff., on conversions to Judaism in this period, though he deals mainly with the diaspora. See also Smallwood, *Jews*, p. 469 (Antoninus Pius), p. 475, re Septimus Severus, on Roman attempts to ban circumcision of gentiles, with the repetition of the prohibition indicating the continuation of infringements.
169. Cf. the "majority Anglo-Saxon opinion," in the *Oxford Dictionary of the Christian Church*, 2nd ed., s.v. "Didache."
170. Notoriously, Peregrinus Proteus—cynic, Christian, Brahmin, and suicide; see Lucian, *De Morte Peregrini.*
171. H. Chadwick, *Origen: Contra Celsum* (Cambridge, 1953), p. xvii.
172. In the *De Abstinentia*: Y. Baer, "Israel, the Christian Church and the Roman Empire," *Scripta Hierosolymitana* 7 (1961): 116.
173. Sifre Deut. 307, p. 346.
174. Gentile followers of Jesus (Mark 7: 26 etc.); H. Chadwick, *Origen: Contra Celsum*, p. xx: "all pagans know that Moses was an expert magician."
175. t A. Zar. 2: 4 (Z., p. 462): one is forbidden to sell to gentiles—therefore the gentiles would want to buy?
176. Acts 8: 27: the Ethiopian eunuch reading Isaiah though he does not understand it; t A. Zar. 3: 7 (Z., p. 463): a gentile scribe who writes out holy books in Sidon for sale to Jews. (When he was reported to the rabbis, they permitted him to continue.)
177. t Ber. 5: 21 (L., p. 28): if a gentile says blessings over food, the rabbis say that one should reply, "Amen."
178. Capernaum (Luke 7: 5, re the centurion); in general t Meg. 2 (3): 16 (L., p. 362), re a gentile donating a beam to a synagogue with a dedication to the Almighty inscribed upon it; and for gentile donors outside Palestine,

see B. Lifshitz, *Donateurs et Fondateurs dans les Synagogues juives* (Paris, 1967), p. 21, no. 13 (Phocaea); pp. 26-29, nos. 19-21 (Sardis); p. 32, no. 30 (Tralles).

179. *Beth Shearim* 2: 89, no. 109: εἰς θεὸς β[οήθει].
180. M. Schwabe, "A Jewish inscription from ed-Dumeir near Damascus," *EI* 2 (1953): 161-65 (Heb.).
181. Epiphanius, *Panarion* 30. 12. 8.
182. *IGLS* V 2134, etc. These are clearly Christian, from the crosses inscribed alongside; cf. W. Liebeschuetz, "Epigraphic evidence on the Christianisation of Syria," in J. Fitz, ed., *Limes: Akten des XI Internationalen Limeskongresses* (Budapest, 1977), p. 485.
183. Cf. *BJ* 2. 463, on the prevalence of "Judaizers."
184. Matt. 23: 15: "scribes and pharisees travel over sea and land to get one proselyte"; cf. Simon, *Verus Israel*, pp. 47, 318 ff.
185. t Ber. 6: 2 (L., p. 33).
186. Simon, *Verus Israel*, p. 325.
187. Sifre Deut. 353, p. 279.
188. E.g., t Kel. B.B. 2: 4 (Z., p. 592): the equipment of Onkelos's butcher is checked by Gamaliel and eighty-five elders. Onkelos's piety must surely be exceptional.
189. The use of baptism at this date is uncertain but likely, cf. G. D. Kilpatrick, "Dura-Europus: The Parchments and the Papyri," *Greek, Roman and Byzantine Studies* 5 (1964): 215, about Dura; Simon, *Verus Israel*, p. 333.
190. *Vita* 113, 149.
191. t A. Zar. 3: 12 (Z., p. 464); *Digest* 48. 8. 11. 1.
192. Smallwood, *Jews*, pp. 429-31.
193. *BJ* 2. 560, in Damascus.
194. m Dem. 6: 10.
195. *Encyclopedia Judaica* 13: 1184; appreciation of the possibility of incest I owe to D. Daube, in Littman Lectures, Oxford, 1977.
196. Hegesippus, ap. Eusebius, *Hist. Eccl.* 3. 19, 20; Nerva's claim to have removed the *calumnia* of the tax is likely to refer to proselytes (H. Mattingly et al., eds., *Coins of the Roman Empire in the British Museum* (London, 1923-   ) 3: 15, 17, 19).
197. Cf. *Compendia* 2: 756-60, re comparative leniency in checking on the virginity of brides (and illegitimate offspring); t Ket. 1: 4 (L., pp. 57-58).
198. Cf. E. Schürer, *History of the Jewish People in the Age of Jesus Christ*, 2 vols., so far, revised by G. Vermes, F. Millar, and M. Black (Edinburgh, 1973-79) 1: 217-18.
199. *Encyclopedia Judaica* 13: 1183.
200. At the most extreme form, this requires complete acceptance of all rabbinic teachings, according to R. Yosi b. Judah (MdRashbi Bo, p. 37, 1. 14).
201. See Epstein, *Marriage Laws*, p. 195, for Jewish status passing through the female line in the second century.

Chapter 5

1. See above, p. 19; E. M. Meyers, A. T. Kraabel, and J. F. Strange, eds., "Ancient Synagogue Excavations at Khirbet Shema', Israel, 1970-1972," *AASOR* 42 (1976): 168, on the steady supply of Tyrian coins at Khirbet Shema', suggesting that exports outweighed imports.

2. J. F. Strange, "The Capernaum and Herodium Publications," *BASOR* 226 (1977): 72, with references to discussions of "Galilean bowls."
3. t B.M. 3: 20 (Z., p. 377).
4. *Compendia* 2: 687: old market day was Friday, but Monday and Thursday by Mishnaic times; but m B.M. 4: 6 and t B.M. 3: 20 (Z., p. 377) suggest that Friday continues, with Monday and Thursday for public religious and political meetings.
5. Mark 6: 56; for the equivalence of שׁוּק and ἀγορά, cf., e.g., J. Cantineau, J. Starcky, and J. Teixidor, eds., *Inventaire des Inscriptions de Palmyre*, 11 fascs. (Beirut and Damascus, 1930–56) 3: 28–31, no. 22: the רב שׁוּק is the ἀγορανόμος.
6. *EAEHL* 3: 860.
7. Z. Yeivin, "Excavations at Khorazin," *EI* 11 (1975): 145 (Heb.).
8. t B.M. 3: 29 (Z., p. 379): cheating by disguising the weight.
9. Sifre Deut. 75, p. 140: Eleazar b. Azariah claims that meat is normally bought in the market; m Hull. 2: 9: animals may be slaughtered in the market or at home (depending presumably on ease of transport for the carcase). Purchase of meat is treated surprisingly casually since it cannot have been too plentiful; cf. above, pp. 23–24.
10. t Dem. 3: 2: greenstuff; m Peah 3: 3: onions.
11. t B.M. 9: 21 (Z., p. 392), but herbs are sometimes sold straight from the fields.
12. m Maas. 2: 1: fig sellers hawking their wares in the market; t Maas. 2: 4 (L. p. 232) = t Toh. 9: 7 (Z., p. 672): problem when grapes taken to market are left unsold; t B.K. 11: 8 (Z., p. 370): fruit stalls left in the care of a hired guard.
13. t B.M. 2: 3 (Z., p. 373): so common that it would be impossible to ascertain the true owner of a string of fish if it got lost in the market place.
14. Ibid.; t A. Zar. 4 (5): 12 (Z., p. 467): apple wine bought from gentiles (therefore not a Galilean market?).
15. t Eduy. 2: 5 (Z., p. 458).
16. m Hall. 2: 7; m Pes. 2: 5: wafers; t Hall. 1: 6 (L., p. 276); t Hall. 2: 8 (L., p. 276): bread sold in market by bakers with a staff of women production assistants.
17. E.g., m B.B. 2: 3: a man makes utensils at home to sell in the market.
18. See p. 56, re crafts.
19. m M. Sh. 4: 1.
20. t B.M. 4: 9 (Z., p. 379).
21. m B.M. 7: 1; cf. t Dem. 4: 26 (L., p. 83), re gentile ass drivers.
22. t B.M. 7: 14 (Z., p. 387): they are available for hire; but note m A. Zar. 5: 4: Jew leaves wine barrels in a wagon outside a village while bathing inside.
23. m Maas. 1: 5; t Ter. 2: 8 (L., p. 113); cf MdRi Vayassa' 7: 21–22, for desirability of having an animal for transport.
24. m Ned. 4: 8; cf. y Shab. 6: 9, 39a: sellers of sweets by the roadside.
25. MdRi Pisha 7: 2–4: R. Yosi haGalili asserts that "one should be alert"; MdRi Pisha 11: 66–7: night travel is foolish.
26. t Ter. 2: 8 (L., p. 113): fruit being stolen while taking it to be sold.
27. Finding suitable witnesses for documents is described usually as "getting one from the שׁוּק" (e.g., m Pes. 9: 11), which assumes that most people there are adult male Jews, eligible as witnesses.
28. m Hall. 2: 7.

29. t B.K. 11: 7 (Z., p. 370).
30. t M. Sh. 4: 9 (L., pp. 264-65); t B.K. 11: 7 (Z., p. 370).
31. E.g., m B.B. 2: 3 (in a courtyard); t B.B. 3: 1 (Z., p. 401) (opening into courtyard and/or street).
32. t Dem. 3: 10 (L., p. 75).
33. *EAEHL* 3: 860.
34. m Ned. 11: 2. Perhaps only one offers credit.
35. t B.K. 11: 7 (Z., p. 370).
36. t Maksh. 3: 10 (Z., p. 675).
37. E.g., t B.M. 6: 13 (Z., p. 384).
38. t Maksh. 3: 10 (Z., p. 675).
39. t Pes. 2: 1 (L., p. 144): turnover of baker's produce is far faster in the big towns.
40. t A. Zar. 4 (5): 12 (Z., p. 467).
41. m M. Kat. 2: 5.
42. See above, n. 31.
43. m B.K. 2: 2.
44. m B.K. 6: 6: camel load set alight by shop candle (but this must be early second century, before R. Judah).
45. t A. Zar. 7 (8): 14 (Z., p. 472); cf. J. Brand, *Klei ha Heres be Sifrut ha Talmud (Ceramics in Talmudic Literature)* (Jerusalem, 1953) (Heb.).
46. t Maksh. 3: 9 (Z., p. 675).
47. t Shebi. 6: 22 (L., p. 193).
48. m B.M. 2: 4: all money found in shop belongs to the finder unless it lies between the place where the shopkeeper sits and the counter.
49. m Maas. 2: 2: customers sitting in a shop succumb to a passing fig seller's call to "Take figs."
50. t B.M. 2: 14 (Z., p. 374).
51. m Betz. 3: 8; t Yom Tob 3: 6, 7 (L., p. 294), re a man's favorite butcher or baker.
52. m Ned. 4: 7.
53. m Shebu. 7: 1, 5; there may be significance in the use of the Greek word 'πίνακες' for this institution.
54. m Shebu. 7: 6.
55. In Khirbet Shema', it is suggested that variations in standard in the building of the first synagogue indicate cooperation between local (bad) craftsmen and visiting experts (from Lower Galilee?): E. Meyers, Kraabel, and Strange, "Synagogue at Kh. Shema'," pp. 48-49.
56. MdRi Nezikin 1: 66 (specialists); t Kidd. 5: 15 (Z., pp. 297-98) on the need to gain an honorable skill.
57. m B.B. 2: 2.
58. t B.K. 6: 25 (Z., p. 356).
59. m B.K. 10: 10.
60. m. M. Kat. 2: 4.
61. Meiron (E. M. Meyers, C. L. Meyers, and J. F. Strange, "Excavations at Meiron in Upper Galilee—1974, 1975: Second Preliminary Report," *AASOR* 43 [1976]: 78); Khorazin (S. Applebaum and M. Gihon, eds., *Israel and her vicinity in the Roman and Byzantine Periods* [Tel Aviv, 1967], p. 16).
62. I. Mendelsohn, "Guilds in Ancient Palestine," *BASOR* 80 (1940): 19; y Peah 1: 1, 5a, re flax traders.
63. t B.M. 11: 25-26 (Z., p. 397), re such insurance for ass drivers and boat

men who lose their ass or their ship; it is applied to other occupations by Mendelsohn, "Guilds," only by analogy.

64. t B.M. 11: 24–25 (Z., p. 397).
65. *Compendia* 2: 681–84.
66. See above, n. 2. For imported red slip in the fourth century, see D. E. Groh, "Galilee and the Eastern Roman Empire in Late Antiquity," *Explor* 3 (1977): 82.
67. m Kel. 5: 9: in pieces for erection at home.
68. m Kel. 17: 17; 29: 6.
69. See above, p. 21.
70. This information comes from Dina Castel.
71. Metal working is not included in the *Compendia* list, except in Jerusalem. See above, n. 65.
72. See above, p. 37; despite Mendelsohn, "Guilds," p. 19, on guilds of weavers.
73. *AJ* 18. 314.
74. m B.K. 9: 4.
75. m Shab. 1: 3.
76. m Pes. 4: 6; tailors with many customers sewed tags on the clothes to indicate ownership (m Kil. 9: 10).
77. m Ket. 7: 10.
78. m B.B. 2: 9. Akiba comments on the rule, so it must be early.
79. t Kidd. 2: 2 (L., p. 282).
80. D. Sperber, *Roman Palestine 200–400: Money and Prices* (Ramat-Gan, 1974), only tries to deal with Roman state currency, not city issues.
81. m Kel. 12: 7: old coins in use; Y. Meshorer, "Coins from the Excavations at Khorazin," *EI* 11 (1973): 158–62 (Heb.): coins in Khorazin hoard date from Hadrian to A.D. 340.
82. Meshorer, "Coins from Khorazin": Khorazin coins from Sepphoris, Hippos, Caesarea, and Tyre; idem, "A hoard of coins from Migdal," *Atiqot* 11 (1976): 54–71 (Heb.): Migdal hoard shows same spread of city origins and dates (A.D. 74–222).
83. *Compendia* 2: 687, n. 1.
84. A. Ben-David, "Jewish and Roman Bronze and Copper Coins: Their Reciprocal Relations," *PEQ* (1971): 120: R. Shimon b. Gamaliel relaxed rules about using Tyrian currency in divorce payments because of its scarcity. See now R. S. Hanson, *Tyrian Influence in the Upper Galilee* (Cambridge, Mass., 1980), in which arguments about trade are based on the coin evidence. I have not, unfortunately, seen this work.
85. Ben-David, "Jewish and Roman Bronze and Copper Coins," p. 123, for bronze weights in scattered finds. For monetary values put on land, see the sale document in DJD 2: 145, no. 30; for a loan, see DJD 2: 240–41, no. 114; for monetary arrangements on divorce, see DJD 2: 248–49, no. 115. This degree of monetarization in a rural economy is striking given the arguments of M. Crawford, "Money and Exchange in the Roman World," *JRS* 60 (1970): 43–45, that coin was not much used for transactions in the countryside in Italy and northern provinces.
86. On this whole subject, cf. E. Lambert, "Les changeurs et la monnaie en Palestine, du Ier au IIIe siècle de l'ère vulgaire," *REJ* 51 (1906): 217–44; 52 (1906): 24–42.
87. m B.M. 4: 6.
88. MdRashbi Mishpatim 160, 1.25.: a money changer has a job "for the public."

89.. t B.M. 4: 9 (Z., p. 379).

90. t Ket. 6: 5 (L., p. 76).

91. Sifre Deut. 306, p. 338.

92. Ibid., p. 339.

93. m M. Sh. 4: 2. Perhaps this was sometimes excessive, cf. Matt. 21: 12.

94. Matt. 25: 27.

95. For general complaints about usurious loans properly signed and sealed, see m B.M. 5: 10.

96. m B.M. 2: 4.

97. m Kel. 12: 5.

98. H. Hamburger, "Minute Coins from Caesarea," *Atiqot* 1 (1955): 115-38; cf. L. I. Levine, *Caesarea under Roman Rule* (Leiden, 1975), pp. 41-42.

99. m Shebu. 7: 6.

100. t B.M. 4: 2 (Z., p. 379).

101. Ibid.

102. Sifre Deut. 13, p. 22.

103. t B.M. 3: 15 (Z., p. 377); m B.M. 4: 6: checking coins on request.

104. m Shebu. 7: 6.

105. m B.M. 3: 11.

106. m B.M. 9: 12.

107. J. Jeremias, *Jerusalem in the Time of Jesus*, translated by F. H. Cave and C. H. Cave (London, 1969), p. 56.

108. Unless this is the origin of the fifth-century coins in Capernaum? See M. Avi-Yonah, "Editor's Note," *IEJ* 23 (1973): 44.

109. Sifre Deut. 307, p. 344: leaving a valuable cup with a friend.

110. Sifre Deut. 357, p. 428.

111. E.g., m Kidd. 4: 14.

112. Lambert, "Changeurs et Monnaie," 51, p. 221; cf. the wealthy Palmyrene buried at Beth Shearim (*Beth Shearim* 1: 173).

113. m Ned. 9: 2. The activities of *soferim* in copying and correcting biblical texts had considerable religious effect but perhaps less social importance (S. Lieberman, *Hellenism in Jewish Palestine*, 2nd ed. [New York, 1962], p. 31; E. Schürer, *History of the Jewish People in the Age of Jesus Christ*, 2 vols. so far, revised by G. Vermes, F. Millar, and M. Black [Edinburgh, 1973-79] 2: 332-36).

114. m Gitt. 3: 1.

115. N. Avigad et al., "The Expedition to the Judaean Desert, 1961," *IEJ* 12 (1962): 235 ff.

116. t Shab. 8 (9): 12 (L., p. 32): debt repayment receipts; t Gitt. 2: 2 (L., p. 252): divorce documents kept locked in a chest or box.

117. See below, p. 72.

118. m Eduy. 2: 3.

119. E.g., m B.M. 5: 11 about usurious loans; t A. Zar. 1: 1 (Z., p. 460): especially for loans to gentiles.

120. m B.B. 10: 3.

121. DJD 2: 156, no. 42.

122. m Gitt. 3: 2.

123. H. J. Polotsky, "Three Greek Documents from the Family Archive of Babatha," *EI* 8 (1967): 51 (Heb.).

124. m Gitt. 8: 8.

125. m B.B. 10: 3.

126. MdRashbi Mishpatim, p. 160, 1.25: a job "for the public."

127. t Sot. 3: 16 (L., p. 65, Erfurt Ms.); cf. A. Büchler, *The Political and the Social Leaders of the Jewish Community of Sepphoris in the Second and Third Centuries* (Oxford, 1909), p. 17; cf. S. Lieberman, *Tosefta Ki-fshutah: A Comprehensive Commentary on the Tosefta* (New York, 1955–   ), ad loc.

128. m Sanh. 2: 5; t A. Zar. 3: 5 (Z., p. 463).

129. The rabbis insist it be of money, not goods (m Tem. 6: 4).

130. m Meg. 4: 9; and a rather higher class girl down by the Mediterranean in Sifre Num., pp. 128–29, Shalah 115: she has a slave girl and gold furniture, and charges 400 dinars, payable in advance.

131. t Hor. 2: 5–6 (Z., p. 476).

132. Cf. Bardaisan, in H. J. W. Drijvers, ed., *The Book of the Laws of Countries: Dialogue on Fate of Bardaisan of Edessa* (Assen, 1965), pp. 46–48: not Oriental but German.

133. m Kel. 24: 16; 28: 9.

134. t B. B. 10: 6 (Z., p. 412); cf. Mark 5: 26: doctors' fees for twelve years to stem a blood flow; E. Sachau, ed., *Syrische Rechtsbücher*, 3 vols. (Berlin, 1907) 1: 180, R III 123.

135. *Beth Shearim* 2: 57–58, no. 81 (= *CIJ* II 1100): ὁ ἰατρός ; Sachau, *Syrische Rechtsbücher* 1: 178, R III 117: doctors in χώρα as well as towns; but cf. G. M. Harper, "Village Administration in Syria," *YCS* 1 (1928): 153: there is no record of public expenditure on health care in the villages.

136. Christian: Mark 7: 25, and passim, re Jesus himself; Justin Martyr, *Second Apology* 16, re exorcists; Epiphanius, *Panarion* 30. 4: Jewish patriarch gets a bishop to come to him when he is ill, disguised as a doctor; t Hull. 2: 22 (Z., p. 503): Jacob of Kfar Sama tries to cure R. Eleazar b. Dama of snake bite in the name of Yeshua b. Pantera. Jewish: y Yoma 3: 7, 18b, re curing by the divine name; G. Vermes, *Post-Biblical Jewish Studies* (Leiden, 1975), pp. 178–214, re Hanina b. Dosa. Pagan: Asclepius' cures for Aelius Aristeides, discussed in C. A. Behr, *Aelius Aristides and the Sacred Tales* (Amsterdam, 1968), pp. 38–39.

137. E.g., Cos; cf. G. W. Bowersock, *Greek Sophists in the Roman Empire* (Oxford, 1969), p. 64; cf. also the snobbishness of Origen about Greek medicine (Origen, *c. Celsum* 3. 12).

138. m Ohol. 1: 8: 248.

139. Trepanation: t Ohol. 2: 6 (Z., p. 599); cf. Z. Goldman, "Surgical Trepanation in Ancient Times," *Yediot* 25 (1961): 258–59 (Heb.), re a skull in Hellenistic Akko; abortions, m Bekh. 8: 1; removal of boils, m Ker. 3: 8; warts, t B.K. 6: 20 (Z., p. 356); abscesses, t Eduy. 1: 8 (Z., p. 455).

140. m Pes. 2: y: cures of septic wounds using wheat grains; t Shab. 12 (13): 10 (L., p. 53): cures of toothache; t Shab. 12 (13): 11 (L., p. 53): cures of headache.

141. m Yom. 8: 6.

142. t Shab. 4 (5): 9 (L., pp. 18–19).

143. m Shab. 6: 10: R. Meir argues against the sages on the appropriate category for locust and other similar cures.

143a. Also, to earn cash for payment of taxes (cf. hoards of Tyrian coins in Upper Galilee); see below, p. 132.

144. t Ber. 3: 7 (L., p. 13); t B.M. 8: 25 (Z., pp. 389–90): ass drivers sometimes went in convoy.

145. t Ber. 6 (7): 16 (L., p. 37): Ben Azzai, about the כרכים.

146. m Ket. 5: 6: not more than a week, for the rabbis reckon it reasonable to

insist that the ass driver have intercourse with his wife at least once a week.

147. t B.M. 4: 8 (Z., p. 379).
148. t Dem. 4: 20 (L., p. 81): the תגר.
149. t Dem. 4: 21 (L., p. 81): same agricultural goods may have been bought direct or via the תגר.
150. t A. Zar. 1: 9 (Z., p. 461): the תגרים tell each other whether a fair is in progress or not.
151. t B.M. 8: 25 (Z., pp. 389-90).
152. For evidence that camels were used in Galilee, note the technical vocabulary of camel drivers used in R. Ishmael's parable (Sifre Num., p. 181, 1.15, Pinhas 135), though this may belong to Judaea or the coast.
153. t Toh. 8: 9 (Z., p. 669): perhaps a shorter period; m A. Zar. 5: 4; cf. t B.M. 3: 25 (Z., p. 378): ass drivers asking at city entrance for supplies.
154. t A. Zar. 7 (8): 12 (Z., p. 472): one can leave wine barrels there while going into the settlement. But there is no archaeological evidence of such places.
155. t Yeb. 14: 10 (L., p. 55).
156. m Dem. 3: 5.
157. In first century Ophel, the ξενῶνα : *CIJ* II 1404.
158. Ibid. See H. Shanks, *Judaism in Stone: The Archaeology of Ancient Synagogues* (New York and London, 1979).
159. See above, p. 17.
160. t A. Zar. 1: 16 (Z., p. 461).
161. m Erub. 1: 8.
162. m Sukk. 2: 3.
163. *CIJ* II 873: a Beirut Jewish silk merchant; H. Z. Hirshberg, "New Jewish Inscriptions in the Nabataean Sphere," *EI* 12 (1975): 142 (Heb.): Jews in trading oases in the third century.
164. m B.M. 2: 8. Or just those most likely to be damaged by use?
165. See above, p. 21.
166. Mark 14: 5: flask of ointment for 300 denarii.
167. m Arak. 6: 5: taking pearls to kerakh to sell.
168. See above, p. 24.
169. m Kel. 30: 3 (R. Yosi).
170. At Meiron: E. M. and C. L. Meyers, "Digging the Talmud in Ancient Meiron," *Biblical Archaeology Review* 4, no. 2 (June 1978): 38; by Dead Sea: Y. Yadin, *The Finds from the Bar Kokhba Period in the Cave of Letters,* Judaean Desert Studies, Vol. 1 (Jerusalem, 1963), p. 101 ff., *contra Compendia* 2: 741.
171. Sifre Deut. 306, p. 338.
172. Sifre Deut. 306, p. 339.: בית איליים.
173. E.g., John of Gischala exporting to Paneas (*Vita* 74) or Syria (*BJ* 2. 591).
174. t A. Zar. 3 (4): 18 (Z., p. 465). Cf. Osrhoenian slave sold in Tripolis, Phoenicia (POxy., 3053).
175. t Kel. B.K. 6: 19 (Z., p. 576): R. Meir says this, since the inspector may have made a swift libation to a pagan deity.
176. t A. Zar. 7 (8): 6 (Z., p. 471): an actual case involving wine rendered suspect by an *agaronomos*. The sages who were asked ordered it to be sold off to gentile market officials.
177. A. Zar. 2: 3.
178. Ibid. It is interesting to see sacrificial meat being sold off like this.

179. t A. Zar. 1: 6 (Z., p. 460).
180. t A. Zar. 1: 9 (Z., p. 461).
181. t A. Zar. 1: 5 (Z., p. 460).
182. t A. Zar. 3 (4): 19 (Z., p. 465).
183. See above, p. 48.
184. t A. Zar. 1: 7 (Z., pp. 460-61): given by מלכות, מדינה או גדולי המדינה.
185. E.g., Gerasa: C. Y. Kraeling, ed., *Gerasa: City of the Decapolis* (New Haven, 1938), pp. 153-58.
186. t Ohol. 18: 16 (Z., p. 617).
187. y Shab. 16: 7, 81a.
188. Cf. W. A. L. Elmslie, *The Mishna on Idolatry: 'Aboda Zara* (Cambridge, 1911), p. 12; Pliny, *Ep.* 39; G. A. Cooke, *A Text-Book of North Semitic Inscriptions* (London, 1963), pp. 276-77, no. 119, for semitic use of the term.
189. t Ohol. 18: 18 (Z., p. 617).
190. t Toh. 7: 14 (Z., p. 668). Professor Brunt suggests that these buildings might be *horrea.* If so, this might suggest some cooperation between individuals in the storing of grain.
191. The courtyard of Hammata near Tiberias (i.e., Hammat Tiberias?) is also considered to be like a basilica (ibid.).
192. t Toh. 7: 12 (Z., p. 668).
193. E.g., t Toh. 7: 13 (Z., p. 668): "the doors directly opposite one another."
194. Ibid.

Chapter 6

1. Even if Alexander did not intend all the changes that followed him, he certainly caused most of them; for this rather more simplistic view, cf. M. I. Rostovtzeff, "La Syrie Romaine," *Revue Historique* 65 (1935): 11; S. Lieberman, *Greek in Jewish Palestine* (New York, 1942), p. 6. Continued differences between Greek colonies founded by Hellenistic kings (e.g., Dura) and semitic towns granted city status (e.g., Palmyra) must be borne in mind, though few distinctions are likely still to linger by the second century A.D.
2. H. Seyrig, *Antiquités Syriennes,* Extracts from Syria, 6 vols. (Paris, 1934-66), no. 2, "Notes épigraphiques," 1: 8: Palmyrene bath dedicated in Greek only; F. Millar, "Paul of Samosata, Zenobia and Aurelian," *JRS* 61 (1971): 2: Greek replaces Nabataean in Provincia Arabia after 106 as official language. Almost all purely Greek texts from Palmyra are official and come from the agora.
3. Most strikingly in the documents from the Judaean Desert: DJD 2: 243-56, nos. 115-16; N. Avigad et al., "The Expedition to the Judaean Desert, 1960," *IEJ* 11 (1961): 53-62; idem, "The Expedition to the Judaean Desert, 1961," *IEJ* 12 (1962): 258-62.
4. See above, p. 46.
5. N. Jidejian, *Baalbek: Heliopolis, "City of the Sun"* (Beirut, 1975), pp. 22-23; L. I. Levine, *Caesarea under Roman Rule* (Leiden, 1975), pp. 42-43.
6. Seyrig, *Antiquités Syriennes,* no. 26, "La grande statue parthe de Shami et la sculpture palmyrénienne," 3: 13.
7. Mark 7: 26.
8. J. Cantineau, J. Starcky, and J. Teixidor, eds., *Inventaire des Inscriptions de Palmyre*, 11 fascs. (Beirut and Damascus, 1930-65) 10: 89, no. 145, and many other inscriptions.

9. Ibid. 10: 22, no. 29.

10. R. Savignac and J. Starcky, "Une inscription Nabatéenne provenant du Djôf," *RB* 64 (1957): 216, citing early Nabataean inscription and third century Palmyrene stones.

11. *CIS* II 195 (A.D. 39).

12. *CIJ* 1374; cf. *CERP*, pp. 228-30, for the significance of the continuation of old place names.

13. F. Millar, "The Background to the Maccabean Revolution," *JJS* 29 (1978): 4.

14. Seyrig, *Antiquités Syriennes*, no. 13, "Le culte de Bel et de Baalshamin à Palmyre," 1: 87-102.

15. See above, p. 47; the feasts (מרזחא): G. A. Cooke, *A Text Book of North-Semitic Inscriptions* (London, 1903), p. 302, no. 104; the priests (כמר): Cantineau, Starcky, and Teixidor, *Inscriptions* 9: 29, no. 19.

16. Rostovtzeff, "La Syrie Romaine," p. 26.

17. Cf. M. A. R. Colledge, *The Art of Palmyra* (London, 1976), p. 21.

18. E.g., Berytus, whose official inscriptions were a mixture of Latin and Greek; cf. R. Mouterde and J. Lauffray, *Beyrouth Ville Romaine: Histoire et Monuments* (Beirut, 1952), pp. 15-16.

19. E.g., the Palmyrene customs inscription: *CIS* II 3913; *OGIS* II 629.

20. Eusebius, *Mart. Pal.*, p. 4 (Syriac text), re Procopius.

21. Avigad et al., "Expedition, 1961," p. 235; cf. C. Rabin, in *Compendia* 2: 1009, and E. Schürer, *History of the Jewish People in the Age of Jesus Christ*, 2 vols. so far, revised G. Vermes, F. Millar, and M. Black (Edinburgh, 1973-79) 2: 27-8.

22. J. K. Stark, *Personal Names in Palmyrene Inscriptions* (Oxford, 1971), pp. 131-41.

23. Some transcriptions are mistaken, which suggests a lack of comprehension, see below, p. 151.

24. M. Avi-Yonah, *Oriental Art in Roman Palestine* (Rome, 1961), pp. 66 ff.

25. E.g., southern Palestine. Cf. Avi-Yonah, *Oriental Art*, p. 64.

26. Colledge, *Art of Palmyra*, passim.

27. C. H. Kraeling, ed., *The Excavations at Dura Europus: Final Report*, Vol. 8, pt. 1, *The Synagogue* (New Haven, 1956), pp. 390-95: the synagogue is a mixture of semitic, Greek, and Iranian elements, but the semitic predominates.

28. E.g., Nabataeans (Avi-Yonah, *Oriental Art*, pp. 43-57).

29. E.g., Antioch; cf. D. Levi, *Antioch Mosaic Pavements,* 2 vols. (Princeton, 1947): a strong hellenic tradition.

30. J. B. Segal, *Edessa, "the Blessed City"* (Oxford, 1970), p. 31.

31. Odenath, Waballath, and Zenobia. Cf. H. M. D. Parker, *A History of the Roman World from A.D. 138 to 337* (London, 1935), pp. 190-92, 198-200.

32. Millar, "Background to Maccabees," pp. 4-5, gives what evidence there is.

33. Colledge, *Art of Palmyra*, p. 23 and passim.

34. E.g., M. Hengel, *Judaism and Hellenism: Studies in their Encounter in Palestine during the Early Hellenistic Period*, 2 vols., translated by J. Bowden (London, 1974).

35. *AJ* 20. 263-64; but lack of fluency may only refer to his literary style.

36. E.g., t A. Zar. 1: 20 (Z., p. 461): R. Joshua.

37. S. Lieberman, *Hellenism in Jewish Palestine*, 2nd ed. (New York, 1962), pp. 100-114.

38. M. Avi-Yonah, *The Jews of Palestine: A Political History from the Bar*

Kokhba War to the Arab Conquest (Oxford, 1976), p. 66, for theories of continued "zealot" movements.

39. Cf. Rabin, in *Compendia* 2: 1025 ff.; Schürer, *History* 2: 20–21.
40. E.g., *BJ* 1: 3: Josephus wrote the *Bellum* originally in Aramaic.
41. Matt. 27: 46.
42. Mark 5: 41.
43. E.g., in lower synagogue in Gischala (*EAEHL* 4: 1135).
44. E.g., *EAEHL* 2: 460, 467.
45. E.g., in Tiberias synagogue (fourth century?): M. Schwabe, "Recently Discovered Jewish Inscriptions," *Yediot* 18 (1954): 161 (Heb.).
46. Schürer, *History* 2: 25, re names on ossuaries.
47. E.g., Sifre Deut. 303, p. 321: formulaic declaration about poor tithes may be in any language; m Ber. 4: 3: abbreviated prayers for the unlearned.
48. Avigad et al., "Expedition, 1960," pp. 46–47, no. 12; Schürer, *History* 2: 27.
49. *EAEHL* 3: 705.
50. *EAEHL* 2: 464.
51. Epiphanius, *Panarion* 30. 3.
52. E.g., Sifre Deut. 333, p. 383 (R. Meir): to deserve Paradise, it is sufficient to live in Palestine, say the Shema, and speak Hebrew.
53. Schürer, *History* 2: 27–28.
54. Schürer, *History* 2: 25.
55. See above, p. 66.
56. The scroll of Esther on Purim: t Meg. 3 (4): 13 (L., p. 356); 2: 6 (L., p. 349).
57. L. I. Levine, *Caesarea under Roman Rule* (Leiden, 1975), p. 70.
58. Note the qualification; cf. N. R. M. de Lange, *Origen and the Jews* (Cambridge, 1976), pp. 10, 22.
59. *Beth Shearim* 2: 219; H. B. Rosen, "Palestinian κοινή in rabbinic illustration," *JSS* 8 (1963): 56–72, tries to reconstruct a specifically Palestinian dialect of Greek.
60. E.g., "Σάβερος υἱὸς Σάβινο ἀρχιβαφθος" (B. Lifshitz, "Beiträge zur palästinischen Epigraphik," *ZDPV* 78 [1962]: 64).
61. *Beth Shearim* 2: 219–21.
62. *Beth Shearim* 2: 220.
63. *CIJ* II 991.
64. Schwabe, "Recently Discovered Inscriptions," p. 161, though a marble worker might well be a visiting craftsman given the lack of marble found naturally in Galilee and therefore the improbability of an indigenous marble industry.
65. E. M. Meyers, "Galilean Regionalism as a Factor in Historical Reconstruction," *BASOR* 221 (1976): 97.
66. E. M. Meyers and C. L. Meyers, "Digging the Talmud in Ancient Meiron," *Biblical Archaeology Review* 4, no. 2 (June, 1978): 42.
67. For Greek and Hebrew signatures to Hebrew documents: DJD 2: 142, no. 29.
68. S. Krauss, *Griechische und Lateinische Lehnworter im Talmud, Midrash und Targum*, 2 vols. (Berlin, 1898–99); Schürer, *History* 2: 72 ff.
69. Compare the use of French words in English; cf. Schürer, *History* 2: 74.
70. S. Lieberman, *Formation of the Caesarean Talmud*, supplement to *Tarbiz* 2, no. 4 (Jerusalem, 1931) (Heb.).
71. Levine, *Caesarea*, p. 70.

72. H. A. Harris, *Greek Athletics and the Jews*, edited by I. M. Barton and A. J. Brothers (Cardiff, 1976), p. 45.
73. Sifre Deut. 306, p. 336: ערך 'is לשון כנעני.
74. Cf. the modern spread of American culture among non-English speakers in the Middle East.
75. Schürer, *History* 1: 384-86; 2: 59.
76. *AJ* 15. 276.
77. V. Sussman, "Early Jewish Iconoclasm," *Atiqot* 7 (1974): 95-96 (Heb.).
78. E. L. Sukenik, *Ancient Synagogues in Palestine and Greece* (London, 1934), p. 21.
79. MdRi Bahodesh 6: 58 ff.: comprehensive prohibition of all graven images; MdRi Bahodesh 10: 101: no gods made of silver just for adornment.
80. E. E. Urbach, "The Rabbinical Laws of Idolatry in the Second and Third Centuries in the Light of Archaeological and Historical Facts," *IEJ* 9 (1959): 154 ff.; Schürer, *History* 2. 59: "second and third centuries."
81. t A. Zar. 5 (6): 1 (Z., p. 468).
82. t A. Zar. 5 (6): 2 (Z., p. 468).
83. y A. Zar. 2: 19 (Leningrad ms.).
84. Avigad et al., "Expedition, 1960," p. 50.
85. Avigad et al., "Expedition, 1961," p. 230.
86. Sukenik, *Ancient Synagogues,* pp. 61-67; and for the dates, see below, p. 85.
87. *Beth Shearim* 1: Plate xv, no. 2, etc.
88. *EAEHL* 1: 221.
89. m A. Zar. 4: 4.
90. t A. Zar. 5 (6): 5 (Z., p. 468).
91. Kraeling, *Dura Europus Synagogue*, p. 392, suggests that synagogue wall-painting might have been an established genre long before the first century, but not necessarily in Palestine.
92. Avigad et al., "Expedition, 1960," p. 39: Roman booty?
93. E. J. Bickerman, "Sur la Théologie de l'Art Figuratif," *Syria* 44 (1967): 131-61, against E. R. Goodenough, *Jewish Symbols in the Greco-Roman Period*, 13 vols. (New York, 1953-68).
94. E.g., Edessa church mosaic of the fifth century, which has a very pagan content (J. Leroy, "Mosaïques funéraires d'Édesse," *Syria* 34 [1957]: 323).
95. Cf. the mosaics of the Hammat Tiberias synagogue and those of Beth Alpha.
96. G. Foerster, in *Compendia* 2: 1002, dates the change too early, to the period immediately following the Bar Kokhba war; there is almost a half century after this until the Beth Shearim sarcophagi.
97. m A. Zar. 3: 1, 2; see above, n. 90.
98. E. M. Meyers, A. T. Kraabel, and J. F. Strange, "Ancient Synagogue Excavations at Khirbet Shema', Israel, 1970-72," *AASOR* 42 (1976): 250-53.
99. Cf. Avi-Yonah, *Oriental Art*, pp. 29-42.
100. Ibid., p. 32: "the current Greco-Syrian style in its Hauranic variety."
101. G. Foerster, in L. I. Levine, ed., *Ancient Synagogues Revealed* (Jerusalem, 1981), pp. 47-48.
102. *Beth Shearim* 1: 26; E. Meyers, Kraabel, and Strange, "Synagogue at Kh. Shema'," pp. 119-22.
103. E.g., Kh. Shema'. See E. Meyers, Kraabel, and Strange, "Synagogue at Kh. Shema'," p. 260.

104. M. Avi-Yonah, "Oriental elements in the Art of Palestine in the Roman and Byzantine Periods," *QDAP* 11 (1944): 105-51; 13 (1948): 128-65.
105. *EAEHL* 1: 240, 242.
106. Colledge, *Art of Palmyra*, p. 58 ff.
107. Palmyrene Jews (*Beth Shearim* 1: 197); Palmyrene cemetries (Colledge, *Art of Palmyra*, p. 58 ff.).
108. N. Avigad, "Ancient Jewish Art in Galilee," *EI* 7 (1964): 18-23 (Heb.).
109. Ibid.
110. Avi-Yonah, *Oriental Art*, p. 33 ff.
111. S. Applebaum, *Prolegomena to the Study of the Second Jewish Revolt* (Oxford, 1976), p. 26: after A.D. 70.
112. Particularly Goodenough, *Jewish Symbols*, Vol. 12.
113. *EAEHL* 4: 189; this is not to deny possible symbolism in the mosaics, just their connection with the traditions behind Dura-Europus.
114. Kraeling, *Dura Europus Synagogue*, p. 398 ff.
115. G. M. Harper, "Village Administration in Syria," *YCS* 1 (1928): 153, cites an inscription from near Antioch: a village school, presumably privately funded, unlike the publicly supported *grammatikoi* of the larger Greek cities.
116. m Ab. 5: 21: Judah b. Tema on the stages of education. The rapidity of progress from stage to stage may well be idealistic, the passage is missing in some mss., and the meaning of "talmid" is obscure, but the first stage would anyway be likely. On schools in general, see Schürer, *History* 2: 417 ff.; on stages in education, ibid., 2: 421-42, n. 41.
117. m Ber. 4: 3.
118. m Bikk. 3: 7.
119. m Sukk. 3: 10.
120. Y. Yadin, in N. Avigad et al., "Expedition, 1961," pp. 253-54, re כתב על נפשה not meaning that the individual concerned signed on his own behalf. If this is so, some of those concerned may well be illiterate. The term מפמרא ("from his dictation") presumably indicates illiteracy since one would expect signatures at least to be those of the individual concerned (e.g., DJD 2: 159, re no. 42, where the handwriting is very different in the signatures of the scribe and the witnesses).
121. t Yad. 2: 11-12 (Z., p. 683); H. I. Marrou, *A History of Education in Antiquity*, translated by G. Lamb (London, 1956), pp. 269-71.
122. t Yad. 2: 11 (Z., p. 683): problems over the sanctity of copybooks once such prayers have been copied out in them.
123. m Ned. 4: 3 (in some mss.); note the literacy of Babata.
124. Marrou, *History of Education*, pp. 265-66.
125. t Hag. 1: 2 (L., p. 375).
126. *Compendia* 2: 952 (from Genesis Rabba).
127. MdRi Pisha 18: 111-13: swimming is ascribed to Akiba, "civics" (Lauterbach's translation) to R. Judah ha Nasi.
128. Schürer, *History* 2: 418-19.
129. *AJ* 16: 203: this is a translation of "κωμογραμματεῖς." The sons of Herod were fitted for the post by their παιδεία, so the post is therefore presumably not political.
130. m Kidd. 4: 13; t Kidd. 5: 10 (L., p. 297): such a man should not teach scribes (*soferim*).
131. Marrou, *History of Education*, p. 267.
132. m Shab. 1: 3.

133. m Ned. 4: 3.
134. t Kel. B.B. 1: 2 (Z., p. 591).
135. Sifre Deut. 160, p. 211: a *luaḥ* as an alternative to paper.
136. DJD 2: 216–31: accounts etc., on skins in Greek; DJD 2: 87–92: similar trifles in Hebrew.
137. E.g., DJD 2: 90–92, nos. 10, 11.
138. Marrou, *History of Education*, p. 274 ff. The evidence used by Marrou will not have applied to the inhabitants of many Egyptian villages, where literacy was rare (H. C. Youtie, *Scriptiunculae*, 2 vols. (Amsterdam, 1973) 2: 611–27).
139. Harris, *Greek Athletics and the Jews*, p. 91.
140. m Ab. 5: 21. I take this to be the meaning of משנה ("repetition") and מצות ("duties"), but this is clearly only speculative; cf. Josephus, *Contra Apionem* 1. 60 (12); 2. 204 (25): Schürer, *History* 2: 421, n. 41.
141. *Vita* 8: μνήμη and σύνεσις
142. Origen, *c. Celsum* 2. 34.
143. *AJ* 20. 263.
144. *Beth Shearim* 2: 220; 2: 97 ff.; cf. J. Brand, "Concerning Greek culture in Palestine during the Talmudic period," *Tarbiz* 38 (1968–69): 13–17 (Heb.), for the origin of Justus.
145. t A. Zar. 1: 20 (Z., p. 461).
146. De Lange, *Origen and the Jews*, p. 22.
147. Lieberman, *Hellenism in Palestine*, p. 100 ff.
148. Levine, *Caesarea*, pp. 70–71.
149. See above, n. 144.
150. Origen, *c. Celsum* 1: 67.
151. Tertiary education: Marrou, *History of Education*, pp. 284 ff.; political influence of the sophists: F. Millar, *The Emperor in the Roman World (31 B.C.–A.D. 337)* (London, 1977), pp. 83, 424.
152. *AJ* 17. 226.
153. *Vita* 40: a good demagogue; *Vita* 356: made secretary to Agrippa.
154. *EAEHL* 2: 409; but the hermit Hilarion from Gaza finished his Greek education in Alexandria in the early fourth century according to Jerome, *Vita Hilarionis* 2 (J. P. Migne, ed., *Patrologia Latina*, 221 vols. [Paris, 1879–90] 23: 30).
155. N. Jidejian, *Tyre through the Ages* (Beirut, 1969), p. 90; C. P. Jones, "Two enemies of Lucian," *Greek, Roman and Byzantine Studies* 13 (1972): 490, re Hadrian of Tyre (though Hadrian *studied* at Antioch).
156. *AJ* 20. 264.
157. Justin Martyr, *Dial. c. Trypho.* 58: Trypho accuses Justin of expertise in rhetoric. Cf. the deliberate Christian *sermo humilis*: see, e.g., Augustine, *Epist.* 17, which is in deliberate contrast to the eloquence of his pagan correspondent.
158. S. Sandmel, *Philo of Alexandria: an Introduction* (New York and Oxford, 1979).
159. E.g., Numenius reckoning Plato to be the Greek Moses (De Lange, *Origen and the Jews*, p. 69).
160. Origen believed that the Bible taught the Greeks their philosophy (ibid., p. 67).
161. Jidejian, *Tyre*, p. 90.
162. On such imitations, cf. E. Bickerman, *Four Strange Books of the Bible* (New York, 1967), pp. 143–45.

163. Cf. Lucian, *Vitarum Auctio* 9–11; E. Bickerman, *Four Strange Books*, p. 144.
164. The thesis of H. A. Fischel, *Rabbinic Literature and Greco-Roman Philosophy: a Study of Epicurea and Rhetorica in Early Midrashic Writings* (Leiden, 1973), is not at all convincing. A few rabbinic texts are twisted to agree with Epicurean evidence culled from widely disparate sources. This is not enough to show a "common tradition" (ibid., p. 89).
165. Marrou, *History of Education*, pp. 187–92.
166. A. H. M. Jones, "Inscriptions from Jerash," *JRS* 18 (1928): 151, inscr. no. 2.
167. Eusebius, *Mart. Pal.* p. 4 (Syriac text).
168. Lieberman, *Hellenism in Palestine*, pp. 180–93 (on science), p. 73 (on mathematics).
169. See above, p. 60.
170. C.J. 10. 50. 1.
171. S. Krauss, "Outdoor Teaching in Talmudic times," *JJS* 1 (1948–49): 82–84. Cf. t Kil. 1: 4 (L., pp. 262–63): a pupil giving purity instruction in the market place.
172. Origen, *c. Celsum* 3. 50–51.
173. Justin Martyr, *Dial. c. Trypho.* 92: remarks on the crowd listening; for Galilee, S. Krauss, "Outdoor Teaching," p. 83.
174. H. Chadwick, *Origen: Contra Celsum* (Cambridge, 1953), p. xi.
175. Compare the broadly ethical considerations of Sifre to the legal preoccupations of Mishnah and Tosefta.
176. t Shebu. 3: 6 (Z., pp. 449–50).
177. t Hull. 2: 24 (Z., p. 503).
178. m A. Zar. 3: 4. Cf. the philosopher Iamblichus performing miracles at Hammat Gader, according to Eunapius, *Vitae Phil. et Soph.* 459.
179. Midrash Tannaim 26: 19 (ed. Hoffman, p. 262).
180. L. Wallach, "The Colloquy of Marcus Aurelius with the Patriarch Judah I," *JQR* 31 (1940/1): 274–77.
181. De Lange, *Origen and the Jews*, p. 21: "I once heard a Jew."
182. Ibid., pp. 75–102; A. Büchler, *Studies in Jewish History* (London, 1956), p. 250.
183. Justin Martyr, *Dial. c. Trypho.*, passim.
184. G. Vermes, *Post-Biblical Jewish Studies* (Leiden, 1975), Chapter 2, "The Decalogue and the Minim," especially p. 177, suggests that the *minim* were "hellenistic" Jews, but not from Palestine.
185. De Lange, *Origen and the Jews*, p. 34.
186. See below, p. 86.
187. m Ber. 4: 2.
188. D. Urman, "Jewish inscriptions from Daburra, Golan," *Qadmoniot* 4 (1971): 133 (Heb.), from Daburra; dating these inscriptions between the second and fourth century A.D. is speculative.
189. m Ter. 11: 10.
190. m Shab. 18: 1: the propriety of clearing such straw to make room on the Sabbath.
191. E.g., Deir Aziz (*EAEHL* 2: 466).
192. E. Meyers, Kraabel, and Strange, "Synagogue at Kh. Shema'," p. 87, n. 65.
193. Personal observation in the Rockefeller Museum in Jerusalem.
194. E.g., m Eduy. 2: 4.

195. Krauss, "Outdoor Teaching," pp. 82-84.
196. m Ab. 1: 4 urges the good man to let sages meet in his house.
197. t Pes. 2: 16 (L., p. 147): deduced from "this is what *we* learnt on that day."
198. t Maas. 2: 1 (L., p. 230): R. Yohanan b. Zakkai, in Beror Hail near Yabneh.
199. t Nidd. 6: 6 (Z., p. 647); t Par. 4: 9 (Z., p. 633).
200. *AJ* 20. 264.
201. J. Neusner, *A History of the Mishnaic Law of Purities*, 22 parts (Leiden, 1974-77) 21: 13 and passim, re purity law; De Lange, *Origen and the Jews*, p. 105, re Jewish exegesis.
202. Preservation of ancient customs to help the Jewish nation should the Temple ever be rebuilt is possible, but cf. the lack of response to the Emperor Julian's attempts to bring this about in 362 (Avi-Yonah, *Jews of Palestine*, p. 196).
203. m B.B. 10: 8.
204. J. Neusner, *The Rabbinic Traditions about the Pharisees before 70*, 3 parts (Leiden, 1971) 3: 319. These form the subject matter of over half the Mishnah.
205. I.e., Maase Bereshit and Merkabah mysticism. Cf. G. Scholem, *Major Trends in Jewish Mysticism*, paperback edition (New York, 1961), pp. 40-79; m Hag. 2: 1 on restrictions on the students allowed to study such matters.
206. m Dem. 2: 3; cf. Matt. 5: 33-37, re oaths.
207. m Dem. 4: 6.
208. t Kidd. 3: 9 (L., p. 288).
209. t Taan. 1: 7 (L., pp. 324-25); Sifre Deut. 306, p. 339.
210. A. Büchler, *Der galiläische 'Am-ha'Ares des zweiten Jahrhunderts* 1906 (repr. Hildesheim, 1968); A. Oppenheimer, *The 'Am Ha-aretz: a Study in the Social History of the Jewish People in the Hellenistic-Roman Period*, translated by I. H. Levine (Leiden, 1977), p. 161 ff. Rules to be an *haver* are stricter than those to be *ne'eman*; t Dem. 2: 10 (L., p. 70 ff.) has a detailed discussion; see below, pp. 102-4.
211. m Hor. 3: 8.
212. E.g., t A. Zar. 3 (4): 9 (Z., p. 464): intermarriage; t A. Zar. 7 (8): 2 (Z., p. 471): helping an impure baker to bake bread. This is a new, more lenient ruling.
213. E.g., Sifre Deut. 48, p. 112: *all* are required to learn Torah.
214. See below, Chapter 7, on the extent of rabbinic authority.
215. Cf. L. Blau, "Early Christian Archaeology from the Jewish point of view," *HUCA* 3 (1926): 210, re similarity of special rabbinic dress to that of philosophers.
216. Sifre Deut. 344, p. 400.
217. De Lange, *Origen and the Jews*, p. 35; for tefillin in use in this period in the Judaean Desert, see DJD 2: 80 ff., no. 4 and others.
218. Sifre Num. p. 129, 1. 6, Shalah 115.
219. E.g., m Betz. 2: 3 on the need of one group (haburah) to re-kosher utensils used by another group.
220. Neusner, *Pharisees before 70* 3: 317.
221. m Ket. 5: 6.
222. Matt. 10: 37.
223. *AJ* 17. 42; 18. 12 ff.
224. E.g., Josephus; cf. *BJ* 1.648 ff.: young men with time to study every

day; *Vita* 191: Simon b. Gamaliel is of "high family"; *Vita* 197: deputation of three high-ranking (?) Pharisees from Jerusalem; see below, p. 93, for the change.

225. *BJ* 2. 162 ff., and elsewhere.
226. *AJ* 17. 155, Judas the Galilean is called "sophist" also; cf. *BJ* 2. 118.
227. Sifre Deut. 305, p. 324; Sifre Num. p. 63, 11. 22–23, Behaalotekha 68.
228. Cf. t Kel. B.B. 2: 3 (Z., p. 592): R. Eleazar asking a complex purity question of his father, R. Zadok.
229. t Kel. B.K. 4: 17 (Z., pp. 573–74): the daughter of R. Hanania b. Teradion gave better halakha on one occasion than her brother.
230. t Sanh. 7: 9 (Z., p. 426): the sons of the sages may not understand the proceedings but are nevertheless privileged.
231. See below, p. 93.
232. G. Alon, *Jews, Judaism and the Classical World* (Jerusalem, 1977), pp. 436–57, using rather late evidence.
233. Sifre Num., p. 141, 11. 5 ff., Korah 118.
234. m Ab. 4: 12.
235. t Ned. 5: 1 (L., p. 115): it takes a fixed amount of time.
236. E.g., Sifre Deut. 32, p. 57, re Tarfon, Joshua, Eleazar b. Azariah and Akiba visiting R. Eliezer.
237. Justin Martyr, *Dial. c. Trypho.* 112 sneers at those who study to get it (from Matt. 23: 7); Sifre Deut. 41, p. 85, warns against the same practice; *Beth Shearim* 1: 196, etc. reveals the title in use.
238. t B.M. 2: 30 (Z., p. 375). This is despite the term apparently equivalent to "rabbi" used in Beth Shearim (*Beth Shearim* 2: 95, no. 124).
239. Sifre Deut. 182, p. 224; t B.K. 9: 11 (Z., p. 364).
240. E.g., m B.M. 2: 11; one should ransom one's *rab* before one's father, etc.
241. MdRi Nezikin 1: 63, reasonably taken as reflecting earlier conditions from parallels with John the Baptist carrying the shoes of Jesus (Matt. 3: 11) and Jesus reversing the role by washing the disciples' feet (John 13: 5 ff.).
242. m Erub. 3: 5; Sifre Deut. 48, p. 110, suggests that one should start with a local rabbi and only later go elsewhere.
243. H. L. Strack, *Introduction to the Talmud and Midrash*, English translation (Philadelphia, 1931), p. 105 ff.
244. t A. Zar. 6 (7): 18 (Z., p. 471).
245. Lieberman, *Hellenism in Palestine*, pp. 83–84, suggests that the whole Mishnah was edited by such oral repetition; cf. the literal meaning of the word "tanna" as "a man who repeats."
246. t Zab. 1: 5 (Z., p. 676): R. Akiba puts in order the *zab* rules for his students.
247. t Pes. 3 (2): 11 (Z., p. 154).
248. Sifre Deut. 305, p. 324: a new *rab* will only be trusted if he spoke up while his rab was alive.
249. t Zeb. 2: 17 (Z., p. 483).
250. m Erub. 1: 2.
251. m Neg. 9: 3.
252. Sifre Num., p. 141, 11. 6 ff., Korah 118.
253. Sifre Num., p. 195, 11. 5–12, Pinhas 148.
254. t M. Sh. 5: 16 (L., pp. 271–72).
255. t Ohol. 16: 8 (Z., p. 614): wrong answers given deliberately to "spur them on."

256. Sifre Num., p. 158, 11. 15-17, Hukat 124.
257. D. M. Goodblatt, *Rabbinic Instruction in Sasanian Babylonia* (Leiden, 1975).
258. Above, n. 234: teaching groups are centered round the one *rab*.
259. m Ab. 5: 15; there seems to be some significance in the act of sitting down, cf. t Hag. 2: 1 (L., p. 380): Yohanan b. Zakkai insists on doing so before discussing the Chariot of Ezekiel; but t Taan. 2: 5 (L., p. 331) has R. Yohanan b. Nuri rise to his feet to defend a halakha.
260. t Sanh. 7: 8-10 (Z., p. 426). This, and the parallel in m Sanh. 4: 3-4, refers to the Sanhedrin as *court*, but references to the *talmidei ḥakhamim* suggest this is only the Academy in formal guise.
261. See below, p. 109.
262. M. Aberbach, "Educational Institutions and Problems during the Talmudic age," *HUCA* 37 (1966): 107-20.
263. m Yad. 4: 3: reply was about tithes.
264. t Sot. 7: 9 (L., p. 193).
265. Ibid.
266. t Dem. 8: 8 (L., p. 102). Evidently a weekday, because it is suggested that he might be separating tithes, which would be forbidden on the Sabbath.
267. Sifre Num. p. 133, 1. 17, Korah 116: Tarfon had been busy eating tithes.
268. t Yom Tob. 4: 6 (L., p. 301): borrowing a shirt from a friend to go to the beth midrash, though this was perhaps special, being on a festival.
269. E.g., the dispute in m Maksh. 6: 8; but the Mishnah and Tosefta evolve law precisely out of such displays of disputatiousness.
270. Philostratus, *Vitae Soph.* 531 (re Polemo) and passim; cf. Eunapius, *Vitae Phil. et Soph.* 486 (re initiation of students in Athenian schools), 483 (re feuds between schools).
271. Cf. *Compendia* 2: 963.
272. E.g., y Shab. 2: 7, 20b: professedly of the pupils of R. Eliezer, but perhaps reflecting later customs.
273. I.e., to be attracted by hellenistic philosophy. See above, n. 184; below, p. 105.
274. Ed. Frezouls, "Recherches sur les Théâtres de l'Orient syrien," *Syria* 36 (1959): 202-7; 38 (1961) : 54-86.
275. *EAEHL* 2: 471; S. Applebaum, "The Roman Theatre at Beth Shean," *Yediot* 25 (1961), p. 147 (Heb.): the Beth Shean theater is late second century.
276. *AJ* 15. 268.
277. Levine, *Caesarea*, p. 27.
278. L. Waterman, *Preliminary Report of the University of Michigan Excavation at Sepphoris, Palestine, in 1931* (Michigan, 1937), p. 29.
279. t A. Zar. 2: 5 (Z., p. 462); there was similar partial opposition in the first century to the use of the theater in Caesarea (*AJ* 19. 332-34).
280. E.g., Origen, *c. Celsum* 3. 56. Cf. Tertullian, *de Spectaculis.*
281. Lucian, *de Saltatione*; Frezouls, "Théâtres," 38 (1961): 82.
282. H. J. W. Drijvers, ed., *The Book of the Laws of Countries: Dialogue on Fate of Bardaisan of Edessa* (Assen, 1965), p. 50, 1. 8: Syria is not one of the areas excluded from such delights.
283. John Chrysostom, *Oratio contra Judaeos* 1. 2.
284. From personal observation in the Israel Museum.
285. A. W. Pickard-Cambridge, *The Dramatic Festivals of Athens*, 2nd ed., revised by J. Gould and D. M. Lewis (Oxford, 1968), p. 297.

286. t A. Zar. 2: 6 (Z., p. 462).
287. M. I. Rostovtsev, *Caravan Cities*, translated by D. Talbot Rice and T. Talbot Rice (Oxford, 1932), p. 76.
288. E.g., at Baalbek (Jidejian, *Baalbek*, p. 30).
289. In Caesarea, cf. Eusebius, *Mart. Pal.*, p. 11 (Syriac text).
290. t A. Zar. 2: 5 (Z., p. 462). Cf. n. 279, above.
291. Frezouls, "Théâtres," 38 (1961): 58.
292. Saccaea (*IGR* III 1192); Gerasa (Frezouls, "Théâtres," 38 [1961]: 85).
293. Frezouls, "Théâtres," 38 (1961): 64; cf. *AJ* 17. 161: Herod uses amphitheater for political purposes; *BJ* 2. 490, re Alexandria; F. Millar, *The Emperor in the Roman World (31 B.C.–A.D. 337)* (London, 1977), p. 37: Titus hears the Antiochean-Jewish debate in the Antioch theater.
294. A Büchler, *The Economic Conditions of Judaea after the Destruction of the Second Temple* (London, 1912), p. 64.
295. See below, pp. 84–87; G. Foerster, "The Synagogues at Masada and Herodium," *EI* 11 (1973): 224–28 (Heb.).
296. Drijvers, *Book of Laws of Bardaisan*, p. 52, l. 20.
297. *BJ* 2. 618; *Vita* 331.
298. *Vita* 132.
299. y Erub. 6: 31b: נפשה דסיריקין is probably a "Syrian monument."
300. m Shab. 22: 6: the question is whether it can be done on the Sabbath. Cf. *BJ* 4. 91: the training of a wrestler.
301. t Shab. 5 (6): 11 (L., p. 21).
302. Harris, *Greek Athletics and the Jews*, pp. 96–101. My conclusions are much less extreme than his.
303. Philo, *De Specialibus Legibus* 2. 230; but Jewish interest in gymnasia may be largely politically motivated in the hope of gaining Greek citizenship, cf. PLond., 1912; see A. D. Nock, "Downey's Antioch: a Review," *Greek, Roman and Byzantine Studies* 4 (1963): 51, n. 8, for the gymnasium as the center of Egyptian-Greek paganism.
304. The wrestlers and runners mentioned in the rabbinic texts are assumed to be amateurs (above, notes 300–301), since they are allowed, in the end, to practice on the Sabbath.
305. *IGR* III 1012 (A.D. 221).
306. Jidejian, *Tyre*, p. 111.
307. Idem, *Baalbek*, p. 29 (from coins).
308. Rostovtsev, *Caravan Cities*, p. 75.
309. *AJ* 15. 268–9.
310. *AJ* 17. 175.
311. R. Mouterde and J. Lauffray, *Beyrouth Ville Romaine*, p. 12.
312. *EAEHL* 2: 423.
313. L. Robert, *Les Gladiateurs dans l'Orient Grec* (Paris, 1940), p. 241.
314. *AJ* 15. 341; still in use in 300. Cf. Eusebius, *Mart. Pal.*, p. 11 (Syriac text).
315. Harris, *Greek Athletics and the Jews*, p. 34.
316. t Ohol. 18: 16 (Z., p. 617).
317. Ibid.
318. E.g., m A. Zar. 1: 7: no helping a gentile to build *stadia*; cf. Y. Baer, "Israel, the Christian Church and the Roman Empire," *Scripta Hierosolymitana* 7 (1961): 93.
319. According to K. G. Bruns and E. Sachau, eds., *Syrisch-Römisches Rechtsbuch aus dem fünften Jahrhundert* (Leipzig, 1880), p. 7 (Syro-Roman Law Book L9), no professional in athletic games can be made heir in Roman law.

320. *Beth Shearim* 1: 184.
321. m Kel. 23: 2: R. Yosi, but obscure.
322. MdRashbi Beshallah p. 52, 1. 14; MdRi Beshallah 2: 204-7; *Digest* 21. 1. 38. 14, re three-horse chariot teams.
323. *AJ* 14. 210: Hyrcanus gets special seats at Roman gladiatorial show.
324. After 70: *BJ* 7. 37 (Caesarea).
325. Cf. Philostratus, *Life of Apollonius of Tyana* 1. 16, on the strong feelings in Antioch and Ephesus for ensuring the continuance of the baths, and the Arab delight on finding baths in Syria after their conquest.
326. Exceptions: the orgies at the hot baths near Gadara (Epiphanius, *Panarion* 30. 7); the Jewish use of a ritual *mikveh* for purification and conversion (see p. 107, below).
327. m B.B. 4: 7.
328. Meiron has one of sorts (E. M. Meyers, C. L. Meyers, and J. F. Strange, "Excavations at Meiron in Upper Galilee—1974, 1975: Second Preliminary Report," *AASOR* 43 [1976]: 81), but other sites (e.g., Khirbet Shema', Khorazin) have not revealed any.
329. G. Tchalenko, *Villages Antiques de la Syrie du Nord: Le Massif du Bélus à l'Époque Romaine*, 3 vols. (Paris, 1953-58), p. 25 ff.: baths were quite common.
330. E.g., *Vita* 65: John of Gischala wants cure in Tiberias; *EAEHL* 4: 1179, re Tiberias; *EAEHL* 2: 469, re Gadara.
331. m B.B. 4: 6; t B.B. 3: 3 (Z., p. 402).
332. m Kil. 9: 3.
333. t Kel. B.M. 2: 12 (Z., p. 580): but this is from R. Gamaliel, therefore not in Galilee; cf. t Yom Tob. 2: 7 (L., p. 291) (re strigils?).
334. t Shab. 3 (4): 3 (L., p. 12), referring in fact, to early second century Bnei Barak in Judaea.
335. t Toh. 8: 7, 8 (Z., p. 669).
336. The *balanarios* . Cf. m Zab. 4: 2.
337. W. A. L. Elmslie, *The Mishna on Idolatry: 'Aboda Zara* (Cambridge, 1911), p. 14; public baths: m B.B. 4: 6 (it "belongs to *ha'ir*"); Epiphanius, *Panarion* 30. 12 (Tiberias); private baths hired out: m Ned. 5: 3.
338. m A. Zar. 1: 9; t A. Zar. 2: 9 (Z., p. 463) (R. Shimon b. Gamaliel).
339. m Meil. 5: 4; t B.B. 11: 12 (Z., p. 414); t M. Sh. 1: 4 (L., p. 244).
340. t Toh. 8: 8 (Z., p. 669): clothes are put in locker in *olearium* to stop gentiles touching them; m Maksh. 2: 5: bath heated on Sabbath for gentile use; m A. Zar. 3: 4: Gamaliel in baths at Akko.
341. m A. Zar. 1: 7: a Jew is even permitted by the tannaim to help gentiles build their bath-houses, apart from the pedestal for idolatrous statues.
342. t Mikw. 6: 4 (Z., p. 658): used only by day with Jewish attendants; t A. Zar. 3: 4 (Z., p. 463): dangerous to be alone with a gentile in a bath.
343. t A. Zar. 4 (5): 8 (Z., p. 466).
344. Cf. the Roman custom adopted in this period in much of the eastern Empire in place of the Greek gymnasium (*Oxford Classical Dictionary*, 2nd ed., s.v. "Baths").
345. m Shab. 22: 6.
346. t Makk. 3 (4): 3 (Z., p. 441); t Ter. 10: 10 (L., p. 162).
347. Sifre Deut. 258, p. 282; m A. Zar. 3: 4; t Ber. 2: 20 (L., p. 10): attempts to pray and discuss religious matters are allowed only in parts of bathhouse where everyone is dressed.
348. Acts 6: 9, and elsewhere.

349. *BJ* 2. 285.
350. Matt. 4: 23; Luke 7: 5 (Capernaum); *Vita* 277: προσευχή in Tiberias is a μέγιστον οἴκημα.
351. G. Foerster, "Synagogues at Masada and Herodium," pp. 224-28.
352. D. Saltz, "Surveys, Salvage and Small Digs in Israel," *American Schools of Oriental Research Newsletter*, no. 10 (May 1977): 3.
353. H. Shanks, *Judaism in Stone: The Archaeology of Ancient Synagogues* (New York and London, 1979), p. 76.
354. This tendency to assume any public building to be a synagogue without confirmation is found most of all on the Golan in the later Roman period: *EAEHL* 2: 460 (Qisrin), 464 (Kh. Dabya and Bathyra), 466 (En Nateh).
355. Sukenik, *Ancient Synagogues*, p. 27.
356. G. Foerster, "Ancient Synagogues in Eretz-Israel," *Qadmoniot* 5 (1972): 39, for distribution map; F. F. Hüttenmeister and G. Reeg, *Die antiken Synagogen in Israel*, 2 vols. (Wiesbaden, 1977), for a list of archaeological remains, literacy references, and inscriptions; Shanks, *Judaism in Stone*, for a useful summary of work so far.
357. *EAEHL* 1: 190 (Gaza synagogue also).
358. Sukenik, *Ancient Synagogues*, p. 27.
359. Shanks, *Judaism in Stone*, pp. 50-51.
360. Ibid., p. 50: the basilica type.
361. Ibid., p. 98: the broadhouse plan in late third-century Khirbet Shema' is particularly disconcerting.
362. E. Meyers, C. Meyers, and Strange, "Meiron Second Preliminary Report," p. 84.
363. Capernaum has numerous later Roman coins under a floor of an "early" design building (S. Loffreda, "The Late Chronology of Capernaum," *IEJ* 23 [1973]: 41); note the heroic attempt of Avi-Yonah to deny the weight of this evidence (M. Avi-Yonah, "Editor's Note," *IEJ* 23 [1973]: 43-5). The Gischala synagogue of apparently c. A.D. 250 has an "experimental" design (*American Schools of Oriental Research Newsletter* no. 3 [Nov. 1972]: 8); the Kh. Shema' broadhouse plan is dated by sealed layers of pottery and coins (E. Meyers, Kraabel, and Strange, "Synagogue at Kh. Shema'," p. 79); Kh. Neburaya has a small, "early" style synagogue with Hebrew inscription dating to A.D. 564, though this may only indicate use over a long period (*EAEHL* 3: 711).
364. As on the Golan: *EAEHL* 2: 467 ("second to fourth centuries").
365. E. Meyers, C. Meyers, and Strange, "Meiron Second Preliminary Report," p. 84.
366. *Beth Shearim* 1: 17-18.
367. Z. Yeivin, "Excavations at Khorazin," *EI* 11 (1973): 157 (Heb.) (largely dated by style).
368. Applebaum, *Prolegomena*, p. 18.
369. Beth Shearim: *Beth Shearim* 1: 16; Arbel: A. Segal, ed., *Ancient Sites of the Holy Land in the Classical Period: Selected Plans* (Beer-Sheva, 1978) (Heb.), plan 20; cf. Z. Yeivin, "Survey of the Settlements in Galilee and the Golan from the Period of the Mishnah in the Light of the Sources," (Ph.D. diss., Hebrew University of Jerusalem, 1971), p. vii.
370. t Meg. 3 (4): 22 (L., p. 360); Sukenik, *Ancient Synagogues,* pp. 50-52; the problem can be tackled by treating "east" as meaning "towards Jerusalem," cf. ibid., p. 52.
371. t Meg. 3 (4): 23 (L., p. 360); cf. Beth Shearim, Meiron, Kh. Shema', the

upper synagogue at Gischala, Arbel, Khorazin, etc.—all prominent buildings visible from afar; opposed to the earlier Halicarnassus document that claims that it is Jewish custom to make προσευχαί by the seaside (*AJ* 14. 258). It is at least possible that synagogues in the second century looked no different from any other houses, and hence the failure to recognize them in the archaeology. m Ned. 9: 2 records a second-century discussion that assumes that a private house might be *turned into* a synagogue.

372. M. Simon, *Verus Israel: Étude sur les Relations entre Chrétiens et Juifs dans l'empire Romaine (135-425)* (Paris, 1948), p. 51.
373. Schürer, *History* 2: 239.
374. Nehemiah 8: 8.
375. *Vita* 277 (Tiberias); *CIJ* II 1404 (Ophel).
376. A. Büchler, "Triennial Cycle: The Reading of the Law and the Prophets," *JQR* 5 (1893): 420-68; Mark 6: 2; *CIJ* II 1404; Luke 4: 16-21 (Isaiah); R. le Déaut, *Introduction à la literature targumique* (Rome, 1966), p. 32 ff.
377. Matt. 6: 5: disapproves of hypocrites who like to be seen praying in the synagogues; see Shanks, *Judaism in Stone*, pp. 19-20.
378. Matt. 23: 6.
379. Luke 4: 16-21 (Isaiah).
380. *Vita* 276-77 in Tiberias; Foerster, "Synagogues at Masada and Herodium," pp. 224-8: "like theatres"; *Compendia* 2: 942.
381. *CIJ* II 1404: the *xenona.*
382. Ibid. Cf. B. Lifshitz, *Donateurs et Fondateurs dans les Synagogues juives* (Paris, 1967). All the later names seem to have contributed only a part to the cost rather than build it all themselves. Theodotus in *CIJ* II 1404 may in fact be exceptional, since synagogues in Jerusalem would have a special function for the use of pilgrims that would not be required in Galilee.
383. E.g., m Meg. 4: 4.
384. t Maas. 2: 20 (L., p. 236): this is to be derived from the fact that the synagogue is apparently sometimes to be accounted a dwelling place for purity purposes.
385. t Sukk. 2: 5 (L., p. 262), with t B.B. 8: 14 (Z., p. 409): money is promised on the Sabbath, to be paid later.
386. Z. Yeivin, in *EAEHL* 1: 300.
387. *EAEHL* 2: 460.
388. J. Ben Zevi, "A third century Aramaic inscription in Er-rama," *JPOS* 13 (1933): 94-6; *CIJ* II 979.
389. Justin Martyr, *Dial. c. Trypho.* 117.
390. Justin Martyr, *Dial. c. Trypho.* 16; m Ber. 2: 3.
391. Exodus 15: 1-18; t Sot. 6: 2-3 (L., pp. 183-84); cf. G. Sarfatti, "Three comments regarding some tannaitic sources," *Tarbiz* 32 (1962-63): 139-42. The suggestion that the Shema was also sung in the synagogue is missing in the Vienna Codex for t Sot. 6: 2-3.
392. m R. Sh. 3: 7; m Sukk. 3: 13; cf. Hallel being sung: MdRashbi Beshallah 72: 18; and M. Avigad et al., "Expedition, 1960," pp. 48-49, doc. 15, for Sukkot being kept by Bar Kokhba. Festival celebrations in pre-70 Cyrenian synagogue: J. and G. Roux, "Un Décret du Politeuma des Juifs de Bérénikè en Cyrénaïque au Musée Lapidaire de Carpentras," *Revue des Études Grecques* 62 (1949): 283.
393. t B.K. 8: 11 (Z., p. 362): meat.

394. t Moed 2: 13 (L., p. 372).
395. For marriages, see *Compendia* 2: 757; for circumcisions, see m Shebi. 7: 4; Sifre Deut. 343, p. 398; for funerals, see m Ket 7: 5 (women going); *BJ* 2. 1: an expensive public funeral considered necessary for a holy man; Avi-Yonah, *Jews of Palestine*, p. 57; *Compendia* 2: 783; m M. Kat. 1: 5, re the funeral oration and expenses; m M. Kat. 3: 7, re mourners' meal with contributions.
396. Gischala lower synagogue (*EAEHL* 4: 1135).
397. m Ned. 5: 5: synagogue belongs to the town.
398. E. M. Meyers, J. F. Strange, C. L. Meyers, and R. S. Hanson, "Preliminary Report on the 1977 and 1978 Seasons at Gush Halav," *BASOR* 233 (Winter 1979): 35–37.
399. Cf. S. Sandmel, *Judaism and Christian Beginnings* (New York, 1978).
400. See above, pp. 46–49.
401. Shanks, *Judaism in Stone*, p. 51. See above, p. 70, on synagogue architecture.
402. b Shab. 72b.
403. *CERP*, p. 172.
404. D. Schlumberger, *La Palmyrène du Nord Ouest* (Paris, 1951), pp. 143–77.
405. John Chrysostom, *Hom. ad pop. Ant.* 19. 1.
406. De Lange, *Origen and the Jews*, p. 151, n. 56; S. Applebaum, "Judaea as a Roman province: the Countryside as a Political and Economic Factor," *ANRW* II (Principate) 8 (1977): 371, with wholly inadequate evidence.
407. *AJ* 18. 36; *Vita* 33–37.
408. *Vita* 39.
409. *Vita* 39, 375 (Sepphoris); 99, 381 (Tiberias).
410. S. Zeitlin, "Who were the Galileans?," *JQR* 64 (1973): 203.
411. E.g., *Vita* 375 ff.
412. G. Vermes, *Jesus the Jew: a Historian's Reading of the Gospels* (London, 1973), pp. 48–49.
413. S. G. F. Brandon, *Jesus and the Zealots* (Manchester, 1967), for political interpretation of Jesus' ministry.
414. t Nidd. 6: 9 (Z., p. 648) (כרך opposed to כפר); t Sot. 3: 16 (L., p. 165) (specifically Sepphoris and Tiberias).
415. See below, p. 139.
416. Harper, "Village Administration," pp. 112–15; also referring to Batanea and Trachonitis, *CERP*, p. 286, notes that large villages and cities differed only in prestige.
417. M. Ben-Dov, "Fragmentary Synagogue Inscription from Tiberias," *Qadmoniot* 9 (1976): 79–80 (Heb.).
418. Strack, *Introduction to Talmud*, p. 65.
419. Ibid., p. 118, re R. Judah ha Nasi.
420. See above, pp. 81–82.
421. E. M. Meyers, J. F. Strange, and D. E. Groh, "The Meiron Excavation Project: Archaeological Survey in Galilee and Golan, 1976," *BASOR* 230 (1978): 22; *EAEHL* 4: 1171, re Tiberias.
422. Cf. *Vita* 65 for Agrippa's magnificent palace. It was destroyed in A.D. 66, but other buildings must have remained—though it is strange to see how little of first century date has been found at Tiberias: *EAEHL* 4: 1171 (mostly late Roman).
423. Unless the *minim* are such men? If so, their numbers and importance are limited; see below, p. 105.

Chapter 7

1. The whole argument of this chapter is based on acceptance of the view that, before A.D. 132, most Galileans were nonrabbinic Jews (see, among others, G. Vermes, *Jesus the Jew: A Historian's Reading of the Gospels* [London, 1973], pp. 42–57. Cf. also the name of R. Yosi ha Galili, which would be strange if many other rabbis came from Galilee). A Oppenheimer, *The 'Am Ha-aretz: a Study in the Social History of the Jewish People in the Hellenistic-Roman Period*, translated by I. H. Levine (Leiden, 1977), pp. 200–217, has recently argued that this view is incorrect, but he does not convince: the evidence he adduces shows that Galileans were Jews who venerated the Bible but not that Galileans shared to any great extent the distinctive rabbinic interest in tithing and purity. On tithes, the only apparently persuasive case that he puts forward (p. 208) is from t Dem. 4: 13 (L., p. 80), which concerns beans in the market of Meiron, and a question sent on the subject to R. Akiba; this text is referred by S. Lieberman, *Tosefta Ki-fshutah: a Comprehensive Commentary on the Tosefta* (New York, 1955–   ), ad loc., to the use of Sabbatical Year produce. On the Sabbatical Year itself, t Shebi. 4: 13 (L., p. 182) is taken by Oppenheimer (p. 209) to show voluntary submission of a case by the Sepphoritans (taking the text to say: "They came and asked"), although the better ms. (Lieberman text) has: "the matter came before the sages," i.e., the sages in Beth Shearim got to hear of illicit customs only a few miles away. On purity, only t Maksh. 3: 5 (Z., p. 675), re R. Yosi and the obedience of the Sepphoritans over the watering of their cucumbers, is convincing (p. 209), and that, because of the date of R. Yosi, is likely to be post-A.D. 135. Stories of individual sages operating in Galilee are largely found in later texts and may project familiar Galilean geography onto by now semi-mythical figures. Nonetheless, Oppenheimer's work enjoins caution: *most*, rather than *all*, rabbis were immigrants from Judaea. Cf., similarly, S. Klein, *Eretz haGalil miyeme haaliyah miBavel ad ḥatimat haTalmud*, edited by Y. Eltizur (Jerusalem, 1967), p. 75 (Heb.).

2. S. Applebaum, in *Compendia* 2: 684.

3. E. E. Urbach, "Class status and leadership in the World of the Palestinian Sages," *Proceedings of Israel Academy of Sciences and Humanities* 2, pt. 4 (1966): 68, though his evidence for patriarchate or charitable support is all late.

4. See n. 2, above.

5. M. Avi-Yonah, *The Jews of Palestine: a Political History from the Bar Kokhba War to the Arab Conquest* (Oxford, 1976), p. 54; cf. J. Ostrow, "Tannaitic and Roman Procedure in Homicide," *JQR* 48 (1957–58): 352–70; 52 (1961–62): 160–67, 245–63: rabbis judge like Roman magistrates alongside a *quaestio* system (i.e., the beth din). This whole view is based ultimately on the reconstruction of rabbinic history by R. Sherira ha Gaon. Cf. J. Neusner, *A History of the Mishnaic Law of Purities*, 22 parts (Leiden, 1974–77) 21: 4–5.

6. E. Schürer, *History of the Jewish People in the Age of Jesus Christ*, 2 vols. so far, revised by G. Vermes, F. Millar, and M. Black (Edinburgh, 1973–79) 2: 210.

7. Neusner, *Purities*, passim. The argument is summarized ibid., part 22.

8. MdRi Nezikin 18: 55–63, about the last conversation of R. Shimon and R. Ishmael.

9. t Ohol. 4: 14 (Z., p. 601). This does not seem to be an actual case since it concerns Nazarites; cf. Sifre Deut. 48, p. 112: "our rabbis allowed them to go from '*ir* to '*ir* . . . to deal with purity cases."
10. t Kel. B.B. 2: 2 (Z., p. 591).
11. Ibid.
12. t Maksh. 3: 5 (Z., p. 675).
13. m Yad. 3: 1.
14. m Kel. 5: 4.
15. t Kel. B.M. 5: 3 (Z., p. 583).
16. t Kel. B.B. 1: 3 (Z., p. 590).
17. t Nidd. 4: 6 (Z., p. 644).
18. m Nidd. 8: 3.
19. t Nidd. 8: 3 (Z., p. 649).
20. t Nidd. 4: 3 (Z., p. 644).
21. m Shek. 1: 1; see below, pp. 121–22.
22. t Ohol. 16: 11 (12) (Z., p. 614).
23. t Ohol. 4: 2 (Z., p. 600).
24. t Nidd. 8: 7 (Z., p. 650).
25. MdRi Amalek 4: 20–21.
26. MdRi Kaspa 3: 62–66.
27. Sifre Deut. 152, p. 205: niddah and other issues of blood; ibid.; "*nega*'" ("injury" *R.S.V.*) is taken as "leprosy sign."
28. m Bekh. 4: 4.
29. t Hull. 2: 13 (Z., p. 502).
30. m Maksh. 3: 4: the exact place is not certain.
31. t Kil. 1: 4 (L., pp. 203–4).
32. t Kil. 1: 3 (L., p. 203).
33. m Kil. 6: 4.
34. m Kil. 4: 9.
35. t Shebi. 4: 13 (L., p. 182). Note the use by Oppenheimer, '*Am Ha-aretz*, p. 209, of the wrong edition of this text (see above, n. 1).
36. m Kil. 7: 5.
37. Oppenheimer, '*Am Ha-aretz*, p. 23 ff., gives a clear account of tithes owed.
38. m Bekh. 4: 5.
39. m Bekh. 6: 8.
40. m Bekh. 6: 9.
41. m Bekh. 6: 6.
42. t Bekh. 4: 8 (Z., p. 539).
43. Sifre Num., p. 133, 11. 16–19, Korah 116. Josephus speaks in the present tense of the tithes owed to him as a priest (*Vita* 80); Sifre Deut. 352, p. 409: "most priests are rich" should be still relevant in the second century (why not "*were* rich" otherwise?); cf. the special plot for Cohanim in Beth Shearim (*Beth Shearim* 2: 31); *Compendia* 2: 584; Oppenheimer, '*Am Ha-aretz*, p. 42 ff.
44. m Ter. 4: 13.
45. t Shebi. 5: 2 (L., p. 186).
46. m Shab. 16: 7; 22: 3.
47. m Betz. 3: 5.
48. m Erub. 10: 10.
49. m Shab. 3: 4.
50. t Erub. 4 (6): 16 (L., p. 110).

51. m Erub. 7: 7 and t Moed 2: 15-16 (L., p. 372), on the use of golden slippers, etc.
52. m A. Zar. 5: 2.
53. m A. Zar. 3: 7.
54. m A. Zar. 4: 12.
55. t Meg. 3 (4): 35 (L., p. 363).
56. t Hag. 2: 13 (L., p. 386).
57. t Meg. 3 (4): 21 (L., p. 359); *CIJ* II 991: the *archsynagogi* of Tyre and Sidon at Sepphoris; cf. below, pp. 123-24.
58. m Yeb. 16: 7.
59. m R. Sh. 1: 6; 2: 8.
60. E.g., m R. Sh. 1: 3.
61. t Pes. 2 (1): 16 (L., p. 147).
62. m Gitt. 4: 7.
63. m Ned. 9: 5.
64. m Ned. 5: 6. Cf. the New Testament on pharisaic preoccupation with the validity of oaths (Matt. 5: 34; 23: 16); and Qumran in the *Damascus Rule* (G. Vermes, *The Dead Sea Scrolls in English* (Harmondsworth, 1962), pp. 108-9).
65. t Taan. 2 (3): 13 (L., p. 334).
66. G. Vermes, *Post-Biblical Jewish Studies* (Leiden, 1975), p. 189; m Taan. 3: 8.
67. t Taan. 1: 7 (L., p. 325); cf. Matt. 6: 16: "In fasts, do not be like the hypocrites who make their faces unsightly."
68. m Taan. 2: 5.
69. m Taan. 3: 9.
70. m Taan. 3: 8.
71. *Compendia* 1: 405.
72. See below, p. 128.
73. t A. Zar. 1: 8 (Z., p. 461) (R. Yosi and Yoseph ha Cohen); t Nidd. 6: 6 (Z., p. 647) (Hanania b. Khinai); t Par. 4: 9 (Z., p. 633) (Hanina b. Gamaliel).
74. m A. Zar. 3: 7: the tree.
75. t Nidd. 4: 6 (Z., p. 644): *niddah*.
76. m Gitt. 4: 7.
77. See below, p. 126.
78. See below, pp. 126-27, 160-61.
79. E.g., MdRi Nezikin 18: 58-59: it is the *client* who comes to ask for judgment.
80. Luke 11: 46: complaint against the *νομικοί* for loading men with burdens hard to bear.
81. Oppenheimer, *'Am Ha-aretz*, has discussed this issue in detail, not always convincingly. His criticism of the approach of Zeitlin is excellent, but his disagreement with Büchler (p. 5) is asserted rather than argued, and he has a tendency both to amalgamate evidence from different periods and to assume that each term used in the text refers to a separate group without reference to the intentions of the authors of the text. But it is a very useful work in clarifying the rabbis' view of the opposition to them. See also above, n. 1.
82. See below, pp. 104-7.
83. A. Büchler, *Studies in Jewish History* (London, 1956), p. 239.
84. m Bekh. 4: 10.

85. m Toh. 7: 3 (R. Meir); m Toh. 10: 3.
86. m Toh. 10: 1 (R. Shimon).
87. m Ter. 9: 2 (R. Akiba).
88. Mark 7: 3–4: Pharisees and all Jews wash hands before eating and cleanse vessels by ritual dipping. This may show a general acceptance of the principles of purity (cf. G. Alon, *Jews, Judaism and the Classical World* (Jerusalem, 1977), pp. 190–234), but not a general attention to the pharisaic minutiae (Oppenheimer, *'Am Ha-aretz*, pp. 58–62).
89. m Hull. 7: 1, though the sages did not agree.
90. t Dem. 4: 9 (L., p. 79).
91. t Hull. 1: 1 (Z., p. 500).
92. *AJ* 14. 261; cf. the figs and nuts eaten by priests sent to Rome (*Vita* 14).
93. Origen, *c. Celsum* 8. 29.
94. m A. Zar. 4: 9.
95. t A. Zar. 7 (8): 2 (Z., p. 471).
96. t Maksh. 3: 10 (Z., p. 675).
97. t Maksh. 3: 8 (Z., p. 675).
98. m Shek. 1: 2: R. Judah on the increase in Kilaim nonobservance, in the mid second century. The need to insure efficient use of land in more crowded conditions after 135 may be part of the reason.
99. E.g., MdRi Shabbata 1: 118.
100. m Ab. 5: 9; t A. Zar. 7 (8): 10 (Z., p. 472).
101. m R. Sh. 1: 8 = m Sanh. 3: 3.
102. m Shebi. 5: 8.
103. E.g., m Shebi. 8: 11: profiting by using a bath heated with Shebiit straw is permitted, but not approved.
104. t Dem. 3: 17 (L., p. 78).
105. E.g., *AJ* 14. 475, re c. 37 B.C.
106. DJD 2: 125, no. 24. This does not prove that Bar Kokhba enforced the Sabbatical Year, *contra Compendia* 2: 652.
107. Y. Sussman, "A halakhic inscription from the Beth-Shean valley," *Tarbiz* 43 (1973–74): 88–158 (Heb.).
108. See Oppenheimer, *'Am Ha-aretz*, p. 29 ff., for slightly muddled discussion.
109. t A. Zar. 3: 10 (Z., p. 464): ruling of the sages against R. Meir.
110. Cf. m Bekh. 4: 10.
111. t M. Sh. 3: 18 (L., pp. 261–62).
112. m Bekh. 4: 9 (R. Judah).
113. m Bekh. 4: 7.
114. m Ab. 5: 9.
115. m M. Sh. 5: 15. This may, however, refer to new legislation by Yohanan.
116. t Erub. 5 (7): 18 (L., p. 115).
117. t Shab. 3 (4): 3 (L., p. 12).
118. H. J. W. Drijvers, ed., *The Book of the Laws of Countries: Dialogue on Fate of Bardaisan of Edessa* (Assen, 1965), p. 58; cf. the observance of Sabbath during the first revolt: *Vita* 159–61; *BJ* 2. 392–93.
119. t A. Zar. 7 (8): 10 (Z., p. 472).
120. t Gitt. 3: 7 (L., p. 257): the ruling is "for the public order."
121. E. E. Urbach, "The Rabbinical Laws of Idolatry in the Second and Third Centuries in the Light of Archaeological and Historical Facts," *IEJ* 9 (1959): 160–61.
122. m Ab. 3: 10.
123. t Meg. 2: 5 (L., p. 349).

124. See above, p. 99.
125. t B.K. 8: 14 (Z., p. 362).
126. t B.M. 2: 33 (Z., p. 375).
127. t B.M. 5: 7 (Z., p. 381).
128. t Shebi. 3: 13 (L., p. 177).
129. N. J. McEleney, "Orthodoxy in Judaism in the First Christian Century," *JSJ* 9 (1978): 83-88: if there was *any* orthodoxy in first century Judaism it applied only to a very few tenets, e.g., some belief in the validity of the Mosaic Law.
130. t B.M. 2: 33 (Z., p. 375).
131. N. R. M. de Lange, *Origen and the Jews* (Cambridge, 1976), p. 44; *contra* Büchler, *Studies in Jewish History*, pp. 247-73, whose claim that Jewish *minim* were only found in pre-Bar Kokhba Judaea is not substantiated.
132. m Meg. 4: 9; Sifre Deut. 86, p. 150; 218, p. 251; 320, p. 367; 330, p. 381. None of these passages gives a clear idea of the *kind* of theological heresy of which complaints are being made.
133. M. Simon, "Les sectes juives d'après les témoignages patristiques," *Studia Patristica* 1 (1957): 526-39, especially 532.
134. De Lange, *Origen and the Jews*, p. 37. This is despite the existence of sects *among* the Samaritans after 130 (M. Gaster, *The Samaritans* [London, 1923], p. 38; Origen, *c. Celsum* 1. 57).
135. For a discussion of tannaitic and later references to belief by some Jews in two powers, see A. F. Segal, *Two Powers in Heaven: Early Rabbinic Reports about Christianity and Gnosticism* (Leiden, 1977). Segal makes it clear (p. 121) that only in the *amoraic* period, if at all, was opposition to such beliefs dominant in Palestine. In the second century the only theological stance that needed countering in Galilee was the tendency of some Hellenistic Jews outside Palestine to seek a mediation between man and God. Cf. also Vermes, *Post-Biblical Jewish Studies*, p. 169 ff. Whether the hellenized Jews described by Celsus existed in Galilee is dubious, cf. de Lange, *Origen and the Jews*, p. 63 ff., especially p. 69, but some rabbinic arguments may be directed against ideas of Greek philosophers. See H. A. Fischel, *Rabbinic Literature and Greco-Roman Philosophy: a Study of Epicurea and Rhetorica in Early Midrashic Writings* (Leiden, 1973); Sifre Deut. 12, p. 20.
136. R. T. Herford, *Christianity in Talmud and Midrash* (London, 1903); B. Bagatti, *Excavations in Nazareth: From the Beginnings till the XII Century*, translated by E. Hoade (Jerusalem, 1969), p. 19; *contra* P. Benoit, "Review of W. D. Davies, *The Gospel and the Land* (London, 1974)," *RB* 83 (1976): 594, where the existence of any distinct "Galilean Christianity" is roundly denied. The speculation on this topic in S. Freyne, *Galilee from Alexander the Great to Hadrian, 323 B.C.E. to 135 C.E.* (Notre Dame, 1980), pp. 344-91, is not at all convincing, as Freyne himself admits (p. 379).
137. Epiphanius, *Panarion* 30. 11.
138. Epiphanius, *Panarion* 30. 5; cf. 30. 9, which concerns another rabbinic Jew living further south who was said to be afraid to convert to Christianity because of his fellow Jews.
139. Origen, *c. Celsum* 1. 52; cf. J. Wilkinson, *Jerusalem Pilgrims before the Crusades* (Warminster, 1977), p. 151.
140. Eusebius, *Onomasticon* 248; though Wilkinson, *Jerusalem Pilgrims*, pp. 20-28, shows that early pilgrims did not go to Galilee but stuck to the main Roman roads.

141. Epiphanius, *Panarion* 30. 3.

142. Matt. 28: 16.

143. Cf. the Protoevangelion of James, the brother of Jesus.

144. Bagatti, *Excavations in Nazareth*, p. 11.

145. De Lange, *Origen and the Jews*, p. 12 and passim.

146. Epiphanius, *Panarion* 30.

147. Above, n. 137.

148. V. C. Corbo, *The House of St. Peter at Capharnaum: a Preliminary Report of the First Two Campaigns of Excavations*, translated by S. Saller (Jerusalem, 1969).

149. Ibid., p. 71.

150. For grafitti, see V. C. Corbo, S. Loffreda, A. Spijkerman, and E. Testa, *Cafarnao*, 4 vols. (Jerusalem, 1972–75), Vol. 4, *I Grafitti della casa di S. Pietro*.

151. Bagatti, *Excavations in Nazareth*, p. 137.

152. t Hull. 2: 21 (Z., p. 503): advising complete separation from the *minim*.

153. t Hull. 2: 20 (Z., p. 503), re their bread, wine, and books, and the tithing of their produce.

154. t Hull. 1: 1 (Z., p. 500), re validity of their ritual slaughtering.

155. MdRi Pisha 15: 19, 20.

156. V. Burr, *Tiberius Julius Alexander* (Bonn, 1955).

157. S. Applebaum, *Prolegomena to the Study of the Second Jewish Revolt (A.D. 132–135)* (Oxford, 1976), p. 7: cf. MdRi Shabbata 1: 113 ff.

158. Justin Martyr, *Dial c. Trypho* 46.

159. m Hor. 1: 3.

160. See below, pp. 136, 138; cf. Justin Martyr, *Dial. c. Trypho.* 16: the only mark of Jews is the fleshly circumcision.

161. Meiron before Bar Kokhba (E. M. Meyers, C. L. Meyers, and J. F. Strange, "Excavations at Meiron in Upper Galilee—1974, 1975: Second Preliminary Report," *AASOR* 43 (1976): 81); Khirbet Shema' (E. M. Meyers, A. T. Kraabel, and J. F. Strange, "Ancient Synagogue Excavations at Khirbet Shema', Israel, 1970–1972," *AASOR* 42 (1976): 39–41; Khorazin (*EAEHL* 1: 300).

162. Cf. Aristophanes, *Lysistrata* for enforced abstention from sexual relations as a woman's weapon.

163. Assumed by Sifre Deut. 35, p. 63 and Justin Martyr, *Dial. c. Trypho.* 46; cf. the tefillin found in the Judaean desert (DJD 2: 83–85, no. 4; DJD 2: 85–86, no. 5, for possible *mezuza*).

164. See above, p. 102.

165. C. L. Grabbe, "Orthodoxy in First Century Judaism," *JSJ* 8 (1977): 152, re first century; cf. M. Avi-Yonah, "The Caesarean Inscriptions of the 24 Priestly Courses," *EI* 7 (1964): 24–28 (Heb.): Caesarean fourth to sixth century zodiac mosaic suggests continued importance of calendar element in religion. The Samaritan calendar had a mystical significance (Gaster, *Samaritans*, p. 66).

166. G. Vermes, *The Dead Sea Scrolls: Qumran in Perspective* (London, 1977), p. 176.

167. Avi-Yonah, *Jews of Palestine*, p. 62.

168. *AJ* 18. 15.

169. Matt. 23: 6–7.

170. t Kidd. 3: 9 (L., p. 288).

171. t B.K. 2: 13 (Z., p. 349).

172. t B.K. 6: 5 (Z., p. 354).
173. Special cases: Hanina b. Dosa (Vermes, *Post-Biblical Jewish Studies*, pp. 189 ff.); Honi the Circle-Maker (W. S. Green, "Palestinian Holy Men: Charismatic Leadership and Rabbinic Tradition," *ANRW* II (Principate) 19. 2. (1979): 619–47). Green points out that this emphasis on miraculous powers for rabbis is a third-century phenomenon (ibid., p. 646).
174. Sifre Deut. 357, p. 429.
175. Sifre Deut. 316, p. 358.
176. Luke 4: 2: Jesus' forty days in the desert.
177. E.g., Josephus in *Vita* 11.
178. Origen, *c. Celsum* 7. 9; cf. the Essenes and their power of prophecy (*AJ* 15. 379).
179. Neusner, *Purities* 21: 302 ff.
180. A limited circle of mystics, according to Origen, *c. Celsum* 1. 8.
181. G. Scholem, *Jewish Gnosticism, Merkabah Mysticism and Talmudic Tradition* (New York, 1960); *Encyclopedia Judaica* 10: 507: Sefer Yetzirah may be third century; J. A. Goldstein, "Review of E. R. Goodenough, *Jewish Symbols in the Greco-Roman Period*," *Journal of Near Eastern Studies* 28 (1969): 215 ff.: Dura Europus paintings concentrate on the topics at the center of rabbinic mysticism, and especially on the Merkabah.
182. P. S. Alexander, unpublished Littman Lectures, Oxford 1977.
183. Scholem, *Jewish Gnosticism*, pp. 36–42.
184. S. Lieberman, in Scholem, *Jewish Gnosticism*, pp. 118–26.
185. Despite prohibitions on learning Torah in order to get rich (Sifre Deut. 41, p. 87) and evidence that some rabbis enter the schools after a life spent in other, sometimes lucrative occupations—e.g., Yohanan b. Zakkai (Sifre Deut. 357, p. 429)—and complaints in the gospels of the Pharisees being φιλάργυροι (Luke 16: 14), there is little evidence of rabbis being wealthy.

    However, cf. M. Stern, in *Compendia* 2: 620, citing M. Beer, for examples of richer sages, and below, p. 113, for the rabbinic patriarchs. Gamaliel was rich (e.g., m B.M. 5: 8: generous to his tenants); Yohanan b. Mattia could afford to hire workers (m B.M. 7: 1); R. Ishmael gave a poor girl nice clothes to help her get married (m Ned. 9: 10). Rabbinic sarcophagi of the *third* century in Beth Shearim are very fine (cf. *Beth Shearim* 1: 39–41), but perhaps there was public help in paying for them; cf. the public mourning for R. Gamaliel (Avi-Yonah, *Jews of Palestine*, p. 57). Anyway, magnificent funerals had long been an important feature of pious Palestinian Judaism whether the family could afford it or not (*BJ* 2. 1).

    On the whole question of rabbinic occupations, see Urbach, "Class-Status and Leadership."
186. A Büchler, *The Political and the Social Leaders of the Jewish Community of Sepphoris in the Second and Third Centuries* (Oxford, 1909), p. 5.
187. *Compendia* 2: 620.
188. Büchler, *Political and Social Leaders*, p. 66, assumes that scholars in Sepphoris are maintained by the community and quotes (p. 75) Jerome, who asserts, remarkably given his own career, that rabbis live off funds donated by wealthy women; but all tannaitic texts assume that rabbinic occupations must bring no reward (m Ab. 4: 5; *AJ* 20. 265: "scarce two or three Jewish scholars are rewarded for their pains") except in the spiritual sense, t Hor. 2: 7 (Z., p. 476).

189. Büchler, *Political and Social Leaders*, p. 5; cf. *AJ* 18. 15: Pharisees operate through control of the populace.
190. t Sanh. 7: 7–8: 2 (Z., pp. 426–27). There are a number of passages in Sifre justifying the claim of the rabbinic court to authority equal to that of the pre-70 Sanhedrin (e.g., Sifre Deut. 144, p. 209: it is the rightness of the judgment that matters). In Sifre Deut. 153, p. 206, the words "Priests and Judge" in Deut. 17: 9 are taken to refer to the court at Yabneh and it is asserted that this court is valid without either Levite or Cohen (perhaps after this had been challenged).
191. t Sanh. 7: 7–11 (Z., pp. 426–27). Cf. the rather different picture in t Sanh. 8: 1 (Z., p. 427), re Yabneh (R. Gamaliel with two rabbis to his right and the elders to his left).
192. t Gitt. 3: 10 (L., p. 258).
193. t Ohol. 18: 17 (Z., p. 617). Decisions were taken by "24 elders," probably therefore a formal beth din. Note that both are lenient decisions. H. Mantel, *Studies in the History of the Sanhedrin* (Cambridge, Mass., 1961), p. 231, claims that the small court of R. Judah ha Nasi was a separate institution from the "great court" or Sanhedrin of his day. This is possible but unproven, and unnecessary as an explanation of the evidence.
194. E.g., m R. Sh. 1: 7; 2: 5; cf. above, notes 59–60.
195. t Ohol. 4: 14 (Z., p. 601); m A. Zar. 3: 7; m Gitt. 4: 7; m Bekh. 6: 9; possibly t Mikw. 6: 2 (Z., p. 658), re Hanina b. Teradion.
196. The first three references cited in n. 195, above.
197. *Compendia* 1: 409.
198. b Sanh. 14a; cf. H.-P. Chajes, "Les Juges juifs en Palestine de l'an 70 à l'an 500," *REJ* 39 (1899): 42.
199. y Hag. 1: 7, 6a (cf. Mantel, *Studies*, p. 194).
200. y Yeb. 12: 6, 69a.
201. J. Neusner, *Eliezer b. Hyrcanus: the Traditions and the Man*, 2 parts (Leiden, 1973) 2: 384–86, re Eliezer.
202. See below, p. 179.
203. H. L. Strack, *Introduction to the Talmud and Midrash*, trans. of 5th ed. (Philadelphia, 1931), pp. 116–18; Klein, *Eretz haGalil*, pp. 78 ff.
204. m Gitt. 5: 6; t Gitt. 3: 10 (L., p. 257): the easing of the *sikarikon* laws. This might be seen as an attempt to be fair both to the Judaean immigrants (who would want moral confirmation of their right to any property they usurp) and to the local Galileans. But the texts concentrate on Judaea and the problem may be only theoretical for Galilee. Klein, *Eretz ha-Galil*, p. 58, interprets the *hazakah* (possession) laws of m B.B. 3: 2 as attempts to protect the rights in *Judaea* of those who have taken refuge in Galilee.
205. See above, pp. 102–4.
206. References in Mantel, *Studies*, p. 4, notes 17, 18.
207. Strack, *Introduction to Talmud*, pp. 107–8.
208. Mantel, *Studies*, p. 4, n. 21.
209. Ibid., pp. 52–53.
210. E. Schürer, *History of the Jewish People in the Age of Jesus Christ*, 2 vols. so far, revised by G. Vermes, F. Millar, and M. Black (Edinburgh, 1973–79) 2: 210.
211. Mantel, *Studies*, p. 35; cf. De Lange, *Origen and the Jews*, p. 33.
212. J. Juster, *Les Juifs dans l'Empire Romain: Leur Condition Juridique, Économique et Sociale*, 2 vols. (Paris 1914) 1: 393, n. 3; Avi-Yonah, *Jews of Palestine*, p. 56 ff.

213. All the old petty kingdoms of the Eastern Empire are incorporated into provinces with normal direct Roman administration by the mid second century.
214. *Compendia* 1: 409; cf. ibid. 1: 378, for recognition under the Severans.
215. Mantel, *Studies*, pp. 1–53, discusses the evidence for the use of the title "Nasi" but comes to very different conclusions by pushing all the evidence (including that from late sources) to the limit.
216. The first attested use of ἐθνάρχης in this sense is in Origen in the mid third century (see below, n. 288, and "patriarchus" in C. Th. 16. 8. 2.). The term "ethnarch," referring to diaspora, Herodian, or Hasmonean leaders in the first century, does not seem to be connected (Schürer, *History* 2: 271).
217. m Hag. 2: 2; t Hag. 2: 8 (L., pp. 382–83).
218. Schürer, *History* 2: 217; Mantel, *Studies*, pp. 39–41, for arguments denying the importance of this.
219. A list of *nesiim* based on Talmud and Sherira ha Gaon was compiled by Graetz. It is cited in Mantel, *Studies*, p. 2, n. 4.
220. t Pes. 4: 13–14 (L., p. 165).
221. t Shab. 7 (8): 18 (L., p. 28); t Sanh. 4: 3 (Z., p. 420). The interest here lies in the insistence of the proselyte Onkelos in carrying out this rather unJewish rite in honor of his teacher.
222. Ezekiel 45: 7 and elsewhere.
223. t Sanh. 8: 1 (Z., p. 427).
224. Y. Yadin, *Bar-Kokhba* (London, 1971), p. 124.
225. Some rabbis were friendly to Bar Kokhba and others not (Mantel, *Studies*, p. 36), but not even R. Akiba can safely be said to have cooperated in his rebellion (see now G. S. Aleksandrov in Neusner, *Eliezer b. Hyrcanus* 2: 422–36).
226. Given the disjunction noted above between rabbinic claims and achievement, this was quite possible. Would the Messianic Nasi of the Qumran sect have been recognized outside Qumran? (*Damascus Rule* 7); cf. Vermes, *Dead Sea Scrolls in English*, p. 104.
227. See above, notes 220–21.
228. For dates, Strack, *Introduction to Talmud*, pp. 110–11, 116.
229. Mantel, *Studies*, p. 179.
230. m R. Sh. 2: 7.
231. Mantel, *Studies*, p. 187.
232. m Taan. 2: 1.
233. Sifre Deut. 16, p. 26: license to Yohanan b. Nuri and Eleazar Hisma to teach pupils.
234. t Pes. 3 (2): 11 (L., p. 154): Zonin the *memuneh* did the routine training while Gamaliel sat facing the scholars.
235. Sifre Deut. 318, p. 74.
236. Ibid. 351, p. 408.
237. Ibid. 344, p. 401.
238. m A. Zar. 2: 4.
239. m Eduy. 7: 7. What was he doing there? Much argument has raged over whether the term "רשות" indicates that Gamaliel was given power over Palestine by the governor of Syria. But "permission to teach" is a far more plausible rendering.
240. m M. Sh. 5: 9, and elsewhere. Again, the journey with four other rabbis

may not be for administrative purposes, though an embassy to the imperial court is not impossible and would explain why it is remembered. Cf. Josephus' journey on behalf of fellow priests at the age of twenty-six (*Vita* 13-16).

241. To Emmaus to buy an animal for a feast in honor of his son (Sifra 16a, col. 2); to Tiberias (t Shab. 12 (14): 2 (Z., p. 57); m Erub. 10: 10); from Akko to Tyre with a crowd of disciples following (t Pes 2 (1): 15 (L., pp. 146-47)).

242. m Erub. 10: 10: Gamaliel and his elders in Tiberias.

243. E.g., m Kel. 5: 4; m Yad. 3: 1 (Gamaliel asked by a woman to rule for her).

244. t Pes. 2 (1): 16 (L., p. 147). Cf. the grant of permission not to circumcise a child after death of his brothers, using similar "holy man" authority (t Shab. 15 (16): 8 (L., p. 70)).

245. m Gitt. 1: 5: divorce with Samaritan witnesses (Gamaliel); m B.M. 8: 8: bath-house hired in Sepphoris for "one year at twelve dinars, one dinar a month" in a leap year of thirteen months (R. Shimon b. Gamaliel with R. Yosi).

246. t M. Sh. 3: 9 (L., p. 259) (R. Shimon b. Gamaliel).

247. t Shebi. 6: 27 (L., p. 194) (R. Shimon b. Gamaliel, lenient over Sabbatical Year olives.)

248. *Contra* Mantel, *Studies*, p. 176 ff.

249. Ibid., pp. 188 ff, 198 ff.

250. Ibid., p. 190 ff.

251. Ibid., p. 195 ff.

252. Ibid., p. 206 ff.

253. Ibid.

254. Ibid., p. 235.

255. Urbach, "Class-Status and Leadership," p. 62.

256. Above, n. 229.

257. Above, p. 109.

258. Above, n. 185.

259. See below, pp. 129, 148.

260. t Sot. 15: 8 (L., pp. 241-42). Speaking Greek because they are "close to the government" (זכות למלכות , which is an ambiguous phrase).

261. Above, n. 218. According to m Ned. 5: 5, R. Judah stated that, with regard to the assigning of public property to the Nasi in order to avoid breaking a vow not to benefit from the goods of a fellow citizen, "the people of Galilee need not specifically assign their share since their fathers have done so for them already." This might seem to indicate an earlier use of the title, as Mantel, *Studies*, p. 45 ff. points out, but, since the passage clearly refers to a purely technical assignment for religious purposes only (ibid., p. 48, n. 271), even if this use does date back to before Judah ha Nasi it reveals nothing of the secular power of any earlier nasi.

262. More than a third of the Mishnah.

263. Urbach, "Class-Status and Leadership," p. 69.

264. It is, however, puzzling not to find more evidence of his power and influence in the Tosefta.

265. Urbach, "Class-Status and Leadership," p. 70.

266. t Sanh. 7: 8 (Z., p. 426), etc.

267. Mantel, *Studies*, p. 227 ff.

268. Urbach, "Class-Status and Leadership," p. 73.

269. Ibid., p. 70.
270. J. Neusner, *A History of the Jews in Babylonia*, 5 vols. (Leiden, 1965-70) 1: 116 ff.
271. Mantel, *Studies*, p. 243. It has been suggested that this relationship was invented to bolster his claim to authority (L. I. Levine, "The Jewish Patriarch (Nasi) in Third Century Palestine," *ANRW* II (Principate) 19. 2 [1979]: 659).
272. Mantel, *Studies*, p. 243.
273. S. Krauss, *Antoninus und Rabbi* (Vienna, 1910).
274. See above for the extent of opposition and indifference to rabbinical religious ideas.
275. G. W. Bowersock, *Greek Sophists in the Roman Empire* (Oxford, 1969), p. 58; F. Millar, *The Emperor in the Roman World (31 B.C.-A.D. 337)* (London, 1977), p. 83 and passim.
276. See below, p. 179.
277. Ibid.
278. Ibid.
279. Ibid.
280. Taken as vital evidence by Juster, *Les Juifs* 1: 393, n. 4.
281. De Lange, *Origen and the Jews*, pp. 23-24.
282. Ibid., with other suggestions.
283. Origen, *Peri Archon* 4. 3 (J. P. Migne, ed., *Patrologia Graeca*, 163 vols. [Paris, 1857-1936] 11: 348); idem *Ep. ad Africanum de Hist. Susannae* 14 (Migne, *Patrologia Graeca* 11: 81-83).
284. Origen, *Peri Archon* 4. 3 (Migne, *Patrologia Graeca* 11: 348).
285. Mantel, *Studies*, p. 238.
286. Genesis 49: 10.
287. De Lange, *Origen and the Jews*, p. 89 ff.
288. Origen, *Ep. ad Africanum de Hist. Susannae* 14 (Migne, *Patrologia Graeca* 11: 81-83).
289. J. R. Vieillefond, ed., *Les "Cestes" de Julius Africanus: Étude sur l'Ensemble des Fragments* (Florence, 1970), pp. 14, 17 (birth), 26 (whereabouts at time of the letter); cf. Levine, "Jewish Patriarchs," pp. 649-88, especially 663-80.
290. Evidence in Mantel, *Studies*, Chap. 5.
291. y Hag. 1: 7, 6a. Compare this to the account of R. Judah ha Nasi being *asked* to send a man to administer Simonias.
292. Mantel, *Studies*, p. 199 ff.
293. Urbach, "Class-Status and Leadership," p. 72.
294. Mantel, *Studies*, p. 221.
295. Most obviously Palmyra, cf. M. A. R. Colledge, *The Art of Palmyra* (London, 1976), p. 21.
296. The Stobi inscription from Macedon (*CIJ* I 694), most recently dated to the late third century, refers to a fine payable to the patriarchs. But these may be local figures or the patriarchs of the Old Testament, and it is not clear who is to collect the fine. See B. Lifshitz in J. B. Frey, ed., *Corpus of Jewish Inscriptions*, 2 vols., Vol. 1, revised by B. Lifshitz (New York, 1975), pp. 76-77, citing Heichelheim and Hengel.
297. Mantel, *Studies*, pp. 190-98.
298. C. Th. 16. 8. 14.
299. Justin Martyr, *Dial. c. Trypho.* 17.
300. Eusebius, *Commentaria in Hesaiam* 18. 1.

301. Jewish messengers are portrayed as being sent from *Jerusalem* to slander the Church. The context seems most likely to be first century and to refer to the early struggle of nascent Christianity against the diaspora synagogues.
302. *Oxford Classical Dictionary*, 2nd ed., s.v. "Epiphanius,"
303. Ephiphanius, *Panarion* 30. 11. 2.
304. Epiphanius is unreliable when he can be checked in his account of other heresies (e.g., F. L. Horton, *The Melchizedek Tradition: a Critical Examination of the Sources to the 5th century A.D.* [Cambridge, 1976], Chap. 4). In the present case, he has heard a story "a long time ago" from the principal character, Joseph, when Joseph was over seventy and living in fear in Beth Shean (*Panarion* 30. 5. 1-2.).
305. I. Bidez and F. Cumont, eds., *Flavii Claudii Iuliani Epistulae . . .* (Paris, 1922), pp. 279–80.
306. M. Adler, "The Emperor Julian and the Jews," *JQR* 10 (1893): 624, n. 1: "The Talmud knows nothing of it."
307. Jews in the fourth century diaspora may well have remained unrabbinic.
308. C. Th. 16. 8. 14 (April 399).
309. Mantel, *Studies*, pp. 175–253, presents a good portrait of the nasi in *this* period since all the evidence he cites for earlier periods is genuinely applicable in the late fourth century. If, despite n. 305 above, it is considered preferable to believe the Emperor Julian responsible for advancing the patriarchate to prominence (Avi-Yonah, *Jews of Palestine*, pp. 194–95) it would be easy to find a reason for such behavior in his anti-Christian policy, but it seems to me that the silence of the Codes and Libanius before the late 380s makes a Theodosian date more likely.
310. R. Syme, *Emperors and Biography: Studies in the Historia Augusta* (Oxford, 1971), pp. 17–29.
311. C. Th. 16. 8. 22, depriving Gamaliel of his rank as praetorian prefect in A.D. 415.
312. C. Th. 16. 8. 11: forbidding insults to the illustrious patriarchs in A.D. 396.
313. C. Th. 16. 8. 13: admitting the power of the illustrious patriarchs over other administrators in A.D. 397.
314. Ibid.: "Such Jews shall obey their own laws."
315. C. Th. 16. 8. 14: forbidding the collection of dues in the diaspora for the patriarch in A.D. 399 (ban lifted in A.D. 404, cf. C. Th. 16. 8. 17).
316. Syme, *Emperors and Biography*, pp. 23–24, from a letter by Jerome of A.D. 395 or 396.
317. Libanius, (ed. Foerster) *Epistulae* 914, 917, 973, 1084, 1097, 1098, 1105.
318. Over 1,200 letters written before A.D. 388 survive. They comprise over four-fifths of the collection according to the dates suggested in R. Foerster, ed., *Libanii opera*, 12 vols. (Leipzig, 1903–27), Vols. 10, 11.
319. N. Q. King, *The Emperor Theodosius and the Establishment of Christianity* (London, 1961), especially p. 118, with a mild verdict on Theodosius' policy toward the Jews.
320. C. Th. 16. 8. 22, compared to the end of the patriarchate assumed in C. Th. 16. 8. 29.
321. There is no good evidence in the archaeological remains of any decline in the early fifth century; on the contrary, the ending of settlement at Khirbet Shema', Meiron, and Khorazin in the mid *fourth* century is in stark contrast to a profusion in the fifth century of new building in old sites in Lower Galilee, in, e.g., Tiberias (*EAEHL* 4: 1178, 1182), Beth Alpha (*EAEHL* 1: 190), the Capernaum synagogue (see above, Chap. 6,

n. 363), and the Hammat Gader synagogue (*EAEHL* 2: 472–73). Note also the buildings in at least twenty-six entirely new sites on the Golan (*EAEHL* 2: 457, though recent surveys by Dr. C. Dauphin have revealed even more), which there is no reason to assume to be non-Jewish; cf. the useful article by D. E. Groh, "Galilee and the Eastern Roman Empire in Late Antiquity," *Explor: A Journal of Theology* 3 (1977): 78–93, especially pp. 78–85.

Chapter 8

1. See also below, pp. 128–29. The article by E. E. Urbach, "Class-Status and Leadership in the World of the Palestinian Sages," *Proceedings of the Israel Academy of Sciences and Humanities* 2, pt. 4 (1966): 38–74, is mostly concerned with the pre 70 period and is disappointing for the second century. Urbach derives wide-ranging conclusions about Palestinian society from a few, mostly late texts. His article is primarily interested in the role of the sages, treated (explicitly, p. 62) as a separate class. Throughout, Urbach projects talmudic conditions back onto the tannaitic period.

2. See E. Schürer, *History of the Jewish People in the Age of Jesus Christ*, 2 vols. so far, revised by G. Vermes, F. Millar, and M. Black (Edinburgh, 1973–79) 2: 427, and G. Alon, *Toledot ha Yehudim be Eretz Yisrael be Tekufat ha Mishnah vehaTalmud*, 2 vols., Vol. 1, 2nd ed. (Tel Aviv, 1967), Vol. 2 (Tel Aviv, 1961) 2: 80 ff.

3. E.g., Caesarea. What happened after 70 is not, however, clear. A Jewish community is only certainly attested in the mid third century (L. I. Levine, *Caesarea under Roman Rule* (Leiden, 1975), p. 34; N. R. M. de Lange, *Origen and the Jews* (Cambridge, 1976), p. 2).

4. E.g., in Alexandria (E. R. Goodenough, *The Jurisprudence of the Jewish Courts in Egypt* [New Haven, 1929]), though little is known of the community after A.D. 117 and it may have been wiped out (De Lange, *Origen and the Jews*, p. 8; V. A. Tcherikower, "The Decline of the Jewish Diaspora in Egypt in the Roman Period," *JJS* 14 (1963): 31); see also Sardis in the first century B.C. (*AJ* 14. 235), etc.

5. The "elders of the Jews" in Caesarea (*BJ* 2. 267: γεραιοί).

6. *BJ* 2. 287: "great men of the Jews" (δυνατοί); a fourth-century πατήρ is found in Mantinea (B. Lifshitz, *Donateurs et Fondateurs dans les Synagogues juives* (Paris, 1967), p. 16, no. 9: πατὴρ λαὸς διὰ βίος) and Stobi (Lifshitz, *Donateurs*, p. 18, no. 10: πατὴρ τῆς ἐν Στόβοις συναγωγῆς), both men having the money to donate privately for synagogue construction.

7. Magnes (Lifshitz, *Donateurs*, p. 17, no. 9a); Olbia (ibid., p. 19, no. 11: restoring the synagogue); Cyrenaica (ibid., p. 81, no. 100).

8. Ibid., p. 30, nos. 22–25 (Sardis: four βουλευταί, one of them a goldsmith).

9. Ibid., p. 38, no. 37: fifth-century Pamphylia.

10. Ibid., p. 22, no. 14 (fourth-century Smyrna); ibid., p. 34, no. 22 (third-century Dura Europus).

11. E.g., at Teos (ibid., p. 23, no. 16).

12. Ibid., passim; J. Juster, *Les Juifs dans l'Empire Romain: Leur Condition Juridique, Économique et Sociale*, 2 vols. (Paris, 1914) 1: 450.

13. Cf. Lifshitz, *Donateurs*, p. 41, no. 40: ἄζζαν and διάκονο , c. A.D. 400 in Apamaea, must have liturgical functions. They donated the mosaic.

14. C. Th. 16. 8. 13: the term ἱερεῖς is used in the same period by Jews to refer to Cohanim (*Beth Shearim* 2: 153, no. 180: ἱερεὺς ραβι Ἱερώνυμος)

but the Roman legal texts can hardly have the same reference—they are equating Jewish communal leaders to Christian clergy (A. Linder, "The Roman Imperial Government and the Jews under Constantine," *Tarbiz* 44 (1974–75): 95–143 (Heb.)).

15. For purity, cf. J. Neusner, *A History of the Mishnaic Law of Purities*, 22 parts (Leiden, 1974–77) 22: 137–99.
16. *Compendia* 1: 415, re Yabneh, though it is not clear here whether Safrai assumes that the leaders are rabbis after 70.
17. *BJ* 3. 35 ff.
18. G. Alon, *Jews, Judaism and the Classical World* (Jerusalem, 1977), p. 465.
19. G. M. Harper, "Village Administration in Syria," *YCS* 1 (1928): 116.
20. See below, p. 130.
21. See below, p. 131.
22. Harper, "Village Administration," pp. 105–68; *CERP*, pp. 282–4, re Batanea etc., though Jones denies, ibid., p. 284, similar independence to Jewish villages, without good reason.
23. m Erub. 5: 6, on the עיר של יחיד ; cf. above, p. 33.
24. S. Applebaum, *Prolegomena to the Study of the Second Jewish Revolt (A.D. 132–135)* (Oxford, 1976), pp. 13–14; but see below, pp. 144–46, for Galilee.
25. *CERP*, p. 284.
26. t B.M. 11: 23 (Z., pp. 396–97); the "people of an עיר" are defined as those who have been in residence over twelve months (*Compendia* 1: 413).
27. t B.M. 11: 23 (Z., pp. 396–97). "*Reshut*" probably refers to Roman authority since it is seen as intrinsically evil. Alon, *Toledot*, p. 387, refers to such functions as those of "citizens' tribunals."
28. t Shek. 1: 1 (L., p. 200): through the agents of the beth din.
29. t Shek. 1: 2 (L., p. 200): also through the agents of the beth din.
30. t Shek. 1: 4 (L., p. 200). Cf. Diocletianic boundary stones between κῶμαι on the Golan (Y. Aharoni, "Three new boundary stones from the Western Golan," *Atiqot* 1 (1955): 109–14; idem, "Two additional boundary stones from the Huleh Valley," 2 (1959): 152–54).
31. *Beth Shearim* 1: 22.
32. See above, p. 71.
33. *Beth Shearim* 1: 132–33; 2: 202.
34. Unlike elsewhere (*CIJ* II 799 (Bithynia) etc.); cf. the use of curses instead (*Beth Shearim* 2: 112–13, 223–24); on earlier Judaea, cf. A. D. Nock, *Essays on Religion and the Ancient World*, edited by Z. Stewart, 2 vols. (Oxford, 1972) 2: 527.
35. m B.B. 6: 8: selling a place for a grave; *Beth Shearim* 2: 6: owners of halls in Beth Shearim necropolis have names on lintels; J. Cantineau, "Textes funéraires Palmyréniens," *RB* 39 (1930): 548, no. 14: Nabatean woman sells a share of her tomb to a man.
36. Cf. the fine sarcophagi in Beth Shearim; V. Tzaferis, "Tombs in Western Galilee," *Atiqot* 5 (1969): 72–5 (Heb.): Yehi'am third-century tombs with glass and jewels; F. Vitto, "Notes and News: Gush Halav," *IEJ* 24 (1974): 282: fine fourth-century mausoleum in Gischala with second and third-century sarcophagi; m M. Kat. 1: 6: apparatus for burial.
37. Elaborate mourning ceremonies were performed before burial: expensive *hesped* (m M. Kat. 1: 5); cf. *BJ* 2. 1 on funeral feast expected of a pious man. At the grave itself there was the ceremony of transferring bones from *arcosolia* to *kokhim* (*Beth Shearim* 1: 57, 135) and of regular mourning

visitations (t Shebi. 3: 5 (L., pp. 175-76)): clearing paths to the cemetery is essential, partly, presumably, to preserve solemnity in carrying the corpse if there should be a new death). The "judges of Sepphoris" (דייני ציפורי) defined for these purposes the area of ground required next to the grave for mourners (m B.B. 6: 7).

38. Hidden graves could pollute (m Naz. 9: 3; Luke 11: 44); hence m B.B. 2: 9: cemeteries should be fifty cubits from any settlement. But this was ignored, it seems, in the building of Khirbet Shema' in the mid third century (E. M. Meyers, A. T. Kraabel, and J. F. Strange, "Ancient Synagogue Excavations at Khirbet Shema', Israel, 1970-1972," *AASOR* 42 (1976): 121-22.

39. *Beth Shearim*, Vol. 1, passim. Money may come from the estate of the deceased (t Shek. 1: 12 (L., p. 204), but the text is not clear) and can be very considerable (J. Cantineau, "Textes funéraires," p. 40, no. 9: money for נפש runs out before completion).

40. J. Cantineau, "Textes funéraires," passim; H. Seyrig, *Antiquités Syriennes*, Extracts from Syria, 6 vols. (Paris, 1934-66), no. 71, "Bractées Funéraires," 6: 31: little is known about burial ceremonies in Syria, but gold plaques were used to cover the eyes (ibid., p. 57).

41. m Meg. 1: 1-2; m Ket. 1: 1.

42. *Vita* 277 ff.

43. Cf. the mass decisions by the populace in admittedly exceptional circumstances in first-century Jerusalem (*BJ* 4. 162); Matt. 18: 17: a sinner is to be rebuked by the ἐκκλησία.

44. Harper, "Village Administration," pp. 151-52; cf. Libanius, *Oratio* 47. 11: village lands possibly divided into open strips.

45. See above, p. 86.

46. *Compendia* 1: 414.

47. Harper, "Village Administration," p. 136, re the ἔκδικος.

48. t Shek. 1: 12 (L., p. 204); 2: 8 (L., p. 208).

49. m Peah 8: 7, re the fund for travelling beggars: collected by (at least?) two and distributed by (at least?) three.

50. t Gitt. 3: 13 (L., p. 259).

51. t Meg. 2 (3): 15 (L., p. 352).

52. *Compendia* 1: 413.

53. M. Avi-Yonah, *The Jews of Palestine: A Political History from the Bar Kokhba War to the Arab Conquest* (Oxford, 1976), p. 101. Cf. Sifre Deut. 306, p. 339: a man may be identified as a *talmid ḥakham* once he is appointed to be פרנס על הציבור but this is not enough to justify *Compendia* 1: 416: "the central institutions in Usha had overwhelming influence on the appointment of public leadership throughout the country."

54. t Meg. 2 (3): 12 (L., p. 351).

55. t R. Sh. 1 (2): 18 (L., pp. 311-12). A. Büchler, *The Political and the Social Leaders of the Jewish Community of Sepphoris in the Second and Third Centuries* (Oxford, 1909), pp. 13-14, wants to distinguish the "parnas of the public" from the parnas of communal charity, but without justification.

56. Sifre Deut. 162, p. 212; 305, p. 324.

57. m Dem. 3: 1; t B.M. 8: 26 (Z., p. 390): "their repentance is hard"; t Peah 4: 15 (L., p. 59).

58. m B.K. 10: 1.

59. t Dem. 3: 16 (L., p. 77).

60. t Toh. 8: 5 (Z., p. 669).

61. Ibid.
62. Matt. 17: 24: at Capernaum, οἱ τὰ δίδραχμα λαμβάνοντες ; t Men. 13: 21 (Z., p. 533): "slaves of the High Priest came and beat us with sticks."
63. DJD 2: 165, no. 46: Euphronius b. Eliezer is commanded *qua* ". . . the poor and burying the dead."
64. See below, pp. 157-60.
65. See below, p. 159.
66. The evidence for councils in other villages is very slight: Harper, "Village Administration," pp. 143-45 (hypothetical); *OGIS* II 488: Castellus, a village in Lydia, has a γερουσία and ἐκκλησία. Cf. the seven-man councils set up by Josephus (*BJ* 2. 570-71), according to Josephus' own claim.
67. t Shek. 1: 1-4 (L., p. 200).
68. t Shek. 1: 3 (L., p. 200): disapproval was indicated by pronouncing the crops of the guilty "hefker", i.e., ownerless.
69. t Gitt. 3: 9 (L., p. 257).
70. t Gitt. 3: 8 (L., p. 257).
71. E.g., t Ter. 1: 1 (L., p. 107), for those incapable of running their own affairs; t B.B. 8: 13 (Z., p. 409).
72. N. Avigad et al., "The Expedition to the Judaean Desert, 1961," *IEJ* 12 (1962): 260.
73. See below, p. 163.
74. E.g., t Gitt. 1: 1 (L., p. 245).
75. t Gitt. 3: 1 (L., p. 253). There is a clear problem here to distinguish the village beth din from that set up by the rabbis (see above, p. 109) for important decisions. The term simply means "house of judgment." Only the context can make it clear in any particular case which court is under discussion.
76. t Gitt. 3: 8 (L., p. 257).
77. See above, notes 67-68.
78. t B.B. 3: 5 (Z., p. 402). Selling of an '*ir* may be purely theoretical—no case is attested in tannaitic texts. However, it would not be impossible. Cf. the gift of Jamnia to Livia by Salome (Schürer, *History* 1: 443).
79. t B.B. 3: 5 (Z., p. 402).
80. y B.M. 8: 3, 30b; y B.B. 4: 7, 14a.
81. t Makk. 5 (4): 12 (Z., p. 444).
82. t Meg. 3 (4): 21 (L., p. 359).
83. *IGLS* IV 1321.
84. Cf. Schürer, *History* 2: 427 ff.
85. See above, p. 119.
86. m Ned. 5: 5.
87. Luke 13: 14: they act against Jesus teaching in the synagogue; Mark 5: 23, 35-8: the ἀρχισυνάγωγος in Capernaum.
88. S. Sandmel, *Judaism and Christian Beginnings* (New York, 1978): Schürer, *History* 2: 433-36.
89. t Meg. 3 (4): 21 (L., p. 359).
90. t Ter. 2: 13 (L., p. 115). The problem over tithes was solved by R. Gamaliel, who was passing through.
91. *CIJ* II 991: but this almost certainly refers to men of Sidon and Tyre and is fourth century. All other inscriptions in Galilee definitely refer to men from outside the area: *Beth Shearim* 2: 190-91, no. 203 (Jacob of Caesarea, originally from Pamphylia).
92. t Meg. 3: 21 (L., p. 359); N. Avigad, "An Aramaic Inscription from the

Ancient Synagogue of Umm el-'Amed," *Yediot* 19 (1955): 183 (Heb.): third century Galilean Aramaic inscription about a donation by a חזן.

93. t Sukk. 4: 6 (L., p. 273): R. Judah relates this.

94. m B.M. 5: 7, re prices; Sifre Deut. 294, p. 312: "local custom" is to be followed in measuring and weighing produce (the problem is over the heaping up or levelling off of measuring vessels). It has been claimed that market authorities only supervised measures, not prices, in Palestine: L. Jacobs, "The Economic Conditions of the Jews in Babylon compared with Palestine," *JSS* 2 (1957): 349), but this is based on a text referring explicitly to Jerusalem alone (t B.M. 6: 14 (Z., p. 384)).

95. Sifra 91a, col. 2: the ἀγορανόμος controls weights and measures; Sifre Deut. 294, p. 313: cheating over measures is the concern of the *agoranomos*.

96. See above, Chap. 4, n. 75.

97. Applebaum, *Prolegomena*, p. 18: Jewish agoranomos in Jaffa in A.D. 107. Cf. C. Th. 16. 8. 10: preventing gentile intereference in the self-regulation of prices in Jewish markets.

98. *IGR* III 1020: ἀγορηταί.

99. See above, Chap. 5, passim. Of course, supervision of this sort might have been undertaken by the polis (see *IGR* III 1020, for polis interference in markets), but there is no hint of antagonism in the texts.

100. *AJ* 18. 149.

101. See below, pp. 158–59.

102. Harper, "Village Administration," pp. 105–68.

103. Alon, *Jews, Judaism and Classical World*, pp. 464–65: Hauran, Bashan, and Trachonitis.

104. *Supplementum Epigraphicum Graecum* VIII (1937), no. 2: Qadesh Naftali (συγγένια); *IGR* III 1156; *OGIS* II 616: ἐθνάρχος and στρατηγὸς νομάδων, referring to an Arab chief.

105. *OGIS* II 488: Castellus in Lydia; *Supplementum Epigraphicum Graecum* VIII (1937), no. 2: ἐπιμεληταί.

106. *IGLS* V 2089: Borg el Qaʻi, A.D. 196–197; *IGLS* V 2118: Hamairiya, A.D. 226; *IGR* III 1009: Kefar Nebo, A.D. 248.

107. E.g., baths: *IGR* III 1155, c. A.D. 230 (Zaravae). See above, pp. 81–84.

108. Harper, "Village Administration," pp. 116–41.

109. *OGIS* II 488.

110. *IGR* III 1146: overseeing building work, A.D. 208.

111. See n. 108 above.

112. Suggested by J. T. Milik, in DJD 2: 157, on no. 42.

113. Lifshitz, *Donateurs*, p. 62, no. 76.

114. t B.B. 10: 5 (Z., p. 412): what to do with the financial responsibility if one of two brothers jointly owning property is made *epimeletus* or *gabbay*.

115. Harper, "Village Administration," pp. 130–32.

116. *IGLS* V 2089, 2118; *IGR* III 1009, 1138.

117. F. F. Abbott and A. C. Johnson, *Municipal Administration in the Roman Empire* (Princeton, 1926), p. 22.

118. *IGLS* VI 2804: villages reserve places in the temple compound.

119. The Byzantine τετρακωμία : M. Avi-Yonah, *The Holy Land from the Persian to the Arab Conquests (536 B.C. to A.D. 640): A Historical Geography* (Grand Rapids, 1966), pp. 133–35.

120. *EAEHL* 2: 472–73.

121. DJD 2: 155–59, no. 42.

122. Avigad et al., "Expedition, 1961," pp. 249–50, doc. 44. Although Honi

b. Ishmael in doc. 43 may be a *conductor* of land from Bar Kokhba rather than a *parnas*.

123. DJD 2: 124, no. 24B.
124. *OGIS* II 488.
125. Harper, "Village Administration," p. 151.
126. A. Marmorstein, "La Réorganisation du doctorat en Palestine au 3e siècle," *REJ* 66 (1913): 50.
127. Sifre Deut. 162, pp. 212–13.
128. t Hag. 3: 34 (L., p. 393).
129. m Hag. 3: 6.
130. t Dem. 3: 4 (L., p. 74).
131. *Contra* the assertion of Alon that an end to *semikha* meant an end to Jewish courts (Alon, *Toledot* 2: 44). See below, pp. 158–60.
132. MdRi Amalek 4: 60–70.
133. Ibid.
134. Ibid.
135. t Sanh. 5: 1 (Z., p. 422).
136. J. Neusner, *A Life of Yohanan ben Zakkai, Ca. 1–80 C.E.*, 2nd ed. (Leiden, 1970), pp. 70–72.
137. t B.K. 8: 14 (Z., p. 362).
138. A. N. Sherwin-White, *Roman Society and Roman Law in the New Testament* (Oxford, 1963), p. 133.
139. See below, pp. 157–59; Schürer, *History* 2: 186–87.
140. DJD 2: 100–104, no. 18 (A.D. 55–56).
141. DJD 2: 104–9, no. 19: A.D. 111; the ruling about marrying a second wife is R. Joshua's in m Gitt. 9: 3.
142. DJD 2: 254–56, no. 116.
143. DJD 2: 118–21, no. 22.
144. y B.B. 8: 8, 26a.
145. R. Yaron, *Gifts in Contemplation of Death in Jewish and Roman Law* (Oxford, 1960), p. 20 ff.
146. See below, p. 160.
147. t Gitt. 1: 3 (L., p. 246): the question was whether a particular village counted as part of Israel or the territory of Akko for the purpose of giving evidence; cf. the purely local relevance of some of the terms of the Yerushalmi inscription in Rehov (Y. Sussman, "The Boundaries of Eretz-Israel," *Tarbiz* 45 (1975–76): 213–57 (Heb.)).
148. m Gitt. 1: 5: again, relevantly, on the border of Galilee and Samaria.
149. m Kidd. 2: 7.
150. m B.B. 10: 8.
151. t Makk. 1: 3 (Z., p. 438). Compare to these cases, Luke 12: 13–14: someone comes to Jesus to have an inheritance case sorted out but Jesus refuses to act as *kritēs*.
152. m B.K. 8: 6.
153. See below, pp. 180–81.
154. See above, pp. 110–11.
155. Büchler, *Political and Social Leaders*, passim.
156. T. Rajak, "Justus of Tiberias," *Classical Quarterly* n.s. 23 (1973): 347, re Tiberias.
157. S. Yeivin, in L. Waterman, *Preliminary Report of the University of Michigan Excavation at Sepphoris, Palestine, in 1931* (Michigan, 1937), p. 17 ff.; *Vita* 37.

158. E.g., Palmyra; cf. M. A. R. Colledge, *The Art of Palmyra* (London, 1976), p. 21.
159. See above, p. 31; Büchler, *Political and Social Leaders*, p. 5: rabbis in Sepphoris in the second century; A. Ovadiah, "A Jewish Sarcophagus at Tiberias," *IEJ* 22 (1972): 229: second to third century Jewish inscription " Σιμωνος βαρ Σεμια " on Tiberias sarcophagus.
160. A. D. Nock, "Downey's Antioch: a Review," *Greek, Roman and Byzantine Studies* 4 (1963): 50.
161. Rajak, "Justus," p. 346; cf. the *archōn* in Tiberias (*BJ* 2. 599).
162. Eusebius, *Mart. Pal.*, p. 29 (Syriac text); though this may be a mistake for "Diospolis" referring to Lydda.
163. E.g., Avi-Yonah, *Jews of Palestine*, p. 46.
164. *Digest* 5. 2. 3. 3.
165. Avi-Yonah, *Jews of Palestine*, p. 46.
166. Waterman, *Excavation at Sepphoris*, p. 20.
167. *CERP*, p. 278.
168. E. M. Smallwood, *The Jews under Roman Rule from Pompey to Diocletian* (Leiden, 1976), p. 423.
169. *CERP*, p. 227: emperors, Hygeia, and Cornucopiae are, according to Jones, to be considered "typically Jewish" symbols for the city's coinage from 70-135.
170. C. F. Hill, *Catalogue of the Greek Coins of Palestine*, Catalogue of the Greek coins in the British Museum, (London, 1914), pp. 1-10: Temple of Zeus in Tiberias (Tiberias, no. 23) and Sepphoris (Sepphoris, no. 26) is like that in Sebaste (ibid., pp. 81-82, nos. 12, 15) and Aelia Capitolina (ibid., p. 82, no. 1); Nike in Tiberias (Tiberias, no. 32) appears in Neapolis (ibid., p. 52, no. 51); city goddess in Tiberias (Tiberias, nos. 3, 37) and Sepphoris (Sepphoris, no. 21) appears in Neapolis (ibid., p. 57, no. 80), etc. These coin types are mundane.
171. E.g., Hygeia in Tiberias under Trajan (Hill, *Catalogue*, p. 6, re Tiberias, no. 10); city goddess of Tiberias with *chitōn* and *peplos*, also under Trajan (Tiberias, no. 3).
172. Rajak, "Justus," p. 346; *Vita* 32: the "respectable citizens" are the wealthy; *Vita* 64: the πρῶτοι of Tiberias.
173. *Vita* 169; *BJ* 2. 639.
174. *BJ* 2. 639; *Vita* 69, 296; Schürer, *History* 2: 180, n. 518.
175. Lifshitz, *Donateurs*, p. 59, no. 74 (Sepphoris).
176. Büchler, *Political and Social Leaders*, passim, especially p. 4.
177. Sifre Deut. 309, p. 348.
178. Ibid.
179. Rajak, "Justus," p. 357.
180. A. H. M. Jones, *The Greek City from Alexander to Justinian* (Oxford, 1940), pp. 273-74 (little administrative interference), p. 244 (no land tax), warns against exaggeration; but cf. ibid., p. 268: "the cities were economically parasitic on the countryside."
181. Avi-Yonah, *Holy Land*, pp. 127-29, on the methods used.
182. Ibid.
183. A. Büchler, *Studies in Jewish History* (London, 1956), p. 197.
184. Y. Soreq, "Rabbinical Evidences about the Pagi Vicinales in Israel," *JQR* 65 (1975): 221-24, using material from the Jerusalem Talmud (but no tannaitic sources).
185. Büchler, *Studies*, pp. 180, 216; better arguments are based on the require-

ment for a divorce document brought out of one jurisdiction (מדינה) into another in order to be subjected to stricter rules of evidence (m Gitt. 1: 1); but t Gitt 1: 3 (L., p. 246) bases such a ruling on *proximity* to a big town rather than official boundaries.

186. J. F. Strange, "The Capernaum and Herodium Publications," *BASOR* 226 (1977): 73.

187. See above, pp. 88–89.

188. See above, pp. 119–26.

189. Aristeides, *Roman Oration* 94, in J. H. Oliver, "The Ruling Power: a Study of the Roman Empire in the Second Century after Christ through the Roman Oration of Aelius Aristides," *Transactions of the American Philosophical Society*, n.s. 43 (1953).

190. *CERP*, p. 281, though the size of the Byzantine *tetracomia* is nowhere indicated. There was no reason why the territory of a city should not lie many miles away from the city, so long as it brought in a steady income. For salutary uncertainty about city territories, cf. R. P. Duncan-Jones, *The Economy of the Roman Empire: Quantitative Studies* (London, 1974), pp. 260–61.

191. The function of city law courts will be discussed below, pp. 161–65. It might be expected that cities would be resented if they extorted taxes, but, in fact, individual *mokhsin, not* the city authorities are blamed.

192. t B.M. 8: 26 (Z., p. 390).

193. t B.K. 10: 22 (Z., p. 368); m B.K. 10: 1.

194. Mark 2: 14 (Levi b. Alphaeus); Luke 3: 12 (τελῶναι coming to John to be baptised are told not to exact too much); *BJ* 2. 287 (Jewish *publicani* in Caesarea); *BJ* 2. 405 (Roman tax collected by ἄρχοντες καὶ βουλευταί who "divide themselves into the villages").

195. Matt. 5: 46; 9: 10; 18: 17.

196. t B.M. 8: 26 (Z., p. 390).

197. Luke 5: 29; 19: 2. The story in y Sanh. 6: 6, 28b (= y Hag. 2: 2, 11a) concerns Ashkelon and purports to date from the first century B.C., so it is only very indirect evidence.

198. E.g., t B.M. 8: 25 (Z., p. 390).

199. Matt. 9: 9.

200. t B.K. 10: 22 (Z., p. 368).

201. t B.M. 7: 12 (Z., p. 386).

202. m B.K. 10: 2.

203. t B.B. 7: 3 (Z., p. 407): there is advantage in pretending that a slave is a son but not vice versa; the reason must be that property tax was not payable on a son.

204. m Kil. 9: 2.

205. m Kel. 17: 16.

206. t Kel. B.M. 1: 1 (Z., p. 578): the "big utensil" used to "collect" (לגבות) the tax (מכס) (translation of לגבות as "escape" in J. Neusner, *The Tosefta translated from the Hebrew* [New York, 1977], ad loc., has no justification that I can see).

207. m Shab. 8: 2: size is used as a measurement for the Sabbath laws.

208. t Shab. 8 (9): 11 (L., p. 32): the *baal hamekhes.*

209. Sifra 91b, col. 1.

210. Abbott and Johnson, *Municipal Administration*, p. 121. Nothing in tannaitic texts would prevent *mokhsin* from being village rather than city officials, and perhaps this is more likely outside city territories. But, unlike the

liturgy in Egypt, the job is clearly voluntary. Cf. tax collection by the metropolis *boule* in Egypt after 200 (A. K. Bowman, *The Town Councils of Roman Egypt* [Toronto, 1971], p. 122).

211. I. L. Merker, "A Greek Tariff Inscription in Jerusalem," *IEJ* 25 (1975): 238–44.

212. Edessa (A. R. Bellinger and C. B. Welles, "A third century contract of sale from Edessa in Osrhoene," *YCS* 5 (1935): 131); Palmyra probably, cf. the *Lex Vectigalis* (*OGIS* II 629).

213. m Ned. 3: 4: would the Roman tax authorities take cognisance?

214. G. A. Smith, *The Historical Geography of the Holy Land* (London, 1894), p. 429. Capernaum is probably close to the main Damascus road, but Sherwin-White, *Roman Society and Law*, p. 126, points out the lack of evidence for such taxes.

215. See above, n. 203.

216. See above, n. 210.

217. t Shebu. 2: 14 (Z., p. 448); m Ned. 3: 4.

218. In general: Jones, *Greek City*, pp. 212–13; for policing in cities, cf. ῥαβδοῦχοι in Philippi (Acts 16: 27–28); for policing the countryside, cf. Hierapolis παραφύλακες sent out to control villages in the second century (Abbott and Johnson, *Municipal Administration*, p. 443, no. 117).

219. *BJ* 2. 269; *AJ* 19. 308.

220. *BJ* 2. 641 (Tarichaeae); *BJ* 2. 269 (Caesarea).

221. Matt. 18: 30.

222. *BJ* 2. 229.

223. t Ber. 2: 13 (L., pp. 8–9); cf. the clearly gentile קסדור (quaestor) in t Erub. 5 (8): 22 (L., pp. 115–16), who comes to town for thirty days; this may be just a vague term for some Roman officer, but it cannot be intended to bear its precise meaning of the magistrate in charge of finance in a senatorial province.

224. Avi-Yonah, *Holy Land*, pp. 144–45, on the territory of Caesarea.

225. Sifre Deut. 309, p. 348.

226. B. S. Jackson, *Theft in Early Jewish Law* (Oxford, 1972), p. 255.

227. t B.B. 3: 5 (Z., p. 402).

228. Harper, "Village Administration," p. 153.

229. Abbott and Johnson, *Municipal Administration*, p. 80.

230. Y. Meshorer, "Jewish coins in ancient historiography," *PEQ* (1964): 47.

231. See above, Chap. 5.

232. Migdal: Y. Meshorer, "A hoard of coins from Migdal," *Atiqot* 11 (1976): 54–71, etc.; cf. Sherwin-White, *Roman Society and Law*, p. 125.

233. See above, p. 60.

234. See above, p. 33. *Contra Compendia* 2: 663, admittedly referring to the first century.

235. A. Oppenheimer, *The ʿAm Ha-aretz: a Study in the Social History of the Jewish People in the Hellenistic-Roman Period*, translated by I. H. Levine (Leiden, 1977), pp. 19–20.

236. See above, Chap. 5, passim.

237. Bashan: POxy., 3054 (A.D. 263: semitic tribes, overlaid with Greek forms); Edessa: Bellinger and Welles, "Contract of Sale from Edessa," p. 135 (third-century tribal basis, with βουλή).

238. Cf. the fragments of a second-century inscription at Beth Shean set up by the βουλή and δῆμος to a provincial governor (S. Applebaum, "The Roman Theatre at Beth Shean," *Yediot* 25 (1961): 147 (Heb.)).

239. See above, p. 129; Sifre Deut. 309, p. 348.
240. Rajak, "Justus," pp. 346-47.
241. t Eduy. 2: 4 (Z., p. 457); as opposed to הפרכיות in t Gitt. 6: 3 (L., p. 270).
242. J. A. Goldstein, "The Syriac Bill of Sale from Dura-Europus," *Journal of Near Eastern Studies* 25 (1966): 1-16.
243. Above, p. 133.
244. The boundaries of Palmyra were fixed by the Roman legate and procurators: *IGLS* V 2549-50 (second century Khirbet Bil'as).
245. Tiberias and Sepphoris (*Vita* 37); Tiberias and Hippos (*EAEHL* 2: 521).
246. Most famously, Antioch, reduced to a village by Septimus Severus in A.D. 196 (G. Downey, *A History of Antioch in Syria* (Princeton, 1961) p. 241).

Chapter 9

1. E. M. Smallwood, *The Jews under Roman Rule from Pompey to Diocletian* (Leiden, 1976), pp. 331-32, 340 (under Trajan), 463 (renaming).
2. B. Isaac and I. Roll, "Judaea in the Early Years of Hadrian's reign," *Latomus* 38 (1979): 54-66.
3. Smallwood, *Jews*, p. 546 ff.
4. See below, pp. 141-43.
5. See above, pp. 128-34.
6. M. Avi-Yonah, *The Holy Land from the Persian to the Arab Conquests (536 B.C. to A.D. 640): A Historical Geography* (Grand Rapids, 1966), p. 111: "the fundamental process of the period under discussion."
7. L. I. Levine, *Caesarea under Roman Rule* (Leiden, 1975), p. 41.
8. *Not* implied by the title "$\mu\eta\tau\rho\acute{o}\pi o\lambda\iota\varsigma$" according to G. W. Bowersock, "A Report on Arabia Provincia," *JRS* 61 (1971): 231-32, against Yadin, but cf. the remarks of J.-P. Rey-Coquais, "Syrie Romaine, de Pompée à Dioclétien," *JRS* 68 (1978): 54; the title was only given to Caesarea under Severus Alexander (N. R. M. de Lange, *Origen and the Jews* [Cambridge, 1976], p. 1).
9. G. H. Stevenson, *Roman Provincial Administration till the Age of the Antonines* (Oxford, 1939), pp. 85-88, with F. Millar et al., *The Roman Empire and its Neighbours* (London, 1967), pp. 61-62.
10. S. L. Wallace, *Taxation in Egypt from Augustus to Diocletian* (Princeton, 1938), p. 1.
11. *Contra* A. N. Sherwin-White, *Roman Society and Roman Law in the New Testament* (Oxford, 1963), p. 128, who reckons it to be pure chance that the village clerks and toparchies are not mentioned in the Gospels as not relevant.
12. E.g., *AJ* 17. 25: Batanea; *BJ* 2. 509: Narbatene.
13. *DJD* 2: 248, no. 115: Herodian toparchy (A.D. 124); N. Avigad et al., "The Expedition to the Judaean Desert, 1961," *IEJ* 12 (1962): 252, n. 42: Jericho toparchy (A.D. 127).
14. All the precise indications of locality given by Eusebius are given as the distance from the nearest *polis*.
15. E.g., Tiberias toparchy (*BJ* 2. 252).
16. *CERP*, p. 274.
17. Ibid., p. 273.
18. Ibid., pp. 272-73: the last recorded *strategus* comes from the second century B.C.

19. E.g., *BJ* 3. 55.
20. Avi-Yonah, *Holy Land*, p. 111: Sepphoris takes the toparchy of Araba under Hadrian; Smallwood, *Jews*, p. 493: toparchies remain administrative units until, presumably, at least A.D. 200.
21. See above, n. 16.
22. Cf. B. Bar Kochva, "Gamla in Gaulanitis," *ZDPV* 92 (1976): 61: the term "Lower Gaulanitis" in Josephus is also a geographical term, not an administrative one; S. T. Parker, "The Decapolis Reviewed," *JBL* 94 (1975): 437–41, re the Decapolis, with a similar analysis.
23. Avigad et al., "Expedition, 1961," pp. 239–41, doc. 2; p. 242, doc. 6.
24. F. Millar, *The Emperor in the Roman World (31 B.C.–A.D. 337)* (London, 1977), pp. 420–34, for the importance of requests from below.
25. In general, see S. Lieberman, "The ·Martyrs of Caesarea," *Annuaire de l'Institut de Philologie et d'Histoire Orientales et Slaves* 7 (1939–44): 426–28.
26. Above, p. 6, for the timelessness of the texts.
27. m Erub. 10: 1: tefillin; m M. Sh. 4: 11: separating terumah for priests; m Shab. 19: 1: circumcision; t Erub. 5 (8): 24 (L., p. 117): reading Torah on roof; t Meg. 2: 4 (L., p. 349): reading Esther at night on Purim; t Sukk. 1: 7 (L., p. 257): makeshift tabernacle built out of ladders.
28. t Shab. 15 (16): 9 (L., p. 71).
29. J. Geiger, "The ban on circumcision and the Bar Kokhba Revolt," *Zion* 41 (1976): 143–47 (Heb.); G. Alon, *Toledot haYehudim be Eretz Yisrael be Tekufat haMishnah vehaTalmud*, 2 vols., Vol. 1, 2nd ed. (Tel Aviv, 1967), Vol. 2 (Tel Aviv, 1961) 2: 45.
30. Despite Origen's claim that only Christianity encourages martyrdom (Origen, *c. Celsum* 1. 26).
31. Sifre Deut. 308, p. 347; t Gitt. 7: 1 (L., p. 263).
32. List in t Yeb. 14: 4 (L., p. 52): lions, burning, hanging, bleeding, snakes, drowning in oil or wine. But some of these may only be theoretical accidents.
33. Sifre Deut. 32, p. 58: Akiba, Shimon b. Yohai, Nehemiah, Yosi b. Judah, Meir.
34. E.g., R. Haninah b. Teradion (Sifre Deut. 307, p. 346).
35. Lieberman, "Martyrs," pp. 417–20; Alon, *Toledot* 2: 56, notes the similarity of this persecution to that by Antiochus Epiphanes. This may reflect simply the typology of martyrdom stories.
36. m Ket. 9: 9: R. Shimon b. Gamaliel (mid second century) states that one can no longer assume safekeeping of a *get* or *prozbul* document since the "time of danger."
37. The *mazikin*, cf. M. Avi-Yonah, *The Jews of Palestine: a Political History from the Bar Kokhba War to the Arab Conquest* (Oxford, 1976), p. 29.
38. m Gitt. 4: 6; t Ket. 4: 5 (L., p. 67): wife.
39. Sifre Num., p. 170, 11. 7–10, Balak 131; precisely true of the Severus who was appointed commander against Bar Kokhba (Smallwood, *Jews*, p. 448).
40. Sifre Deut. 204, p. 240: *tormenta, ballista*, and other words corrupted in transmission (but knowledge of siege weapons may come rather from the first revolt than the second).
41. t Yom Tob. 2: 6 (L., p. 287): Judah b. Baba entertains a squadron unwillingly; cf. m A. Zar. 5: 6: in time of war, no squadron would have time to get at a Jew's wine, whereas in peacetime soldiers would be bound to help themselves. This is not sufficiently detailed information for the details

of the Roman campaign to be elicited, despite the efforts of S. Applebaum, *Prolegomena to the Study of the Second Jewish Revolt (A.D. 132-135)* (Oxford, 1976), p. 23 (taken, with some imagination, from t Erub. 4 (6): 11 (L., p. 108)).

42. Above, p. 93.
43. *Contra* A. Oppenheimer, *The 'Am Ha-aretz: a Study in the Social History of the Jewish People in the Hellenistic-Roman period*, translated by I. H. Levine (Leiden, 1977), p. 216, who relies on very late, obscure, and inconclusive texts; cf. Alon, *Toledot* 2: 17.
44. Applebaum, *Prolegomena*, pp. 22-35.
45. P. Bar-Adon, in M. Kochavi, ed., *Judaea, Samaria and the Golan: Archaeological Survey 1967-1968* (Jerusalem, 1972), p. 25, map 2: roads, forts, etc., as part of the Roman effort against the Jews in the Judaean Desert.
46. Among those who believed that the revolt was confined to this area were Büchler, Alon, and Avi-Yonah (Applebaum, *Prolegomena*, p. 22). Applebaum's suggestion (ibid., p. 25) that the huge losses recorded by Dio would only come from a wider conflict is question-begging.
47. H. Hamburger, "A Hoard of Syrian tetradrachms from Tiberias," *Atiqot* 2 (1959): 133-45.
48. Applebaum, *Prolegomena*, p. 23.
49. Ibid.
50. See now P. Schäfer, *Der Bar Kokhba Aufstand: Studien zum zweiten Jüdischen Krieg gegen Rom* (Tübingen, 1981), pp. 103-35.
51. Applebaum, *Prolegomena*, p. 59: they call one another.
52. Ibid., p. 22.
53. Ibid., p. 23.
54. E.g., Kh. Shema': E. M. Meyers, A. T. Kraabel, and J. F. Strange, "Ancient Synagogue Excavations at Kh. Shema', Israel, 1970-1972," *AASOR* 42 (1976): 169.
55. DJD 2: 159-61, no. 43: obscure letter about Galileans in Judaea during the revolt.
56. Cf. the attacks on Jews outside Palestine in A.D. 66 (*BJ* 2. 559 ff., in Damascus).
57. Geiger, "Circumcision," p. 145: "the circumcision ban is never differentiated from other forms of persecution in the rabbinic sources."
58. Justin Martyr, *Dial. c. Trypho.* 16, 47, 108; Origen, *c. Celsum* 2. 8.
59. S. Safrai, "The Holy Congregation in Jerusalem," *Scripta Hierosolymitana* 23 (1972): 62-78.
60. The Temple in ruins before 132: Sifre Deut. 43, p. 95; Bar Kokhba seems to use Jerusalem for propaganda purposes on coins but not as a military base (Applebaum, *Prolegomena*, p. 27).
61. *Contra* Geiger, "Circumcision," p. 147, who believes it to be a local ban by a vindictive governor.
62. G. W. Bowersock, "Old and New in the History of Judaea," *JRS* 65 (1975): 185.
63. H. J. W. Drijvers, ed., *The Book of the Laws of Countries: Dialogue on Fate of Bardaisan of Edessa* (Assen, 1965), p. 56: "Romans have recently conquered Arav and removed all their customs, including circumcision." Cf. Rome's refusal to let Christians castrate themselves (Justin Martyr, *First Apology* 29.)
64. Origen, *c. Celsum* 2. 13.
65. Smallwood, *Jews*, p. 469.

66. Ibid., pp. 467, 471.
67. See above, p. 107.
68. The *fiscus Judaicus: CPJ* II 160–229; Smallwood, *Jews*, pp. 375–78.
69. m B.K. 10: 5: the "blow to the State" (מכת מדינה) includes the stealing of fields by oppressors (*mazikin*).
70. H.-P. Chajes, "Les Juges juifs en Palestine," *REJ* 39 (1899): 42.
71. H. Mantel, *Studies in the History of the Sanhedrin* (Cambridge, Mass., 1961), pp. 140–45.
72. Cf. Trajan forbidding fire brigades to be formed in Bithynia (Pliny *Epp.* 10. 33–34).
73. Cf. the wild account of Y. Baer, "Israel, the Christian Church and the Roman Empire," *Scripta Hierosolymitana* (1961): 79–149.
74. Applebaum, *Prolegomena*, pp. 17–21.
75. Hegesippus, ap. Eusebius, *Historia Ecclesiastica* 3. 19–21; Smallwood, *Jews*, p. 425, re Julianus and Pappus martyrdom stories.
76. Strikingly, after the revolt in Egypt: *CPJ* II 435, col. 3, 11. 16–17: "Not even ἡγεμών can execute Jews ἀκρίτους"; though for the biases inherent in administering the law, cf. P. Garnsey, *Social Status and Legal Privilege in the Roman Empire* (Oxford, 1970).
77. Granted at the very beginning of Roman rule (*AJ* 14. 267, and passim); still intact in mid second century (Drijvers, *Book of Laws of Bardaisan*, pp. 56, 58).
78. Though there is a gap in Eusebius, *Mart. Pal.* between Symeon (A.D. 107) and the whole group martyred in the Decian persecution of 251 in Caesarea.
79. Though some are serving by the end of the fourth century (C. Th. 16. 8. 24.).
80. Smallwood, *Jews*, pp. 469, 473.
81. t Sot. 15: 10 (L., p. 242): R. Shimon b. Gamaliel: "Since they issue a decree against learning Torah, Jews might as well not produce children." This text is found only in the less good Erfurt ms. and not in the main versions, which have instead the vaguer phrase "since they are rooting out Torah" (L., p. 243).
82. E.g., Tertullian; *contra* Baer, "Israel, Christians and Romans," p. 86.
83. Origen, *c. Celsum* 3. 8.
84. Lieberman, "Martyrs," p. 417: *contra* Baer, "Israel, Christians and Romans," and A. Linder, "The Roman Imperial Government and the Jews under Constantine," *Tarbiz* 44 (1974–75): 95–143 (Heb.), who believes that Constantine resurrected Hadrian's persecution policies at the end of his life.
85. Safrai's assertion (*Compendia* 1: 405), that Jews were *dediticii* after 70, is based on a rash assertion of Mommsen and is completely unfounded; such treatment of rebellious subjects is not attested elsewhere in the Empire in the imperial period and would need to be backed up by very good evidence. None is forthcoming, cf. H. Wolff, *Die Constitutio Antoniniana und Papyrus Gissensis 40.1* (Cologne, 1976).
86. MdRashbi Mishpatim, p. 169, 1.7. For pagan martyrdom stories concerning Trajan, see H. A. Musurillo, ed., *The Acts of the Pagan Martyrs: Acta Alexandrinorum* (Oxford, 1954), p. 162.
87. F. A. Lepper, *Trajan's Parthian War* (London, 1948), pp. 99–100, 131–32, 205–13.
88. Smallwood, *Jews*, p. 431.

89. M. Hecker, "The Roman Road Legio-Zippori," *Yediot* 25 (1961): 175.
90. In A.D. 175–176, according to Amminus and Cassius Dio (Smallwood, *Jews*, pp. 482–83).
91. De Lange, *Origen and the Jews*, p. 1.
92. Baer, "Israel, Christians and Romans," pp. 123, 127.
93. MdRashbi Bo, p. 14, 11. 13–14.
94. MdRi Bahodesh 8: 72–76.
95. MdRashbi Beshallah, p. 73, 11.25 ff.; 78, 11.8 ff.; 124, 1.13.
96. m A. Zar. 4: 6.
97. Millar, *Emperor*, p. 28.
98. Sifre Num. p. 85, 11.1–4, Behaalotekha 85.
99. In the twelfth-century compilation, Midrash Tannaim 16: 19, of Hadrian; cf. M. D. Herr, "The Historical Significance of the Dialogues between Jewish Sages and Roman Dignitaries," *Scripta Hierosolymitana* 22 (1971): 123.
100. E.g., *colonia* status granted to Caesarea by Vespasian, and to Sebaste by Severus and Caracalla (Smallwood, *Jews*, pp. 342–43, 490).
101. Sifre Deut. 26, p. 40. The description fits well the position of Severus after the protracted struggle for the purple in A.D. 193–197; the amount of building in Sebaste and the city's elevated status perhaps caught the imagination of rabbis (Smallwood, *Jews*, p. 490).
102. E.g., Caesarea? See L. I. Levine, *Caesarea under Roman Rule* (Leiden, 1975), p. 44.
103. *OGIS* II 614: third-century wall in village Der'at put up ἐκ δωρέας τοῦ Σεβαστοῦ.
104. Acts 25: 11: καίσαρα ἐπικαλοῦμαι ; perhaps reflected in MdRi Amalek 2: 30–37, where המושל הגדול (the great ruler) is the last in line to bear responsibility for a decree.
105. E.g., re validity of a bequest to the *universitas* of Jews in Antioch by a Roman woman (C.J. 1. 9. 1.).
106. Millar, *Emperor*, p. 530; see below, pp. 165–67.
107. G. P. Burton, "Proconsuls, Assizes and the Administration of Justice under the Empire," *JRS* 65 (1975): 92–106.
108. Millar, *Emperor*, p. 41: using royal palaces as *praetoria*; for the use of Latin in Caesarea, see Levine, *Caesarea*, pp. 36–37.
109. In first century: Mark 15: 16; John 18: 28.
110. De Lange, *Origen and the Jews*, p. 10: "Caesarea is the source of every harsh verdict."
111. Sifre Deut. 37, p. 72: no administrator is satisfied till he has *praetoria* and villas in Eretz Israel to show his prestige.
112. *AJ* 18. 262, 269 ff.
113. *AJ* 20. 130; Babata declared her property in 127 (Avigad et al., "Expedition, 1961," p. 260).
114. Sifre Num. p. 80, 11.10–14, Behaalotekha 84. Cf. Burton, "Proconsuls, Assizes and Justice," pp. 99–102.
115. Cf. Babata perhaps having to go to Petra to see the governor (Avigad et al., "Expedition, 1961," p. 261).
116. m Maksh. 2: 5–6.
117. Cf. *AJ* 14. 188 ff.: Josephus' collection of decrees about Jews in the late Republic and the early Empire; S. Lieberman, *Hellenism in Jewish Palestine*, 2nd ed. (New York, 1962), pp. 7–8.
118. By this time the terms were conventional; cf. Gaius *Libri XXXII ad edictum provinciale*.

119. t Shab. 17 (18): 8 (L., p. 82): a matter of urgency for the *medinah* (which may mean either "the city" or "the public" in general).
120. Sifre Deut. 33, p. 59.
121. Millar, *Emperor*, pp. 207-8, 314, for governors passing matters onto the emperor for decision. See also Burton, "Proconsuls, Assizes and Justice," passim.
122. *IGLS* VII 4016 bis: decree by *boulē* follows the *epikrima* of the governor; F. F. Abbott and A. C. Johnson, *Municipal Administration in the Roman Empire* (Princeton, 1926), pp. 381-83, no. 65a: governor intervenes in Antioch in famine in A.D. 93, etc.
123. *OGIS* II 618: water supply to village Kanata by the *presbeutēs Sebastou.*
124. MdRi Bahodesh 5: 3-7; though this may only refer to the archetype of a good king (see below, pp. 152-54).
125. Compare the career of the younger Pliny in Bithynia.
126. y Kidd. 3: 2, 34a.
127. For the census as the governor's job in the second century, see Avigad et al., "Expedition, 1961," pp. 240, 260, re Babata declaring her property to the governor in Provincia Arabia; for the census being resented, see *BJ* 2. 118, re A.D. 6, cf. Luke 2: 1-2.
128. Avi-Yonah, *Holy Land*, p. 112.
129. Applebaum, *Prolegomena,* p. 52.
130. *EAEHL* 2: 258.
131. *Contra* Applebaum, *Prolegomena,* pp. 28-31, whose theory of a series of small forts (burgi) blocking every pass in a hostile Galilee is based on idiosyncratic interpretation of obscure passages in the Jerusalem Talmud and is entirely unsubstantiated by archaeology, unlike the numerous forts he correctly identifies in the Judaean Desert (ibid., pp. 53-54).
132. B. Isaac, "Milestones in Judaea, from Vespasian to Constantine," *PEQ* (1978): 47-59, with map on p. 48.
133. Ibid., correcting Avi-Yonah, *Holy Land*, pp. 181-87. A Roman road from Tiberias to Damascus is often postulated, but there is no evidence for it.
134. Smallwood, *Jews,* p. 494, on road building from Pertinax to Caracalla in Palestine.
135. Applebaum, *Prolegomena,* p. 31: at Ḥurvat Ḥazon, west of Meiron ("probably second century").
136. Ibid., p. 6; M. Avi-Yonah, "Newly discovered Latin and Greek inscriptions," *QDAP* 12 (1946): 91; a centurion(?) called Pompeius, but rustic lettering may suggest a local craftsman rather than a military engraver; ibid., p. 88: T. Antoninus Augurinus, aged twenty-two; ibid., p. 87: wife of a solider buried in 'Arab near the plain of Sepphoris. On the other hand, Alon, *Toledot* 2: 59, is wrong to cite a diploma of A.D. 135 from Nazareth since the stone was originally found on the Hauran (H. de Villefosse, "Diplome Militaire," *RB* 2 (1897): 598-604). The centurion in Capernaum in Matt. 8: 5-13 is more likely to be a Herodian than a Roman soldier.
137. R. Macmullen, *Soldier and Civilian in the Later Roman Empire* (Cambridge, Mass., 1963), p. 77 ff.
138. Despite reductions under Antoninus (Smallwood, *Jews,* p. 481).
139. Avigad et al., "Expedition, 1961," p. 259.
140. Ibid.; DJD 2: 240-43.
141. E.g., Matt. 17: 54: presiding over crucifixions; Acts 21: 23-24; Eusebius, *Mart. Pal.,* p. 37 (Syriac text): martyrs caught at gate of Caesarea by soldiers. The resident freedman of the emperor at Gerasa is rather more

formally in control of the city, perhaps because Gerasa lies near the frontier (C. H. Kraeling, ed., *Gerasa: City of the Decapolis* (New Haven, 1938), p. 51).

142. A. H. M. Jones, "Inscriptions from Jerash," *JRS* 18 (1928): 150, no. 10: centurion in Severan Gerasa; *IGR* III 1017: centurion at Aradi.

143. E.g., aqueduct at Caesarea (Levine, *Caesarea*, p. 37): Dura Europus amphitheater for soldiers' own use (Macmullen, *Soldier and Civilian*, p. 83). Cf. R. Macmullen, "Roman imperial building in the provinces," *Harvard Studies in Classical Philology* 64 (1959): 207–35.

144. t Dem. 1: 13 (L., p. 65): grain in the "storehouse of kings"; t Dem. 6: 3 (L., p. 94): payment to (gentile?) granary distinguished from payment to קיטרון, which may be translated "centurio" or perhaps, as Lieberman suggests (*Tosefta Ki-fshutah: a Comprehensive Commentary on the Tosefta* (New York, 1955–), ad loc.), "actores."

145. See below, pp. 147–48.

146. t Taan. 2: 10 (L., p. 333).

147. m A. Zar. 5: 6.

148. t Yom Tob 2: 6 (L., p. 287); cf. the protection against illegal exactions of *xenōnia* requested by villages from the *ekdikos* (*OGIS* II 609: Phaenae).

149. Sifre Deut. 309, p. 348.

150. See above, n. 136.

151. *BJ* 3. 31.

152. t Shab. 13 (14): 9 (L., p. 60); S. Klein, *Eretz haGalil miyeme haaliyah miBavel ad ḥatimat haTalmud*, ed. Y. Eltizur (Jerusalem, 1967), p. 80 (Heb.), reckons these to be the soldiers of Agrippa in the first century, perhaps rightly.

153. y B.B. 2: 11, 7b.

154. t A. Zar. 2: 6 (Z., p. 462).

155. t A. Zar. 2: 7 (Z., p. 462).

156. t M. Sh. 1: 6 (L., p. 244).

157. Macmullen, *Soldier and Civilian*, p. 84.

158. Cf. R. Judah ha Nasi in t Ohol. 18: 12 (Z., p. 617): gentiles dwell in *castra*, etc.

159. Smallwood, *Jews*, p. 482.

160. *Beth Shearim* 1: 182–83.

161. J. Kaplan, "A Mausoleum at Kfar Giladi," *EI* 8 (1967): 110 (Heb.).

162. C. Th. 16. 8. 24.

163. E.g., in Roman Britain.

164. S. Applebaum and M. Gihon, eds., *Israel and her vicinity in the Roman and Byzantine periods* (Tel Aviv, 1967), pp. 47–49.

165. E.g., Emmaeus (Smallwood, *Jews*, p. 341).

166. Only one discharge certificate from the Golan east of Hippos belies this: *CIL* XVI 87 (A.D. 139)—perhaps a local pagan called up to fight Bar Kokhba further south.

167. Sifre Num., p. 169, 11.8–11, Balak 131.

168. MdRashbi Beshallah, p. 52, 1.17 (R. Shimon b. Eleazar); MdRashbi Beshallah p. 53, 11.21–22 (a formation apparently learnt from Egypt by the Romans!); MdRashbi Beshallah 49, 1.3 (top) (Egyptian actores accompanying Israelites in the desert).

169. Millar, *Emperor*, p. 62.

170. Applebaum, *Prolegomena*, p. 21 ff.

171. Sifre Num., p. 91, 11.18–20, Behaalotekha 91: in a parable, a man requests that he be killed but his sons be spared as he goes out to execution.

172. אספקלריא (MdRi Amalek 4. 65).

173. Applebaum, *Prolegomena*, p. 9.
174. A. Büchler, *The Economic Conditions of Judaea after the Destruction of the Second Temple* (London, 1912), p. 61.
175. Avi-Yonah, *Holy Land*, p. 112.
176. Millar, *Emperor*, p. 185, n. 75; cf. J. T. Milik in DJD 2: 123, no. 24: Bar Kokhba leases with *conductor* and *coloni* seem to concern expropriated imperial property.
177. S. Applebaum, "The Agrarian Question and the Revolt of Bar Kokhba," *EI* 8 (1967): 283 (Heb.).
178. *AJ* 14. 207.
179. *Vita* 119.
180. Avi-Yonah, *Holy Land*, p. 141.
181. *Compendia* 2: 657.
182. *Vita* 71: τὸν κάισαρος σῖτον . Though this could show that the area was already imperial land by A.D. 66 (and this is its produce). Clearly, "imperial corn" could either be rent or corn taken as taxation (M. I. Rostovtzeff, *The Social and Economic History of the Roman Empire*, 2nd ed., revised by P. M. Fraser, 2 vols. (Oxford, 1957), p. 661).
183. *BJ* 7. 216: it is not clear what is included in πᾶσα γῆ τῶν Ἰουδαίων .
184. See above, p. 139.
185. Avi-Yonah, *Holy Land*, pp. 112, 115.
186. Ibid., p. 115.
187. A. H. M. Jones, *The Later Roman Empire 284–602: A Social, Economic and Administrative Survey*, 3 vols. (Oxford, 1964) 2: 712–13.
188. See below, p. 147. Much of the kingdom of Agrippa II in Lebanon became imperial domain on his death, but the survival of numerous inscriptions there to this effect points up the contrast with Galilee (J.-P. Rey-Coquais, "Syrie Romaine," p. 53).
189. In *CERP*, p. xvii, A. H. M. Jones assumes that directly administered, non-city territory became Roman public land and therefore, under the Principate, gradually indistinguishable from imperial land. But for arguments against this view, and in favor of private ownership of such land, see Millar, *Emperor*, p. 623.
190. Avi-Yonah, *Holy Land*, p. 112.
191. Smallwood, *Jews*, p. 341.
192. t Dem. 1: 13 (L., p. 65) c. A.D. 150, cf. Millar, *Emperor*, pp. 484–85; similarly t A. Zar. 1: 7 (Z., pp. 460–1) permits use of a fair (יריד) given by the מלכות ; such a fair took place, presumably, on imperial estates, which in this case were most likely to be in the Jezreel valley.
193. The immensely complicated question of the status and whereabouts of the "mountain of the king" (הר המלך) is not relevant here since it clearly lies in Judaea (Avi-Yonah, *Holy Land*, p. 95); so too the problem of land illegally usurped after the revolt by *mazikin*, Jewish or gentile, in the absence of their owners, on which problem there is a great deal of modern and ancient halakhic discussion (e.g., Applebaum, *Prolegomena*, p. 10).
194. The *sikarikon* laws have been taken to concern such imperial land (e.g., D. Rokeah, "Comments on the Revolt of Bar Kokhba," *Tarbiz* 35 (1965–66): 122–31 (Heb.), but actually refer to any confiscation that is illegal in Jewish eyes (see now, S. Applebaum, "Judaea as a Roman Province: the Countryside," *ANRW* II (Principate) 8 (1977): 388–89).
195. *AJ* 18. 3–4 (A.D. 6); Matt. 22: 17: should the census be paid to Caesar or not?; cf. *AJ* 18. 4: complaint of Judas of Galilee against the tax.

196. See above, pp. 131–32.
197. *Vita* 429.
198. *Vita* 71; though see above, n. 182, for other possibilities.
199. t Dem. 6: 3 (L., p. 94) (though this may be *annona*).
200. t M. Sh. 3: 8 (L., p. 259).
201. *AJ* 14. 202.
202. Smallwood, *Jews*, p. 479, from Appian, *Syr.* 50.
203. Ibid., pp. 375–78.
204. *CIL* VI 8604: *procurator ad capitularia Iudaeorum*.
205. See above, p. 131, on *mokhsin*; *AJ* 14. 250: Rome imposed customs on all goods exported from Judaea in c. 40 B.C.
206. G. M. Harper, "Village Administration in Syria," *YCS* 1 (1928): 155, for taxes in some Syrian village markets in third century.
207. Avigad et al., "Expedition, 1961," p. 246, doc. 8: fine to emperor stipulated for non-observance of contract in wine sale, A.D. 122; *IGR* 1150: 3 unciae fine for tomb violations in Hauran (though the word "$\tau\alpha\mu\varepsilon i\omega$" is conjecture). But how often did Roman courts hear such civil cases? See below, pp. 166–70.
208. Confiscation of the goods of *damnati*: *Digest* 48. 8. 3. 5.; t Sanh. 4: 6 (Z., p. 421): "the property of a man killed by a king goes to the king", despite the belief expressed by some sages that it should go to the heirs, suggesting that this is only theory for a *Jewish* king.
209. Sifre Num., p. 129, 1. 8. Shalah 116: gentile prostitute gives a third of her profits to the emperor (מלכות); cf. Suetonius, *Gaius* 40; Millar, *Emperor*, p. 429.
210. Tacitus, *Annals* 2. 42.
211. Sifre Deut. 333, p. 382.
212. Sifre Deut. 330, p. 380; cf. the revolt in c. A.D. 248 in Syria and Cappadocia against excessive tax.
213. Cf. Wallace, *Taxation in Egypt*, pp. 23–25; S. M. Mitchell, "Requisitioned Transport in the Roman Empire: a New Inscription from Pisidia," *JRS* 66 (1976): 106–31.
214. Macmullen, *Soldier and Civilian*, p. 56.
215. t Bekh. 2: 2 (Z., p. 535): animals of the ארנונה compared to those known to be ownerless; but the *annona* animal is judged to be different because its origin is known and therefore its first born is due to the Temple.
216. t Hall. 1: 4 (L., p. 275): the dough is still wet (עיסה), cf. Büchler, *Economic Conditions of Judaea*, p. 64: the government consumes property by customs, baths, theaters, and annona.
217. Sifre Deut. 200, p. 237.
218. Matt. 5: 41.
219. Mark 11: 3.
220. Mark 15: 21.
221. m B.M. 6: 3.
222. y Ber. 1: 1, 6a.
223. y B.M. 6: 3, 26b: in קפנדריא (?) as opposed to *basilica*.
224. m B.B. 9: 4. The text says literally that "it falls between them," i.e., the consequences, good or bad, are shared.
225. t B.B. 4: 7 (Z., p. 403).
226. y B.M. 4: 2, 15a (R. Hiya b. Joseph, in the late third century.)
227. t Ohol. 9: 2 (Z., p. 606) (preferring Jastrow's translation, *Dictionary*,

s.v. רחיים, to J. Neusner, *The Tosefta translated from the Hebrew* (New York, 1977-   ), ad loc.).

228. t Yeb. 14: 7 (L., pp. 53-54): the gentile members have news of the death of a Jew who had gone with them.

229. MdRi Bahodesh 1: 31-32. Perhaps this is not surprising. On locals' responsibility for roads, see J. Pekary, *Untersuchungen zu den römischen Reichsstrassen* (Bonn, 1968). However, this Mekhilta passage may well be interpolated (Isaac, "Milestones in Judaea," p. 56, n. 32).

230. Survey of rabbinic views of Rome in G. Vermes, *Post-Biblical Jewish Studies* (Leiden, 1975), pp. 215-24, and in N. R. M. de Lange, "Jewish Attitudes to the Roman Empire," in P. D. A. Garnsey and C. R. Whittaker, eds., *Imperialism in the Ancient World* (Cambridge, 1978), pp. 255-81. The latter work makes a good attempt at distinguishing changes in reaction over a time span, but with somewhat uncritical use of sources.

231. t R. Sh. 2 (4): 12 (L., p. 317): R. Yosi in the mid second century introduces lamentations into a New Year liturgy for disasters caused by the gentiles.

232. t Taan. 2 (3): 13 (L., p. 335): R. Yosi hopes a flood or plague will come and destroy the gentiles, thus heralding the Messiah—referring perhaps to the great plague of the 160s.

233. De Lange, "Jews and the Roman Empire," p. 272; Vermes, *Post-Biblical Jewish Studies*, p. 223.

234. *Vita* 21, re Pharisees at start of the revolt of A.D. 66.

235. Stories in Origen and Eusebius about a Jewish and Samaritan revolt in 194 refer either to a local disaffection (Smallwood, *Jews*, p. 489) or, more probably, to support by some Palestinians of the imperial pretender Niger (J. Neusner, *A History of the Jews in Babylonia*, 5 vols. [Leiden, 1965-70] 1: 81). For revolts in the 330s, see Avi-Yonah, *Jews of Palestine*, pp. 176-81.

236. Cf. D. Daube, *Collaboration with Tyranny in Rabbinic Law* (London, 1965), though he notes the continuation of some opposition even then (ibid., p. 40 ff.).

237. See below, n. 243.

238. P. A. Brunt, "Josephus on Social Conflicts in Roman Judaea," *Klio* 59 (1977): 149-53.

239. Ibid.

240. See above, p. 33.

241. See above, p. 129.

242. t Ned. 2: 2 (L., p. 104): it is possible to save goods from the hands of mazikin ("oppressors") by saying that they belong to particular Jews (of high standing, presumably).

243. Cf. C. S. Walton, "Oriental Senators in the service of Rome," *JRS* 19 (1929): 38-66.

244. Baer, "Israel, Christians and Romans," p. 91.

245. Kaplan, "Mausoleum at Kfar Giladi," pp. 104-13.

246. Sifre Deut. 351, p. 408: Agnitus the ἡγεμών asked R. Gamaliel how many laws were given to Israel; Sifre Deut. 344, p. 401: visit of the officials to the academy either of R. Gamaliel or Shimon b. Gamaliel at Usha (should be Yabneh?) to check on what is going on there; t B.M. 3: 11 (Z., p. 376): a man asks R. Yosi and the sages detailed questions about halakha and aggadah; S. Krauss, *Antonius und Rabbi* (Vienna, 1910): stories about philosophical discussions between R. Judah ha Nasi and an emperor, but

all stories about specific political matters being discussed by them are very late.

247. b. Sanh. 11a.
248. B. Jackson, *Theft in Early Jewish Law* (Oxford, 1972), p. 255; but this comes from late talmudic evidence.
249. Neusner, *History of Jews in Babylonia* 1: 82–83.
250. De Lange, *Origen and the Jews*, p. 11.
251. Above, p. 117.
252. B. Lifshitz, *Donateurs et Fondateurs dans les Synagogues juives* (Paris, 1967), p. 59, no. 74.
253. I.e., after A.D. 212, the Constitutio Antoniniana. Cf. Wolff, *Die Constitutio Antoniniana*.
254. Millar, *Emperor*, pp. 394–410, for such requests.
255. See above, pp. 71–81.
256. Millar, *Emperor*, p. 9.
257. Ibid., p. 10; cf. Josephus' embassy on behalf of fellow priests in A.D. 61 (*Vita* 13–16).
258. Acts 24: 1: the High Priest uses a rhetor called Tertullian in the governor's court.
259. Herr, "Dialogues between Sages and Romans," pp. 123–50.
260. Ibid., p. 125.
261. E.g., ibid., p. 140: Eccl. Rabb. 10: 7, re a eunuch who is high up in the government attacking R. Akiba, which would be impossible in the second century, though not implausible in the fourth.
262. Above, n. 258.
263. Sifre Deut. 343, p. 394.
264. *AJ* 20. 264: Jews do not value eloquence highly.
265. Millar, *Emperor*, passim.
266. m Gitt. 8: 5. The Jerusalem Talmud observes that Persian and Seleucid dates are no longer relevant (y Gitt. 8: 5, 47a).
267. Avigad et al., "Expedition, 1961," p. 242, doc. 6.
268. Ibid. (Arabia); cf. t Gitt. 6 (8): 3 (L., p. 270): a divorce can be dated by the היפרכין (i.e. ὑπαρχεία, province?); DJD 2: 105, no. 19: "6th year of (Bostra) eparchy."
269. See above, n. 267.
270. Avi-Yonah, *Holy Land*, p. 129; *CIJ* II 1423: Aramaic inscription of A.D. 306, dated according to the local era of the city of Bostra. This may be taken from the city's foundation or some other event of local importance (Rey-Coquais, "Syrie Romaine," pp. 44–46).
271. See above, p. 134, for the exception.
272. t Gitt. 6 (8): 3 (L., p. 270). Lieberman, *Tosefta Ki-fshutah*, ad loc., gives variant readings and meanings for the second word (ארכינות), but no other suggestion seems satisfactory.
273. *CIJ* II 1208: Aramaic, south of the Dead Sea in A.D. 433; DJD 2: 22: "the exile of Israel."
274. A. H. M. Jones, "Numismatics and History," in idem, *The Roman Economy: Studies in Ancient Economic and Administrative History*, edited by P. A. Brunt (Oxford, 1974), pp. 61–63.
275. E.g. Meiron (C. L. Meyers, E. M. Meyers, and J. F. Strange, "Excavations at Meiron in Upper Galilee—1971, 1972: a Preliminary Report," *BASOR* 214 (1974): 23; Khirbet Shema' (E. Meyers, Kraabel, and Strange, "Synagogue at Kh. Shema'," pp. 149–50).

276. A. Kindler, *The Coins of Tiberias* (Tiberias, 1961), p. 87 (Hadrian), etc.

277. G. A. Cooke, *A Text-book of North Semitic Inscriptions* (London, 1903), p. 278, no. 121: a Palmyrene inscription of A.D. 242–243, with Greek parallel text.

278. *CIS* II 34/3, 1. 121 = *OGIS* II 629, 1. 168 (*Lex Vectigalis* of Palmyra).

279. J. Cantineau, J. Starcky, and J. Teixidor, eds., *Inventaire des Inscriptions de Palmyre*, 11 fascs. (Beirut and Damascus, 1930–65) 3: 16–17, no. 12.

280. Ibid., 3: 23, no. 17.

281. Ibid., 3: 28–29, no. 22 (actually ἡγησαμένου given as הינמוניא).

282. Ibid., 3: 15, no. 10: ἐπίτροπος (אפטרופא); Cooke, *North Semitic Inscriptions*, p. 287, no. 127: δουκενάριος (דוקנרא); *CIS* II 3913, 1. 53: *senator* (סנקלטיקא); M. G. Bertinelli Angeli, *Nomenclatura Pubblica e Sacra di Roma nelle Epigrafi Semitiche* (Genoa, 1970), pp. 69, 83: *fiscus* (פסקום).

283. Cantineau, Starcky and Teixidor, *Inventaire* 10: 62, no. 102.

284. J. Teixidor, "Bulletin d'Épigraphie Semitique," *Syria* 49 (1972): 440, no. 149, with רב פרשיא for *praefectus alae* also attested.

285. J.-B. Chabot, *Choix d'Inscriptions de Palmyre* (Paris, 1922), p. 57.

286. Angeli, *Nomenclatura*, p. 76.

287. E.g., Avigad et al., "Expedition, 1961," p. 242, doc. 6: dating of a deed of gift.

288. Sifre Deut. 317, p. 360.

289. E.g., m Maksh. 2: 5.

290. m Gitt. 1: 1; t Gitt. 1: 1 (L., p. 245): originally מדינה (πόλις), then שכונה ("area"), then (mid second century) הגמוניה ("province"); cf. the long discussion of Lieberman, *Tosefta Ki-fshutah*, ad loc.

291. It would, for instance, be difficult to tell territorial boundaries between Scythopolis and Tiberias without a physical marker, but none such survive from Galilee.

292. The great work on this subject is I. Ziegler, *Die Königsgleichnisse des Midrasch beleuchtet durch die römische Kaiserzeit* (Breslau, 1903), a remarkable book that suffers from over-enthusiasm in trying to pinpoint exact references for vague rabbinic remarks and an uncritical acceptance of stories from all periods.

293. Themes about kings that could apply to Herodians: kingly behavior consisting in sitting on a throne and hearing lawsuits (*AJ* 17. 232), the power of pedagogues (*AJ* 16. 242), the use of trusted agents to run their kingdoms (*AJ* 15. 65; *Vita* 126: the ἐπίτροπος), and plenty of scandalous detail about ungrateful sons and unfaithful wives. Sherwin-White, *Roman Society and Law*, pp. 134–36, refers Gospel parables to Eastern client kings like the Herods.

294. Sifre Deut. 157, p. 209: the Jewish king has the right to a horse, throne, and scepter and not to be seen naked, barbered, or bathed; by inference, in Sifre Deut. 26, p. 36, where a parable has a woman sent to the arena (?) for breaking the Sabbatical Year laws, the king concerned must be Jewish, else he would not care.

295. In particular, stories derived from the picture of Ahasuerus in the book of Esther.

296. Into this category must go, presumably, all those stories that cannot be fitted in elsewhere; they form a good proportion of these collected by Ziegler, *Die Königsgleichnisse*.

297. See below, p. 153, and compare to Millar, *Emperor*, pp. 15–131.

298. *IGLS* I 39: wrong titles for Septimus Severus on an inscription set up to mark bridge rebuilding.

299. For the legend of Nero in the East, see S. J. Bastomsky, "The Emperor Nero in Talmudic Legend," *JQR* 59 (1968-69): 321-25; for Antoninus, see Krauss, *Antoninus und Rabbi*; for Diocletian, see Lieberman, *Hellenism in Palestine*, p. 5. Diocletian is remembered because of the persecution of Christians, cf. Eusebius, *Mart. Pal.*, p. 29 (Syriac text) for Jews looking on at executions.

300. Sifre Deut. 3, p. 11: soldiers demand hot loaves in the desert but the king's *eparchus* points out that he has no mills or stoves; cf. Mekhilta stories (MdRi Shirata 4: 54-7; MdRashbi Beshallah, p. 82, 11. 18 ff.: king is beset by petitions from neighboring states but refuses to deal with them until he returns victorious from war.

301. E.g., MdRashbi Bo, p. 32, 11.22-23: it is normal for a king to take his valuables and treasury with him on going to war, in order to prevent insurrection in his rear.

302. See above, pp. 139-40.

303. Sifre Deut. 307, p. 72.

304. Millar, *Emperor,* p. 28.

305. Sifre Num., p. 78, 1.7. The term has been taken by others as *antecessor*—a soldier who goes before the army to find a place to camp—since the word ἀντικαίσαρ is otherwise unknown in Greek. Cf. the obscure דיתוכוס (= διάδοχος ?) in Sifre Deut. 27, p. 44, of whom a king is said to be afraid as he sits on his βῆμα .

306. Ziegler, *Die Königsgleichnisse*, p. v (Erstes Capitel, no. xxvii); cf. Domitian's insistence on being addressed as "Domine," resented by Dio Chrysostom (Dio Chrysostom, *Oratio* 45. 1).

307. E.g., Sifre Deut. 343, p. 398: a king in his palace will have around him better men than himself.

308. Sifre Deut. 308, p. 74: a feature far more of the early Empire than of the Empire after the third century, but perhaps this is too general a remark to be significant.

309. E.g., Sifre Deut. 11, p. 19; 306, p. 331. The Roman parallel would be the *praefectus urbis* in Rome, but the idea of "handing over the keys to the kingdom" to a trusted friend is more likely to be Herodian (*AJ* 15. 65: Herod, summoned to Antonius, left Joseph as procurator for his government and for public affairs).

310. Sifre Deut. 26, p. 38; 312, p. 353; 349, p. 407: leased-out land and the danger to the lessee from nonpayment of rent.

311. Evidence in Mekhilta: the Almighty goes through Egypt like a king going from place to place (MdRashbi Bo, p. 14, 11.13-14).

312. m A. Zar. 4: 6.

313. MdRashbi Beshallah 73, 1.25.

314. Avi-Yonah, *Jews of Palestine*, p. 127.

315. See above, p. 46; Eusebius, *Mart. Pal.* (Syriac text), p. 5: Caesarean festival for twenty years of emperor's reign; *IGR* 1132: Arabs build τύχεα to Severus in A.D. 213.

316. m A. Zar. 1: 3: a gentile town will usually observe his birthday and the accession day of the emperor.

317. There is no such abuse apart from MdRi Shirata 8: 27-28, despite the obvious opportunity to compare Roman emperors and Egyptian Pharaohs in this regard. See below, Chap. 11, n. 10.

318. *CPJ* II 427, 11. 18-24: Jew in Egypt in A.D. 101 swears by Trajan; Avigad et al., "Expedition, 1961," p. 260: Babata declares property in census, swearing by τύχη of the Lord Caesar in A.D. 127.

319. Sifre Num., p. 199, 1.12, Matot 203: vows by life of king or king himself; t Sot. 6: 1 (L., p. 182): R. Joshua or R. Judah: one should swear by the life of a king only if one likes him.
320. Sifre Deut. 29, p. 47; 43, p. 98; 306, p. 331 (R. Nehemiah); 352, p. 413; Sifre Num., p. 85, 11.15-16, Behaalotekha 86; p. 182, 11.7-9, Pinhas 135.
321. There are no stories of sons actually being put to death for bad behavior as might have been expected if the Herodian background was the most important.
322. Sifre Deut. 343, p. 397; 347, p. 404.
323. Sifre Deut. 352, p. 412: in this case given to the youngest son for his modesty (to the amazement of the rabbis though less so to Romans who do not assume primogeniture).
324. Sifre Num., p. 187, 11.16-19.
325. Perhaps this is not so inaccurate. Herodian considers that Severus' expedition to Britain had the main aim of reconciling his two sons (Herodian 3. 14. 2); see J. D. Thomas, "An Imperial Constitutio on Papyrus," *Bulletin of Institute of Classical Studies, University of London* 19 (1972): 103-12, especially 108, re the two sons of Antonius Pius in his public *consilium*.
326. E.g., Sifre Deut. 306, p. 330.
327. Ziegler, *Die Königsgleichnisse*, p. xciv, Siebentes Capitel, no. II.
328. Sifre Deut.354, p. 421.
329. Sifre Deut. 346, p. 403 (R. Shimon b. Yohai). The bridge of boats built by Gaius Caligula shows that the astonishment of the rabbis was misplaced; see Suetonius, *Gaius Caligula* 19.
330. Compare the stereotyped tyrant emperor painted by Alexandrian pagans in Musurillo, *Acts of the Pagan Martyrs*. Other examples are lacking.
331. E.g., Britain (Tacitus, *De Vita Agricolae* 21).
332. *Contra* Applebaum, *Prolegomena*, pp. 49-52, 128-31.
333. Cf. Aelius Aristeides, *Roman Oration* 94; R. Macmullen, *Roman Social Relations 50 B.C. to A.D. 284* (New Haven, 1974), p. 28.
334. C. R. Whittaker, "Review of M. Bénabou, *La résistance africaine à la Romanisation* (Paris, 1976)," *JRS* 68 (1978): 192, sees the same non-relationship between Rome and the locals in African villages. This lack of interest is a better explanation for the failure of Galilean villages to develop into cities than Sherwin-White's alternative that they were suppressed by native (Herodian) rule (Sherwin-White, *Roman Society and Law*, pp. 129-32).

Chapter 10

1. L. Mitteis, *Reichsrecht und Volksrecht in den östlichen Provinzen des Römischen Kaiserreichs* (Leipzig, 1891); R. Taubenschlag, *The Law of Greco-Roman Egypt in the Light of the Papyri 332 B.C.-640 A.D.*, 2nd ed. (Warsaw, 1955), p. 20: conflicts between Greek and Egyptian law may continue in the Roman period, but this is not certain.
2. y Meg. 3: 2, 24b, cf. S. Lieberman, "The Martyrs of Caesarea," *Annuaire de l'Institut de Philologie et d'Histoire Orientales et Slaves* 17 (1939-44): 397.
3. b B.M. 58a.
4. C.J. 1.9.1. (Antoninus to A. Claudius Tryphoninus in A.D. 213).
5. C.J. 6.2.2.; cf. R. Yaron, "Reichsrecht, Volksrecht and Talmud," *RIDA* 3rd ser. 11 (1964): 281; and D. Daube, in B. S. Jackson, ed., *Jewish Law*

in Legal History and the Modern World, Jewish Law Annual, Suppl. Ser. 2 (Leiden, 1980), pp. 45–60. I have also gained much from B. S. Jackson, "On the Problem of Roman Influence on the Halakha and Normative Self-Definition in Judaism," in E. P. Sanders et al., eds., *Jewish and Christian Self-Definition,* 2 vols (London, 1980–81) 2: 157–203.

6. See above, p. 110.
7. Mitteis, *Reichsrecht,* p. 159 ff.
8. m Gitt. 9: 8.
9. t Yeb. 12: 13 (L., p. 44).
10. H.-P. Chajes, "Les Juges juifs en Palestine, de l'an 70 à l'an 500," *REJ* 39 (1899): 42.
11. MdRashbi Mishpatim 211, 1.26; but the text is obscure.
12. MdRi Nezikin 1: 12–18 (reading בדיני, not בדיני).
13. t B.K. 4: 2 (Z., p. 351), though אין תם ומועד בנזקי הגוי may refer only to the position of the gentiles in Jewish law.
14. y B.B. 8: 1, 21b.
15. y Gitt. 1: 4, 7a.
16. Mitteis, *Reichsrecht,* pp. 11–12; for the advantage of the Talmud as a guide to the precise concepts being opposed by the emperors, cf. Yaron, "Reichsrecht, Volksrecht and Talmud," pp. 281–98.
17. For Roman law of property, especially *cessio,* being opposed by Jewish *ḥazakah* and *sikarikon* rules, see M. Gil, "Land Ownership in Palestine under Roman Rule," *RIDA* 3rd ser. 17 (1970): 11–53; for Greek ideas of ἐμφύτευσις affecting the *ḥazakah* ruling, see Y. Soreq, "Hellenistic-Roman Land Tenancy System as reflected in Talmudic Literature," *Zion* 39 (1974): 217–23 (Heb.).
18. Sifre Deut. 144, p. 197; 205, p. 241, where it is assumed that an *'ir* with no court is *possible* but unlikely. Contra Chajes, "Les Juges juifs," p. 52, who claims that there were only "juges isolés," based on the lack of rabbinic stories. But there is no reason to expect such stories. See, for discussion of these courts, pp. 126–27, above.
19. t B.K. 8: 14 (Z., p. 362): legendary?
20. t A. Zar. 8 (9): 4 (Z., p. 473).
21. See above, pp. 122–23.
22. t Shebi. 8: 7 (L., p. 201).
23. DJD 2: 100–104, no. 18.
24. See n. 8, above.
25. E.g., Sifre Deut. 14, p. 24: bringing a gift to a judge; E. E. Urbach, *The Sages: Their Concepts and Beliefs,* translated by I. Abrahams (Jerusalem, 1975), p. 539: punishment of sinners is needed to free the community from responsibility.
26. E.g., N. Avigad et al., "The Expedition to the Judaean Desert, 1961," *IEJ* 12 (1962): 244, doc. 7: the marriage contract of Babata, c. A.D. 128.
27. E.g., DJD 2: 152, no. 36: a Hebrew contract, which is unlikely to have been only valid during the revolt. Passages that might seem to imply the end of Jewish jurisdiction (e.g., Origen, *c. Celsum* 7. 26: Jews cannot condemn to burning or stoning *qua* subject to Rome; MdRi Shabbata 1: 118: "the laws (*dinim*) were taken from Israel") only *limit* jurisdiction and probably refer to the end of the national Sanhedrin acting as an appeal court, which is implied elsewhere (m Makk. 1: 10; m Sot. 9: 11).
28. K. G. Bruns and E. Sachau, eds., *Syrisch-Römisches Rechtsbuch aus dem*

fünften Jahrhundert (Leipzig, 1880), pp. 23-24 (Syro-Roman Law Book L94-95).

29. E.g., Sifre Deut. 14, p. 24; cf. A. Büchler, *The Political and the Social Leaders of the Jewish Community in Sepphoris in the Second and Third Centuries* (Oxford, 1909), pp. 21-22, 26-27.

30. E.g., Sifre Num., p. 79, 1.9, Behaalotekha 79.

31. *Pace* G. Alon, *Jews, Judaism and the Classical World* (Jerusalem, 1977), p. 395. Alon sees a rivalry among the rabbis as to who ought to be a judge in an ideal world.

32. Luke 18: 2.

33. *BJ* 2. 570-71.

34. See above, p. 126.

35. Alon, *Jews, Judaism and Classical World*, p. 394.

36. Sifre Deut. 17, p. 27; same sentiment in Sifre Deut. 144, p. 198.

37. Sifre Deut. 110, p. 197.

38. Certainly not the patriarch, if the arguments put forward above, pp. 111-18, are accepted.

39. See above, p. 126. Note that these warnings on how to appoint come from Midrash aimed at the wider community, not the inward looking halakhic texts.

40. *Compendia* 1: 505.

41. Mitteis, *Reichsrecht*, p. 91 ff.: personal, family and inheritance law were under local control.

42. Taubenschlag, *Law of Greco-Roman Egypt*, pp. 2, 6-7.

43. DJD 2: 152, no. 36.

44. Avigad et al., "Expedition, 1961," p. 244, doc. 7.

45. Ibid., p. 241 ff., doc. 6.

46. S. Zeitlin, "Slavery during the Second Commonwealth and the Tannaitic Period," *JQR* 53 (1962-63): 216: such manumissions are valid simply through a document from the master, according to tannaitic law.

47. This must be so, since gentiles compel Jews to carry out the decision of Jewish courts (m Gitt. 9: 8).

48. Zeitlin, "Slavery," p. 196.

49. B. S. Jackson, *Theft in Early Jewish Law* (Oxford, 1972), p. 230.

50. With slight changes, this is the opinion of Jackson, *Theft*, p. 251. He, however, believes that rabbinic leniency was intended to *attract* Jews to Jewish courts in the hope of acquittal. If that was the purpose, it was rather foolish, since Jewish courts would then be filled with criminal cases they had prevented themselves deciding properly by their own rules.

51. A debated point for the first century; cf. E. Schürer, *The History of the Jewish People in the Age of Jesus Christ*, 2 vols. so far, revised by G. Vermes, F. Millar, and M. Black (Edinburgh, 1973-79) 2: 219-23. But Origen, *c. Celsum* 7. 26 seems to point to it clearly enough by the third.

52. Sifre Deut. 276, p. 295.

53. m Sanh. 1: 4-6: three; above, Chap. 8, notes 137-38: one; Schürer, *History* 2: 187: seven, based on the actions of Josephus.

54. Sifre Deut. 276, p. 229.

55. This is the view of Büchler, *Political and Social Leaders*, p. 22.

56. Collected in Alon, *Jews, Judaism and Classical World*, pp. 395-98; for the earlier period, the law of the Qumranic Temple Scroll would be an example, though doubtless largely theoretical.

57. H. Albeck, cited in G. G. Porton, "Hanokh Albeck on the Mishnah," in

J. Neusner, ed., *The Modern Study of the Mishnah* (Leiden, 1973), p. 223; cf. J. Neusner, *A History of the Mishnaic Law of Purities*, 22 parts (Leiden, 1974–77) 21: 13, for purity law.

58. H. F. Jolowicz and B. Nicholas, *Historical Introduction to the Study of Roman Law*, 3rd ed. (London, 1972), p. 464, re the Theodosian Code.

59. *AJ* 16. 1: Herod introduced exile and slavery as a punishment.

60. Avigad et al., "Expedition, 1961," p. 244, doc. 7; DJD 2: 109–14, no. 20; DJD 2: 243–54, no. 115 (remarriage).

61. DJD 2: 104–9, no. 19 and commentary.

62. Avigad et al., "Expedition, 1961," p. 251 ff., doc. 6.

63. DJD 2: 100–104, no. 18 and commentary.

64. DJD 2: 118–21, no. 22 and commentary.

65. DJD 2: 122–34, no. 24 and commentary.

66. E.g., DJD 2: 118–21, no. 22; 144–48, no. 30. For land sales, see R. Yaron, "The Murabba at Documents," *JJS* 11 (1960): 168.

67. DJD 2: 101, no. 18, in recognition of debt; see R. Yaron, "Note on a Judaean deed of sale of a field,' *BASOR* 150 (1958): 278.

68. Yaron, "Murabba'at Documents," p. 170.

69. M. R. Friedman, "Annulling the Bride's Vows: a Palestinian Ketubba Clause," *JQR* 61 (1970–71): 233: tannaitic practices different from the later talmudic ones were retained in the eleventh-century Cairo Genizah in Galilean Aramaic. This may reflect continued tannaitic practices in Byzantine Galilee.

70. See above, n. 66. Some texts simply allow for gentiles being outside the courts' control, e.g., t Ohol. 18: 1 (Z., p. 616): a Jewish court cannot stop gentiles burying impure abortions in houses; other texts bend the law to keep the peace (cf. the terms תיקון העולם and דרכי שלום); but still others assume a Jewish court hearing a civil case even between two gentiles, especially t B.K. 4: 2 (Z., p. 351): the ox of one gentile goring the ox of another.

71. See above, pp. 127–28.

72. Chajes, "Les Juges juifs," p. 52.

73. C.J. 1. 13. 1, taking *iamdudum placuit* to refer not to previous express permission by Constantine (from A.D. 307 to 316) but to the tacit non interference of earlier emperors.

74. P. Brown, "The Rise and Function of the Holy Man in Late Antiquity," *JRS* 61 (1971): 80–101.

75. A. Ehrman, "The Talmudic Concept of Sale," *JJS* 8 (1957): 177–86: the tannaitic curse for breach of faith in a contract; N. R. M. de Lange, *Origen and the Jews* (Cambridge, 1976), p. 41: Origen is aware of the use of the Korban curse to render the property of a bad debtor useless to him.

76. Sifre Deut. 16, p. 26.

77. Sifre Deut. 16, p. 27.

78. See above, pp. 93–118.

79. S. Lieberman, "Interpretations in Mishna," *Tarbiz* 40 (1970–71): 9 (Heb.), on m Gitt. 9: 4: it is wrong for a witness to sign an undated divorce document, but, once done, the divorce is valid; R. Yaron, *Gifts in Contemplation of Death in Jewish and Roman Law* (Oxford, 1960), discusses methods assumed in rabbinic texts for circumventing the letter and spirit of biblical inheritance law through informal bequests such as *fideicommissa*.

80. On Greek ideas in Jewish law in general, cf. Schürer, *History* 2: 78, n. 265, for bibliography.

81. Mitteis, *Reichsrecht*, pp. 91 ff.; Acts 19: 23–41 (Paul at Ephesus); *Digest* 50. 1. 29; 50. 9. 6; *FIRA* 1: 202–19, nos. 23–24; *Inscriptiones Graecae Bulg.* IV 2263, 11.12 ff.; Philostratus, *Vit. Soph.* 532; cf. G. P. Burton, "Proconsuls, Assizes and the Administration of Justice under the Empire," *JRS* 65 (1975): 100, n. 83.

82. Mitteis, *Reichsrecht*, p. 91 ff.

83. *FIRA* 2: 502 (*Vatican Fragments* 191).

84. See below, pp. 164–65; A. R. Bellinger and C. B. Welles, "A Third-century Contract of Sale from Edessa in Osrhoene," *YCS* 5 (1935): 111–20 (slave sale).

85. Acts 19: 38.

86. Mitteis, *Reichsrecht*, p. 91 ff.; the distinction between criminal and civil actions is much less clear in Greek law where all accusations would be privately brought (including that against St. Paul); but cf. Origen, *c. Celsum* 4. 70, re criminals condemned to public works by the city.

87. Avigad et al., "Expedition, 1961," p. 260. Other legal actions brought by Babata are probably in the Petran court, but unfortunately this is not clearly attested in the skimpy report of the papyri so far published: Babata requesting help for the orphan's upkeep uses an *epitropos ad actum*, which suggests a Greek-style, i.e., *polis*, court (see *Compendia* 1: 507: not Jewish, therefore Greek; Mitteis, *Reichsrecht*, p. 218 ff.: not Roman but Greek practice). The argument over Babata's husband's estate (Avigad et al., "Expedition, 1961," p. 261) *may* be before the same court since the governor seems to require more strictly *Roman* legal forms; see below, p. 168.

88. Matt. 5: 25–26; Luke 12: 58–59: the last drop of money owed will be squeezed out.

89. m Ket. 2: 9; see n. 88, above.

90. t Yeb. 12: 13 (L., p. 44).

91. MdRi Nezikin 1: 12–18.

92. See above, p. 129, for the Jewish administration in these cities.

93. t Toh. 7: 11 (Z., p. 668); not in the translation by J. Neusner, *The Tosefta translated from the Hebrew* (New York, 1977–   ), ad loc. Such buildings are public property for purity, but private property for Sabbath purposes; this may suggest that they are closed on Sabbath and therefore under Jewish control.

94. Man who סרח מין העיר.

95. t Sot. 15: 7 (L., p. 241) (two versions in different manuscripts; see S. Lieberman, *Tosefta Ki-fshutah: A Comprehensive Commentary on the Tosefta* (New York, 1955–   ), ad loc., for references to parallels); it would be possible to twist the reference to "sticks" to make it refer to the *fasces* of a city magistrate (Lieberman, ibid., takes the בעל זמורה to mean ῥαβδοῦχος , i.e., a city policeman), but this is speculative.

96. m Ab. 4: 11.

97. Sifre Deut. 349, p. 408.

98. MdRashbi Mishpatim 219, 1.24.

99. Mitteis, *Reichsrecht*, pp. 30, 32; *contra* W. Selb, *Zur Bedeutung des syrische-römischen Rechtsbuches* (Munich, 1964), who sees the law as basically semitic. There is clearly a mixture of the two, as in Palestine in the second century.

100. M. I. Rostovtzeff and C. B. Welles, "A parchment contract of loan from Dura-Europus," *YCS* 2 (1931): 64 (c. A.D. 122).

101. Bellinger and Welles, "Contract from Edessa," pp. 117-18: A.D. 243; νόμος refers here to local city law (ibid., p. 107).
102. Yaron, "Reichsrecht, Volksrecht and Talmud," pp. 281-82.
103. Mitteis, *Reichsrecht*, p. 313 ff., presents the evidence, though he prefers to emphasize the Greek element.
104. H. J. Wolff, "Le Droit Provincial dans la Province Romaine d'Arabie," *RIDA* 3rd ser. 23 (1976): 286, though in Roman law a guardian *could* sometimes be necessary until the age of twenty-five; cf. Wolff, ibid., p. 288: local law left untouched in Provincia Arabia, after annexation, with regard to marriage, property, contracts, and wills.
105. Bellinger and Welles, "Contract from Edessa," p. 118.
106. J. A. Goldstein, "The Syriac Bill of Sale from Dura-Europus," *Journal of Near Eastern Studies* 25 (1966): 14.
107. *FIRA* 3: 433-36, no. 135 (fourth century A.D.).
108. Avigad et al., "Expedition, 1961," pp. 236-38: tied deeds in the Greco-Roman style; Greek clauses in Aramaic admission of debt (DJD 2: 101, no. 18); Jewish contract of remarriage written in Greek (DJD 2: 243-54, no. 115). But Nabatean law is more striking in its affinities with Jewish law (Avigad, et al., "Expedition, 1961," p. 238).
109. Taubenschlag, *Law of Greco-Roman Egypt*, pp. 13, 19.
110. See above, n. 100.
111. POxy., 3054. It might just mean "in the Greek language," but, if so, why say it?
112. Wolff, "Droit Provincial," p. 278; even Roman terminology is sometimes found (ibid., p. 282).
113. F. F. Abbott and A. C. Johnson, *Municipal Administration in the Roman Empire* (Princeton, 1926), p. 74 ff.
114. Ibid., p. 288.
115. See above, notes 8, 9; below, n. 121.
116. See below, p. 170, for the degree of hellenization of Jewish law as reflected in tannaitic literature.
117. M. Rostovtzeff, "Seleucid Babylonia: Bullae and Seals of Clay with Greek Inscriptions," *YCS* 3 (1932): 57-58; PDura., 28: Edessa slave sale signed by an inspector of documents A.D. 243; POxy., 3054: Bostra slave sale.
118. *Vita* 6 (Josephus' pedigree) and Josephus, *c. Apionem* 1. 31; *BJ* 2. 427: records of debts were under the control of the keeper of records, so that destruction of records apparently is believed to release debtors from all obligations.
119. *Vita* 38; Bellinger and Welles, "Contract from Edessa," p. 119.
120. m Gitt. 1: 5.
121. Ibid.
122. t A. Zar. 1: 8 (Z., p. 461); cf. y Sanh. 3: 2, 14a: Resh Lakish says that, in the archives of Syria, a party to a suit can refuse the judge he has nominated, but not in the law of the Torah.
123. t Moed 1 (2): 12 (L., p. 368); cf. Rostovtzeff, "Seleucid Babylonia," p. 58.
124. t B.B. 8: 2 (Z., p. 409); Sifre Num., p. 135, 1.2, Korah 117.
125. t A. Zar. 6 (7): 2 (Z., p. 469).
126. t B.M. 6: 17 (Z., p. 385); cf. re loans before 70 in Jerusalem, n. 118, above.
127. m Gitt. 1: 5: gentile archives; y Gitt. 1: 4, 6a: Jewish archives, from which a cry is said to go out at insufficiently witnessed divorce documents.

128. m Gitt. 1: 5.

129. *FIRA* 2: 783 (Syro-Roman Law Book 94: *coram* ἀρχειωτῇ *civitatis*).

130. t B.B. 8: 2 (Z., p. 409): ערכיין is not illuminating.

131. *BJ* 2. 427: "keepers of records"; Goldstein, "Syriac Bill of Sale," p. 1: inspector of documents; Bruns and Sachau, *Syrisch-Römisches Rechtsbuch*, pp. 24–25 (Syro-Roman Law Book L95): οἰκονόμος ; E. Sachau, ed., *Syrische Rechtsbücher*, 3 vols. (Berlin, 1907) 1: 170 (R III 95): רשא in בית ארכא ; ibid., 1: 23–24 (L94): ארביומא דמדינתה.

132. On the importance of such archives in general in legal administration by cities, cf. Burton, "Proconsuls, Assizes and Justice," p. 103.

133. Ibid., pp. 105–6.

134. See above, p. 140.

135. P. Garnsey, *Social Status and Legal Privilege in the Roman Empire* (Oxford, 1970), p. 121: *iurisdictio* is inherent in the office of governor.

136. y Shab. 1: 4, 10a: whenever R. Yonathan (in Sepphoris in third century) saw an "important man" (בר נש רב) come to town (קרתיה), he used to greet him in order to win favor if he should judge about orphans or widows. The source is fourth century, but cf. C.J. 5. 4. 1. (A.D. 199): if tutors, mother, and relatives cannot decide on a husband for an orphan girl, then the governor must decide.

137. Avigad et al., "Expedition, 1961," p. 261; even then, this was only achieved after long wrangling.

138. *Digest* 1. 18. 13; in practice the governor had little control over theft, cf. Jackson, *Theft*, p. 256.

139. E.g., trial for "heresy," i.e., Christianity, of R. Eliezer (t Hull. 2: 24 (Z., p. 503)).

140. *FIRA* 1: 414–16, no. 69. But the origins of the stone are dubious (see, e.g., A. D. Nock, *Essays on Religion and the Ancient World*, ed. by Z. Stewart, 2 vols. (Oxford, 1972) 2: 527 ff.: probably from Decapolis and of local application only, though others would disagree): cf. *Beth Shearim* 2: 123, for inscription against disturbers of the grave.

141. t Yeb. 4: 5 (L., p. 11—*Kapotakiya*).

142. MdRi Shirata 10: 44–48. Cf. the brigand Barabbas (John 18: 40).

143. Burton, "Proconsuls, Assizes and Justice," p. 103; *FIRA* 2: 507 (*Vatican Fragments* 223) (Ulpian): special officals to keep them; Taubenschlag, *Law of Greco-Roman Egypt*, p. 31, re Egypt.

144. Sifre Num., p. 180, 1. 21, Pinhas 134, taking קונטרימים to mean *commentarii*.

145. Sifre Deut. 9, p. 17; Sifre Deut. 27, p. 44.

146. Cf. Eusebius, *Mart. Pal.*, p. 27 (Syriac text): governor sits על בים in his pride.

147. S. Lieberman, "Roman Legal Institutions in Early Rabbinics and in the Acta Martyrum," *JQR* 35 (1944–45): 1–57; but cf. Acts 22: 24: examination is μάστιξιν .

148. Garnsey, *Social Status and Legal Privilege*, p. 97; cf. the civilized warning given by a governor to a man to change his style of life (C.J. 2. 11. 19) (A.D. 284).

149. Garnsey, *Social Status and Legal Privilege*, p. 221 ff.

150. m Gitt. 3: 4: someone who "goes out to be killed"; t Sanh. 4: 6 (Z., p. 421): property of a man killed by emperor (the מלך) goes to the emperor (unless this is theory for a Jewish king?).

151. t Sanh. 9: 10 (Z., p. 429): "the authorities always use the sword"; cf. *FIRA* 2: 571 (*Mos. et Rom. Leg. Coll.* 11. 7. 1–2), re Baetica: *gladium* for

cattle rustling is reserved, according to Hadrian, for places like Spain where the problem is serious; it is considered a deliberately harsh measure. There is less about crucifixion (despite *BJ* 2. 253, re robbers being crucified) or the use of wild beasts (Eusebius, *Mart. Pal.*, p. 12 (Syriac text)) or prisons (MdRi Shirata 10: 46; Luke 23: 19—but here it is only in temporary use until condemnation).

152. Sifre Deut. 343, p. 394.
153. Apuleius, *Apologia sive Pro se de magia* 36, 48.
154. Burton, "Proconsuls, Assizes and Justice," p. 105.
155. E.g., *FIRA* 2: 577 (*Mos. et Rom. Leg. Coll.* 14. 3. 1.) (Ulpian): procurators have usurped the trials of kidnappers from governors.
156. C.J. 3. 26. 3; C.J. 3. 13. 1, etc.
157. E. M. Smallwood, *The Jews under Roman Rule from Pompey to Diocletian* (Leiden, 1976), pp. 555-67.
158. See above, p. 146.
159. Sifre Num. p. 102, 11.14-16, Behaalotekha 103.
160. MdRi Amalek 2: 30-36.
161. Lieberman, "Roman Legal Institutions," p. 35.
162. See n. 160, above.
163. See above, p. 142.
164. See above, Chap. 9, n. 84.
165. A. H. M. Jones, *Studies in Roman Government and Law* (Oxford, 1960), p. 135; Mitteis, *Reichsrecht*, p. 5, re development of a Vulgarrecht.
166. E. R. Goodenough, *The Jurisprudence of the Jewish Courts in Egypt* (New Haven, 1929), pp. 230, 242.
167. Jones, *Studies*, pp. 131-32: *peregrini* cannot inherit from Roman citizens.
168. See P. A. Brunt, "The Administrators of Roman Egypt," *JRS* 65 (1975): 134, re advisers to Roman authorities on local law.
169. Cf. Jolowicz and Nicholas, *Historical Introduction*, p. 470; provincial knowledge of Roman law would come mainly from the provincial edict, with further information from the few available juristic commentaries and perhaps *iurisprudentes* giving lectures in Beirut.
170. Mitteis, *Reichsrecht*, pp. 102-4.
171. True also after 212—see, e.g., C.J. 7. 9. 1 (Gordian); C.J. 11. 30. 4 (Diocletian)—though only under Constantine did emperors start giving way to local ideas in conflict with Roman law (Jolowicz and Nicholas, *Historical Introduction*, p. 471).
172. Wolff, *Droit Provincial*, p. 290: to explain the Babata documents.
173. Eunapius, *Vit. Phil. et Soph.* 484: in the fourth century, a governor is found strictly enforcing formalities (Mitteis, *Reichsrecht*, p. 141).
174. Jolowicz and Nicholas, *Historical Introduction*, p. 469 ff.
175. *Digest* 46. 1. 6. (Ulpian): contracts using only Greek or Aramaic are dubious, but cf. *FIRA* 2: 294 (Ulpian 25. 9): *fideicommissa* in Greek are fine, but formal legacies must be in Latin.
176. *FIRA* 2: 196 (Gaius, *Institutes* 3. 154): simple unformulaic contracts are acceptable by *ius gentium*.
177. DJD 2: 240-43, no. 114 (in Greek).
178. Avigad et al. "Expedition, 1961," p. 259 (presumed).
179. DJD 2: 239, no. 113.
180. Avigad et al., "Expedition, 1961," p. 246, doc. 8.
181. H. J. Polotsky, "Three Greek Documents from the Family Archive of Babatha," *EI* 8 (1967): 51 (Heb.).

182. Avigad et al., "Expedition, 1961," p. 261.
183. Some formulae could be very loosely worded (Jolowicz and Nicholas, *Historical Introduction*, p. 199 ff.).
184. "ξενοκριταί" appears in POxy., 3016, where it designates assessors who are particularly strict in their use of Roman forms, even to the extent of employing Latin (in contrast to the Egyptian practices permitted in POxy. 3015 and POxy. 3285). The meaning *recuperatores*, suggested by P. J. Parsons in the commentary to POxy., 3016, may well apply here too. A. Biscardi interprets the term to refer to judges from a different jurisdiction to the litigant (A. Biscardi, "Sulla identificazione degli 'xenokritai' e sulla loro attivita in P. Oxy 3016," in H. Hubner et al., eds., *Festschrift für Erwin Seidl zum 70 Geburstag* (Cologne, 1975), pp. 15-24), an attractive suggestion which would mean that their appearance in a case would render it less, rather than more, likely that local law would be used.
185. Gil, "Land Ownership," p. 39, but this is pure speculation, as is much of the article.
186. m Gitt. 9: 8, re divorces (see above, notes 8, 24); t Yeb. 12: 13 (L., p. 44), re *halizah*: "among the gentiles, they bind him and say to him: 'Do what Rabbi X says to you.' "; see reference below, n. 189.
187. This presumably lies behind *Compendia* 1: 408, which asserts, without good evidence, that Roman use of Jewish law was *normal*. If indeed rabbis were *often* used by the governor for such advice this would be an important factor in their rise to secular power, but the lack of evidence makes it improbable.
188. See above, pp. 161-62.
189. A Mekhilta passage (MdRi Nezikin 1: 12-17) envisages the decision of a gentile court being in accordance with Jewish law and proclaims it none-theless invalid (R. Eleazar b. Azariah). Later texts cited in *Compendia* 1: 408 may refer to the acknowledgment of Volksrecht by governors by the mid fourth century when these texts were edited.
190. For *halizah*, see t Yeb. 12: 13 (L., p. 44).
191. Wolff, "Droit Provincial," p. 285; though see above, n. 183, for the loose-ness of some formulae.
192. t Sot. 15: 7 (L., p. 241); see above, n. 97.
193. B. Cohen, *Jewish and Roman Law: A Comparative Study*, 2 vols. (New York, 1966); Schürer, *History* 2: 78, n. 265, for Greek influence on *halakha*.
194. Cohen, *Jewish and Roman Law*, 1: 18-19, 21-22; 2: 538 ff.; Yaron, "Murabba'at Documents," *JSS* 11 (1960): 159: DJD 2: 104 ff., no. 19.
195. Yaron, *Gifts*, pp. 18, 23-24.
196. D. Daube, "Rabbinic Methods of Interpretation and Hellenistic Rhetoric," *HUCA* 22 (1949): 239-64; Jolowicz and Nicholas, *Historical Introduction*, pp. 79, 469; but see A. Watson, *Law Making in the Later Roman Republic* (Oxford, 1974), Chap. 16, arguing against there being much Hellenistic influence on Roman law in the republic.
197. P. Collinet, *Histoire de l'École de Droit de Beyrouth*, Études historiques sur le droit de Justinien, Vol. 2 (Paris, 1925), p. 20: a school was found there certainly in the third century and probably from the late second.
198. R. Yaron, "Semitic Elements in Early Rome," in A. Watson, ed., *Daube Noster: Essays in Legal History for David Daube* (Edinburgh and London, 1974), pp. 343-57: semitic influence on Roman international contract law came from Carthage in the sixth to fifth centuries B.C.; J. J. Rabinowitz,

"Manumission of slaves in Roman Law and Oriental Law," *Journal of Near Eastern Studies* 19 (1960): 42: Roman slave manumissions were affected early by Oriental law.

199. E.g., perhaps, the changes in dowry law in Jewish and Roman law in the mid third century, cf. Cohen, *Jewish and Roman Law* 2: 350; this is especially likely since Greek influence on Roman law is known to have increased after 212 (Mitteis, *Reichsrecht*, passim).

200. Suggested in Jackson, "Roman influence on the Halakha," pp. 191–92.

201. Taubenschlag, *Law of Greco-Roman Egypt*, pp. 21–22, 40 ff.

202. For the tannaitic texts, cf. Yaron, *Gifts*, p. 18; for Judaean Desert evidence, see DJD 2: 247, on no. 115.

203. Cohen, *Jewish and Roman Law*, passim. Some of these talmudic texts claim to refer to earlier tannaitic rabbis, but their claim is not reliable.

Chapter 11

1. M. Avi-Yonah, *The Jews of Palestine: A Political History from the Bar Kokhba War to the Arab Conquest* (Oxford, 1976), pp. 35–36; S. Applebaum, *Prolegomena to the study of the Second Jewish Revolt (A.D. 132–135)* (Oxford, 1976), p. 64, conclusion number 8.

2. See above, pp. 143–44.

3. See, e.g., F. Millar et al., *The Roman Empire and its Neighbours* (London, 1966), pp. 245–6.

4. F. Millar, *The Emperor in the Roman World (31 B.C.–A.D. 337)* (London, 1977), pp. 15–16; H. H. Scullard, *From the Gracchi to Nero*, 5th ed. (London, 1982), pp. 260–65.

5. Millar, *Emperor*, pp. 394–410.

6. Cf. K. Hopkins, "Rules of Evidence," *JRS* 68 (1978): 178–86, who complains that the patterns observed in the sources are bound to be only those of conscious participants.

7. See above, Chap. 6, passim. No artefacts can ever indicate political changes of this sort. It is foolish to assess, e.g., the romanization of Roman Britain from the spread of villas, use of Samian Ware, etc.

8. See above, pp. 71–81, and especially p. 74.

9. H. I. Marrou, *A History of Education in Antiquity*, translated by G. Lamb (London, 1956), pp. 265–91, for the standard Greek curriculum; J. B. Segal, *Edessa, "the Blessed City"* (Oxford, 1970), p. 165 and passim, for the function of Church Syriac-speaking schools and monasteries as a distinctively Syriac culture emerged in full in the fourth to fifth centuries.

10. See above, Chap. 1, n. 39. Mekhilta passages that fit better into the picture of a second-century emperor than that of an eighth-century caliph: MdRi Pisha 7: 22; 11: 78; Beshallah 1: 214; 2: 206; Shirata 3: 32; 6: 100; 8: 27 (especially significant since only emperors are appropriate targets for abuse about kings who call themselves god, cf. remarks above, Chap. 9, n. 317). There are many other examples.

11. Admitted even by A. Oppenheimer, *The 'Am Ha-aretz: a Study in the Social History of the Jewish People in the Hellenistic-Roman Period*, translated by I. H. Levine (Leiden, 1977), pp. 215–16.

12. See above, pp. 86, 103–4.

13. G. Vermes, *Jesus the Jew: A Historian's Reading of the Gospels* (London, 1973), p. 72 ff.

14. *AJ* 14. 37–38.

15. *BJ* 3. 41–42.
16. See above, pp. 32–33, both for increase in population and for the immigrants being Jewish.
17. See above, pp. 110–11.
18. See above, pp. 102–4.
19. See above, pp. 75–81, for rabbis as educators; above, pp. 102–4, for rejection of rabbinic teachings.
20. J. Neusner, *A History of the Mishnaic Law of Purities*, 22 parts (Leiden, 1974–77) 21: 30 ff., re *kelim*. Earthenware would be very cheap, but surely still burdensome to replace.
21. Planting crops under olive trees and vines was a common practice in the ancient world (K. D. White, *Roman Farming* (London, 1970), pp. 226, 237).
22. t A. Zar. 4 (5): 2 (Z., p. 465).
23. See above, p. 109. Oppenheimer, *'Am Ha-aretz*, tries to bring evidence of tithes payable on manufactured goods, but the evidence is late and unconvincing.
24. E. E. Urbach, "Class-Status and Leadership in the World of the Palestinian Sages," *Proceedings of the Israel Academy of Sciences and Humanities* 2, pt. 4 (1966): 70.
25. *Encyclopedia Judaica* 16: 712; cf. Urbach, "Class-Status and Leadership," for a rapprochement between rabbis and the Galilean rich in the third century.
26. Avi-Yonah, *Jews of Palestine*, p. 109.
27. S. Safrai, "The Practical Implementation of the Sabbatical Year after the Destruction of the Second Temple," *Tarbiz* 35 (1965–66): 304–28; 36 (1966–7): 1–21 (Heb.).
28. Avi-Yonah, *Jews of Palestine*, p. 109.
29. Oppenheimer, *'Am Ha-aretz*, p. 66. For third-century embarrassment about the purity status of Tiberias, see now, L. Levine, "R. Simeon b. Yohai and the Purification of Tiberias: History and Tradition," *HUCA* 49 (1978): 143–86.
30. The Yerushalmi drops the distinction between the *ḥaver* and the *am haareẓ* as being dependent on scrupulous tithes and purity observance; cf. Oppenheimer, *'Am Ha-aretz*, pp. 43, 46–48, 117.
31. Avi-Yonah, *Jews of Palestine*, p. 109.
32. Ibid.
33. m A. Zar. 2: 6. This could be something of a problem for the argument since it can hardly be argued that oil-exporting Galilean farmers *needed* gentile oil. Perhaps Galilean oil was all of one (superior?) grade and different oil would be imported for different purposes (such as lighting, cooking, washing, etc.) from elsewhere, e.g. the Decapolis olive groves (cf. *Compendia* 2: 654, re Galilean oil being a better quality than oil from Decapolis; *Compendia* 2: 674, re Decapolis oil being exported). S. Applebaum, "Judaea as a Roman Province: the Countryside as a Political and Economic Factor," *ANRW* II (Principate) 8 (1977): 372, n. 84, suggests that Galilean oil was sold by a single middleman so that different crops might well get mixed up whether the olives came from Jewish or gentile farmers. The change in the law would therefore be intended to encourage non-Galilean Jews to use Galilean oil with a clear conscience and thereby stimulate Galilean exports to, e.g., Caesarea. Z. A. Steinfeld, "Concerning the Prohibition against Gentile Oil," *Tarbiz* 49 (1980): 264–77, shows how

an amoraic dispute over the basis of the original prohibition helped Babylonian rabbis to *accept* the lifting of the ban, but he does not discuss the reasons for the change having occurred in the first place.

34. J. Neusner, *The Rabbinic Traditions about the Pharisees before 70*, 3 parts (Leiden, 1971) 3: 319, re purity and tithes among pre-70 Pharisees; Neusner, *Purities* 22: 269 ff., puts forward the suggestion originally made by Noam Chomsky that mishnaic purity law ceased to preoccupy because it was in some sense complete.

35. Avi-Yonah, *Jews of Palestine*, p. 108; Oppenheimer, '*Am Ha-aretz*, pp. 47, 65; G. Alon, *Toledot haYehudim be Tekufat haMishnah vehaTalmud*, 2 vols., Vol. 1, 2nd ed. (Tel Aviv, 1967), Vol. 2 (Tel Aviv, 1961) 2: 153; and many others.

36. W. A. L. Elmslie, *The Mishna on Idolatry: 'Aboda Zara* (Cambridge, 1911), p. 38.

Abbreviations

AASOR	*Annual of the American Schools of Oriental Research.*
AJ	Josephus, *Antiquitates Judaicae.*
ANRW	H. Temporini and W. Haase, eds., *Aufstieg und Niedergang der römischen Welt: Geschichte und Kultur Roms im Spiegel der neueren Forschung*, Series 1, Republic, Series 2, Principate, Berlin, 1972–
b	Babylonian Talmud (= Babli).
b.	Ben or bar, meaning "son of."
BASOR	*Bulletin of the American Schools of Oriental Research.*
Beth Shearim	B. Mazar, M. Schwabe and B. Lifshitz, *Beth She'arim: Report on the Excavations during 1936-40*, 2 vols., Jerusalem, 1973-74.
BJ	Josephus, *Bellum Judaicum.*
CERP	A. H. M. Jones, *The Cities of the Eastern Roman Provinces*, 2nd ed., revised by M. Avi-Yonah et al., Oxford, 1971.
CIJ	J.-B. Frey, ed., *Corpus of Jewish Inscriptions*, 2 vols., Vol. 1, revised by B. Lifshitz, New York, 1975, Vol. 2, Rome, 1936.
CIL	T. Mommsen et al., eds., *Corpus Inscriptionum Latinarum*, Berlin, 1863–
CIS	E. Renan et al., eds., *Corpus Inscriptionum Semiticarum*, Parts 1 (3 vols.), 2 (3 vols.), 4 (3 vols.), 5 (1 vol.), Paris, 1881-1951.
C.J.	Codex Justinianus.
Compendia	S. Safrai and M. Stern, eds., *The Jewish People in the First Century: Historical Geography* . . ., Compendia Rerum Iudaicarum ad Novum Testamentum: Section 1, 2 vols., Assen, 1974-76.
CPJ	V. A. Tcherikover and A. Fuks, eds., *Corpus Papyrorum Judaicarum*, 3 vols., Cambridge, Mass., 1957-64. (Vol. 3 was edited by V. A. Tcherikover, A. Fuks and M. Stern, with an epigraphical contribution by D. M. Lewis).
C. Th.	Codex Theodosianus.
DJD 2	P. Benoit, J. T. Milik, and R. de Vaux, *Les Grottes de Murabba'at*, Discoveries in the Judaean Desert, Vol. 2, Oxford, 1960.
EAEHL	M. Avi-Yonah and E. Stern, eds., *Encyclopedia of Archaeological Excavations in the Holy Land*, 4 vols., London and Oxford, 1975-78.
EI	*Eretz Israel.*

FIRA	S. Riccobono et al., eds., *Fontes Iuris Romani Anteiustiniani*, 3 vols., Florence, 1968.
Heb.	Hebrew.
HUCA	*Hebrew Union College Annual.*
IEJ	*Israel Exploration Journal.*
IGLS	L. Jalabert and R. Mouterde, eds., *Inscriptions Grecques et Latines de la Syrie*, Paris, 1929-
IGR	R. Cagnat, ed., *Inscriptiones Graecae ad res romanas pertinentes*, 4 vols. (Vol. 2 never published), Paris, 1906-27.
JBL	*Journal of Biblical Literature.*
JJS	*Journal of Jewish Studies.*
JPOS	*The Journal of the Palestine Oriental Society.*
JQR	*Jewish Quarterly Review.*
JRS	*Journal of Roman Studies.*
JSJ	*Journal for the Study of Judaism in the Persian, Hellenistic and Roman Period.*
JSS	*Journal of Semitic Studies.*
m	Mishnah.
MdRashbi	Mekhilta de R. Shimon bar Yohai.
MdRi	Mekhilta de R. Ishmael.
OGIS	W. Dittenberger, ed., *Orientis Graeci Inscriptiones Selectae*, 2 vols., Leipzig, 1903-5.
PEQ	Palestine Exploration Quarterly (= Palestine Exploration Fund Quarterly Statement).
POxy.	B. P. Grenfell et al., eds., *Oxyrhynchus Papyri*, London, 1898-
QDAP	*Quarterly of the Department of Antiquities in Palestine.*
R.	Rabbi.
RB	*Revue Biblique.*
REJ	*Revue des Études Juives.*
RIDA	*Revue Internationale des Droits de l'Antiquité.*
Sifra	Sifra to Leviticus.
Sifre Deut.	Sifre to Deuteronomy.
Sifre Num.	Sifre to Numbers.
t . . . (L., p. . . .)	Tosefta, cited by tractate, chapter, verse and page in the relevant volume of S. Lieberman, *The Tosefta according to Codex Vienna with variants*, New York, 1955- .
t . . . (Z., p. . . .)	Tosefta, cited by tractate, chapter, verse and page in M. S. Zuckermandel, *Tosefta based on the Erfurt and Vienna codices*, 2nd ed., 1937, reprinted Jerusalem, 1970.
Vita	Josephus, *Vita.*
y	Yerushalmi (= Jerusalem or Palestinian Talmud).
YCS	*Yale Classical Studies.*
ZDPV	*Zeitschrift des deutschen Palästina-vereins.*

Abbreviations of the tractates by which the Mishnah, Tosefta, and Talmuds are cited follow the alphabetical list of H. Danby, *The Mishnah translated from the Hebrew* (Oxford, 1933), p. 806.

Glossary of Hebrew Terms

Transliteration of semitic words

I have used the simplified transliteration system given in *Encylopedia Judaica* 1: 90, with the exception that those words that are commonly found in a different form (e.g., "beth din"), place names (e.g., "Beth Shearim"), and book titles are given in their more usual spelling. Numbers in brackets refer to the pages in the text where fuller explanations are given.

Ab beth din	"Father of the Court." An important rabbi.
aggadah	Interpretation of Scriptural verses by means of edifying stories.
amidah	The main daily prayer, spoken standing up.
amme haarez	"People of the Land," i.e., the ignorant (pp. 102–4).
amora	Rabbinic teachers who taught between c. A.D. 200 and c. A.D. 500.
angareia	The provision of transport to the state under compulsion.
baal habayit	"Master of the House," i.e., householder (p. 34).
baraita	Quotation in later rabbinic compilations of tannaitic (q.v.) statements.
beit ha kneset	"House of meeting," i.e., synagogue.
bekhorot	Firstling animals due for sacrifice.
beth din	"House of judgment," i.e., court.
beth ha midrash	"House of interpretation," i.e., academy.
Cohen	Priest.
demai	Produce from which it is doubtful whether tithe has been separated.
dinar	Denarius.
Eretz Israel	Land of Israel.
erub	Ceremony to permit use of particular nonprivate property on Sabbath.
gabbai	Treasurer (p. 122).
haftarah	The portion of the Prophets read after the Torah (q.v.) reading on the Sabbath.
hakham	Wise man.
halakha	Rabbinic law.
halizah	Ceremony by which a man refuses to marry his brother's widow.
Hallel	Selection of Psalms for recitation on prescribed days.
hasid	Pious man.
haver	A "fellow" (p. 77).
havura	A "fellowship."

ḥazakah	Rabbinic rules of possession.
ḥazan	Superintendent.
'ir	Town or settlement (p. 28).
kashrut	The quality of being kosher (q.v.).
kefar	Village (p. 28).
kerakh	Big city (p. 28).
ketubah	Marriage contract.
kilaim	The law forbidding mixed kinds of vegetables, clothes etc.
kosher	"Strict," especially "in accordance with rabbinic law."
maah	One-sixth of a dinar (q.v.).
malchut	Kingdom, or empire.
maneh	100 dinars (q.v.).
matana	"Donation," especially "donation as prescribed by biblical law."
maẓikin	"Oppressors," especially "usurpers of land."
menorah	Candelabra.
meshumad	Rebellious man.
mezuzah	Rolled parchment containing passages from Deuteronomy and fastened to doorpost.
midrash	Interpretation of scripture, verse-by-verse.
mikveh	Pool for ritual cleansing.
min	Heretic.
mina	100 dinars (q.v.).
mokhsin	Tax collectors (p. 131).
nasi	President, patriarch (p. 111).
niddah	Female impurity during and after menstruation.
Omer	"Sheaf." The first sheaf of the harvest, requiring special rites.
parnas	Administrator (pp. 121–22).
perutah	The smallest copper coin current (a notional currency).
prozbul	Legal device to avoid abolition of debt in the Sabbatical Year.
rab	Master (p. 78).
Sanhedrin	Court, especially the great court of pre-70 Jerusalem.
sela	4 dinars (q.v.).
semikha	Ordination of one rabbi by another.
shebiit	Sabbatical Year.
shema	Daily prayer consisting of three passages from Pentateuch.
shofar	Ram's horn, blown on prescribed ritual occasions.
sikarikon	Rabbinic ruling about rights to usurped land.
talmid ḥakham	A wise man's pupil.
tanna	Rabbi teaching before the compilation of the Mishnah, c. A.D. 200.
tebillah	Ritual immersion in water.
tefillin	Phylacteries, worn on head and arm.
terumah	Heave offering.
Torah	"The Law," both written (i.e., Pentateuch) and oral (i.e., halakha (q.v.)).
zab	Man with a flux.
zugot	The "pairs," cf. m Ab. 1: 4–12, re pre-70 sages.
zuz	Another name for "dinar" (q.v.).

Guide to References in Rabbinic Texts

General introduction to the rabbinic literature:
    H. L. Strack, *Introduction to the Talmud and Midrash,* translation of 5th German edition, Philadelphia, 1931;
    E. Schürer, *The History of the Jewish People in the Age of Jesus Christ,* 2 vols. published, English edition based on 4th German ed., 1909, revised by G. Vermes, F. Millar, and M. Black (Edinburgh, 1973-79) 1: 68-122.

Concordances:
    to Mishnah, in H. Y. Kasovsky, *Otzar Leshon ha Mishnah,* 4 vols., 2nd ed., Jerusalem, 1956-60;
    to Tosefta, in idem, *Otzar Leshon ha Toseftah,* 6 vols., edited by M. Kasowski, Jerusalem, 1932-61;
    to tannaitic midrashim, in B. Kosovsky, *Otzar Leshon ha Tannaim,* 13 vols., Jerusalem, 1965-74.

Babylonian Talmud (= Bablí): cited by tractate and folio number.
    Editions are standard.
    Translation in I. Epstein, ed., *The Babylonian Talmud translated into English,* London, 1935-52.

Mishnah: cited by tractate, chapter, and verse.
    Edition in H. Albeck and H. Yalon, *Shisha Sidrei Mishnah,* 6 vols., Jerusalem and Tel Aviv, 1952-58.
    Translation in H. Danby, *The Mishnah translated from the Hebrew,* Oxford, 1933.

Mekhilta de R. Ishmael: cited by tractate, chapter, and line.
    Edition and translation in J. Z. Lauterbach, ed., *Mekilta de-Rabbi Ishmael,* 3 vols., Philadelphia, 1933-35.

Mekhilta de R. Shimon b. Yohai: cited by tractate, page, and line.
    Edition in J. N. Epstein and E. Z. Melamed, eds., *Mekhilta d'Rabbi Simon ben Jochai,* Jerusalem, 1955.

Sifra to Leviticus: cited by folio number and column.
    Edition in I. H. Weiss, ed., *Siphra: a Halachic Midrash to Leviticus,* Vienna, 1862.

Sifre to Deuteronomy: cited by chapter and page.
    Edition in L. Finkelstein, ed., *Sifre on Deuteronomy,* based on edition by H. S. Horovitz, Berlin, 1939, reprinted New York, 1969.

Sifre to Numbers: cited by page, line, tractate, and chapter.
    Edition in H. S. Horovitz, ed., *Siphre d'Be Rab: Siphre ad Numeros adjecto Siphre Zutta,* Leipzig, 1917, reprinted Jerusalem, 1966.
    Translation into German in K. G. Kuhn, *Der tannaitische Midrasch: Sifre zu Numeri,* Stuttgart, 1959.

Tosefta: cited by tractate, chapter, verse, and page number in relevant edition.
    Editions in M. S. Zuckermandel, *Tosephta based on the Erfurt and Vienna*

codices, with parallels and variants, 2nd ed., with "Supplement to the Tosefta" by S. Lieberman, 1937, reprinted Jerusalem, 1970; S. Lieberman, *The Tosefta according to Codex Vienna with variants etc.*, New York, 1955-   (only orders Zeraim, Mo'ed, and Nashim so far published).

Translations into German in G. Kittel and K. H. Rengstorf, *Rabbinische Texte: Erste Reihe: Die Tosefta: Text, Übersetzung, Erklärung*, Stuttgart, 1953-   , (incomplete); into English in J. Neusner, *The Tosefta translated from the Hebrew*, New York, 1977-82.

Yerushalmi (i.e., Jerusalem or Palestinian Talmud): cited by tractate, chapter, verse, and folio.

Edition in Vilna edition, 8 vols., Vilna, 1922.

Translation into (inaccurate) French in M. Schwab, *Le Talmud de Jerusalem* 6 vols., Paris, 1871-88, reprinted, Paris, 1977; into English in a forthcoming translation by J. Neusner, *The Talmud of the Land of Israel: A Preliminary Translation and Explanation*, 35 vols., Chicago, 1983-

Bibliography

Abbott, F. F. and Johnson, A. C., *Municipal Administration in the Roman Empire*, Princeton, 1926.

Aberbach, M., "Educational Institutions and Problems during the Talmudic Age," *HUCA* 37 (1966): 107-20.

Abramson, S., "A New Fragment of the Mekhilta de-Rabbi Shim'on bar Yohai," *Tarbiz* 41 (1971-2): 361-72 (Heb.).

Adler, M. "The Emperor Julian and the Jews," *JQR* 10 (1893): 591-651.

Aharoni, Y., "Three New Boundary Stones from the Western Golan," *Atiqot* 1 (1955): 109-14.

—— "Two Additional Boundary Stones from the Huleh Valley," *Atiqot* 2 (1959): 152-54.

Alon, G., *Toledot haYehudim be Eretz Yisrael be Tekufat haMishnah veha-Talmud*, 2 vols., Vol. 1, 2nd ed., Tel Aviv, 1967, Vol. 2, Tel Aviv, 1961. Vol. 1 is now translated into English as G. Alon, *The Jews in their Land in the Talmudic Age*, translated by G. Levi, Jerusalem, 1980.

—— *Jews, Judaism and the Classical World*, Jerusalem, 1977.

Alt, A., "Die Stätten des Wirkens Jesu in Galiläa territorialgeschichtlich betrachtet," *ZDPV* 68 (1949): 51-72.

Amiran, D. H. K., "The Population of Galilee," *Yediot* 18 (1954): 223-44 (Heb.).

Angeli, M. G. Bertinelli, *Nomenclatura publica e sacra di Roma nelle epigrafi semitiche*, Genoa, 1970.

Applebaum, S. "The Roman Theatre at Beth-Shean," *Yediot* 25 (1961): 147-49 (Heb.).

—— and Gihon, M., eds., *Israel and her vicinity in the Roman and Byzantine periods*, Notes offered to delegates to the Seventh International Congress of Roman Frontier Studies, Tel Aviv, 1967.

—— "The Agrarian Question and the Revolt of Bar Kokhba," *EI* 8 (1967): 283-87 (Heb.).

—— *Prolegomena to the Study of the Second Jewish Revolt (A.D. 132-135)*, British Archaeological Reports Supplementary Series, Vol. 7, Oxford, 1976.

—— "Judaea as a Roman Province: The Countryside as a Political and Economic Factor," *ANRW* II (Principate) 8 (1977): 355-96.

Avigad, N., "An Aramaic Inscription from the Ancient Synagogue of Umm el-'Amed," *Yediot* 19 (1955): 183-87 (Heb.).

—— et al., "The Expedition to the Judaean Desert, 1960," *IEJ* 11 (1961): 1-72.

—— et al., "The Expedition to the Judaean Desert, 1961," *IEJ* 12 (1962): 167-262.

—— "Relics of Ancient Jewish Art in Galilee," *EI* 7 (1964): 18-23 (Heb.).

—— "The Tomb of Jacob's Daughters at Sepphoris," *EI* 11 (1973): 41-44 (Heb.).

Avi-Yonah, M., "Oriental elements in the Art of Palestine in the Roman and Byzantine Periods," *QDAP* 10 (1944): 105-51; 13 (1948): 128-65.
—— "The Foundation of Tiberias," *IEJ* 1 (1950-51): 160-69.
—— *Oriental Art in Roman Palestine*, Rome, 1961.
—— "Scythopolis," *IEJ* 12 (1962): 123-34.
—— "The Caesarean Inscription of the 24 Priestly Courses," *EI* 7 (1964): 24-28 (Heb.).
—— *The Holy Land from the Persian to the Arab Conquests (536 B.C. to A.D. 640): A Historical Geography*, Grand Rapids, 1966.
—— *The Jews of Palestine: A Political History from the Bar Kokhba War to the Arab Conquest*, Oxford, 1976.
—— and Stern, E., eds., *Encyclopedia of Archaeological Excavations in the Holy Land*, 4 vols., London and Oxford, 1975-78.
Baer, Y., "Israel, the Christian Church and the Roman Empire," *Scripta Hierosolymitana* 7 (1961): 79-149.
Bagatti, B., *Excavations in Nazareth: From the Beginning till the XII Century*, translated by E. Hoade, Jerusalem, 1969.
Bar-Kochva, B., "Gamla in Gaulanitis," *ZDPV* 92 (1976): 54-69.
Bastomsky, S. J., "The Emperor Nero in Talmudic Legend," *JQR* 59 (1968-69): 321-25.
Bellinger, A. R. and Welles, C. Bradford, "A Third Century Contract of Sale from Edessa in Osrhoene," *YCS* 5 (1935): 93-154.
Ben Amos, D., "Narrative Forms in the Aggadah: Structural Analysis," Ph.D. diss., University of Indiana, 1967.
Ben-David, A., "Jewish and Roman Bronze and Copper Coins: their Reciprocal Relations in Mishnah and Talmud from Herod the Great to Trajan and Hadrian," *PEQ* (1971): 109-29.
Ben-Dov, M., "Fragmentary Synagogue Inscription from Tiberias," *Qadmoniot* 9 (1976): 79-80 (Heb.).
Ben Zevi, J., "A Third Century Aramaic Inscription in Er-rama," *JPOS* 13 (1933): 94-96.
Benoit, P., Milik, J. T., and De Vaux, R., *Les grottes de Murabba'at,* Discoveries in the Judaean Desert, Vol. 2, Oxford, 1960.
Bickerman, E., *Four Strange Books of the Bible*, New York, 1967.
—— "Sur la Théologie de l'Art Figuratif à Propos de l'Ouvrage de E. R. Goodenough," *Syria* 44 (1967): 131-61.
Bietenhard, H., *Caesarea, Origenes und die Juden*, Stuttgart, 1974.
Biscardi, A., "Sulla identificazione degli 'xenokritai' e sulla loro attivita in P. Oxy. 3016," in H. Hubner et al., eds., *Festschrift für Erwin Seidl zum 70 Geburtstag*, Cologne, 1975, pp. 15-24.
Blidstein, G. J., "The Sale of Animals to Gentiles in Talmudic Law," *JQR* 61 (1970-1): 188-98.
Bokser, B. M., *Samuel's Commentary on the Mishnah: its Nature, Forms and Content*, Leiden, 1975.
Bowersock, G. W., *Greek Sophists in the Roman Empire*, Oxford, 1969.
—— "A Report on Arabia Provincia," *JRS* 61 (1971): 219-42.
Brand, J., *Klei haHeres be Sifrut haTalmud (Ceramics in Talmudic Literature)*, Jerusalem, 1953 (Heb.).
—— "Concerning Greek culture in Palestine during the Talmudic period," *Tarbiz* 38 (1968-69): 13-17 (Heb.).
—— "Indications of Jewish Vessels in the Mishnaic Period," *EI* 9 (1969): 40-41 (Heb.).

Brown, P., "The Rise and Function of the Holy Man in Late Antiquity," *JRS* 61 (1971): 80–101.

Bruns, K. G. and Sachau, E., eds., *Syrisch-Römisches Rechtsbuch aus dem fünften Jahrhundert*, Leipzig, 1880.

Brunt, P. A., "Josephus on Social Conflicts in Roman Judaea," *Klio* 59 (1977): 149–53.

Büchler, A., "Triennial Cycle: the Reading of the Law and Prophets in a Triennial Cycle," *JQR* 5 (1893): 420–68.

—— *Der galiläische 'Am-ha'Ares des zweiten Jahrhunderts*, 1906, repr. Hildesheim, 1968.

—— *The Political and the Social Leaders of the Jewish Community in Sepphoris in the Second and Third Centuries*, Oxford, 1909.

—— *The Economic Conditions of Judaea after the Destruction of the Second Temple*, London, 1912.

—— *Studies in Jewish History*, London, 1956.

Burton, G. P., "Proconsuls, Assizes and the Administration of Justice under the Empire," *JRS* 65 (1975): 92–106.

Cantineau, J., "Textes Funéraires Palmyréniens," *RB* 39 (1930): 522–51.

Cantineau, J., Starcky, J., and Teixidor, J., eds., *Inventaire des Inscriptions de Palmyre*, 11 fascs., Beirut and Damascus, 1930–65.

Chabot, J.-B., *Choix d' inscriptions de Palmyre*, Paris, 1922.

Chadwick, H., *Origen: Contra Celsum*, Cambridge, 1953.

Chajes, H.-P., "Les Juges juifs en Palestine, de l'an 70 à l'an 500," *REJ* 39 (1899): 39–52.

Cohen, B., *Jewish and Roman Law: A Comparative Study*, 2 vols., New York, 1966.

Colledge, M. A. R., *The Art of Palmyra*, London, 1976.

Collinet, P., *Histoire de l'École de Droit de Beyrouth*, Études historiques sur le droit de Justinien, Vol. 2, Paris, 1925.

Conder, C. R. and Kitchener, H. H., *The Survey of Western Palestine: Memoirs of the Topography, Orography, Hydrography and Archaeology*, 7 vols., 1881–88, Vol. 1, *Galilee*, London, 1881.

Cooke, G. A., *A Text-Book of North Semitic Inscriptions*, London, 1903.

Corbo, V. C., *The House of St. Peter at Capharnaum: a Preliminary Report of the First Two Campaigns of Excavations*, translated by S. Saller, Jerusalem, 1969.

—— Loffreda, S., Spijkerman, A., and Testa, E., *Cafarnao*, 4 vols., Jerusalem, 1972–75.

Daube, D., "The Civil Law of the Mishnah: the Arrangement of the Three Gates," *Tulane Law Review* 18 (1944): 351–407.

—— "Rabbinic Methods of Interpretation and Hellenistic Rhetoric," *HUCA* 22 (1949). 239–64.

—— *Collaboration with Tyranny in Rabbinic Law*, London, 1965.

Dauphin, C., "The Golan in the Mishnaic and Talmudic Period," typescript, Jerusalem, 1979.

De Lange, N. R. M., *Origen and the Jews: Studies in Jewish-Christian Relations in Third Century Palestine*, Cambridge, 1976.

—— "Jewish Attitudes to the Roman Empire," in P. D. A. Garnsey and C. R. Whittaker, eds., *Imperialism in the Ancient World*, Cambridge, 1978, pp. 255–81.

Dinur, B. Z., "The Tractate Aboth (Sayings of the Fathers) as an Historical Source," *Zion* 35 (1970): 1–34 (Heb.).

Downey, G. *A History of Antioch in Syria*, Princeton, 1961.

Drijvers, H. J. W., ed., *The Book of the Laws of Countries: Dialogue on Fate of Bardaisan of Edessa*, Assen, 1965.

Duncan, J. G., "The Sea of Tiberias and its Environs," *PEQ* (1926): 15–22, 65–74.

Ehrman, A., "The Talmudic Concept of Sale," *JJS* 8 (1957): 177–86.

Elmslie, W. A. L., *The Mishna on Idolatry: 'Aboda Zara*, Cambridge, 1911.

Epstein, J. N., *Mevo'ot lesifrut hatannaim (Introduction to Tannaitic Literature)*, edited by E. Z. Melamed, Jerusalem, 1957.

Epstein, L. M., *Marriage Laws in the Bible and the Talmud*, Cambridge, Mass., 1942.

Fischel, H. A., *Rabbinic Literature and Greco-Roman Philosophy: A Study of Epicurea and Rhetorica in Early Midrashic Writings*, Leiden, 1973.

Foerster, G., "Notes on Recent Excavations at Capernaum (Review Article)," *IEJ* 21 (1971): 207–11.

—— "Ancient Synagogues in Eretz-Israel," *Qadmoniot* 5 (1972): 38–42 (Heb.).

—— "The Synagogues at Masada and Herodium," *EI* 11 (1973): 224–28 (Heb.).

—— "Tibériade: Communication," *RB* 82 (1975): 105–9.

Freyne, S., *Galilee from Alexander the Great to Hadrian, 323 B. C. E. to 135 C. E.*, Notre Dame, 1980.

Frezouls, Ed., "Recherches sur les Théâtres de l'Orient syrien," *Syria* 36 (1959); 202–27; 38 (1961): 54–86.

Friedman, M. R., "Annulling a Bride's Vows: a Palestinian Ketubba Clause," *JQR* 61 (1970–71): 222–33.

Garnsey, P., *Social Status and Legal Privilege in the Roman Empire*, Oxford, 1970.

Gaster, M., *The Samaritans*, London, 1923.

Geiger, J., "The Ban on Circumcision and the Bar-Kokhba Revolt," *Zion* 41 (1976): 139–47.

Gil, M., "Land Ownership in Palestine under Roman Rule," *RIDA*, 3rd Ser., 17 (1970): 11–53.

Goldstein, J. A., "The Syriac Bill of Sale from Dura-Europus," *Journal of Near Eastern Studies* 25 (1966): 1–16.

Goodblatt, D. M., *Rabbinic Instruction in Sasanian Babylonia*, Leiden, 1975.

Goodenough, E. R., *The Jurisprudence of the Jewish Courts in Egypt*, New Haven, 1929.

—— *Jewish Symbols in the Greco-Roman Period*, 13 vols., New York, 1953–68.

Grabbe, L. L., "Orthodoxy in First Century Judaism: What are the Issues?" *JSJ* 8 (1977): 149–53.

Grant, M., *The Jews in the Roman World*, London, 1973.

Green, W. S., "Palestinian Holy Men: Charismatic Leadership and Rabbinic Tradition," *ANRW* II (Principate) 19, pt. 2 (1979): 619–47.

Groh, D., "Galilee and the Eastern Roman Empire in Late Antiquity," *Explor* 3 (1977): 78–92.

Hadas-Lebel, M., "Le paganisme à travers les sources rabbiniques des IIe et IIIe siècles: Contribution à l'étude du syncrétisme dans l'empire romain," *ANRW* II (Principate) 19, pt. 2 (1979): 397–485.

Hamburger, H. "Minute Coins from Caesarea," *Atiqot* 1 (1955): 115–38.

—— "A Hoard of Syrian Tetradrachms from Tiberias," *Atiqot* 2 (1959): 133–45.

Hanson, R. S., *Tyrian Influence in the Upper Galilee*, Cambridge, Mass., 1980.

Har-El, M., "The Zealots' Fortresses in Galilee," *IEJ* 22 (1972): 123-30.
Harper, G. M., "Village Administration in the Roman Province of Syria," *YCS* 1 (1928): 102-68.
Harris, H. A., *Greek Athletics and the Jews*, edited by I. M. Barton and A. J. Brothers, Cardiff, 1976.
Hecker, M., "The Roman Road Legio-Zippori," *Yediot* 25 (1961): 175-185 (Heb.).
Heichelheim, F. M., in T. Frank, ed., *An Economic Survey of Ancient Rome*, 5 vols., 1933-40, Vol. 4, *Roman Syria*, Baltimore, 1938, pp. 121-258.
Heinemann, J. H., "The Status of the Labourer in Jewish Law and Society in the Tannaitic Period," *HUCA* 25 (1954): 263-325.
Hengel, M., *Judaism and Hellenism: Studies in their Encounter in Palestine during the Early Hellenistic Period*, 2 vols., translated by J. Bowden, London, 1974.
Herford, R. Travers, *Christianity in Talmud and Midrash*, London, 1903.
Herr, M. D., "The Historical Significance of the Dialogues Between Jewish Sages and Roman Dignitaries," *Scripta Hierosolymitana* 22 (1971): 123-50.
Hirschberg, H. Z., "New Jewish Inscriptions in the Nabatean sphere," *EI* 12 (1975): 142-48 (Heb.).
Horsley, R. A., "Josephus and the Bandits," *JSJ* 10 (1979): 37-63.
Hütteroth, W. D. and Abdulfattah, K., *Historical Geography of Palestine, Transjordan and Southern Syria in the Late Sixteenth Century*, Erlangen, 1977.
Hüttenmeister, F. F. and Reeg, G., *Die antiken Synagogen in Israel*, 2 vols., Wiesbaden, 1977.
Isaac, B., "Milestones in Judaea, from Vespasian to Constantine," *PEQ* (1978): 47-60.
—— and Roll, I., "Judaea in the Early Years of Hadrian's Reign," *Latomus* 38 (1979): 54-66.
Jackson, B. S., *Theft in Early Jewish Law*, Oxford, 1972.
Jacobs, L. "The Economic Conditions of the Jews in Babylon in Talmudic times compared with Palestine," *JSS* 2 (1957): 349-359.
—— "How much of the Babylonian Talmud is Pseudepigraphic?" *JJS* 28 (1977): 46-59.
Jeremias, J., *Jerusalem in the Time of Jesus*, translated by F. H. Cave and C. H. Cave, London, 1969.
Jidejian, N., *Tyre through the Ages*, Beirut, 1969.
—— *Sidon through the Ages*, Beirut, 1971.
—— *Baalbek: Heliopolis, "City of the Sun"*, Beirut, 1975.
Jones, A. H. M., "Inscriptions from Jerash," *JRS* 18 (1928): 144-80.
—— "The Urbanization of Palestine," *JRS* 21 (1931): 78-85.
—— *The Greek City from Alexander to Justinian*, Oxford, 1940.
—— *Studies in Roman Government and Law*, Oxford, 1960.
—— *The Cities of the Eastern Roman Provinces*, 2nd ed., revised by M. Avi-Yonah et al., Oxford, 1971.
Juster, J., *Les Juifs dans l'Empire Romain: Leur Condition Juridique, Économique et Sociale*, 2 vols., Paris, 1914.
Kaplan, J., "A Mausoleum at Kfar Giladi," *EI* 8 (1967): 104-13 (Heb.).
Kindler, A., *The Coins of Tiberias*, Tiberias, 1961.
Klein, S., *Neue Beiträge zur Geschichte und Geographie Galiläas*, Palästina-Studien, Vol. 1, Vienna, 1923.
—— *Eretz haGalil miyeme haaliyah miBavel ad ḥatimat haTalmud*, edited by Y. Eltizur, Jerusalem, 1967.

Kochavi, M., ed., *Judaea, Samaria and the Golan: Archaeological Survey 1967–1968*, Jerusalem, 1972, (Heb.).

Kraeling, C. H., ed., *Gerasa: City of the Decapolis*, New Haven, 1938.

—— *The Excavations at Dura-Europus: Final Report*, Vol. 8, pt. 1, *The Synagogue*, New Haven, 1956.

Krauss, S., *Griechische und Lateinische Lehnworter im Talmud, Midrasch und Targum*, 2 vols., Berlin, 1898-99.

—— *Antoninus und Rabbi*, Vienna, 1910.

—— "Outdoor Teaching in Talmudic Times," *JJS* 1 (1948-49): 82-84.

Kreissig, H., "Die landwirtschaftliche Situation in Palästina vor dem Judäischen Krieg," *Acta Antiqua Acad. Scient. Hungaricae* 17 (1969): 223-54.

Lambert, E., "Les changeurs et la monnaie en Palestine, du Ier au IIIe siècle de l'ère vulgaire," *REJ* 51 (1906): 217-44; 52 (1906): 24-42.

Levine, L. I., *Caesarea under Roman Rule*, Leiden, 1975.

—— "R. Simeon b. Yohai and the Purification of Tiberias," *HUCA* 49 (1978): 143-86.

—— "The Jewish Patrarch (Nasi) in Third Century Palestine," *ANRW* II (Principate) 19, pt. 2 (1979): 649-88.

—— ed., *Ancient Synagogues Revealed*, Jerusalem, 1981.

Lieberman, S., *Formation of the Caesarean Talmud*, supplement to Tarbiz 2, no. 4, Jerusalem, 1931 (Heb.).

—— *Greek in Jewish Palestine*, New York, 1942.

—— "The Martyrs of Caesarea," *Annuaire de l'Institut de Philologie et d'Histoire Orientales et Slaves* 7 (1939-1944): 395-446.

—— "Roman Legal Institutions in Early Rabbinics and in the Acta Martyrum," *JQR* 35 (1944-45): 1-57.

—— "Palestine in the Third and Fourth Centuries," *JQR* 36 (1945-46): 329-70; 37 (1946-47): 31-54.

—— *Tosefta Ki-fshutah: A Comprehensive Commentary on the Tosefta*, New York, 1955-

—— *Hellenism in Jewish Palestine*, 2nd ed., New York, 1962.

—— "Interpretations in Mishna," *Tarbiz* 40 (1970-1): 9-17 (Heb.).

Lifshitz, B., "Beiträge zur palästinischen Epigraphik," *ZDPV* 78 (1962): 62-88.

—— *Donateurs et Fondateurs dans les Synagogues juives*, Cahiers de la Revue Biblique, 7, Paris, 1967.

—— "Scythopolis: L'histoire, les institutions et les cultes de la ville à l'époque hellenistique et imperiale," *ANRW* II (Principate) 8 (1977): 262-94.

Linder, A. "The Roman Imperial Government and the Jews under Constantine," *Tarbiz* 44 (1974-5): 95-143 (Heb.).

Loffreda, S., "The Late Chronology of Capernaum," *IEJ* 23 (1973): 37-42.

Lowe, W. H., ed., *The Mishnah of the Palestinian Talmud*, Cambridge, 1883.

Macmullen, R., *Roman Social Relations 50 B.C. to A.D. 284*, New Haven, 1974.

Mantel, H., *Studies in the History of the Sanhedrin*, Cambridge, Mass., 1961.

Marmorstein, A., "La réorganisation du doctorat en Palestine au 3e siècle," *REJ* 66 (1913): 44-53.

Marrou, H. I., *A History of Education in Antiquity*, translated by G. Lamb, London, 1956.

Mazar (Maisler), B., Schwabe, M., and Lifshitz, B., *Beth She'arim: Report on the Excavations during 1936-40*, 2 vols., Jerusalem, 1973-4.

McEleney, N. J., "Orthodoxy in Judaism of the First Christian Century," *JSJ* 9 (1978): 83-88.

Mendelsohn, I., "Guilds in Ancient Palestine," *BASOR* 80 (1940): 17-21.

—— *Slavery in the Ancient Near East . . . from the Middle of the Third Millennium to the End of the First Millennium*, New York, 1949.

Meshorer, Y., "Coins from the Excavations at Khorazin," *EI* 11 (1973): 158–62 (Heb.).

—— "A hoard of coins from Migdal," *Atiqot* 11 (1976): 54–71.

Meyers, C. L., Meyers, E. M. and Strange, J. F., "Excavations at Meiron in Upper Galilee—1971, 1972: A Preliminary Report," *BASOR* 214 (1974): 2–25.

Meyers, E. M., Kraabel, A. T., and Strange, J. F., "Ancient Synagogue Excavations at Khirbet Shema', Israel, 1970–1972," *AASOR* 42 (1976). (The entire volume is devoted to the report of the excavations.)

—— "Galilean Regionalism as a Factor in Historical Reconstruction," *BASOR* 221 (1976): 93–101.

—— Meyers, C. L., and Strange, J. F., "Excavations at Meiron in Upper Galilee—1974, 1975: Second Preliminary Report," *AASOR* 43 (1978): 73–108.

—— Strange, J. F., and Groh, D. E., "The Meiron Excavation Project: Archaeological Survey in Galilee and Golan, 1976," *BASOR* 230 (1978): 1–24.

—— and Meyers, C. L., "Digging the Talmud in Ancient Meiron," *Biblical Archaeology Review* 4, no. 2 (June, 1978): 38–42.

—— Strange, J. F., Meyers, C. L., and Hanson, R. S., "Preliminary Report on the 1977 and 1978 seasons at Gush Halav (el-Jish)," *BASOR* 233 (1979): 33–58.

—— Strange, J. F., and Meyers, C. L., *Excavations at Meiron, Upper Galilee*, Cambridge, Mass., 1981.

Millar, F., "Paul of Samosata, Zenobia and Aurelian: the Church, Local Culture and Political Allegiance in Third Century Syria," *JRS* 61 (1971): 1–17.

—— *The Emperor in the Roman World (31 B.C.–A.D. 337)*, London, 1977.

—— "The Background to the Maccabean Revolution: Reflections on Martin Hengel's 'Judaism and Hellenism'," *JJS* 29 (1978): 1–21.

Mitteis, L., *Reichsrecht und Volksrecht in den östlichen Provinzen des Römischen Kaiserreichs*, Leipzig, 1891.

Mouterde, R., and Lauffray, J., *Beyrouth Ville Romaine: Histoire et Monuments,* Beirut, 1952.

Neusner, J., *A History of the Jews in Babylonia*, 5 vols., Leiden, 1965–70.

—— *A Life of Yohanan ben Zakkai Ca. 1–80 C.E.*, 2nd rev. ed., Leiden, 1970.

—— *The Rabbinic Traditions about the Pharisees before 70*, 3 parts, Leiden, 1971.

—— *Eliezer b. Hyrcanus: the Traditions and the Man*, 2 parts, Leiden, 1973.

—— ed., *The Modern Study of the Mishna*, Leiden, 1973.

—— *The Idea of Purity in Ancient Judaism: the Haskell Lectures 1972–3*, with a critique and commentary by M. Douglas, Leiden, 1973.

—— *A History of the Mishnaic Law of Purities*, 22 parts, Leiden, 1974–77.

—— *The Tosefta translated from the Hebrew*, New York, 1977–82.

—— *A History of the Mishnaic Law of Women*, 5 parts, Leiden, 1980.

—— *A History of the Mishnaic Law of Holy Things*, 6 parts, Leiden, 1980.

Nock, A. D., "Downey's Antioch: a Review," *Greek, Roman and Byzantine Studies* 4 (1963): 49–54.

Oppenheimer, A., *The 'Am Ha-aretz: a Study in the Social History of the Jewish People in the Hellenistic-Roman Period*, translated by I. H. Levine, Leiden, 1977.

Ostrow, J., "Tannaitic and Roman Procedure in Homicide," *JQR* 48 (1957–58): 352–70; 52 (1961–2): 160–7, 245–263.

Ovadiah, A., "A Jewish Sarcophagus at Tiberias," *IEJ* 22 (1972): 229–32.

—— "Greek Cults in Beth Shean/Scythopolis in the Hellenistic and Roman Periods," *EI* 12 (1975): 116-24 (Heb.).

Parker, S. T., "The Decapolis Reviewed," *JBL* 94 (1975): 437-41.

Polotsky, H. J., "Three Greek Documents from the Family Archive of Babatha," *EI* 8 (1967): 46-51 (Heb.).

Rabinowitz, J. J., "Manumission of slaves in Roman Law and Oriental Law," *Journal of Near Eastern Studies* 19 (1960): 42-45.

Rajak, T., "Justus of Tiberias," *Classical Quarterly* n.s. 23 (1973): 345-68.

—— *Josephus: The Historian and his Society*, London, 1983.

Rey-Coquais, J.-P., "Syrie Romaine, de Pompée à Dioclétien," *JRS* 68 (1968): 44-73.

Rokeah, D., "Comments on the Revolt of Bar Kokhba," *Tarbiz* 35 (1965-6): 122-131 (Heb.).

Rosen, H. B., "Palestinian κοινή in Rabbinic Illustration," *JSS* 8 (1963): 56-72.

Rostovtzeff, M. I. and Welles, C. B., "A Parchment Contract of Loan from Dura-Europus on the Euphrates," *YCS* 2 (1931): 1-78.

—— "Seleucid Babylonia: Bullae and Seals of Clay with Greek Inscriptions," *YCS* 3 (1932): 1-114.

—— (Rostovtsev), *Caravan Cities*, translated by D. Talbot Rice and T. Talbot Rice, Oxford, 1932.

—— "La Syrie Romaine," *Revue Historique* 65 (1935): 1-40.

—— *The Social and Economic History of the Roman Empire*, 2nd ed., revised by P. M. Fraser, 2 vols., Oxford, 1957.

Safrai, S., "The Practical Implementation of the Sabbatical Year after the Destruction of the Second Temple," *Tarbiz* 35 (1965-66): 304-28; 36 (1966-67): 1-21 (Heb.).

—— "The Holy Congregation in Jerusalem," *Scripta Heirosolymitana* 23 (1972): 62-78.

—— and Stern, M., eds., *The Jewish People in the First Century: Historical Geography* . . ., Compendia Rerum Iudaicarum ad Novum Testamentum: Section 1, 2 vols., Assen, 1974-6.

Safrai, Z., "Marginal Notes on the Rehob Inscription," *Zion* 42 (1977): 1-23 (Heb.).

Saldarini, A. J., " 'Form Criticism' of Rabbinic Literature," *JBL* 96 (1977): 257-74.

Saltz, D., "Surveys, Salvage and Small Digs in Israel," *American Schools of Oriental Research Newsletter*, no. 10 (1977): 3.

Sanders, E. P. et al., eds., *Jewish and Christian Self-Definition*, 2 vols., Vol. 2, *Aspects of Judaism in the Graeco-Roman Period*, London, 1981.

Sandmel, S., *Judaism and Christian Beginnings*, New York, 1978.

Sarfatti, G., "Three Comments regarding some Tannaitic Sources," *Tarbiz* 32 (1962-63): 136-42 (Heb.).

Schäfer, P., *Der Bar Kokhba Aufstand: Studien zum zweiten Jüdischen Krieg gegen Rom*, Tübingen, 1981.

Schlumberger, D., *La Palmyrène du Nord-Ouest*, Paris, 1951.

Scholem, G., *Jewish Gnosticism, Merkabah Mysticism and Talmudic Tradition*, New York, 1960.

Schürer, E., *The History of the Jewish People in the Age of Jesus Christ*, 2 vols. so far, English edition based on 4th German edition, 1909, revised by G. Vermes, F. Millar, and M. Black, Edinburgh, 1973-79.

Schwabe, M., "A Jewish Inscription from ed-Dumeir near Damascus," *EI* 2 (1953): 161-65 (Heb.).

—— "Recently Discovered Jewish Inscriptions," *Yediot* 18 (1954): 157-63 (Heb.).

Segal, A., ed., *Ancient Sites of the Holy Land in the Classical Period: Selected plans*, Beer-Sheva, 1978 (Heb.).

Segal, A. F., *Two Powers in Heaven: Early Rabbinic Reports about Christianity and Gnosticism*, Leiden, 1977.

Segal, J. B., *Edessa, "the Blessed City"*, Oxford, 1970.

—— "Popular Religion in Ancient Israel," *JJS* 27 (1976): 1-22.

—— "The Jewish Attitude towards Women," *JJS* 30 (1979): 121-37.

Selb, W., *Zur Bedeutung des syrische-römischen Rechtsbuches*, Munich, 1964.

Seyrig, H., *Antiquités Syriennes*, Extracts from Syria, 6 vols., Paris, 1934-66.

Shanks, H., *Judaism in Stone: The Archaeology of Ancient Synagogues*, New York and London, 1979.

Sherwin-White, A. N., *Roman Society and Roman Law in the New Testament*, Oxford, 1963.

Simon, M., *Verus Israel: Étude sur les Relations entre Chrétiens et Juifs dans l'empire Romain (135-425)*, Paris, 1948.

—— "Les sectes juives d'après les témoignages patristiques," *Studia Patristica* 1 (1957): 526-39.

Smallwood, E. M., *The Jews under Roman Rule from Pompey to Diocletian*, Leiden, 1976.

Smith, G. A., *The Historical Geography of the Holy Land*, London, 1894.

Soreq, Y., "Hellenistic-Roman Land Tenancy System as Reflected in Talmudic Literature," *Zion* 39 (1974): 217-23 (Heb.).

—— "Rabbinical Evidences about the Pagi Vicinales in Israel," *JQR* 65 (1975): 221-24.

—— "A Rabbinic Evidence of the Tricomia in Palestine," *JQR* 66 (1976): 236.

Sperber, D., *Roman Palestine 200-400: Money and Prices*, Ramat-Gan, 1974.

—— *Roman Palestine 200-400: the Land: Crisis and Change in Agrarian Society as reflected in Rabbinic Sources*, Ramat-Gan, 1978.

Stark, J. K., *Personal Names in Palmyrene Inscriptions*, Oxford, 1971.

Steinfeld, Z. A., "Concerning the Prohibition against Gentile Oil," *Tarbiz* 49 (1980): 264-72 (Heb.).

Strack, H. L., *Introduction to the Talmud and Midrash*, translation of 5th German edition, Philadelphia, 1931.

Strange, J. F., "The Capernaum and Herodium Publications," *BASOR* 226 (1977): 65-73.

Sukenik, E. L., *Ancient Synagogues in Palestine and Greece*, London, 1934.

Sussman, V., "Early Jewish Iconoclasm," *Atiqot* 7 (1974): 95-96 (Heb.).

Sussman, Y., "A halakhic inscription from the Beth-Shean valley," *Tarbiz* 43 (1973-74): 88-158 (Heb.).

—— "The Boundaries of Eretz-Israel," *Tarbiz* 45 (1975-6): 213-257 (Heb.).

Syme, R., *Emperors and Biography: Studies in the Historia Augusta*, Oxford, 1971.

Taubenschlag, R., *The Law of Greco-Roman Egypt in the Light of the Papyri 332 B.C.-640 A.D.*, 2nd ed., Warsaw, 1955.

Tchalenko, G., *Villages Antiques de la Syrie du Nord: Le Massif du Bélus à l'Époque Romaine*, 3 vols., Paris, 1953-58.

Teixidor, J., *The Pagan God: Popular Religion in the Greco-Roman Near East*, Princeton, 1977.

Tzaferis, V., "Tombs in Western Galilee," *Atiqot* 5 (1969): 72-79 (Heb.).

Urbach, E. E., "The Rabbinical Laws of Idolatry in the Second and Third Centuries in the Light of Archaeological and Historical Facts," *IEJ* 9 (1959): 149-65, 229-45.

—— "The Laws regarding Slavery as a Source for Social History of the Period of the Second Temple, the Mishnah and Talmud," *Papers of the Institute of Jewish Studies, London* 1 (1964): 1-94.

—— "Class-Status and Leadership in the World of the Palestinian Sages," *Proceedings of the Israel Academy of Sciences and Humanities* 2, part 4 (1966): 38-74.

—— *The Sages: their Concepts and Beliefs*, translated by I. Abrahams, Jerusalem, 1975.

Urman, D., "Jewish Inscriptions from Dabbura, Golan," *Qadmoniot* 4 (1971): 131-33 (Heb.).

Vermes, G., *Scripture and Tradition in Judaism: Haggadic Studies*, Leiden, 1961.

—— *Jesus the Jew: A Historian's Reading of the Gospels*, London, 1973.

—— *Post-Biblical Jewish Studies*, Leiden, 1975.

Vitto, F. and Edelstein, G., "The Mausoleum at Gush Halav," *Qadmoniot* 7 (1974): 49-55 (Heb.).

—— "Notes and News: Gush Halav," *IEJ* 24 (1974): 282.

Wacholder, B.-Z., "The Date of the Mekhilta de-Rabbi Ishmael," *HUCA* 39 (1968): 117-44.

Wallach, L., "The colloquy of Marcus Aurelius with the Patriarch Judah I," *JQR* 31 (1940-41): 259-86.

Waterman, L., *Preliminary Report of the University of Michigan Excavation at Sepphoris, Palestine, in 1931*, Michigan, 1937.

Weiss, I. H., *Zur Geschichte der jüdischen Tradition (Dor Dor veDoreshav)*, 5 vols., Vienna and Vilna, 1883-93.

Wilkinson, J., *Jerusalem Pilgrims before the Crusades*, Warminster, 1977.

Wolff, H. J., "Le droit provincial dans la province romaine d'Arabie," *RIDA* 3rd ser., 23 (1976): 271-96.

Yadin, Y., *The Finds from the Bar Kokhba Period in the Cave of Letters*, Judaean Desert Studies, Vol. 1, Jerusalem, 1963.

—— *Bar-Kokhba*, London, 1971.

Yaron, R., "Note on a Judaean Deed of Sale of a Field," *BASOR* 150 (1958): 26-28.

—— *Gifts in Contemplation of Death in Jewish and Roman Law*, Oxford, 1960.

—— "The Murabba'at Documents," *JJS* 11 (1960): 157-71.

—— "Reichsrecht, Volksrecht and Talmud," *RIDA* 3rd ser., 11 (1964): 281-98.

—— "Semitic Elements in Early Rome," in A. Watson, ed., *Daube Noster: Essays in Legal History for David Daube*, Edinburgh and London, 1974, pp. 343-57.

Yeivin, Z., "Two Ancient Oil-Presses," *Atiqot* 3 (1966): 52-63 (Heb.).

—— "Survey of Settlements in Galilee and the Golan from the Period of the Mishnah in the Light of the Sources," Ph.D. diss., Hebrew Univ. of Jerusalem, 1971.

—— "Excavations at Khorazin," *EI* 11 (1973): 144-57 (Heb.).

Zeitlin, S., "Slavery during the Second Commonwealth and the Tannaitic Period," *JQR* 53 (1962-63): 185-218.

—— "Who were the Galileans?" *JQR* 64 (1973): 189-203.

Ziegler, I., *Die Königsgleichnisse des Midrasch beleuchtet durch die römische Kaiserzeit*, Breslau, 1903.

Index

About the Author: Martin Goodman teaches at the University of Birmingham (England) in the department of ancient history and archaeology.